CHILI DOG MVP

DICK ALLEN, THE '72 WHITE SOX AND A TRANSFORMING CHICAGO

JOHN OWENS
AND DAVID J. FLETCHER
EDITED BY GEORGE CASTLE

ECKHARTZ
PRESS

FOREWORD BY GOOSE GOSSAGE

This Strut-Larsen illustration perfectly captures
Dick Allen in mid-home run stride.

Illustration by Rob Larsen

WHITE SOX 1972 SCHEDULE

SUNDAY	MONDAY	TUESDAY	WEDNESDAY	THURSDAY	FRIDAY	SATURDAY

APRIL

2	3	4	5	6 Oakland	7	8 Oakland
9 Oakland	10 Minnesota	11 N Minnesota	12 Minnesota	13	14 N Kansas City	15 Kansas City
16 DH Kansas City	17	18 N Texas	19 N Texas	20	21 N Kansas City	22 Kansas City
23 Kansas City	24	25 N Cleveland	26 Cleveland	27	28 N Detroit	29 Detroit
30 Detroit						

MAY

	1	2 N Baltimore	3 N Baltimore	4	5 N Cleveland	6 Cleveland
7 Cleveland	8	9 N Detroit	10 Detroit	11	12 N Baltimore	13 N Baltimore
14 Baltimore	15 N Minnesota	16 N Minnesota	17 Minnesota	18	19 N California	20 N California
21 California	22 N Texas	23 N Texas	24 N Texas	25	26 N Oakland	27 N Oakland
28 Oakland	29 TN California	30 N California	31 N California			

JUNE

				1	2 N New York	3 New York
4 DH New York	5	6 N Boston	7 N Boston	8	9 N Milwaukee	10 Milwaukee
11 DH Milwaukee	12	13 N New York	14 N New York	15 N New York	16 N New York	17 Boston
18 Boston	19	20 N Milwaukee	21 N Milwaukee	22 Milwaukee	23 N Texas	24 N Texas
25 Texas	26 N Kansas City	27 N Kansas City	28 Oakland	29 TN Oakland	30 N Texas	

JULY

						1 Minnesota
2 DH Minnesota	3	4 N Baltimore	5 Baltimore	6 N Detroit	7 N Detroit	8 Detroit
9 DH Detroit	10 N Cleveland	11 N Cleveland	12 N Cleveland	13	14 TN Baltimore	15 N Baltimore
16 Baltimore	17 N Detroit	18 N Detroit	19 N Detroit	20	21 N Cleveland	22 Cleveland
23 DH Cleveland	24	25 ALL STAR GAME	26	27 N Kansas City	28 N Kansas City	29 Kansas City
30 Minnesota	31 N Minnesota					

AUGUST

		1 N California	2 N California	3 N California	4 N Texas	5 Texas
6 DH Texas	7	8 N California	9 N California	10 N Oakland	11 N Oakland	12 Oakland
13 Oakland	14 N Cubs	15 N Milwaukee	16 Milwaukee	17	18 N Boston	19 Boston
20 DH Boston	21	22 N New York	23 N New York	24	25 N Milwaukee	26 Milwaukee
27 Milwaukee	28 N Boston	29 N Boston	30	31		

SEPTEMBER

					1 N New York	2 New York
3 New York	4 DH Minnesota	5 6PM Minnesota	6 N Oakland	7 N Oakland	8 N California	9 N California
10 California	11 N Kansas City	12 N Kansas City	13 N Kansas City	14	15 N California	16 N California
17 California	18	19 N Oakland	20 N Oakland	21	22 N Texas	23 N Texas
24 Texas	25	26 N Kansas City	27 Kansas City	28	29 N Texas	30 N Texas
OCT. 1 Texas	OCT. 2 Minnesota	OCT. 3 Minnesota	OCT. 4 Minnesota		☐ AWAY GAMES	

HOME GAMES: ▨ TWI-NIGHT DOUBLEHEADERS 5:30 P.M.
▨ ALL DAY GAMES 1:15 P.M.   ▨ NIGHT GAMES 8:00 P.M.

Photo credit: Chicago White Sox

TABLE OF CONTENTS

"Strike it Rich"
For the first time in his career, Dick Allen felt loved
by the fans and was pleased that he helped draw
minority fans to Comiskey Park.

Photo credit: Leo Bauby Collection

FOREWORD

Goose Gossage in 2013 besides the broadcaster that sang his praises in his rookie year in 1972 that launched his 22-year Hall of Fame career.

Photo credit: David Fletcher

By Goose Gossage – August 2021

1972 was the year I was a rookie, and I was just 20. I made the club out of spring training as a non-roster invitee after my 1971 Season at Appleton in Class A, where I went 18-2. I made it to the big leagues in less than two years after scout Bill Kimball signed me for an $8,000 contract after the White Sox selected me in the ninth round of the June 1970 draft.

That season was also the year of the first baseball strike. It was the first of eight MLB strikes that went on. My career started out on that first strike and my career ended on the last strike in 1994.

At the end of '72 spring training, we traveled north from Sarasota to Chicago. They let us off the bus at Comiskey Park the night we went on strike. Here I am, can't rub two nickels together, and I have no place to stay. I'm walking around the streets of Chicago. I couldn't get in touch with my sister Lavone, who lived in the suburbs. So, I spent the night on the Chicago streets, scared to death, sleeping on a bench.

After the strike was settled and the start of the season was delayed, I got into the second game of the year at Municipal Stadium in Kansas City against the Royals in relief of Stan Bahnsen. It was April 16, 1972. Due to the strike, we only played 154 games that year.

I inherited runners at second and third with no outs in the bottom of the fifth. My first big pitch was thrown to Lou Piniella, who would be my manager in my last stop in the majors in 1994 when I pitched for Seattle. I pitched around Lou and ended up walking him to load the bases. I retired the next three hitters and only allowed one inherited runner to score.

The inning before I got in the game, I heard my pitching coach Johnny Sain shout out: "Get Gossage Up!" My heart raced as I went up the steps of the right field bullpen to get to the bullpen mound. But Stan got out of trouble in the bottom of the fourth. I headed back to take a seat back in the bullpen, only to take a header over the steps into the dugout and fall right on my face.

Welcome to the big leagues!

It was also in Kansas City that I first met Dick Allen. He didn't even show up for spring training. And we were so excited because we got Allen. He didn't disappoint us. He put us on his shoulders and carried us for the entire 1972 season.

I never saw anybody ever play the game like Dick, and boy, this is not a slap in the face to anyone else because I played with tremendous, fantastic Hall of Fame players. But little did I know that in 1972 I was watching the greatest exhibition of baseball that I would ever watch in my life. And Dick Allen was the greatest player that I ever had the privilege of playing with.

In 1972, I'm 20 years old and from that first time that he saw me throw in Kansas City, Dick Allen took me under his wing and taught me the game of baseball. He taught me how to locate fastballs and sequences of pitches. It was an education that all the money in the world could not pay for. That's how much this guy means to me. I absolutely loved that man. He was so misunderstood.

He was the ultimate free spirit. There was not an ounce of BS in Dick Allen. He was a man's man. I saw him in the dugout several times, guys would be joking around and not watching the game and screwing around and Dick would go, "Hey, why don't you (bleep) watch the game, you might learn something ... Get your goddamn head in the game." You could hear a pin drop.

I said the stars were aligned when I got into the big leagues in '72 with Johnny Sain — the guru of the off-speed pitch — along with manager Chuck Tanner, who believed in me. And I had Dick Allen take me under his wing and teach me how to pitch.

Johnny and Chuck were so important to my development. During a White Sox off-day in the '71 season, Chuck had even traveled to the Quad Cities where we were playing a road game to teach me the mechanics of throwing the changeup. This middle-of-the-season instruction from the big-league club manager when I was in A-ball really made a difference and helped launch my Hall of Fame career.

Johnny and Dick made me become a serious student of the game by telling me how to pitch and approach hitters. It was an incredible education — Dick is in one ear and Sain in the other ear!

Thirty-six years later, in 2008, I was inducted into the Hall of Fame. Dick and Chuck showed up to surprise me the day before the induction. In my Hall of Fame induction speech and during the pre-ceremony press conference, I credited Dick, Chuck and Johnny Sain for getting me to Cooperstown.

Nineteen seventy-two was also the year I first got called Goose. I roomed with Tom Bradley, who was four years older and had already had three years in the big leagues. Tom, whose IQ exceeded the top speed of his fastball by at least

30 points and was still working on completing his degree in classical studies at the University of Maryland, first called me "Goss." Later, he changed it to "Goose" because he said I resembled a big ol' long-necked goose when was on the mound looking into reading the catcher's signs.

Thanks to Tom Bradley, I was no longer Rich Gossage and would be forever known as Goose.

The big highlight for me during my rookie season in 1972 was my first appearance at Yankee Stadium on September 1 in the bottom of the sixth inning. My dad, Jake Gossage, died in 1968 and he was a Yankees fan and told everyone in Colorado Springs that I would someday pitch in the majors. When I toed that rubber in Yankee Stadium, I had the most incredible feeling knowing that my dad knew that his dream for his youngest son had come true. It was an out of body experience.

After we had been eliminated by Oakland the last week of the season, Chuck had told Wilbur Wood he could go home a couple days early.

I had convinced Chuck that I could start in place of Wilbur in Game 154 in Minnesota on Wednesday October 4, to end the season. The night before we had a celebration party at the Lemington Hotel, and I got only a couple hours sleep and was hung over. I lasted just three innings and gave up nine earned runs and 13 hits. My perfect winning record of 7-0 was blemished with the loss and my ERA ballooned from 3.49 to 4.28 to finish my rookie year.

Chili Dog MVP: Dick Allen, The 1972 White Sox and a Transforming Chicago tells the story of Dick Allen and my 1972 teammates. We almost won the AL West that year. We had erased Oakland's eight-and-a-half-game lead on July 19 to go up by a game-and-a-half on August 26. We finished the year 87-67 and we had the second-best record in the American League.

My '72 White Sox team made it exciting for fans to come to the great cathedral, Comiskey Park. We were 55-23 at home that season!

During my memorable rookie year, I got a first-hand seat to watch Dick Allen have the best year of any baseball player I have ever seen in my 22-year major-league career.

1972 CHICAGO WHITE SOX 1972

FRONT ROW (left to right) Batboys: Jim Riley, Rory Clark, and Joe White.

SECOND ROW (seated) : Carlos May, Luis Alvarado, Bart Johnson, Coach Al Monchak, Coach Joe Lonnett, Manager Chuck Tanner, Coach John Sain, Coach Jim Mahoney, Jorge Orta, Walt Williams, and Jim Qualls.

THIRD ROW (standing) : Trainer Charlie Saad, Equipment Manager Larry Licklider, Batting Practice Pitcher Glen Rosenbaum, Wilbur Wood, Chuck Brinkman, Jim Geddes, Dave Lemonds, Rick Reichardt, Pat Kelly, Mike Andrews, Dick Allen, Traveling Secretary and Statistician Don Unferth, and Visiting Clubhouse Custodian Mike Morris.

BACK ROW (standing on bench) : Ed Herrmann, Bill Melton, Rick Gossage, Terry Forster, Tom Egan, Rich Morales, Jay Johnstone, Tom Bradley, Vicente Romo, Steve Kealey, and Stan Bahnsen.

Photo credit: Chicago White Sox

CHAPTER 1

June 4, 1972:

The "Chili Dog Game"

"Unbelievable! I know it happened, 'cause I can hear that scoreboard going off!"

– New York Yankees radio play-by-play announcer Phil Rizzuto, at White Sox Park on June 4, 1972

On the Sunday afternoon of June 4, 1972, the nerve center of the city of Chicago was at 35th Street and Shields Avenue in the Armour Square neighborhood on the South Side.

Here, on this day, over 51,000 fans congregated at the aging, storied sports venue which opened in 1910 as the "Baseball Palace of the World" — Comiskey Park...or, rather, White Sox Park, the name by which it was known during the 1960s and early 1970s.

They came via the adjacent Dan Ryan Expressway, the massive, 14-lane interstate highway which had opened exactly 10 years earlier. They came on the also-adjacent Lake-Dan Ryan "L", a then new line of urban rail transportation located in the expressway's median strip that had opened only three years before. And they came via the elevated Jackson Park-Howard "L", located three blocks east of the ballpark, in the heart of the Bronzeville neighborhood — the longtime center of African American culture in what was still the nation's second-largest city.

The attraction was a doubleheader between the Chicago White Sox and the team's historic nemesis from the Go-Go Sox days of the 1950s and '60s — the New York Yankees. But the true significance of the long day wouldn't be known until its final moment, which would serve as a true rolling-out party for protagonist Dick Allen and his Sox teammates fondly remembered a half-century later, beyond Allen's death at 78 in 2020.

Ultimately, 8,000 fans would be turned away from the well-worn, 62-year-old stadium. The official attendance was 51,904 — the largest crowd to see the Sox since 1954 and the sixth-largest paid crowd in Chicago history up to that time.

"People were standing on the walkways next to the scoreboard and behind the last rows of grandstands, and sitting in the aisles," recalled then-16-year-old Sox loyalist Ron Eisenstein, perched in the right center field upper-deck with brother Mark. The siblings were crunched in by fellow fans like in none of the 46 other games they attended in 1970, when the Sox attracted just 495,000 fans for the season.

A traditional Bat Day partly accounted for the massive turnout at the ballpark. The hated Yankees, long a South Side draw, could also be factored into the standing-room-only throng.

But the increased fan excitement on this day was mainly ca̤ overachieving team, resurgent in the American League after a fallow th̤ period. From 1968 to 1970, the Sox lost a combined 295 games, finished lasṭ the league in attendance in two of three years and were continually rumored to be moving out of the city.

"There was just a smattering of fans throughout the park during those days," recalled stadium organist Nancy Faust, who was hired as a 23-year-old in 1970. "Where I was originally located, in the center field bleachers, fans practically didn't exist."

But in 1972, the White Sox were generating excitement with their fan base in a way that hadn't been seen on the South Side since the early 1960s. On June 4, the Sox were 23-17 in the American League's Western Division, just 3½ games behind the already-dominant Oakland Athletics. That team, which had charismatic All-Stars ranging from Reggie Jackson to Catfish Hunter to Joe Rudi, was one year removed from its first AL West title and looking forward to a dynastic future with multiple World Series Championships and a place as one of the great teams in baseball history. But the 1972 White Sox were poised to be competitive with the A's.

"They were a great team and every time we played them it was a battle," remembered Stan Bahnsen, a starting pitcher with the '72 Sox.

The reason for the White Sox' rebirth was multifold. Sox manager Chuck Tanner and director of player personnel Roland Hemond — both brought over from the California Angels late in the 1970 season — had created a competitive roster through trades (former Yankees pitcher Bahnsen, former California Angels outfielder Jay Johnstone), the farm system (a talented young bullpen of fireballers Rich "Goose" Gossage, Terry Forster and Bart Johnson) and holdovers (power-hitting third baseman Bill Melton, line-drive hitting Carlos May and veteran knuckleball pitcher Wilbur Wood).

Team owner John Allyn — a modest insurance mogul who took over as sole owner of the team from his brother, Arthur, near the end of the 1969 season — helped foster on-field change and innovation with hires such as Tanner (an early adopter of analytics), Hemond, iconoclastic pitching coach Johnny Sain and Vice President and General Manager Stu Holcomb.

Holcomb, in turn, was responsible for bringing aboard unique talents like broadcaster Harry Caray and organist Faust.

Caray, the bombastic longtime St. Louis Cardinals announcer who started on the South Side in 1971, was making White Sox radio broadcasts a must-listen event, even though he could only be heard on an ad-hoc network of suburban stations — this because none of the major Chicago outlets wanted the team.

Faust was already a popular staple at White Sox Park, through her unique and ultimately revolutionary keyboard work, using pop standards to provide witty commentary on the game itself. She was popular enough to grace the cover of the Sunday *Chicago Tribune Magazine* on this same June 4, posing for the cover in a bare-shouldered black dress ("Fashions are from Saks Fifth Avenue," according to the Tribune) with pearls, along with players Melton and Wood.

"They laugh when she sits down at the mighty Hammond," the Tribune's Evelyn Livingstone wrote of Faust. "But it's only because she plans it that way."

But these were only important supporting characters to the mob of fans who were at White Sox Park to watch the twin bill. The man that they were ultimately there to see was a 5-foot-11-inch power-hitting first baseman with a slim torso and a powerful, compact upper-body akin to a bodybuilder; who sported mutton-chop sideburns, aviator glasses and a moderate Afro; and who exuded the cool demeanor of someone with the utmost confidence in his abilities.

He was known as Richie Allen when he played in Philadelphia and St. Louis and Los Angeles. But in Chicago, for the first time in his career, Richard Anthony Allen was known by his chosen name — Dick Allen.

"Dick was the greatest hitter that I ever saw hit, the greatest that I ever saw in person play the game," said Hall of Fame reliever Rich "Goose" Gossage, a rookie on that '72 Sox team. "He excited the players almost as much as he did the fans."

"He was mercurial," added Bill Melton. "We were in awe of everything that he did."

By 1972, Dick Allen had established himself as one of the game's best players, with five All-Star appearances, averaging nearly 30 homers and 100 RBI during his first eight seasons in the league. But he was also one of the game's most controversial figures — an independent Black athlete who marched to the beat of his own drum and was repeatedly castigated for that independence.

His reputation had been nearly ruined in Philadelphia, where, soon after his NL Rookie of the Year season, things started to go wrong in the summer of 1965. An altercation with teammate Frank Thomas ended with Thomas' bat crashing against Dick's shoulders. When Thomas was released after the incident, Philadelphia fans took it out on Allen. And for rest of his five seasons in Philadelphia, Dick was subjected to endless verbal abuse from the fans, some of it racially motivated. He began wearing a batting helmet in the field to protect himself from debris thrown from the upper decks at Connie Mack Stadium.

Dick's relationship with the media reflected his relationship with the fans in Philadelphia, as negative coverage of his personality whipped up even more resentment. This was in a city where racial strife was at its peak in the 1960s, with incidents of racially motivated civil unrest mirroring similar incidents through-out the country.

But in Chicago, where he was traded in late 1971, the veteran slugger had found a home and was quickly accepted despite some non-conformist stances.

He benefitted by having an empathetic manager in Tanner, who knew Dick Allen from his days growing up as a star high school athlete in Wampum, Pa. He had understanding coaches like Joe Lonnett, a former teammate with the Phillies minor league team in Little Rock who witnessed first-hand the racism Dick experienced in that Arkansas city. He was surrounded almost uniformly by admiring teammates. Even conservative local media was won over. "Is this really a new Dick Allen, or is it that we never really knew him?" pondered *Chicago Tribune* sports columnist David Condon, who always cozied up to the estab-lishment.

In this situation, Dick thrived and became a true idol among White Sox faithful.

"For the first time in my baseball life, I really feel wanted," he would tell re-porters at the time. "And that's what life's about, isn't it? No matter what you do, you want to believe that someone wants you."

His new home, Chicago, was going through its own transformations, espe-cially on the South Side, which the White Sox had called home since 1900, when owner Charles Comiskey moved his St. Paul Saints of the Western League to Armour Square. The team, rechristened as the White Stockings, would become one of the eight charter American League teams in 1901.

The South Side's other great institution, the Union Stockyards — the center of the nation's meat-packing industry — had closed in 1971, 106 years after its inception. Located less than a mile from Sox Park, the Yards were the inspira-tion for poet Carl Sandburg's moniker for Chicago: "The Hog Butcher For the World". But the gradual decline of the Stockyards was a symbol of the slowly disappearing blue-collar jobs that were once the lifeblood of the South Side.

The neighborhoods surrounding Sox Park, especially to its east, were be-coming poorer, with low-income African American residents concentrated in a two-mile-long stretch of public housing high-rise buildings. White Sox Park itself was a boundary line, separating the largely White Bridgeport neighbor-hood on the west from the Black neighborhoods of Bronzeville, Douglas and Kenwood to the east.

Rory Clark, a White Sox batboy in 1972 who lived in the nearby African American neighborhood of Oakland, called Sox Park a "dividing point" be-tween two separate Chicagos.

"If you pissed off the police over in my neighborhood, they wouldn't say anything to you; they would just tell you get in the car and they would drop you off in Bridgeport," Clark recalled with a laugh. "Good luck getting home."

Richard J. Daley, a longtime White Sox booster now in his 18th year as Chicago mayor, lived in Bridgeport, where he presided over a rigorously segregated city. Throughout his career as mayor, Daley had been in the process of re-creating the city — refashioning Chicago from its blue-collar roots to a white-collar city dominated by its world-class, revitalized downtown. But gleaming new central-city and lakefront high rises sometimes served as a Potemkin's Village, obscuring urban despair that resided behind them. Such a stark fact caused his relationship with the Black community that sprawled to the south and west of downtown Chicago to deteriorate. Years of enforced segregation, where redlined Black communities were the subject of decades of economic disinvestment, had produced neighborhoods where poverty was cyclical, and desperation was ever-present.

Other related issues, most notably police brutality in the African American community, symbolized by the December 1969 police raid that killed the two top leaders in the Illinois Black Panther Party, Fred Hampton and Mark Clark, helped deepen a rift between the city's political establishment, led by Daley, and the Black community. The gulf widened even further in the spring of 1972 when one of Daley's top Black Cook County Democratic Party lieutenants, Olympic hero-turned-congressman Ralph Metcalfe, split with the mayor over incidents of police brutality that struck close to home.

But on this cool Sunday afternoon at 35th Street and Shields Avenue, the main story was the hometown White Sox and their doubleheader against the Yankees. Fans bellied up to the bar at McCuddy's Tavern, the venerable Irish tavern across 35th Street from Sox Park, where legend had Babe Ruth making pit stops both before and after games.

Other fans would stop at Tyler's Restaurant, a Black-owned eatery next door to McCuddy's. Opened in the early 1960s, the diner was run by Mississippi transplant Johnnie Mae Tyler. Tyler's was known for its thick, juicy hamburgers. Indeed, in these days before major league baseball teams developed rigorous nutrition plans for its players, Tyler's was a hot spot for players as well, with clubhouse attendants making regular burger runs for Sox players.

"The cheeseburgers, especially, were phenomenal, so more than a few times, Dick would give me some money and tell me to grab some cheeseburgers for the team when you get a chance," recalled clubhouse attendant Jim O'Keefe. "I probably knew Mrs. Tyler better than anyone in the neighborhood at the time."

The set-in-his-ways veteran would arrive late, as usual, at the white-washed, stately baseball edifice, with its arched windows and towering light structures.

"Sox Park looks like a docked paddle-wheel steamer," according to *New Yorker Magazine* baseball writer Roger Angell. On this day, Dick was in the clubhouse about an hour before the 1:15 p.m. start time of the doubleheader.

"[Allen] didn't care about batting practice," Melton said. "He'd say, 'A batting practice pitcher throwing 60 miles an hour won't help me prepare for a game.'"

While players showered and dressed after batting practice before the first game, O'Keefe made a huge vat of chili that they could dine on between games one and two.

"It was a cool day, so I borrowed one of the players cars to go back to my neighborhood to get the ingredients to make the chili," recalled O'Keefe, a Bridgeport resident who attended high school at nearby De La Salle High School.

The Sox took the field for the first game wearing their new uniforms that had been introduced the year before — red pinstripes and red caps, the classic Old English "Sox" logo in red on the chest and white on the caps and a sketch of a white stocking on the calf portion of each player's red hose.

The old ballpark had been "modernized" a few years earlier, with artificial turf added to the infield. But everything else about White Sox Park was old and familiar — from the blue seats that filled the double-decked enclosed structure, to the catwalks that flanked the mammoth exploding 12-year-old center field scoreboard, another innovation remaining from former Sox owner Bill Veeck.

In the first game, the Sox took care of Yankees ace Mel Stottlemyre, led by Carlos May (a bad-hop single that drove in two runs), Bill Melton (his fifth homer of the season) and their star, Allen, who showed off his base-running acumen with a steal of home. The Sox won, 6-1, behind the strong pitching performance of Tom Bradley.

Manager Chuck Tanner then announced that he would rest Dick for the second game. "He's played every inning of every game for one-fourth of the season," Tanner would tell the media in between contests. "These players are human. It's a grind."

"I didn't ask Chuck for a rest, [but] I was glad for it," Dick would tell the media. "I'm no old man, but I'm not 22. I can take a little whirlpool treatment between games. My back's been sore."

John Allyn had stormed into Tanner's office after it was announced that Dick Allen was resting in game two. "Why isn't he playing?" Allyn asked.

"Just gonna rest him," Tanner replied. "I'll use him when we get the bases loaded. He'll hit a homer to win it for us."

As game two started, teammate Jay Johnstone, also off for the nightcap, spied Allen in the whirlpool in the Sox clubhouse. "He was relaxing in there, having a good time, singing, all that stuff," Johnstone would recall over 40 years later.

"He's sitting in the whirlpool, buck naked."

Game two progressed with the Yankees taking a 4-2 lead in the late innings. By the eighth inning, Tanner was looking for Dick. He told batboy Rory Clark to find his star and bring him into the dugout.

Clark found him by his locker, partaking in a chili dog that was fashioned from the vat that O'Keefe had left earlier for players in the clubhouse.

"He wasn't even dressed — he's in a game jersey and his shower shoes," Clark remembered. "And I said 'Dick, Chuck wants you to pinch hit.' And he looked at me like I was a Martian. He said, 'Tell him I'm eating a chili dog.' And I said I'm not going to tell him that. So, he had spilled chili all over his front, right? So he had to get out of that."

On the fly, Dick changed his chili-stained jersey and put on another Sox polyester zip-up top. He was so rushed that he almost neglected to put on his long-sleeved shirt that he normally wore underneath his uniform.

His time came in the bottom of the ninth, with the Sox still down, 4-2. Yankees starter Mike Kekich got Rick Reichardt to fly out to right field for out number one. Melton walked and second baseman Mike Andrews followed with a single to put runners at first and second with one out creating the perfect situation for Dick Allen to pinch hit and win the game.

"I was really worried that I was going to hit into a double play and kill the rally," said Andrews after the game.

Allen then was summoned to pinch hit for shortstop Rich Morales. Yankees closer Sparky Lyle was called on by manager Ralph Houk to pitch to Allen,

"Mike (Andrews) and Sparky were roommates with the Red Sox," Chuck Tanner would later recall. "Mike Andrews told me what he said to Sparky Lyle as he was crossing the infield coming into pitch. Mike said to Sparky, 'You're in deep shit now.'"

Many fans felt the same foreshadowing, the sense of inevitability with their new superstar. They had never enjoyed a hitter with the talents of a Dick Allen in their collective Comiskey Park histories.

"This is the reason why it was one of my high points of my (Sox) fandom," said Ron Eisenstein. "You really had a sense of what was about to happen. Allen was already approaching mythical status with the Sox. We all got up on our feet. There was an electricity coursing through you. He was hitting off a guy who was the premier reliever in the American League."

Houk had a brief conference at the mound with that premier reliever. "Ralph didn't say anything about pitching around him when we talked one-on-one," said Lyle.

Back in New York, Yankees General Manager Lee MacPhail was driving from Yankee Stadium on his way home in Westchester. His concentration was divided between his motoring in the middle of a vicious thunderstorm that had brought traffic to a halt while he went over the George Washington Bridge and listening to the game on the radio.

"I was just getting on the bridge when Ralph had brought in Sparky Lyle with one out, two on, Yanks leading, 4-2," MacPhail recalled.

Dick approached the plate with his 40-ounce bat. He took one strike, and Lyle's second pitch was wide for a ball to even the count at 1-1. The next pitch was a slider, on which the Chicago White Sox leader hit a screaming line drive that appeared to get barely 20 feet off the ground. Despite the low trajectory, Yankees left fielder Roy White knew the ball was gone the moment it was hit, and he headed off the field almost immediately. It landed seven or eight rows into the lower deck seats, seemingly leaving the field of play in no time at all.

Sparky Lyle didn't bother to watch; neither did Yankees third baseman Hal Lanier.

"I could tell by the sound. I used to hear it a lot in the other league. He's in the same class with Mays and Aaron. I can still see some of those shots disappearing over the roof in Philadelphia," said Lanier.

"I knew it was gone as soon as he hit it, there was no issues looking," said Lyle after the game. He remembered the day before in the bottom of the 10th with game tied when he thought Allen hit a game-winning home run off him only to have Bobby Murcer make a catch right in front of the center field fence in the cavernous stadium.

New York GM MacPhail nearly drove his car off the bridge when he heard the fireworks going off in the background as he listened to Phil Rizzuto's call "I knew it was going to happen…" told MacPhail to *New York Daily News* writer Phil Pepe.

Allen's thunderbolt also dampened the spirits of future sportscaster Keith Olbermann, a Yankees fan, who threw his radio out of the second floor window of his parents' house when Allen abruptly ended the proceedings.

Those fans remaining from the sellout throng at White Sox Park were ecstatic, lingering there almost a half-hour after the game had ended. Their screams of joy reverberated through the enclosed structure — they were loud enough to be heard in the Sox and Visitors clubhouses. Perhaps the franchise's most memorable moment since the team clinched the 1959 American League title was now in the books as an all-time Chicago sports highlight.

"I can still see the ball soaring into the left field lower deck," said Eisenstein. "By the time it was at its apex, we were pounding on each other. It was like Michael Jordan hitting the game-winning shot."

"I would have liked to have checked that ball after Dick hit it, [to see] whether it was lopsided or not," Hemond would say later.

After the game, writers approached Allen in the locker room, where he sat next to his immaculately dressed teammate, Pat Kelly. Allen was looking at a telephone message he had just received.

"Supposed to call this guy in area code 704," Dick said. "Wonder where that is?"

"It's probably from Russia," Kelly replied. "Some dude over there probably called up and said: 'Hey, I thought you guys over in America had promised to quit testing those bombs.'"

An almost mythical moment enveloped a player already surrounded by legend. Dick's performance that day would be a key milepost in the year that culminated with his only Most Valuable Player award.

More importantly, it may have been a turning point for an organization which had been in danger of leaving Chicago.

"I keep smiling when I talk about the '72 season because it was one of my favorite seasons in my career," Hemond would recall 40 years later. "Dick had a tremendous year...one of the finest baseball seasons a player could put together. He certainly played a major, major role in keeping the franchise of the White Sox in Chicago 'cause at that time it could have very well happened that they would have ended up in Milwaukee or Toronto or Denver."

Dick Allen truly transformed the White Sox, a sports franchise that, in the summer of 1972, was no longer an afterthought in a transforming Chicago.

Dick Allen watches his game-winning homer against the Yankees sail into the left field stands on June 4, 1972.

Photo credit: Leo Bauby Collection

Dick Allen (left) is among a mob of happy White Sox
(No. 14 Bill Melton, No. 18 Pat Kelly, No. 28 Wilbur Wood)
returning to the dugout to call it a day after he slugged his
Chili Dog Homer on June 4, 1972.

Photo credit: Leo Bauby Collection

CHAPTER 2

December 3, 1971:
'Crash' Allen Traded To Sox

On Dec. 3, 1971, the headlines in the *Chicago Tribune* chronicled a city on the verge of change.

The newspaper was long the bastion of a unique brand of Midwestern conservatism unfriendly to Democratic presidents and permeating much of its usually hefty collection of sections at the direction of blueblood publisher Robert R. McCormick. But the Tribune was in the midst of change itself. Recently- appointed editor Clayton Kirkpatrick had a mission of modernizing the newspaper, getting away from partisan coverage and addressing some of the key issues of the day, most notably involving race relations.

So, on this date, the Page 1 story had this headline: "Door to Success in Jobs Not Open to Us, Blacks Contend." The story detailed how discrimination both in white-collar jobs and in the various labor and trade unions continued to limit professional options for Blacks in Chicago.

"For years, the post office has been filled with highly educated black people who worked as carriers and clerks," Charles Coleman, an African American attorney, said in the article. "We've had highly educated dining car waiters and Pullman porters."

Meanwhile, a cash-strapped Chicago was threatening to close its public schools on the following Tuesday, 12 days before Christmas break, because the city couldn't pay the $23 million to keep them open for the remainder of the fiscal year.

Mayor Richard J. Daley — the city's most pre-eminent White Sox fan, in addition to being the state's most powerful politician and one of the nation's leading Democrats— was in the state capital, Springfield, on this day. He was working with Governor Richard Ogilvie —a former Cook County sheriff and one of the state's moderate Republicans, known for working across the political aisle— and a group of Chicago businessmen in an effort to avoid the 12-day school shutdown. They would eventually work out a deal, borrowing from the 1972 budget, to cover the remainder of teacher's salaries for 1971, a "kick the can down the road" approach which would hurt the city financially in the coming years.

Daley endured a busy time, as he was leading the Democrats' slate-making for the next year's elections.

Daley and the Cook County Democratic organization slated the mayor's son, Richard M. Daley, for an Illinois Senate seat. And Daley slated Lieutenant Governor Paul Simon as the party's sanctioned gubernatorial candidate.

Simon, years away from being a national figure and liberal icon as a U.S Senator, was at this time the machine's man. He would be ultimately pitted against a dynamic independent Democrat attorney named Dan Walker, who also announced his plans to run for governor.

"Simon's an honest man," Walker would tell the press on this day. "But he's a tool of machine politics."

Other independent Democrats in the city were supporting Walker. Backers included liberal White Chicago aldermen Bill Singer and Leon Despres, maverick Black Democrats in Springfield like State Rep. Harold Washington and State Sen. Richard Newhouse. Also in the Walker camp was the already powerful Rev. Jesse Jackson, the leader of the national civil rights organization Operation Breadbasket, which was located about two miles from White Sox Park at 50th Street and Drexel Boulevard.

They all represented the new iconoclasm in the Cook County Democratic Party — and a real challenge to the authority of Daley and the old-school Chicago Democrats.

On this day, Jackson's nonconformity was also putting him at odds with his own mentors. Jackson was suspended with pay for 60 days by his supervisors at the Southern Christian Leadership Conference for essentially going rogue, especially through his creation of Black Expo, a fundraising organization designed to promote Black businesses. Officials with the SCLC —the landmark civil rights organization founded by Bayard Rustin, Martin Luther King, Jr. and others — said Jackson had become too independent and rebellious, making policy decisions without consulting the national SCLC office in Atlanta.

"Rev. Jackson is a valuable man," SCLC President Ralph Abernathy told the press during a news conference at the Marriott Motor Lodge in Rosemont, Ill. "(But) Jackson has repeatedly acted in manners not representative of staff personnel. He has continually disregarded national policy."

An iconoclast was also featured in the top headline in the sports section on Dec. 3, 1971. This one would — at least temporarily — change the fortunes of the White Sox in the coming years, making them relevant again in Chicago in the short term…and perhaps saving the franchise in the long term.

"Sox Trade John, Huntz for Richie" was the headline in the newspaper about baseball's ultimate outsider, who was just acquired by the White Sox.

By mid-summer in 1972, Chicagoans would address "Richie" by his chosen name — Dick Allen.

"It's the White Sox who made themselves the best deal of the week, getting Richie (Allen). That trade ranks right up there with us getting Kenny Holtzman from the Cubs."

– Oakland A's slugger Reggie Jackson in the lobby of the Arizona Biltmore Hotel on Dec. 3, 1971.

Baseball's winter meetings staged in Phoenix that December produced some trades that would transform Major League Baseball in the next decade.

The Cincinnati Reds would send a package featuring slugging first baseman Lee May to the Houston Astros for a return headed by future Hall of Famer Joe Morgan — the last and most essential cog in the Big Red Machine that would dominate the National League in the remainder of the 1970s. The A's would acquire left-hander Holtzman — who threw two no-hitters with the Cubs — in exchange for outfielder Rick Monday, giving Oakland one of their final important contributors to a team which would eventually win three consecutive World Series. And the Dodgers would acquire a Hall of Famer in his twilight years — Frank Robinson.

But the White Sox would also have one of *their* most important off-seasons in team history.

Roland Hemond and Chuck Tanner were on a mission to make dynamic improvements to a young team that over-achieved with a third-place 79-83 record in 1971. Most specifically, the team needed a superstar on offense — one who could be sandwiched within their homegrown offensive talents, Bill Melton and Carlos May.

Hemond, the low-key director of player personnel, and Tanner, the ebullient manager, had been hired from the California Angels organization late in the 1970 season to breathe life into a franchise that would lose 106 games and be dangerously close to becoming an afterthought in the Chicago sports world.

They completely shook up the team in '71, trading for outfielders Pat Kelly, Jay Johnstone and Rick Reichardt, infielders Mike Andrews and Luis Alvarado and pitcher Tom Bradley. These players would be paired with homegrown products like third baseman Melton, outfielder May and fireballing phenom pitchers Bart Johnson and Terry Foster — who joined longtime Sox pitchers Wilbur Wood, Tommy John and Joel Horlen.

The first full year of the Hemond-Tanner regime was a start in the right direction. Led by Melton, who slugged his league-leading 33rd home run on the final game of the season, the White Sox gave fans a glimmer of hope that better times were around the corner. Attendance improved from 495,000 in 1970 to 834,000, which ranked ninth in the American League.

But despite Melton's heroics, Hemond and Tanner realized the team needed more.

They first tried to acquire Frank Robinson at the 1970 winter meetings. Then, following their resurgent 1971 season, the Sox were again after more offense.

Minnesota's perennial batting champ Rod Carew was an early target for the Sox at the '71 winter meetings as Hemond and Tanner wanted Carew to play center field instead of his normal second base. But talks with the Twins fell through.

The Los Angeles Dodgers were desperately looking for a left-handed starter to add to an already experienced pitching staff that included Don Sutton, Claude Osteen and Al Downing. Tommy John had been a reliable mid-rotation starter for the past seven years for the South Siders, making the All-Star team in 1968. But he went only 13-16 in 1971 and was one of the few pitchers who didn't work well with the Sox' brilliant new pitching coach, Johnny Sain.

Meanwhile, Tanner was successful in moving knuckleballer Wilbur Wood from the bullpen to the starting rotation in 1971, with Wood winning 22 games. This made John expendable to the White Sox…and the Dodgers had their eye on him.

Los Angeles was willing to give up Dick, who had been their best player in 1971, leading the team with a 5.4 WAR (Wins Above Replacement), 23 homers and 90 RBI. The Dodgers had replacements — two talented corner infielders coming up from the minors, Steve Garvey and Ron Cey.

The December 3 trade was finalized: John and utility infielder Steve Huntz for Dick. On the same day, to fill John's vacant spot in the rotation, Hemond acquired accomplished right hander Stan Bahnsen from the New York Yankees for utility infielder Rich McKinney.

But Dick was undoubtedly the main acquisition of the day. "We've got a bomber," a delighted Chuck Tanner told the press.

"He's going to give us a little excitement at Comiskey Park," added Stu Holcomb, the team's executive vice president, responsible for hiring both Tanner and Hemond.

Dick Allen had been one of the very best players in the majors from 1964 to 1971, primarily with the Philadelphia Phillies, though also the St. Louis Cardinals (1970) and Dodgers (1971). During that period, he hit 20-plus homers and recorded an OPS (On Base + Slugging Percentage) of .850 every year, something only Hank Aaron could claim during that time.

But to the mainstream media in 1971, Dick was almost universally labeled by an exclusive contingent of older, all-White male sportswriters as "controversial," "moody" or "un-coachable."

At issue were his highly publicized disputes with fans and management in Philadelphia, which started after a notorious batting-cage fight with a White Phillies teammate, Frank Thomas, in 1965 — an incident which ultimately led to Thomas' dismissal from the team. Fans and media in racially divided Philadelphia unfairly blamed "Richie" for the incident, and his relationship with management would deteriorate at that time and after a series of contract disputes.

Upon his acquisition, Chicago media continued to write skeptically, often painting Dick in a negative light.

"(Allen's) been fined for missing games or reporting to the ball park late," wrote the veteran *Chicago Sun-Times'* baseball writer Jerome Holtzman on the day of the trade. "His career in Philadelphia was especially stormy and, to some extent, resulted in the firing of Gene Mauch, who was then the Phillies manager."

Dick would be "the first six-figure salary player in the club's history," added the Tribune's Richard Dozer, alluding to his $100,000 salary. "(But) his eight years in the major leagues have been strewn with controversy."

"Richie comes with a talent that should endear him to every true Sox fan — he reputedly is one of the great beer drinkers in the history of the pastime," wrote *Sun-Times* columnist Bill Gleason, alluding to rumors that Dick had issues with alcohol.

"We'll match him with some of the legendary semi-pro beer drinkers in (ethnic South Side neighborhoods) South Chicago, the East Side and Hegewisch," wrote Gleason, the proud South Side denizen and vocal White Sox fan who first started covering Chicago sports as a newspaper reporter in 1941. He used his columnist's status to become a pioneer in sports talk as co-creator and panelist on the show "The Sports Writers," which started on WGN-AM in 1974 and later was syndicated nationally on television.

"Rowdy Richie" is what *Sun-Times* baseball writer Edgar Munzel called Dick. Munzel predicted contract 'headaches.' "Rowdy Richie has been holding out almost every year since he came up with the Phillies in 1963," wrote Munzel, who first started covering baseball in Chicago in 1929.

But the Hemond-Tanner regime ignored the negative media publicity. In fact, Dick had been on Hemond's radar during the 1970 winter meetings, when he tried without success to acquire him from the Cardinals for the Sox' still-productive future Hall of Famer, Luis Aparicio.

The key to the acquisition was Dick's longtime relationship with Tanner, who knew the Allen family going back to the days when both men were growing up in western Pennsylvania — the Tanner family in New Castle, and the Allens in nearby Wampum.

"I've known Rich for a long time and he's a nice boy," Tanner said. "I know one thing. He gives 100 percent on the ball field. I'll judge Richie Allen on what he does for me — and only that."

"I scouted 90,000 players in my lifetime. Dick Allen was the greatest I ever saw."

– Veteran Philadelphia Phillies scout John Ogden, the man who signed Dick Allen

Richard Anthony Allen was born on March 8, 1942. Wampum is a tiny rural town about 30 miles north of Pittsburgh. He would always be identified as a Wampum resident— one of his later nicknames was the "Wampum Walloper" and he displayed the name "Wampum" on his jersey when he was a member of the Oakland A's years later. But the Allen family actually lived in Chewton, PA, a tiny village adjacent to Wampum.

Dick was one of eight children — five boys and three girls — raised by Era, a domestic worker. Dick's father, Coy Sr., was a truck driver with a trash hauling business, but he left the home for good by the time Dick was 15. So Era Allen provided all income for the family, cleaning homes and doing the laundry for other families in Wampum. "She almost worked herself to death taking in washing to feed us," Dick would recall many years later to a reporter for Ebony Magazine.

Despite the lack of a father figure, all five Allen boys —Coy, Caesar, Hank, Dick and Ron — became involved with athletics. Coy, also known as "Sonny", was the oldest — and he was the primary influence on his four younger brothers.

"Our father didn't play sports at all, and our mother had no interest in sports," Hank Allen recalled years later. "But Sonny was a standout athlete and we all looked up to him."

Coy, Jr. would star on semi-pro and Black barnstorming teams throughout western Pennsylvania in the 1940s and early 1950s. "He reminded you of — when I think about a comparable player— what Jackie Robinson looked like," Hank Allen said. "He hit like him, he used the same bat that he used at that time, and he was a pretty good player, could hit for power and he could run, too."

"I played a pretty good second base and I might have gotten into the majors, but I knew that I would have to spend some time down south in the minor leagues, and I wasn't about to do that," Coy Jr. would say in a 1974 *Chicago Defender* interview. "So I went into the service."

As soon as they could play, the four other Allen sons followed in Coy's footsteps, starring in basketball and baseball at Wampum High School, playing for the legendary Bumper Hennon, who started coaching at the school back in 1933.

In fact, basketball was arguably Dick's best sport.

"All the brothers were good athletes and great basketball players, because that was a year-round sport at Wampum," recalled Tanner, who competed against Coy Allen, Jr. when Wampum High played New Castle High.

"I played against Coy, but I also remember watching Dick playing high school basketball. He was a sensational basketball player. I'm sure he could have played professional basketball. He would have been a Bob Cousy type, super ball-handler and quick enough to get in the open for shots."

But Coy Jr. would educate his brothers about baseball, taking them to games at nearby Forbes Field in Pittsburgh "five or six times a year," according to Hank Allen.

"Sonny had already moved out of the house, but he'd tell our mom, 'Have the boys ready and I'll be back out to pick them up on Sunday to take them to the game,'" Hank Allen recalled. "When we would go to the game, he would buy us a hot dog and a Coke, and he would explain the nuances of the Pirates game to us. This is how we grew to love the game and understand it."

The lessons were successful, because Dick, Hank and Ron would all end up playing in the major leagues, partially because of Coy, Jr.'s interest in his younger brothers. "It makes me emotional now to think about it, because (Coy) has since passed," Hank Allen said in 2021.

"He never got the opportunity to play professionally himself, but he made sure that we learned the game and was able to play professionally. And when we finally were there, as professionals, he followed us and would still give us advice about pitchers."

Although Dick was the starting guard on the Wampum High basketball team, which won the state championship in his senior year (1960), he preferred baseball, where he also excelled early in his high school career.

"As much as he loved baseball, he was an outstanding basketball player, and he had 103 offers to go to various colleges across the country," brother Hank claimed. "Not one time was he deterred by that. 'I want to be a major league baseball player,' he'd say. The college coaches would come there, they'd come down to the school, they get him, bring him to our home and my mother would ask him, 'Dick, come in and talk to this guy.' He would never come in the living room and talk to any of them. And he told Mom, 'I want to play baseball.' He was single-minded, with his purpose and idea that he wanted to be a major-league baseball player.

"When he was 15, Dick wanted to go try out for the Pirates because they had a trial camp up there one day and he asked my Dad if he could use his car, and he let him go and let him drive up to Forbes Field (in Pittsburgh). So he and (brother) Ronnie together went up there at that time. The Pirates, they wanted to sign him that day. They took him aside after he worked out and they wanted to sign. Thank goodness, Coy told him, 'Whatever you do, if somebody asks you to sign, don't you sign anything.'"

Dick also played American Legion ball at age 15. "He played with the older guys, guys in their 20s, 30s, 40s," Hank Allen added. "He put his age up in order to get there. Not only did he play well, he held his own and in the league he played in, they voted him Rookie of the Year at 15 years old."

Veteran Philadelphia Phillies scout John Ogden, a former pitcher who had his major league debut with the New York Giants in 1918, fell in love with Dick when he witnessed his various feats as a high schooler. "I scouted 90,000 players in my lifetime," Ogden would say later. "Dick Allen was the greatest I ever saw. (He) had more power to all fields than any man I've seen."

Coy Allen would help Dick negotiate a $70,000 bonus with the Phillies, the largest such bonus paid to an African American prospect up to that time. About $40,000 of that money went to mother Era for a new house, which got Dick into trouble with the IRS. The IRS case against him is famous and taught in law schools. Dick would be the petitioner in the famous case Allen v. Commissioner, 50 T.C. 466 (1968) wherein he attempted to avoid paying income tax on the $40,000 gift to his mother, the tax court held Allen was both responsible for the taxes and not able to make a trade or business deduction for the amount.

The Phillies would also eventually sign brothers Hank and Ron based on Ogden's recommendations.

But the Phillies organization had a troubled past with African American athletes. The Phillies —led by owner Bob Carpenter, Jr. and GM Herb Pennock— were blatantly opposed to major league integration in 1947, when Jackie Robinson debuted with the Brooklyn Dodgers. "You just can't bring the nigger here," longtime Dodgers executive Harold Parrott claimed Pennock reportedly told Dodger GM Branch Rickey before Robinson's debut at Shibe Park.

Robinson was harassed by Phillies manager Ben Chapman and his players during that Dodgers' initial appearance in Philadelphia. And the Phillies were the last National League team to integrate its roster in 1957 with utility infielder John Kennedy, only three years before Dick Allen was signed.

Dick and Hank began their careers with the Phillies with Elmira in the New York-Penn League in 1960. And Dick, who began wearing glasses that year, dominated the lower minor leagues, slugging 49 homers and driving in 245 runs in a three-year period, starting at his natural shortstop position (which he played as an amateur), before the organization moved him to second base in 1961.

Despite that great run, the Phillies exposed Dick in the 1961 expansion draft, because they were worried about his lack of a set defensive position and his poor eyesight, glasses notwithstanding (he committed 27 errors in 117 games at class C Magic Valley in '61). In what seems shocking in retrospect, neither the woeful New York Mets nor the Houston Colt 45's would spend the $50,000 posting fee to draft Dick. He saw it as blatant disrespect from the organization. "The Phillies didn't really want me from the beginning," Allen would say more than 10 years later.

After a great season in Class-A Williamsport in 1962 (20 homers, 109 RBI), Dick expected to be called up to the big club in 1963. But instead, the team sent him and a few other players of color to its Triple-A farm club in Little Rock, Ark. in 1963. The team had moved that year from Buffalo to Little Rock. The Phillies insensitively decided to integrate their new franchise there. a scant six years after the U.S. Army was dispatched to the city to quell racial attacks against African Americans after Governor Orval Faubus disobeyed a federal court decree to integrate Central High School.

Wampum was a relatively integrated town, so Dick had never really experienced blatant racism. But in Little Rock he would be subjected to intense racial hatred, starting with Opening Night, when fans attending Travelers Field waved posters that read "Let's not NEGRO-ize our baseball". Dick, playing his first game of the season in another unfamiliar position — left field — dropped the first fly ball that he saw, which created even more animosity from the crowd.

The most notable non-White teammate on the Travelers was future Hall of Famer Fergie Jenkins, who came up with the Phillies before being traded to the Cubs in 1966.

"In 1963, it was a bit of a shock to Dick," Jenkins said of their assignment with the Travelers. "The worst thing that happened is he bought a used vehicle and it was papered with hate stuff. He wanted to go home at one point, and his mom dissuaded him."

Dick, as an everyday player, experienced the worst of the racism. He'd write to Hank Allen, who was experiencing similar issues with the Phillies' other Southern-based farm team in Chattanooga, Tenn.

"I remember when he first got to Little Rock, and he shared a story, he didn't want to get off the plane, because they were carrying signs outside on the tarmac that said: 'Don't Nigger-ize Our Team. We're Segregated. Whites Only.' And so, he didn't want to get off the plane," Hank remembered.

"I didn't want to be a crusader," Dick Allen would say years later about his Little Rock experience. "I kept thinking: 'Why me? Why do I have to be the first black ballplayer in Little Rock?'"

His future coach on the '72 White Sox, Joe Lonnett, was the catcher on that Travelers team. Lonnett, who grew up near the Allens in Beaver Falls, Pa., and even refereed some of Dick's high school basketball games, provided support for the young star.

"His bags were packed, and he was ready to leave," Lonnett would recall in that 1972 season. "He was getting threatening phone calls. There were 'Nigger go home' signs on the windshield of his car. He couldn't get served in a restaurant unless a White player went with him. I told him to hang on — that it was either this, or a lunch bucket in the coal mines."

"If it wasn't for Joe Lonnett, I might not be in baseball today," Dick would say in his first year with the White Sox.

Years later, Hank Allen blamed the Phillies organization for not preparing Dick and himself for the traumatic situation, much less protecting them from hostile fans.

"I don't think it was really right for the Phillies at that time to send us to places like Little Rock and Chattanooga, knowing full well what the atmosphere was like, at that time," Hank said.

"We always had to live separate from everybody else on the team. One year in spring training (in Clearwater, Fla.) Dick and I lived in a funeral home (in nearby Plant City, Fla.) because when you got to spring training, they separated Whites from Blacks.

"The Whites went to the hotel, and we went to the other side of the tracks where Black families lived in private homes or wherever they could. Dick said he wasn't staying in that funeral home because the caskets were open in there and you had those dead bodies in there, and Dick didn't take kindly to death. So, there was an empty house the people owned, but there was no heat in it. So we asked, could we stay over there? And so, they put some light in there and had the lights turned on, they put two cots in there, and that's where he and I slept."

Despite these daunting conditions, Dick Allen thrived on the field in Little Rock. He led the International League with 33 homers and 97 RBI in 1963 — those 33 homers would be a Travelers record for a right-handed hitter for the next four decades. His appearance on the team also forced the Travelers to integrate their grandstands at Travelers Field. Dick's spectacular season also forced the Phillies to bring him up in September 1963. He'd never play another minor-league game. Instead, he'd be a fixture at Connie Mack Stadium, but with a new name. Since childhood, he'd been either "Dick" or "Sleepy", a nickname that called attention to his droopy eyelids. But in Philadelphia, he became "Richie", a nod to Richie Ashburn, the Phillies' star center fielder of the 1950s.

Dick continued his dominant hitting straight into 1964, winning the National League Rookie of the Year award as he sparked the Phillies to an unexpected first-place run before being overtaken by the St. Louis Cardinals during an epic collapse in the last two weeks of the season. Placed by manager Gene Mauch at yet another unfamiliar spot, third base, Allen ended up making 41 errors. But he had a spectacular overall stat line: 29 homers, 91 RBI, a league-leading 13 triples to go with 38 doubles, a .318 batting average and an OPS of .939.

Dick exuded confidence and, even in his rookie year, he bristled at any hint of racial stereotyping. He told *Philadelphia Daily News* reporter Larry Merchant his hatred of his White teammates' nickname for Black teammate Wes Covington: "Kingfish," a stereotypical character on the old "Amos 'n' Andy" radio and TV show. And he put a stop to his teammates' attempts to dub him "Sammy Davis." "I'd get out of baseball rather than put up with that," Dick said. He also knew his self-worth as an athlete. "I don't owe the ball club anything but the best nine innings I could play," he'd tell the media at the time.

But the combination of the Allen confidence, his numerous errors at third base and the collapse of the Phillies in the 1964 pennant race all created negativity among fans directed at their rookie star. A race riot that exploded in August 1964 in North Philly near Connie Mack Stadium also helped create resentment among White fans toward Black players in a segregated city. Dick endured booing and verbal harassment, which started in late summer 1964 and didn't let up until he left town five years later.

Such an independent, stick-up-for-myself stance made an impression on other Black players coming up in the turbulent 1960s when it became apparent business-as-usual would no longer stand. Previously, Black players who supported change had to be careful in public comments in an era when their front office employers held most of the cards. 1965 Dodgers sparkplug Lou Johnson, also a two-time Cub, recalled having to hold his tongue with his livelihood on the line.

Nearly 3,000 miles from Philadelphia, in the Sacramento area, a talented young hitter named Johnnie B. Baker, Jr. took note of Dick Allen's style as an influencer.

"I first started liking Dick when I was in high school," said the young player, better known as Dusty Baker in his long playing career and in five managerial jobs, including the Cubs. "I used to like the way he stood up and was a man, wouldn't back down to anything. He motivated me when I became a pro.

"Dick was first guy I heard besides Sandy Koufax and Don Drysdale turn down a contract. I sent a contract back 18 times. They locked me out in spring training. Lou Johnson was right. If you spoke out, they would squash you and get rid of you," recalled Baker in 2021.

No doubt, Dick's 1965 spring training tactics registered with prep star Baker. Dick held out for more money until midway through camp. If players were valued enough by management, holdouts could bring some results. Dick doubled his 1964 salary by getting $20,000 from GM John Quinn, the father-in-law of Roland Hemond. He was criticized for his successful holdout by media and fellow players alike, but —schooled by his older brother, Coy and his longtime financial advisor Clem Capozzoli — Dick would successfully hold out for higher compensation in each of his years with the Phillies. He would have close to a

$100,000 salary by the time he departed Philadelphia in 1970.

Dick Allen's independent personality also attracted the attention of future Hall of Famer Marvin Miller who, as its new executive director, gradually built the Major League Baseball Players Association into arguably the country's most powerful union. Miller presided over a January 1969 MLBPA meeting at which Allen appeared. He described it in his 1991 memoir, *A Whole Different Ball Game: The Sport and Business of Baseball.*

"I recall the positive contributions that many players at the meeting...for some reason I recall most vividly Dick Allen, always an impressive figure, he came to the meeting dressed in the dashiki. He did not speak in the early part of that meeting but later spoke to quiet dignity...He was eloquent and forceful, and the other players listened intently. He didn't speak as a superstar but as a player...I wish some of the writers who were quick so quick to jump on him years later would have seen him in this light," Miller wrote.

Frank Thomas surely was one teammate who did not see Dick as an intelligent franchise player, which he had become in his second year with the Phillies. The veteran slugger, who started with the Pirates in 1951, was winding down his career with the Phillies as a pinch hitter and utility player in 1965. Thomas was known as an "agitator," possessing the 'uncanny knack of saying the wrong thing at the wrong time to the wrong guy," according to Philadelphia Bulletin reporter Sandy Grady. Thomas specialized in using race-baiting language to Black players. In the past, he had teased one Dick Allen with comments like "Shine my shoes, boy."

On July 3, 1965, the two were involved in a skirmish during batting practice before a Saturday night game at Connie Mack Stadium. The details of the fight are shrouded in baseball legend, with witnesses providing different accounts of what happened. But what is clear is that while in the batting cage, Thomas used a racial slur to address Allen.

"We heard that Thomas was taking extra swings," said Ferguson Jenkins, still a minor leaguer in the Phillies system at that time. "Dick was a regular and wanted to get into the cage. The Big 'N' word came out (from Thomas). (So) Dick charged into the cage."

Dick reportedly punched Thomas in the chest. So Thomas responded with an action that was long considered taboo in baseball — he hit Dick in the left shoulder with his bat. "I had the bat in my hand and hit him in the shoulder — it was a reflex action," Thomas would tell the Philadelphia media later that night.

The two men would play in the game against the Cincinnati Reds — Allen went 3-for-4, while Thomas slugged a pinch-hit home run. But Thomas, the marginal player, was placed on waivers by the end of the weekend. After being released, Thomas immediately went to the press to complain. But Allen was told by manager Gene Mauch not to talk publicly about the incident. With Allen barred from telling his side of the story, Philadelphia fans and media blamed him for the incident.

"All (the Phillies) had to do was call a press conference and clear things up," Dick would say in 1973. "They didn't. They had a losing team, they had to get people out to the park, so they said, 'Boo that Black sumbuck. Go ahead, he won't say nothing.'"

The incident created even more resentment among Connie Mack Stadium fans, who began throwing things at Dick from the stands. He starting wearing a batting helmet in the field to protect himself from these flying objects, a practice he continued for the rest of his career. Teammate and future Hall of Fame broadcaster Bob Uecker began calling Dick "Crash," in reaction to the helmet.

"He'd come into the clubhouse and mimic me," Dick would say with a laugh years later. "My name is Crash Helmet. I wear this thing to protect my head from the fans."

While he was being persecuted by some in the Philadelphia crowds, Dick was becoming one of the best players in the National League. After hitting .302 in 1965, he had a year for the ages in 1966, leading the league in slugging (.632), OPS (1.027) and extra base hits (75). He belted a career-high 40 home runs, second in the NL to Hank Aaron.

Dick had power to all fields and with his 40-ounce bat, his homers were legendary, even in what was considered the decade of the pitcher. In May 1965, he was one of the only players in history to hit a homer over the Connie Mack Stadium roof. "Now I know why they (the Phillies fans) boo Richie all the time. When he hits a home run, there's no souvenir," Pirates slugger Willie Stargell said at the time.

"Dick wanted the ball over the plate," said Jenkins who was a worthy Allen adversary with his sharp-breaking slider. "He had that heavy bat. All he wanted to do was get it started. He hit breaking balls, too. He was off the plate (and) he charged the ball, stepped into it."

He was perhaps baseball's most sculpted athlete: A compact 5-11, 180-pound man with seemingly no body fat. "From the waist up he is a defensive end, from the waist down he is a wide receiver," *Sports Illustrated's* Roy Blount, Jr. would write about Dick. But he never, ever lifted weights to maintain that physique. "He was a morning person and he would get up at around 4:30 or 5 a.m. and run, which was all he'd do to stay in shape," said his son, Richard, Jr.

Dick was also developing a reputation as baseball's most talented eccentric. He was one of the best dressers in the league during the 60s and 70s, known for bringing his tailors into the clubhouse to size him up for colorful Nehru jackets, hip-hugger pants and other resplendent combinations of the time.

Dick Allen was also a professional R&B singer for a time, putting out a regional single called "Echoes of November" in 1968 that did reasonably well in the Northeast. A credible tenor, Dick even performed with his group, the Ebonistics, at venues in Philadelphia, including a halftime stint at a 76ers basketball game, where he, of course, was booed.

But Allen's most famous non-baseball predilection was horses. He was a regular at racetracks across the country and began buying horses during his rookie year in Philadelphia. Hank Allen, who later became a celebrated horse trainer and owner himself, recalled their father was the reason for the family interest in equines.

"Our father was born in King George, Va., where his family had a farm and they had horses," Hank said. "When we were living in Pennsylvania, my dad wanted to go back to his roots a little bit, so he bought a horse. So, Dick said, as soon as I get enough money, I'm going to buy a horse. And sure enough, that first year he was in Philadelphia as a rookie, he bought a horse named Blaze and that's where he would spend his afternoons and when the season was over, riding Blaze down there in Fairmount Park, (in the Mount Airy neighborhood in northwest Philadelphia where Dick lived while playing for the Phillies)."

"He would wake up at 4:30 in the morning and he'd be reading up on horses," Richard (Doobie) Allen, Jr. recalled. "He just loved them. I think it was because they were athletic, they were strong and they were respected, and I felt like maybe he thought a little of that was in him."

Dick remained productive throughout his stint in Philadelphia, including the All-Star team in 1965, 1966 and 1967. And he continued to be a tough negotiator in the off-season, ending up with an $85,000 contract for 1967, the highest ever at that time for a fourth-year player.

But in addition to his continued issues with fans and media, injuries and other physical problems began to crop up. Most notably, on an August 1967 day in Philadelphia when he was idle due to a rainout, he severed two tendons and the ulnar nerve in his wrist after his right hand went through the headlight of his 1950 Ford, which he was trying to push up a hill outside of his home. For years afterwards, he would have no sensation in two fingers on that hand.

The combination of injuries and pressure-filled relationships with fans and media were key influences on Allen's drinking problems during his time in Philadelphia. He was never a big fan of batting practice, because as he later said, he didn't like seeing slower pitches before a game. But by 1967, he was starting to routinely show up just a few minutes before games. "My wife would run me out of the house in the afternoon and I'd go to a bar for a couple of hours," Dick would say in 1973.

After his right hand injury in 1967, he had a breakdown. "I went on maybe a 2½-month drunk," Dick recalled. "Nobody could find me. I was driving. In Pittsburgh, my oldest brother gave me some static. I woke up in Mexicali, Mexico once. In LA, my sister gave me some static, I was out of it. I didn't know where I was."

Despite these issues, he still produced for bad Philllies teams in 1968 and 1969, hitting more than 30 homers in both years, including '68's "Year of the Pitcher." At times, the Phillies kicked the tires on an Allen trade. One report had Dick offered to the Cubs in 1968 for either third baseman Ron Santo or outfielder Billy Williams. The Phillies were turned down. His relationship with manager Gene Mauch deteriorated, and when Mauch was fired in mid-'68, Dick was blamed by the media for the dismissal. In July 1969, he jumped the team for 26 days, after he was suspended for arriving late for a game at New York's Shea Stadium. He lost $11,500 in salary during that time. Dick returned to the team only when owner Bob Carpenter finally agreed to trade him in the off-season.

That trade would be completed on Oct. 7, 1969, five days after the season's conclusion, when Allen, Cookie Rojas and Jerry Johnson were sent to the Cardinals for Curt Flood, Joe Hoerner, Tim McCarver and ex-Cub Byron Browne. Ironically, Dick would not be the most controversial player in this deal. Instead, Flood refused to show up to Philadelphia, challenging baseball's reserve clause, an act which foreshadowed free agency.

For a brief period of time, Dick thought he had a home in St. Louis. He continued to produce as one of the best players in baseball, hitting 34 home runs and driving in 101 runs in 1970, even though he missed almost the last two months with a pulled hamstring muscle. "It was a class organization," Dick would say later. "They had super guys like Bob Gibson and Lou Brock and Joe Torre. I wanted to stay there the rest of my career."

But as it turns out, the Cardinals claimed they needed a singles-hitting second baseman more than they needed a powerful Dick Allen in spacious Busch Stadium. After rebuffing the White Sox' offer of future Hall of Famer Aparicio for Allen, Cardinals GM Bing Devine traded him to the Dodgers for middle infielder Ted Sizemore.

A consequence of the turbulent years in Philadelphia was Dick's reputation within certain segments of the baseball establishment of being a "clubhouse cancer." When he was traded from St. Louis, there were hints in the media that the trade was made to "improve team morale," a rumor that hurt Dick, who always prided himself on having a good relationship with teammates. "When the day comes that I can't get along with my teammates, I'll get out of baseball," he said.

This proud veteran was excited about the prospect of playing for Los Angeles — the Dodgers were the team most admired among African Americans at the time, because the franchise was in the forefront of integrating major league baseball a generation before. But his excitement was tamped down when he learned that longtime manager Walter Alston didn't want him on the team. General Manager Al Campanis had to persuade Alston to accept his new slugger.

Then, when Dick got to Los Angeles, he found a scene where baseball seemed secondary. "I got out there and one guy had his fan club over here and another guy had his fan club over there and three of the guys were trying to be actors on the side and another guy spent most of his time banging on a banjo in Vegas," he said. "It was everything but baseball with the Dodgers."

If he winced at some teammates' prima donna personas, Dick was helpful to younger players coming up. He would go on to mentor rookie Goose Gossage when he arrived in Chicago and had always dispensed counsel to others, with a catch: "He would only talk to young players if they were willing to listen," said Dusty Baker, then of the Atlanta Braves.

Baker was all ears. Breaking in with the Braves organization, before he ever met Dick, he crossed paths with the Allen brothers in the minors. He recalled meeting Hank in Buffalo and Ron with the Mets' affiliate in Tidewater, in the Norfolk, Va., area.

Dick Allen took note of Baker's youth among opposing players. "I was always called The Kid because wherever I played, I was the youngest guy," Baker said. "One time I wasn't swinging good. He asked me if I ever played basketball. He said I didn't have any balance on my feet. Another time he asked if I could dance. He said I didn't have any rhythm at the plate. He equated hitting to dancing."

Baker also witnessed close-up how Dick aggravated his bosses by not strictly adhering to pre-game schedules. "It was September 1971 at Dodger Stadium," he said. "I ran into Dick and they said he was late to the ballpark. No, he wasn't. He was upstairs watching batting practice. He said he was up there getting his mind right."

Baker would have another connection with Dick. As a lively, out-on-the-town young man, he dated his niece, Nancy Allen, for a short time.

When Baker encountered Allen at Dodger Stadium, he was finishing a slightly down year, statistically. But in one of the best pitchers' ballparks in the game, he still managed 23 homers, 90 RBI and an .863 OPS for the Dodgers, who would finish just one game behind their archrival San Francisco Giants for the NL West title.

"Players Walk Out...And Allen Walks in"

– Chicago Tribune headline on April 1, 1972 when Dick Allen signed his White Sox contract and Major League Baseball players launched a 13-day strike

Although Dick was traded to the White Sox on Dec. 3, 1971, he was still not a lock to join the team.

At first, he refused to accept the deal. Sox manager Chuck Tanner — whom Dick called "Homey" — drove to Wampum to talk with him and his mother after the deal went down. But once he got there, he saw a dejected Dick Allen, who was still struggling with his injured right hand hurt in 1967 and other assorted ailments, along with a broken reputation and a potential new team that wasn't considered a competitive squad. He told Tanner that he wasn't interested in joining the Sox.

"I told him thank you but I don't intend to play," Dick recalled.

But Era Allen intervened. "She goes 'Dick, Mr. Tanner's a local man and he wants you to play for his team,'" Tanner's son Bruce said: "Dick told his mom 'I don't want to be there with a bunch of kids — I'm too old for that.' And Dick's mom told him, 'You're going to be playing for Mr. Tanner next year, do you hear me?' And Dick's like, 'Yes, mom.'"

While Dick finally gave Tanner his word that he'd join the team, it would take another four months to hammer out a contract. Allen had made $100,000 with the Dodgers, and he was expecting at least $120,000 in 1972. But the White Sox had never had a six-figure contract in team history. Their highest-paid player was Luis Aparicio, who got $85,000 in 1970, including payment for his responsibilities as a part-time scout for the Sox in Venezuela during the off-season. The top salary on the team when the Allen trade was made was Mike Andrews, who made $55,000. Next was Wilbur Wood and Bill Melton, each at approximately $40,000.

The White Sox offered a sizable increase to Allen's 1971 salary — a deal reported to be at or near the $120,000 he apparently wanted. But Allen refused to accept it. When the team opened spring training in Sarasota, Fla. on Feb. 22, 1972, Allen was absent. Nor was he there when the last other unsigned player, longtime pitcher Joel Horlen, finally reported to camp on Feb. 28. Horlen, the last link to the pre-1967 Go-Go Sox teams and the team's player representative, would be released on April 2, 1972 right after the game's first strike of the modern era was authorized by the Major League Baseball Players Association.

Other holdouts who signed included outfielders Jay Johnstone and Rick Reichardt and pitcher Tom Bradley. As Allen's six-figure salary would represent one-fourth of the Sox' $469,000 payroll, these players had to sign for less than they had requested, likely to accommodate the new arrival's paycheck. Reichardt, the team's new co-player representative along with Johnstone, reluctantly settled for a $2,000 pay increase. "I look back at the trade with mixed emotions," Reichardt would say years later. "It's hard to argue about what Dick did on the field, but some of us had to make sacrifices to get him there. Remember, there were no million-dollar contracts at the time. A lot of us worked in the off-season to make ends meet."

Dick had continuously sent conflicting messages to the team. In late February 1972, his accountant told White Sox General Manager Stu Holcomb that he was ready to sign. But that didn't happen. Then, on March 14, he showed up in camp to tell the Sox that he wasn't accepting their updated $125,000 contract offer, which would make him the highest paid pro athlete in Chicago. "We're not even close to terms," he told the media. "I'm going home to Mama."

The decision not to sign surprised Holcomb and owner John Allyn. "I thought once he came in it would be very easy to sign him," Allyn said.

Though Dick said he was returning home to Wampum, teammates heard he was staying at a nearby motor lodge in Sarasota, doing private workouts to get ready for the season. He'd occasionally drive by Sox camp to check out the players from afar. "I watched from center field and thought this was a high school team," he confessed 40 years later.

Meanwhile, in Chicago, the media was urging the White Sox to get rid of the much-ballyhooed newcomer. "This looks like a good time to cut your losses and run," wrote the Tribune's Robert Markus, an early Allen critic who later was won over by the slugger.

Dick, for his part, told a Philadelphia reporter that he was considering sitting out the season and challenging baseball's reserve clause in court, as Curt Flood did two years earlier. "You ever wonder why baseball loves big dumb farm boys?" he asked the reporter. "It's because farm boys don't say very much.

"What say do I have in my professional life?" Dick said. "They tell you to go here, they send you a piece of paper and say this is your salary. Accept it. What if I don't want to play in Chicago?"

Ironically, the latest Allen contract dispute came as talk of the players strike began to ramp up in training camps throughout Florida and Arizona. At issue was the expiration of the league's three-year pension agreement. The players wanted a modest increase in pension payouts, to match inflation. The owners refused. But the players union, strong and unified under Miller, threatened to walk out if the issue wasn't resolved.

On April 1, MLBPA player representatives voted 47-0 to strike, effective immediately.

On that same day, Dick Allen walked into the White Sox-owned Sarasota Motor Lodge, sharply dressed in a dark green suit, a light green shirt and a gold necktie. He met briefly in private with Holcomb. The two, along with Tanner and Allen's agent Alfred Morris, then held a news conference, announcing that Allen had signed a $135,000 contract. "For the first time in my career, I really feel wanted," Allen told the media. "Baseball is all I know, and I do want to play. So, I was a little concerned and came down here on my own."

At the same time and at the same motel lodge, the Team's player reps Johnstone and Reichardt were meeting with players, informing them about the nature of the strike.

Allen said he was happy to be with the Sox and said he wasn't concerned about the club being inferior. "I'm here to help, whether it's a good club or bad club." he said.

What do you want to be called?" a newsman asked.

"Never late for supper," laughed Allen. "Dick will be all right, I guess. I would much rather be called the winner when this thing is over. I don't really mind. I've been called Dick ever since I was a kid, but when I was in Philly, Richie Ashburn was there so he started to call me Richie—that's where it started."

After the press conference, Dick moved to a nearby municipal park, where he employed a college student to throw him batting practice for almost an hour.

Thirteen days later, after the strike was over, the new slugger was at White Sox Park for the first time, where he belted around six home runs during a workout on a frigid day as the Sox prepared for their delayed Opening Day in Kansas City now set for Saturday, April 15.

Allen enjoyed a low-key first official workout with his new team. But he would soon become the dominant figure on the South Side of Chicago, if not in all of baseball.

Dick Allen with his mother, Era Allen - a prevailing, strong influence in his life.

Photo credit: Leo Bauby Collection

A passion that rivaled baseball for Dick Allen was horses.
He involved his brothers in the training and grooming of horses.

Photo credit: Leo Bauby Collection

CHAPTER 3

January 7, 1972:
The Baseball Palace
of the World

Dick Allen had made his name playing in Philadelphia's Connie Mack Stadium, the oldest of the so-called "Jewel Box" ballparks. These were the 14 urban, two-tiered stadiums constructed of steel and concrete for major league baseball teams, built between 1909 and 1923 to replace the wooden structures of the late 19th century.

But one year after Dick was traded from Philadelphia, Connie Mack Stadium was abandoned by the Phillies. The ballpark was replaced in 1971 by Veterans Stadium, one of the new, generic, multi-purpose stadia constructed in the 1960s and 1970s. With Astroturf-covered fields, these structures were generally soulless and derided in future years as "cookie-cutter."

With Dick's trade to the White Sox in late 1971, he would now be playing in Comiskey Park, which was by 1972 the oldest active major league stadium.

The ballyard at 35th and Shields was an expansive, revolutionary concrete-and-steel stadium constructed on a former city dump in the Armour Square neighborhood on the city's South Side, originally seating an unprecedented 32,000. In time, it became one of the most storied sports venues in the United States. The White Sox would eventually play more than 6,000 games and Comiskey would host four World Series, including one for the crosstown Cubs.

The old park was also the site of the major league baseball's first All-Star Game in 1933 and the exclusive home of the Negro League's East-West All Star Game from 1933 to 1950. It hosted famous boxing matches, most notably the 1937 bout between Joe Louis and James J. Braddock, when Louis first became the heavyweight champion of the world. The NFL's Chicago Cardinals would play there for four decades before leaving for St. Louis in 1960. And a panoply of non-sports events were also staged at Comiskey Park over the years — from concerts featuring the likes of the Beatles to roller derby events (attracting 50,000-plus fans) to massive religious convocations. All these events were held in front of a backdrop of the sloping Romanesque arches along the walls of the grandstand.

"To me, it was like playing in a great cathedral," recalled Hall of Fame pitcher Rich "Goose" Gossage, remembering when he first laid eyes on the South Side Palace as a rookie for the White Sox in 1972.

On Jan. 7 of that year, the 62-year-old iconic South Side landmark was sharing headlines on what was an extremely busy news day. Page 1 of the *Chicago Tribune* reported on an explosive device being planted at the First National Bank in downtown Chicago. The alleged perpetrators were the Weathermen, the radical leftist militant group led by Bill Ayers and Bernardine Dohrn, which had been responsible for the violent "Days of Rage" demonstrations in the city during October 1969.

Meanwhile, at Chicago's City Hall, Richard J. Daley, entering his 18th year as mayor, was once again in his role as kingmaker as he met with the media for the first time after returning from a Christmas vacation in the Florida Keys. Democratic presidential candidates were beginning to jockey for position to run against President Richard Nixon in the general election. And Daley, still by far the most powerful Democratic big city mayor in the country, had a favorite candidate — Sen. Edmund Muskie.

Hizzoner had little enthusiasm, however, for Sen. George McGovern, who was fast becoming the favorite among Democratic presidential candidates. McGovern had been critical of Daley after the clashes between Chicago police and anti-Vietnam War protestors at the 1968 Democratic National Convention. Daley, in turn, was lukewarm when asked about McGovern's chances. "Sen. Muskie ran the best campaign in '68, and he's the best candidate in 1972," said the Mayor, without making an official endorsement.

On the sports pages, the main story was about the future of Comiskey Park. For almost 10 years, the White Sox had been in discussions with Daley and with the city's other sports teams about the possibility of playing in a new multi-purpose sports facility. Frequently discussed after the success of Houston's Astrodome was a domed stadium with a retractable roof that would house the Sox, the Cubs and the NFL's Bears. Comiskey Park was aging and whispers abounded about its location near to low-income neighborhoods directly to its east.

Other aging "Jewel Box" stadiums which, like Comiskey, were located in inner-city neighborhoods — Ebbets Field and the Polo Grounds in New York, Connie Mack Stadium in Philadelphia, Crosley Field in Cincinnati and Sportsman's Park in St. Louis — had all been demolished and replaced with modern, multi-purpose facilities. Also seeing the wrecking ball was Pittsburgh's Forbes Field, next to the University of Pittsburgh. The fact that the Sox had drawn just 495,000 in 1970 seemed to prove that the facility had outlived its usefulness.

But on this cold morning, at the team's annual mid-winter luncheon, owner John Allyn doubled down on Comiskey Park, saying that that team would stay on the South Side for the foreseeable future. "I don't believe there will be a joint sport facility in Chicago for an extensive period of time," Allyn said. "In fact, I am going to resign my position on (Daley's) committee for a new stadium because I see no interest in it or money available." Instead, Allyn was planning on small improvements to his aging stadium. Most notably, he was investing in a new sound system which involved the installation of a new state-of-the-art stadium organ underneath the press box over home plate, in order to showcase his brilliant young organist, Nancy Faust.

"I don't think the White Sox will be moving out of our park for a long time," Allyn declared.

When the White Sox held their inaugural game at their new home in 1910, three years before the owner renamed it after himself, the team had already been playing in the South Side neighborhood for almost 10 years. After its founding in 1901, Chicago's American League charter team had been playing at South Side Park at 39th Street and Wentworth Avenue, a venue constructed primarily of wood that seated 7,500 fans. Here, in the first decade of the 20th century, the Sox would establish themselves as a successful sports franchise. They won the first — and only — crosstown World Series against the Cubs in 1906 while playing in that ballpark, which had also served as the home grounds for the Chicago Wanderers cricket team during the 1893 World's Fair.

But White Sox owner and founder Charles A. Comiskey (The "Old Roman") was keeping abreast of all new developments in major league baseball. And he noticed the new trend of concrete-and-steel ballparks which were being constructed by the two National League teams in Pennsylvania. The Phillies opened Shibe Park (later Connie Mack Stadium) in April 1909; the Pirates were playing in Forbes Field by June 1909.

After visiting these stadia in person, Comiskey was intent on constructing his own concrete-and-steel facility as soon as possible. And for him, it was important that the park opened in the same neighborhood where his team was already playing. Part of that was because Comiskey was a native South Sider — he was born there in 1859, the son of a notable early Chicago alderman, "Honest John" Comiskey. And 11-year-old Charles Comiskey watched as his beloved team, the Chicago White Stockings (the team that would eventually become the National League's Chicago Cubs), played their inaugural season in Dexter Park at 47th and Halsted streets.

In 1890, Comiskey returned to Chicago after starring for more than a decade as the player-manager with the St. Louis Brown Stockings, which won four consecutive American Association championships. He came back as player-manager for the Chicago Pirates in the newly-formed but short-lived Players League. Those Pirates also played on the South Side — they were at Brotherhood Park, located at the northwest corner of 35th Street and South Wentworth Avenue where present day White Sox marquee marketing sign is located, just west of Wenworth and visible from the Dan Ryan expressway. There, Comiskey took notice that his team outdrew their National League rival Chicago Colts (the former White Stockings).

The Old Roman knew that a baseball team would do well in that location because the Wentworth Street streetcar ran from downtown Chicago right past the park — the same route that 80 years later would be occupied by the CTA Red Line trains and the Dan Ryan. With excellent access and the right on-field product, Comiskey knew he could cater to the working-class fans who lived nearby in Bridgeport, Canaryville, Washington Park and Back-of -the-Yards. They and their descendants would form the base of his franchise until the present day.

Comiskey kept the spot in mind when he was scouting for his modern baseball home. And on Christmas Day in 1908, he was able to purchase property nearby — at what was formerly a city dump at 35th Street and Shields Avenue. The owner hired architect Zachary Taylor Davis to design the facility. Davis, who apprenticed with Frank Lloyd Wright at the landmark architectural firm Adler and Sullivan, would later design Wrigley Field on the North Side and consult on Yankee Stadium in New York. But he was best known for his work with churches (including the ornate Archbishop Quigley Preparatory Seminary in downtown Chicago).

For this ballpark, Davis designed a kite-shaped, red-bricked stadium with sloping Romanesque arches embedded throughout the ballpark, designed to bring in the late-afternoon sunlight — something that was needed in the days before teams erected lights at their venues. The design blended in with the churches and factories that were commonplace in the nearby Bridgeport, Canaryville and Back of the Yards neighborhoods. Construction started in the late winter of 1910 and required only five months for completion of the $750,000 ballpark.

For good luck, Comiskey planted a brick with Gaelic soil imported from Ireland to commemorate the ground-breaking of the ballpark on St. Patrick's Day 1910. The brick was painted a bright green hue according to legend, but quickly was covered over by Davis, who feared it would be carried away by souvenir hunters.

Comiskey had his star pitcher, "Big Ed" Walsh, consult with Davis on the design. The end result was a pitcher-friendly ballpark with dimensions of 363 feet down the foul lines, a posted 375 feet in the power alleys and 420 feet to straightaway center. Those dimensions would be altered throughout the years. In 1972, for instance, the park was a bit more hitter-friendly: 349 down the lines, still with the posted 375 in the power alleys but only 400 to straightaway center — with the bullpens located on the field by the left and right field foul lines.

Throughout its 80-year history, Comiskey Park remained a pitchers' park. No White Sox batter in team history ever hit 100 homers there — Carlton Fisk came closest, with 94. And 61 years passed before the team would field an American

League home run champ: Bill Melton, who led with 33 homers in 1971.

"The issue with old Comiskey was that the fences from the right and left foul poles were straight across, instead of being rounded off like in a lot of other ballparks," Melton said. "That's why you had the power alleys at [nearly] 380 and center at 420. The depth was a lot further than if they had rounded it off. So you really had to square up the ball to hit it out."

The team christened White Sox Park on July 1, 1910, when 32,000 fans filled the ballpark on one of the hottest days of the year. Temperatures reached 96 degrees. A two-tiered grandstand extended down both the baselines and a single level of wooden bleachers were located behind the outfield wall. "Unfinished as the plant was in spots…the size of the new palace was what most forcibly struck all visitors who were making their first call," an unidentified *Chicago Tribune* scribe reported on the South Side park's opening day. "As each emerged from the sloping inclines which led to the rear of the main stand, he or she stopped for a moment in silent awe, gazing at the broad, sweeping lines of the stands and at the seemingly endless rows of seats."

Only one aspect seemed to mar the opening, in Charles Comiskey's mind. Countering the soil-planting at the ground-breaking, Comiskey believed he had cursed his ballpark and franchise forever because he violated the Irish-Catholic superstition of "Never on a Friday" with the inaugural game taking place on a Friday.

When the new ballpark opened, the White Sox' old stadium, South Side Park, became the home of the Chicago American Giants, the team co-owned by legendary Negro League founder Rube Foster. The small venue was renamed Schorling Park for team owner Foster's White business partner, John C. Schorling, who happened to be Comiskey's son-in-law. The Chicago American Giants leased the grounds until Christmas Day of 1940, when Schorling Park was destroyed by fire. The property would be redeveloped as a still-existing public housing complex, Wentworth Gardens. The American Giants would play their remaining 12 seasons at Comiskey Park.

In short order, Comiskey Park neé White Sox Park became the location for famous — and infamous — events in sports. At their baseball "palace," the Sox defeated the New York Giants in their second World Series in 1917. The franchise would have to wait another 88 years to win another. In 1918, the National League pennant-winning Cubs chose to play their World Series home games against the Boston Red Sox at Comiskey Park instead of Weeghman Park (soon to be renamed Wrigley Field) due to Comiskey's much-larger seating capacity. That series, won by the Babe Ruth-led Red Sox 4-2 at the end of World War I (and staged during the deadly influenza pandemic that would eventually kill more than 675,000 in the U.S.) was later rumored to be fixed. White Sox pitcher Eddie Cicotte alleged that several Cubs took bribes to throw the Series. And in 1919, the Sox played their ill-fated "Black Sox" World Series at Comiskey, as Cicotte and seven of his teammates were accused, acquitted and then banned from baseball for their role in throwing the Fall Classic.

In response to Ruth's incredible popularity on the New York Yankees, Comiskey launched a $1 million ballpark renovation after the 1926 season. The wooden bleachers were replaced and the upper deck was extended to left and right fields, essentially enclosing the stadium. This renovation increased the park's seating capacity to 52,000 and gave it the basic look it would have for the remainder of its long existence.

The Bards Room, the legendary interior dining room and bar for the media and team executives, located underneath the grandstand, opened in 1917. The gathering spot was originally designed, complete with a gigantic fireplace, as a private gentleman's club for the Old Roman and his friends and colleagues. Outside the park, McCuddy's Tavern served both fans and players. Ruth was said to be a regular in the 1920s and early 1930s. An autographed bat from the Babe was displayed behind the tavern for years, until it was demolished in 1989 to make way for Comiskey Park's replacement — the new Comiskey Park, later named U.S. Cellular Field and then Guaranteed Rate Field.

After the "Black Sox" scandal, the Chicago White Sox spent the next 30 years mostly in the second division (lower half of the standings), playing second fiddle to the Cubs in attendance. But Comiskey itself still was the city's primary venue for important national sporting events.

The 1933 All-Star Game, organized by *Chicago Tribune* sports editor Arch Ward and supported by Cubs President William L. Veeck Sr., was supposed to be a one-time only event. But its initial success at Comiskey helped turn the spectacle into an annual national event. The All-Star Game came back to Comiskey Park in 1950, and then fittingly returned for a 50th anniversary gala in 1983.

Meanwhile, the Negro League's East-West All-Star game, which also was launched in 1933, would become a near-annual event at Comiskey. Twenty-eight East-West games were staged at the park from 1933 to 1960. This assemblage would be considered as one of the premier entertainment events nationally for African Americans, who would flock from all over the country to see the best of the Negro Leagues competing against one another. Votes for the All-Stars were tallied by two of the most notable African American newspapers of that time: The *Chicago Defender* and the *Pittsburgh Courier*.

Chuck Comiskey, the forward-thinking grandson of the first Charles, was promoted to the White Sox front office in 1948, while only in his early 20s. He would spearhead stadium improvements, including the park's first electronic center field scoreboard in 1951, somewhat known then for its advertisement of Chesterfield cigarettes. He was also responsible for adding a press box hanging over the third-base box seats, designed for the football Chicago Cardinals.

These stadium improvements occurred while Comiskey and general manager Frank Lane were reviving the franchise, which in 1951 began a 16-year streak as a first-division team. The addition of exciting new talent like Minnie Minoso, Billy Pierce, Nellie Fox and Luis Aparicio heading up consistently winning teams made Comiskey Park the center of major league baseball attention in Chicago during the 1950s and 1960s. The Sox routinely drubbed the Cubs in attendance, even attracting some fans from the North Shore, traditionally Cubs country. P.K. Wrigley's contrarian insistence on day-only baseball killed his Cubs gate on weekdays as the Sox proved lights were needed for decent crowds when the majority of fans worked 9 a.m. to 5 p.m.

Tickets to White Sox-Yankees games were particularly coveted, with more than 40,000 fans routinely showing up for Friday night games and Sunday doubleheaders. Even Monday through Wednesday nights with the Yankees typically drew in excess of 35,000, if not actual full houses.

"We lived in Highland Park and we used to drive there as soon as we got our driver's license as many nights and days as we could — all weekends, certainly Sunday doubleheaders." recalled Emmy Award-winning television producer Tom Weinberg, who started regularly attending Sox games in the early 1950s.

"We moved to the North Shore in 1951, and the Cubs were horrible then." added Weinberg's longtime friend, Roger Wallenstein. "And the White Sox, that was the beginning of the 'Go-Go Sox' era and they were a much more appealing team. We thought it looked like a lot more fun than rooting for a team that loses all the time. And there was nothing more complicated than that. The fact the Cubs were on the North Side vs. the Sox on the South Side never entered into it. It was a question of rooting for a poor team that lost all the time or a team that was up-and-coming, where you could feel good about the team winning. So we took the winners, we were front-runners."

By the 1950s, Comiskey Park had some of the most integrated large crowds in a still largely segregated Chicago.

"There were a lot more Black people in the Fifties and Sixties at Comiskey than there were with the Cubs by far," Weinberg said. "The first game I went to was the Cubs with my dad. He was a Sox fan but for whatever reason we went to see the Cubs, I think it was '48 or '49. I couldn't believe there was a guy named Peanuts Lowrey playing for the Cubs. But I remember that we didn't see any Black people at Wrigley."

The exception, of course, was when Jackie Robinson and the Brooklyn Dodgers came through the North Side. Black fans went far beyond the normal boundaries of the segregated city north to Addison Street to watch the trailblazing Robinson and other first-generation Black major leaguers.

Weinberg, who along with host Wallenstein produced a Sox post-game radio talk show in 1971 on WEAW-FM in Evanston, has an indelible memory of large groups of Black fans congregating near the Comiskey right field foul line.

"They knew their baseball a whole lot more than the people in the box seats," he recalled. Black fans chose that area for specific reasons, according to Kenny McReynolds, the longtime Chicago sports broadcaster who grew up an African American Sox fan in the nearby Ida B. Wells housing project. "The gate that was closest to right field was right off 35th Street," McReynolds recalled. "So most of the Black fans were coming from the neighborhoods to the east of the park and they were coming in off 35th. And all the Blacks would come in that gate near right field and get their (unreserved) seats near where they entered."

Comiskey's convenient location on the South Side meant that the White Sox were the neighborhood team for the Black communities to its immediate east and south: Douglas, Armour Square (south of Comiskey), Bronzeville, Oakland, Kenwood and Woodlawn. And it was the neighborhood team for the White ethnic neighborhoods immediately to its west and north: Bridgeport, Canaryville, McKinley Park, Brighton Park, Gage Park, Back of the Yards, Garfield Ridge and Archer Heights (north of Comiskey).

"It was just so exciting for everyone in the neighborhood every summer, to be able to walk to White Sox Park," said McReynolds, who as a child walked there by himself from his nearby home. "It wasn't expensive to get in —as a kid, I got in for 75 cents. Sometimes I would get an adult to go in with me, because kids under 14 could get in free with an adult. I'd find a White guy and say 'Hey, can I go in with you? It's free.' And they'd always say, yeah, come on. And I would always put my hand out after I got in, shake their hand and say 'Thank you.' Then, I'd pocket the 75 cents my mother gave me and find a seat. I thought the best seat in the ballpark was the left field upper deck."

But, as united as fans of all races were inside Comiskey, the communities outside the ballpark were as segregated as any in the city. The wide train viaduct just to the west of the park was the boundary between the two races. Black residents were careful not to venture west of that viaduct. And Whites were, for the most part, hesitant to go east of the ballpark, with the exception of high school students from Bridgeport and Canaryville who attended Richard J. Daley's alma mater, De La Salle Institute. Daley's sons were De La Salle students. Only Daley's youngest son, William, went to St. Ignatius. Decades later, Bill Daley became a political power broker, serving as secretary of commerce under and briefly chief of staff to President Barack Obama.

That racial divide was reinforced by the ultra-wide South Expressway just to the east of Comiskey Park. Later named the Dan Ryan, it was slated to run from north to south, starting downtown at Halsted near Madison, eventually running through the Bridgeport neighborhood along Normal Avenue. But Daley and the Chicago City Council voted in 1956 to move the route east to the mostly African American area in and near Armour Square, adjacent to north/south Wentworth Avenue. The expressway would displace thousands of residents and clear away hundreds of working-class homes —some of which were substandard—along with the shopping and business districts on Wentworth, including the Seventh Regiment Armory.

But while the new expressway may have destroyed some of the character of the South Armour environs, the mega-highway initially provided a major boost for the Sox. With its opening, Comiskey Park became the most conveniently located of all the stadiums in the city, at least for auto traffic. Part of the interstate expressway system (Interstate 94) launched under the landmark Federal Aid Highway Act of 1956, the Dan Ryan was connected with the recently construct-ed expressways serving the city's West Side and suburbs (the Congress, later the Eisenhower, Expressway) and the Northwest Side and suburbs (the Northwest, later the Kennedy, Expressway).

With large parking lots located immediate south and west, Comiskey offered far more room for cars than any other sports venue in the city. "All Roads Lead to White Sox Park" is how the team advertised in newspapers and its media guide throughout the 1960s and early 1970s. The ads also called the facility "Chicago's Downtown Ball Park", due to its immediate proximity to the expressways that were —in theory, at least — a 10-minute drive from the Chicago Loop.

While changes were taking place outside the stadium gates, Bill Veeck in his first Sox ownership tenure transformed Comiskey and revolutionized sta-dium entertainment. In late 1958, Veeck purchased the majority shares of the team from Grace Comiskey, the granddaughter of Charles. And, in the winter of 1959, after the team made it to the World Series for the first time in 40 years, Veeck turned his attention to the renovating the park in a way that would reflect his fan-friendly ethos. The striking red-bricked exterior was faded and dingy, due to exposure to nearly a half-century of the elements. So Veeck completely white-washed the bricks.

Then, influenced by a scene in the movie version of William Saroyan's play "The Time Of Your Life" featuring an explosive pinball machine, Veeck came up with a truly revolutionary ballpark attraction — the exploding scoreboard.

"It had seemed to me for a long time that the home run, which had once been the single most exciting and spectacular event in a ball game, had become so commonplace that it was being greeted not with cheers but with yawns…I could not see why it should not be possible to put the kick back into the home run by having it trigger something else," Veeck wrote in "Veeck As In Wreck," his 1965 autobiography. "We built a scoreboard at Comiskey Park with 10 mortars bristling from the top for firing Roman candles. Behind the scoreboard, the fireworks crew shot off bombs, rockets and anything else they happened to think of."

But this $300,000, 130-foot scoreboard making its debut on May 1, 1960, didn't offer just fireworks. The structure also had flashing strobe lights and a "Sox-O-Gram" message board which provided electronic greetings for fans, information and statistics, and advertisements. Veeck's brainchild was the most elaborate scoreboard of its time and influenced the massive scoreboards in every stadium built since.

Also in 1960, Veeck also introduced a picnic area under the left field stands. The attraction was created by knocking out a hole in the left field wall and adding benches and tables underneath the stands, which allowed fans to have a field-level view of the action from the outfield. Finally, Veeck was the first owner to add players' names to the backs of their uniforms, both at home and on the road.

"A lot of what made Comiskey special were the things that Bill added," said Weinberg, who later became a minority investor in the Sox during Veeck's second period of ownership with the team from 1975 to 1980. "He made the park fun."

Inside his partially-renovated old stadium, Veeck staged off-beat, entertaining spectacles that were unique in baseball. Longtime fans still remember the night in the pennant-winning season of 1959, when Veeck had a helicopter land behind second base. The chopper was filled with four-foot tall "Martians" who were there to invade the ballpark and "capture" the team's hyper-valuable double-play combination of Luis Aparicio and Nellie Fox. The "Martians" were led by none other than little person Eddie Gaedel, who had his historic at-bat for Veeck's St. Louis Browns in 1951.

As the Sox broke their 40-year wanderings through the pennant wilderness in 1959, the players were far more accessible than today.

Mike Pols, the former city-championship-winning football coach at Sullivan High School in Rogers Park, was turned down for a vendor's job as a teenager at Wrigley Field. So he hopped back on the L and landed a gig at Comiskey Park. For day games, the vendors reported at 9 a.m. and Pols found a number of Sox players sitting in the stands, enjoying some smokes before batting practice. He took the opportunity to chat it up with "Jungle Jim" Rivera, the team's most colorful character. Pols liked vending to a happy crowd when the Sox thumped the Dodgers 11-0 in Game 1 of the World Series. His only concern in that era was safeguarding pockets full of change from his vending profits after night games on the long L ride home to the North Side.

The combination of a pennant-winning team and Veeck's bread and circuses helped Comiskey Park break the city's 31-year-old baseball attendance record in 1960, when the Sox drew more than 1.6 million fans. And the team would continue drawing well into the mid-1960s. Especially on the South and Southwest Side, in some western suburbs and in Northwest Indiana, attending Sox games were the highlight of the summer — the most coveted sports entertainment ticket in town.

"We'd always go to the Sunday doubleheaders," recalled 1980s White Sox slugger Ron Kittle, who grew up 25 miles away in Gary, Ind. "My first vision when I walked into this ballpark was a scoreboard. It was not a player, it was a scoreboard. It looked pretty damn spectacular. It looked huge. It looked like the Sears Tower to me. Seeing the teams and the stats and the numbers up there."

Arthur Allyn, Jr., was an insurance executive and a minority investor in the Veeck ownership group when he bought the majority shares in the team from Veeck in 1961. And Allyn, along with his brother John, who was a quasi-silent partner in the ownership, continued the stewardship of the old ballpark, but without the Veeck flair.

Around this time, a treasured Comiskey Park mascot-of-sorts began just showing up at games. Andy Rozdilsky, who worked as a clerk in the research division of International Harvester's South Side plant, had won a pair of season tickets at a Knights of Columbus neighborhood raffle. Rozdilsky attended the games dressed up as a clown, as he had done for various South Side charity events. Wearing a trademark red bowler hat, white face paint and a flashing red nose, Rozdilsky became a daily presence at Sox games known as "Andy The Clown." His bellowing, trademark chant of "Go Youuuu White Sox!!" was heard repeatedly during games at the old stadium over the next 30 years.

Due to its size and its proximity to the new expressways, Comiskey Park in these years continued to be the preferred venue in Chicago for large, outdoor non-sporting events. Most notably, more than 50,000 screaming fans saw the Beatles perform here during two shows in August 1965. The crowd's well-known screams for the Fab Four were so loud in the walled-in stadium that WLS deejay Clark Weber, standing next to the stage, claimed he could barely hear the quartet's songs. The Allyns also launched a professional soccer team here — the

Chicago Mustangs, who played in the 1967 and 1968 seasons in the failed United States Soccer Association. The team drew no more than 25,000 fans for six contests, combined.

But baseball remained the centerpiece at Comiskey Park or, rather, White Sox Park, as it was renamed by the Allyns starting in the 1962 season. White Sox Park remained the official name through 1975, although many fans still continued to call it Comiskey. At that time, night games started at 8 p.m., and day games including doubleheaders began at 1:15 p.m. The occasional weekday twi-night doubleheader started at 6 p.m.

"They were good, vocal blue-collar fans," said Lloyd Rutzky, a Comiskey Park vendor from the then-predominantly Jewish South Shore neighborhood, who started working there in the mid-1960s. "And a lot of them pretty good drinkers, although I didn't start selling beer at Sox Park until 1973. I sold pizza — Ron Santo pizza (a brand owned by the Cubs and one-season Sox third baseman)." Formally named Pros Pizza, the snack drew poor reviews from many diners, including Santo's own teammates, while it was sold at both Wrigley Field and Comiskey Park.

As the 1970s began, more vocal, younger, brawling fans made their presence known at Sox Park, especially after the boisterous Caray was hired as the team's radio broadcaster beginning in 1971. "Harry totally identified as a beer drinker, as a guy who was an alcohol guy — and there were an awful lot of people who could identify with him," Tom Weinberg said. "It's probably a coincidence, and it was also probably a part of the times, but fans started to become more feisty in the 70s, so you saw more brawls in the stands."

Comiskey also became known throughout the league for its "10th man" — the grounds crew led by longtime head groundskeeper Gene Bossard and his son, Roger, who was hired as his father's assistant in 1967. Gene Bossard had been hired by Grace Comiskey to take over groundskeeping at Comiskey in 1940, when he was only 23. His father, Emil Bossard, had been the head groundskeeper at Cleveland's League Park and Municipal Stadium since the early 20th century.

By the 1960s, Gene Bossard was the most creative and influential groundskeeper in the league. His key responsibility, in addition to maintaining a challenging turf (Comiskey Park didn't have an adequate drainage system until the late '70s), was to provide a home-field advantage for the Sox and their most potent asset in the 1950s and 1960s — the pitching staff. From Billy Pierce, Early Wynn, Dick Donovan and Bob Shaw in the 1950s to Gary Peters, Joel Horlen, Tommy John and Juan Pizarro in the 1960s, all were aided by Bossard's creative field-tending. With the encouragement of managers Al Lopez and Eddie Stanky,

Bossard was known for tilting the foul lines to help bunters with the White Sox, while letting the grass grow in front of home plate and keeping the area around the batter's box moist to deaden ground balls for the opposition.

"The front of home plate was like mud and the grass was always high," Roger Bossard recalled from his office at Guaranteed Rate Field, where he remains the Sox head groundskeeper. "Obviously I would never think of doing that kind of stuff anymore. But back in the day you could do that. You got away with it. Bill Veeck said he thought a groundskeeper was worth maybe six to eight games."

Another trick that the Bossards would use to help pitchers was "freezing baseballs". The groundkeepers would add weight to game balls by putting them in a room with a humidifier for several days.

"Dad and Al Lopez started doing this in the 1950s," Roger Bossard remembered. "After Al Lopez left and Eddie Stanky was hired in 1966, he continued doing it. Dad had two rooms for baseballs at Comiskey. And one of the rooms had the humidifier. Dad was in charge of the baseballs. When Eddie Stanky wanted to use the frozen baseballs, he'd have Dad bring the frozen ones to the umps. And literally, I bet it was probably a half-ounce difference in the ball. I would help my dad bring the balls out and the boxes with the frozen balls were soaking wet. It literally probably made -- got to be at least an eight-to-ten, maybe a 12-foot difference in the flight of the ball. So, you've got Tommy John pitching. He's a low-ball pitcher. The grass is four inches high. It's mud in front of home plate and the balls are damp. That ball's not going anywhere."

Bossard's tricks, along with the other mound and strike zone advantages that pitchers had throughout much of the 1960s, helped a dominant pitching staff that top to bottom might have been more effective than the Dodgers of Sandy Koufax and Don Drysdale.

But those same tricks *hurt* the Sox offense at home. In their pennant-chasing season of 1967, when the White Sox battled Detroit, Minnesota and Boston for the AL title until the last week of the season, the highest batting average for a Sox starter was right fielder Ken Berry's .241. Left fielder Pete Ward led the team with only 18 homers, 62 RBI and a .726 OPS. To a man, the team blamed the rigged conditions as a reason for the anemic offense.

"We could have an eight-month drought in Chicago and there'd be a swamp in front of home plate," Pete Ward recalled to the *Chicago Tribune* in 1998. "During batting practice, with the writers all around the batting cage, guys would hit down on the ball and try to splatter the writers with mud — thinking there'd be a mention of it in the papers. And there'd never be any."

By 1968, Comiskey Park began to experience a significant attendance drop. Between 1951 and 1966, the Chicago White Sox outdrew the Chicago Cubs by a wide margin: 18,966,405 fans to 12,636,867. But after 17 straight seasons of above .500 baseball, the team dropped to the second division in 1968. The Cubs, after years of dormancy, had become a top NL team under manager Leo Durocher, finally outperforming the Sox on the field at the box office.

But, more than anything else, the unspoken "concern" about Comiskey began to bubble to the surface — worries about safety outside the stadium. The mid-1960s were a time of civil unrest in many American cities, including Chicago. In 1967, there were riots in more than 150 American cities. The unrest culminated in more riots after the assassination of civil rights leader Martin Luther King, Jr. on April 4, 1968. When the White Sox opened their season against the Indians at home on April 10, they drew just under 8,000.

Additionally, there where whispers about the neighborhoods to the east and south of White Sox Park. Right before the Dan Ryan was constructed, a group of public housing high rises called Stateway Gardens were erected from 35th to 41st streets, only two blocks southeast of the stadium. Crime became an issue in these low-income units, especially as serious offenses ticked up throughout the U.S. in the 1970s. But much of the innuendo about crime in the area was largely false and racially-driven, a fact that even sportswriters of the time recognized. Year after year, crime statistics in the largely African American neighborhood near Comiskey Park were negligible.

As the issue of safety around Comiskey Park became amplified, due to the shockingly low attendance numbers for the 1968 season opener, *Chicago Sun-Times* columnist Bill Gleason lambasted the whisperers: "[The White Sox] have to go to work now to persuade the sports-buying public of the Chicago area that Comiskey Park is attractively located. They must roll up their sleeves and fight the 'bad neighborhood' slander... Those who say the neighborhood is 'bad' re suffering from vision distorted by racism or fear. [Arthur] Allyn and [General Manager Ed] Short should get out into the neighborhoods where their customers are, stand on the corners, visit the taverns, shake a few hands, and ask fans why they are staying home."

All the while, Arthur Allyn was sending signs that he was dissatisfied with Comiskey Park. In 1967, he introduced a proposal to build a privately financed stadium in the South Loop. He was also dickering with Richard J. Daley about the Mayor's own plan to build that multi-purpose stadium for the city's pro sports teams. But Allyn's most discouraging move involving Comiskey's fate as a future venue was his decision to play 10 home games in Milwaukee's County Stadium in 1968.

The shift to Milwaukee mystified some Chicago sportswriters, who felt there was nothing wrong with the Baseball Palace. Tribune sports columnist David

Condon wrote this impassioned plea to fans to return to the ballpark after the 1968 season:

"During the Bill Veeck era, Comiskey Park was known as a swinging place. It also was clean and remarkably tidy. Lt. John L. Sullivan's police force, with assistance from the Andy Frain usher corps, made the Comiskey Park area one of the safest in Chicago.

"Unfortunately, and mistakenly, Comiskey Park has lost its good image in recent years. Allyn didn't help a bit when he announced plans to build a new stadium in another location, or when he transferred some home games to Milwaukee.

"The truth is that our family of south siders, and our friends, would prefer to go to Comiskey Park rather than assemble at any other arena in town... No arena in this city is more convenient by automobile... There is more than ample parking in the Comiskey Park vicinity.

"(It) isn't the Taj Mahal. Some seats are too narrow for the fatties. But all in all, it is a good, clean baseball park."

But Condon and others in the Chicago media would have been shocked if they knew the real story — that Arthur Allyn was secretly negotiating to sell the team to Milwaukee businessman Bud Selig, who would then abandon Comiskey and Chicago for Milwaukee by 1970.

In response to the perceived safety concerns, Allyn installed brighter lighting for the ballpark parking lots for the 1969 season. But his only significant upgrade inside the stadium that season would be an odd one. Three years earlier, Houston's landmark indoor stadium, the Astrodome, introduced artificial turf to professional sports. After the 1968 season, Allyn spent $110,000 to install Astroturf in his infield.

"This is a great trivia question," Roger Bossard said, with a laugh. "Who's the first team to have outdoor Astroturf? It's the Chicago White Sox. No one — if you're in a bar, ask that question. You'll win a few drinks. And the other thing is, who was the first team to pull out Astroturf on their field? It was the Chicago White Sox when Bill Veeck owned the team."

The Astroturf was one of Arthur Allyn's attempts to make the pitcher-friendly park more inviting to hitters. He also added inner fences in front of the right and left foul poles, which reduced the distance to the poles by 17 feet. The fences were removed for the 1971 season under brother John Allyn's sole ownership with the right- and left-center dimensions restored to 382 feet. But the artificial turf would remain through the 1975 season. Comiskey Park would be the only sports facility in the country with a combination of natural and artificial turf.

"It was the first Astroturf on the market," Bossard said. "So what it was, it was eight inches of gravel, there was a four-inch lift of asphalt over the gravel. And then there was a three-quarter inch cushion — cork cushion — and the short Astroturf on top. So, after the first year, after weather got to it, the cork cushion obviously was a brick. Infielders hated it — Bill Melton really hated it."

"In April and May, it was the roughest place in the world to play because when it gets damp, you call it wet, doesn't have to rain, just that mist in the cold, the ball skids," Melton said. "So, the first hop it skids, so it comes to you twice as fast."

"It was horrible, because it was so hot," added White Sox batboy Rory Clark. "And so if you had a day game after a night game you're tired 'cuz you don't get home until two o'clock. You're back in at 8 in the morning. And then you're out there at Noon, and if it's 95 degrees it's really 120 when that stuff heats up. And the ball took funny bounces for the players. And it was — yuck."

The artificial turf at White Sox Park would be Art Allyn's last contribution — such as it was — to the team. Before he could consummate his deal with Selig to move the team to Milwaukee, Allyn's brother John swooped in to purchase the White Sox in the fall of 1969 and keep the team in Chicago, on the South Side and in the same ballpark. In his first interviews after buying the team, John Allyn talked about his quiet admiration for the Comiskey Park experience. "I've been bringing my family to this park for years and we've never seen an unpleasant incident," he said.

On the same day that that John Allyn announced he had taken over primary ownership of the team, he had more good news about the ballpark. The new $51 million rapid transit system that would run in the median of the Dan Ryan Expressway to 95th Street was opening for a public preview. Sox fans going to Comiskey would no longer have to walk four blocks to and from what was then known as the Jackson Park-Englewood "L" stop located near 35th and State in Bronzeville. Now an "L" train dropped off fans less than one block from a Sox Park gate.

John Allyn's commitment to Comiskey Park would help contribute to its prolonged life-span. The ballyard would outlast most of its "Jewel Box" contemporaries, with the exception of Wrigley Field, Boston's Fenway Park and Detroit's Tiger Stadium.

But generations of cash-poor ownership — from the Comiskeys to Bill Veeck to the Allyns — would not have the necessary financial resources to properly maintain the old South Side ballpark. These owners didn't have the deep pockets of their North Side counterparts, the Wrigley family, who consistently provided upgrades to Wrigley Field in the 1950s and 1960s. Off-season maintenance projects there were reportedly in the six-figure range during P.K. Wrigley's ownership tenure – including rebuilding the upper deck in 1967-68.

Engineers who did annual inspections of Comiskey Park for the then-relatively new White Sox ownership group led by Jerry Reinsdorf and Eddie Einhorn began warning in 1984 about structural deterioration throughout the stadium. By 1986, the engineering firm responsible for monitoring Comiskey Park wrote: "Unfortunately, we foresee the likelihood of significant expenditures on an annual basis to keep the park in safe and usable condition through the 1989 season. Beyond that, there are no realistic long-term solutions, since the deterioration is irreversible. Simply put, Comiskey Park is nearing the end of its useful life."

By 1988, Reinsdorf and Einhorn had spent $20 million on maintenance for Comiskey, which was the same amount the duo and its ownership team had paid to buy the franchise and ballpark from Veeck in 1981.

The Reinsdorf-Einhorn group discussed multiple options for a new stadium — from a city-sanctioned proposal at Roosevelt Road and Clark Street in the South Loop to a move to west suburban Addison, where land was purchased by them in 1984. As had happened in the past, the White Sox were in real danger of moving, as Reinsdorf and Einhorn also seriously contemplated transplanting to the new Suncoast Dome (now Tropicana Field) built to attract a major league team to Tampa-St. Petersburg, Fla. in the late 1980s.

But ultimately, the Sox would reach a deal with the City of Chicago and state of Illinois to keep the team at the intersection of 35th and Shields. A new publicly-funded ballpark would be located on 35th Street, across from the first Comiskey Park — an idea which Mayor Harold Washington had originally floated, to keep the team as a South Side institution and take advantage of the existing infrastructure for baseball there.

A last-second deal was struck with the Illinois General Assembly for a $137 million new stadium. With Gov. James R. Thompson lobbying hard among lawmakers even after the clock struck midnight July 1, 1988 for *official adjournment*, the stadium package was approved in Springfield with the time stamp dated June 30, 1988.

The ballyhooed last game at old Comiskey Park took place on Sunday, Sept. 30, 1990, as a capacity crowd of 42,849 turned out for a 2-1 Sox victory over the Seattle Mariners. Sox players, led by future Hall of Famer Carlton Fisk, saluted the throng after the final out.

An off-season passed quickly before the first game in the new stadium drew 42,191 on Thursday, April 18, 1991. The result was far less satisfying: Detroit Tigers 16, White Sox 0. But there'd be days of glory in the future: Numerous division titles, a 70th anniversary All-Star Game in 2003 and the first two victories of the Sox' four-game sweep over the Houston Astros in the 2005 World Series. The memories of Paul Konerko's grand-slam homer and singles hitter Scott Podsednik's walk-off blast in the rain won't soon fade.

A yeoman's effort for decades got the White Sox through many minefields to these junctures. The effort was at its peak back in 1972, when John Allyn led a renewed effort to get fans back to the Baseball Palace of the World. His acquisition of Dick Allen would be the central act in that effort.

Comiskey Park fireworks go off after a late-inning
Sox home run by #15 Dick Allen.

Photo credit: Leo Bauby Collection

CHAPTER 4

The South Side

It is the perfect snapshot of a moment in time in mid-20th century Chicago.

The scene is Comiskey Park in August 1957. We're looking out from behind home plate, as White Sox left-hander Billy Pierce finishes his warm up pitches to start the sixth inning. Meanwhile, Boston Red Sox slugger Ted Williams — currently hitting .383— waits patiently, eyeing Pierce. In the background, the giant scoreboard installed by Chuck Comiskey in 1950 is illuminated — it's 9:58 p.m. on the huge Longines clock, while a large ad below the clock for Chesterfield cigarettes implores fans to "Smoke For Real".

Over the darkened ballpark, there's a thick haze, which is partially from the cigarette and cigar smoke produced by some of the 25,000 fans in the stands. But the haze is also from the nearby Union Stockyards, which are located less than a mile from the ballpark — covering nearly one square mile, from Halsted Street on the east to Ashland Avenue on the west and from 39th Street on the north to 47th Street on the south.

At its peak, the 345-acre stockyards contained more than 2,300 pens of livestock; and tens of thousands of cattle, hogs and sheep were processed here daily — over 4 million annually. In addition to the haze, the enormous meat-packing facility produced a pungent smell which would waft over the surrounding neighborhoods — Back of the Yards, Canaryville, Bridgeport and South Armour Square — especially when winds blew from the southwest. When Pierce was first traded from the Detroit Tigers to the White Sox in 1949, his first opinions about Comiskey were based on that unforgettable smell. "Comiskey Park was dim, and the nearby stockyards were going full blast and the aroma was terrible," Pierce would recall to author Danny Peary nearly 50 years later.

Those unpleasant effects were symbols of a prosperous industry based on the South Side — an industrial complex which had been headquartered in the area since 1865. At its peak, the Union Stockyards employed more than 40,000 people, many from the nearby neighborhoods. Before World War II, a majority of those employees were White ethnics from the nearby neighborhoods to the south and west of Comiskey Park. After the war, African Americans coming up from the South during the second wave of the Great Migration were growing in numbers at the meat-processing center of the world. By the time Pierce was confronting Williams at Comiskey in August 1957, approximately 80 percent of the employees at the stockyards were African American, according to historian Dominic Pacyga.

But as the 1950s and 1960s faded away, so did the stockyards. In the late 19th and early 20th century, the concentration of the meatpacking industry in Chicago was partly based on the city's location as the nation's hub for the railroads. The development of refrigeration technology helped maintain that status as the world's center for meatpacking — both at the stockyards and in the freight industry, where refrigerated rail cars became commonplace.

After World War II, however, the meatpacking industry became decentralized, due to the development of interstate highways, which allowed farmers to sell their livestock regionally to packers. The development of refrigerated trucks to move the butchered livestock also contributed to the decentralization of the industry. The Big Three packers at the stockyards — Swift and Company, Wilson and Company and Armour and Company — began phasing out their plants at the stockyards in the early 1950s. By the mid-1960s, all three would be gone, moving their butchering operations to regional centers such as Cedar Rapids, Iowa; Kansas City; Omaha and Albert Lea, Minn.

Small, independent packers hung on at the stockyards throughout the 1960s. But by 1969, the number of processed livestock dropped below one million animals for the first time, and hog trading ended there in May 1970. Chicago Mayor Richard J. Daley had worked at the stockyards after graduating in 1919 from De La Salle Institute, the Christian Brothers high school located on 35th Street a few blocks east of Comiskey Park. Daley's job duties at the Stockyards included moving cattle off trucks and some basic clerical work for a commission house.

But Daley had no interest in supporting and maintaining a scaled-down stockyards as mayor — even though his political empire was built in the neighboring Bridgeport community. Daley, instead, had a bigger goal in mind for the city — one that didn't involve the neighborhoods close to Sox Park. Instead, his plan was to concentrate development downtown and in communities near downtown — like the South Loop and the Near West and Near North sides— so that the middle class would be lured back to the city. The plan ultimately worked in a way — emphasizing development downtown and creating a globally connected, white-collar city center, Daley would save Chicago from the fate of other Rust Belt cities like Detroit, Cleveland and St. Louis. But it was a pyrrhic accomplishment, as thousands of unskilled laborers on the South Side, who had for generations relied on the stockyards and other industries, became unemployed.

The closing of the Stockyards was a symbol of the changes taking place in the early 1970s on the South Side — the ancestral home for the Chicago White Sox. One of the nation's largest industrial centers was being affected by changes in the nation's economy — changes which would continue over the next 20 years. In the 1970s, it was the closing of the stockyards; in the late 1970s to the early 1990s, the South Side's two massive steel mills would close — Wisconsin Steel and U.S. Steel's South Works plant. Deindustrialization left behind hundreds of empty factories and warehouses on the South Side, as Chicago moved from being an industrial, blue-collar city to a service-oriented, white-collar city.

The South Side would also be affected by White Flight during the 70s, as the ethnics that dominated the neighborhoods began moving to the suburbs, following the service and industrial jobs that had gone there. In the rigidly segregated city of Chicago, White Flight was also influenced by fear of the "other" — the African Americans who were moving out of the traditional Black Belt communities bursting at the seams to move farther south and west, and Latinos, moving into the same previously all-White neighborhoods.

Finally, South Side politics were changing, as the African American community expanded further south and west. More independent, middle-class Blacks were beginning to express dissatisfaction with a Democratic machine — ruled in Boss-like fashion by Daley -- which had long controlled the minority vote in Chicago.

This was the transforming South Side surrounding Comiskey Park in 1972 — a diverse, storied group of neighborhoods with a storied past...and an uncertain future.

Chicago's South Side is the largest of the three "sides" of the city: North Side, West Side, South Side (Lake Michigan is to the east). Its boundaries are debatable — technically, according to the city's grid system, the South Side begins at Madison Street in Chicago's Loop. But the most commonly accepted boundaries are 12th Street (Roosevelt Road) to the north and 138th Street to the south, with its eastern boundaries being Lake Michigan and the Indiana state line, while the western boundaries vary from north to south. All told, the South Side is larger in area than the North and West sides combined.

The South Side was —and still is— a city within the city of around 800,000 people, more or less. And this city within a city had its own world class amenities — a network of sports arenas, educational institutions and even the world's busiest airport, for a short period of time.

In the early 1970s, the South Side included one venerable, if fading, major league baseball stadium and 50,000 seat outdoor entertainment venue — Comiskey Park. The area also included two aging indoor stadiums. The International Amphitheatre was constructed in 1934 as a 10,000-seat arena and convention hall adjacent to the stockyards. The Chicago Coliseum was an ancient 7,000-seat facility in the South Loop built in 1900, possessing an exterior that was partly culled from a prison for Confederate soldiers in Richmond, Va.

The Amphitheatre hosted five presidential nominating conventions, including the notorious 1968 Democratic National Convention. It was also home to pro basketball, hockey, other sports and concerts. The Coliseum, meanwhile, hosted six of its own presidential nominating conventions. As a sports stadium, the cozy confines would also be the home of the first entry of the National Hockey League's Blackhawks (from 1926 through 1932), and later professional teams. The American Negro Exposition, also known as the Black World's Fair and the Diamond Jubilee Exposition, were held in the Coliseum in the summer of 1940 to mark 75 years since the end of slavery. Notable counter-culture conventions included gatherings of the Black Panther Party and the Students for a Democratic Society.

But by 1972, both the Amphitheatre and Coliseum, which closed that year, were outmoded, replaced by large, new convention centers like the second version of McCormick Place, located along the lakefront. Also corralling sports events, concerts and conventions was the 1929-vintage Chicago Stadium on the West Side and by outlying venues like the Rosemont Horizon near O'Hare Airport. The Amphitheatre had lost much of its luster after the stockyards closed.

The South Side's great landmark of higher education — the University of Chicago — was revolutionized through Robert Maynard Hutchins' "Chicago Plan" for undergraduates. Hutchins' brainchild encouraged liberal education at earlier ages and measured achievement by comprehensive examination rather than by classroom time served. The University of Chicago was also where the nuclear age began.

Three years after Hutchins disbanded his school's Big Ten football program, branding the sport as a distraction from education, physicist Enrico Fermi staged the first controlled nuclear chain reaction under the west grandstands of since-demolished Stagg Field in 1942. The hyper-secret Manhattan Project to develop the first atomic bombs grew out of that achievement. And the South Side was home to the Illinois Institute of Technology, whose new campus, designed by the influential post-modernist architect Ludwig Mies van der Rohe, replaced slums along Federal Street between 31st Street and 35th Street, a mere two blocks east of Comiskey Park.

The University of Chicago also established its own world-class medical center, most enduring of the hospitals that called the South Side home. The local Jewish community spearheaded the growth of Michael Reese Hospital at 29th Street and Ellis Avenue, a major research and teaching hospital that at one juncture was one of the largest hospitals in the city. Provident Hospital, further south on 51st Street, was the first hospital in the U.S. that was owned and operated by African Americans. The world's first open heart surgery by Dr. Daniel Hale Williams in 1893 was conducted at Provident Hospital.

Southwest Side is home to what was America's first great regional airport — Midway Airport, located in the Garfield Ridge neighborhood. Midway was the "World's Busiest Airport" for more than 12 years from 1948 to 1960, before O'Hare Airport took those honors in 1963. By 1972, Midway was clearly the second airport in the region, dwarfed by O'Hare.

The South Side also had a sizable influence on American culture. Some of the most celebrated names of American literature were either born there, spent extensive time there or wrote extensively about the area — Upton Sinclair, James T. Farrell, Nelson Algren, Richard Wright, Saul Bellow and Sam Greenlee. Pulitzer Prize-winning poet Gwendolyn Brooks, Illinois' poet laureate, spent much of her adult life in a home at 74th Street and Evans Avenue, in the Grand Crossing neighborhood.

American music would be unthinkable without the South Side. Only a few blocks east of Comiskey Park, venues like the Pekin Theatre (31st and State) and the Sunset Cafe (315 E. 35th Street) were key to the development of jazz in America. Louis Armstrong became a dynamic solo performer who revolutionized jazz improvisation while playing at the Sunset. At one time, Al Capone also owned a piece of the place. This same building, still standing, became the Grand Terrace Cafe, one of the most famous nightclubs in the country, known for its incredible floor shows and pioneering swing music played by the house orchestras of Earl Hines and Fletcher Henderson. Even Count Basie's Orchestra had its debut outside of Kansas City here.

Farther south in Bronzeville, on 47th Street, the Regal Theatre was the Midwestern bookmark to New York City's Apollo Theatre — presenting the best African American entertainers on its stage for more than 40 years. Chicago blues also were incubated in clubs along 43rd and 47th streets on the South Side, as legends like Muddy Waters, Howlin' Wolf and Little Walter introduced and advanced this vital American music in the same neighborhoods where they lived. Meanwhile, at the Chess Recording studio at 21st and Michigan, some of those same blues musicians teamed up with St. Louis guitarist/singer Chuck Berry to record the music that would become the real foundation of rock and roll, admired the world over. The Rolling Stones recorded "Satisfaction" at Chess during their first U.S. tour in 1964. The building is now the Willie Dixon's Blues Heaven Foundation.

And then there was Black gospel music, which was created by former blues musician-turned-evangelist Thomas A. Dorsey in the early 1930s at Pilgrim Baptist Church, the Adler and Sullivan-designed house of worship at 33rd Street and Indiana Avenue, just a few blocks east of Comiskey Park. This music would become a worldwide phenomenon, especially through vessels like lifelong Chicagoan Mahalia Jackson, the brilliant gospel vocalist best known for her rendition of Dorsey's "Precious Lord, Take My Hand." Jackson lived in a bungalow at

88th Street and Indiana Avenue.

Not surprisingly, Comiskey Park would absorb the music from its nearby neighborhoods. Jimmy Yancey, the pioneering blues pianist who was one of the first inductees into the Rock and Roll Hall of Fame, spent 25 years working as a groundskeeper for the White Sox, from 1925 to 1950. Yancey, whose boogie woogie piano style would go on to influence rock and roll, wrote a signature piece called "White Sox Stomp." Still later, Comiskey Park would employ ground-breaking stadium organists — first Shay Torrent, and then the incomparable Nancy Faust — who would revolutionize the art of music incorporated into a stadium setting.

But by 1972, some of the music from the South Side had disappeared. The Regal had closed. The Grand Terrace Cafe was a hardware store. Chess was sold in 1969, and the label's Chicago studios were closed by the early 1970s. Even Muddy Waters moved from the South Side — he left his longtime home at 4339 S. Lake Park Ave., and moved to southwest suburban Westmont.

———————————————

Neighborhoods throughout the South Side were changing in 1972. To the south and west of Comiskey Park, predominantly-White, ethnic neighborhoods held forth, but Mexican Americans were beginning to move heavily into neighborhoods like Back of the Yards and Pilsen. The Irish had come first in the 19th century. Polish, Scandinavians, Lithuanians and other Eastern and Southern Europeans began arriving in the early 20th century. By the 1920s, these ethnic groups were firmly entrenched in what came to be known as the Bungalow Belt, referring to the similarly-constructed brick, one-story homes built by the thousands in the era, representing much of the Southwest Side's housing stock.

To the southeast, the African American community was finally expanding. During the first half of the 20th century, discriminatory real-estate practices limited Black residents to the "Black Belt" communities. Middle-class and lower-income African Americans shared the area, which was anchored by the two central intersections: 35th and State and 47th and South Parkway (Martin Luther King Drive). Black Chicagoans, restricted from many institutions downtown, established their own businesses, banks and even their own influential newspaper — the Chicago Defender.

But starting in the 1960s, a combination of factors allowed Black families to move farther south and east, and expressways made the suburbs more accessible. The Fair Housing Act of 1968 addressed discrimination in real estate. White flight was also encouraged by panic peddling from unscrupulous realtors. The result was the mass settlement of Black families in previously-White neighborhoods like Englewood, Auburn-Gresham, Chatham, Avalon Park and South Shore. The same also occurred in the mostly upscale far South Side Beverly neighborhood, one of the few which retained White families and would be, along with Hyde Park, a truly integrated neighborhood in the City of Chicago.

Some communities remained solidly middle class after the transition from White to Black: Most notably, Avalon Park, Chatham and Pill Hill. But in other neighborhoods such as Englewood, financial resources dwindled and businesses moved out after the transition. Meanwhile, in the old Black Belt, the city, starting in the mid-1950s, constructed massive public housing complexes, including many cheaply-built high rises like Stateway Gardens and the Robert Taylor Homes, for low-income families. Some 28,000 were crammed into the Stateway and Taylor big boxes. At the same time, street gangs of all races started to organize in economically-challenged neighborhoods.

On the West Side, the Vice Lords were the first major African American street gang organized in the late 1950s. And by 1959, the Blackstone Rangers were the first powerful Black street gang to become a factor on the South Side. These groups would have major influence in the inner-city starting in the 1960s.

Longtime Chicago ballpark vendor Lloyd Rutzky was a native South Sider who came from a Jewish family which lived first in Avalon Park and then the predominantly-White and Jewish Pill Hill neighborhood. He witnessed firsthand the change of these neighborhoods from White to Black.

"It started when it was time for me to go to Hirsch High School (in Chicago's Grand Crossing neighborhood)," Rutzky recalled. "The neighborhood, that's when there was like — they called it the 'exodus.' The neighborhood changed beyond belief. When my brother started in 1959 at Hirsch, the school was, I'd say, 90% White. And then a few years later when I started going there, my brother and I were one of 25 White kids in the whole school."

The heavily Jewish areas ranging from South Shore down Jeffery Boulevard to Jeffery Manor past 95th Street were extremely close-knit, far more than their counterparts on the North Side and northern suburbs. They combined the prosperity of post-war America and the neighborliness of the old Jewish West Side of the earlier 20th century when many residents were recent immigrants from Eastern Europe.

Ron Eisenstein, still a partial White Sox season-ticket holder in 2021, grew up near the corner of 92nd and Bennett. He remembered how doctors or dentists lived at all four corners of the intersection, thus the area's name of "Pill Hill." Old neighborhood ties were binding.

"The neighborhood was so popular, so ingrained, and close friends were still friends (decades later)," he said. "I shared my bar mitzvah date with another boy, there were so many (Baby Boomers) of that age, at Rodfie Sholom Synagogue on May 25, 1968. My haftarah was shorter as a result."

Thousands in Eisenstein's old neighborhood experienced a modern-day exodus, as Rutzky had described it, almost as hurried as in ancient Egypt. Literally, within three to four years at the close of the 1960s, the White residents of the area felt a need to depart their near-Eden, and quickly.

Attempts at orderly integration of middle-class residents of Whites and Blacks on the South Side were heavily covered in the media. WBBM-TV presented a half-hour special, "Decision At 83rd Street," in July 1962, focusing on middle-class Black residents moving into the Marynook subdivision. A decade later in 1972, the *Chicago Today* afternoon newspaper published a multi-part series on local activists of both races trying to promote integration in South Shore.

But even though reports circulated of teenagers of both races becoming friends in the short period of racial balance in these neighborhoods, real and prolonged residential integration never took root. The panic peddlers trying to scare off longtime residents to sell quickly had too big of an impact. Even though the Black newcomers were largely of the same economic class as the incumbent White residents, too much fear of the "other" was ingrained. Whites simply followed their friends and neighbors out of the neighborhood, often to the North Side and northern suburbs while keeping their friendships solidly intact.

But accelerating the White Flight was an incursion of crime from the inner city. Without warning one day late in 1966, a faction of the Blackstone Rangers gang from outside the neighborhood broke into the South Shore High School cafeteria and created chaos. Several White students were injured. Those Jewish residents who were on the fence about moving apparently finalized their plans to leave, according to one of the students injured.

Black middle-class residents who had settled into South Shore and other nearby neighborhoods also wanted to keep their distance from the gangs. That was one of the motivations for the migration of hundreds to a new housing development, developed on a former military base, by 107th and Aberdeen, just south of Mt. Vernon Park. The homes, developed by Andrew R. Malone, all appeared in the mid-and late-1960s with Black purchasers usually their first owners.

Close-knit like the Jews of South Shore, these residents formed a regular car patrol of local men in teams of two who would drive around at night to spot any troublemakers. Connected to a base station by CB radio, the men could thus inform the local police. The neighborhood, adjacent to Morgan Park, but later known as Washington Heights, also started the successful Jackie Robinson West Little League program at Mt. Vernon Park.

Although Washington Heights went from all-White to all-Black within a decade's time, one of the leaders of the newcomers told reporters that she'd prefer residential and school re-segregation if it meant tranquility and security for her children. She was well aware of the history of changing neighborhoods going back several decades.

The transformation of White neighborhoods to Black would lead to tension and conflict between the two groups throughout the 1960s and into the 1970s. Violence actually started in the 1950s, when riots occurred after a Black family moved into the predominantly-White Trumbull Park Homes on the Far South Side in 1953. The violence against Blacks continued into the 1960s, particularly in neighborhoods on the Southwest Side like Gage Park and Marquette Park.

In the summer of 1966, civil rights activist Martin Luther King, Jr. led open-housing marches into White neighborhoods to protest discrimination against Blacks in housing caused by illegal redlining real estate practices. King would be violently attacked in these marches. As gun-toting police officers flanked him, King avoided serious injury when a rock glanced off his head.

"I've been in many demonstrations all across the South, but I can say that I have never seen — even in Mississippi and Alabama — mobs as hostile and as hate-filled as I've seen here in Chicago," King told reporters afterward. In 1972, this area was still a racial powder keg, most notably in Gage Park, where the neighborhood high school would be engulfed in racial violence throughout the year, as White students and parents angrily resisted the increased influx of Black students into the school.

Chicago Mayor Richard J. Daley understood this ethnic tribalism perfectly because it helped shaped him as a politician. Born in 1902 in Bridgeport, Daley's entry into Chicago politics was through the Hamburg Athletic Club, a neighborhood group described by Daley biographers Adam Cohen and Elizabeth Taylor as a "part social circle, part political organization, and part street gang." Along with its counterpart Bridgeport club, "Ragan's Colts," the Hamburg A.C. was the key instigator in the 1919 Chicago Race Riots, where Whites violently attacked Blacks in street skirmishes based on racial boundaries. The riots, which lasted for six days, claimed 38 lives and injured thousands, the majority of whom were African American. They began after a weekend of racial skirmishes at a Lake Michigan beach, culminating in the drowning of a Black teenager named Eugene Williams who had been stoned by a White mob, incensed that he swam into a so-called "whites only" area.

Daley was a member of the Hamburg Athletic Club during those riots and in 1924 was elected its president. But Daley also coldly understood the importance of the Black vote. As he progressed in county and state politics in Illinois, he became acquainted with the pioneering, powerful Black politician Rep. William Dawson. First elected to the U.S. House in 1942, serving the First Congressional District, Dawson was only the third African American to serve in Congress nationally since Reconstruction. He followed two other South Siders, Oscar De Priest and Arthur Mitchell, also African American congressmen serving the First District. Dawson would have absolute control of the African American vote on Chicago's South Side, closely aligning with the city's Democratic machine along with Daley.

With Dawson's help, Daley had been able to use a majority of Black Chicago's support as a base to first get elected as Chicago's mayor in 1955. His base of support in the Black community would carry him through successful re-elections to six terms through 1975. With Dawson and his ward henchmen pulling the ballot strings, Daley did not have to actively court the Black vote. He could pay lip service to civil rights, even uttering false homilies that all was well in his duchy. He could smile and wave to the crowd during the 1956 Bud Billiken Parade, riding atop an open convertible with former President Harry S Truman and *Chicago Defender* Founder and Publisher Robert Sengstacke Abbott.

Early in his first term, Daley said Chicago had no slums. In 1956, he outdid himself with this proclamation: "We believe that we do not have segregation in Chicago. Here we recognize every man, regardless of race, nationalistic origin, or creed, and they are all entitled to their rights as provided in the United States Constitution and the Constitution of Illinois."

Daley's background in Bridgeport, from where he could advance as far the WASP establishment's tolerance allowed an Irish-Catholic in mid-century, no doubt influenced this response to a civil-rights activist nun who visited him: Blacks should "lift themselves up by their bootstraps like our grandparents did…take care of their children…work hard…take care of their houses." He left out the fact an Irish-American could more easily blend in to a discriminatory, caste-system society simply by the color of his skin.

But the political system of gratitude-and-reward did not work for Chicago's communities of color, for all their electoral loyalty to the machine. Daley was no doubt startled when he won a far-below optimum (by Democratic standards) race for re-election to his third term in 1963. Pitted against former Cook County State's Attorney Ben Adamowski, a Polish-American, Daley's plurality was 137,531, or 55 percent of the vote. Preventing real trouble for Daley was a 138,769 margin for his candidacy in 14 wards out of 50 that were already predominately Black or nearly majority Black. These wards delivered an 82 percent majority vote for Daley, who got just 49 percent of the overall White vote.

Rather than using his immense political power to insure the Black vote was happy and satisfied by improving their economic and social conditions, Daley doubled down and began pandering to the White ethnic vote. Despite increasing frustration and even hopelessness, the Black vote had nowhere else to go with no strong, pro-civil rights challengers to Daley in subsequent elections. Chicago Republicans were a near after-thought. When Daley romped to victory for his fourth term in 1967, eight black South and West Side wards gave Daley a 120,408 to 14,275 swamping of hapless Republican challenger John Waner.

South Side frustration was expressed in other ways than mayoral elections. Communities there were angry over overcrowding in schools, where mobile portable classrooms (dubbed "Willis Wagons" in honor of Chicago Public Schools Superintendent Benjamin Willis) were used for overflow students, instead of placing these kids in nearby all-White schools which had plenty of classroom space. Inspired by the August 1963 March on Washington, thousands of demonstrators poured into downtown Chicago weeks later to protest the segregated schools. When Daley spoke at a 1963 NAACP event in Grant Park, he was booed.

Amid the constant rancor, Daley was unable to impede all progress. Willis was long gone by 1970, when the Chicago Board of Education could no longer ignore overcrowded inner-city schools. A "permissive transfer" program was instituted in which high school students could apply to attend majority-White schools across the city. This was "busing" without busing – the students would be on their own via public transportation to attend their new schools.

Although conflicts erupted at some schools with the arrival of Black students, success stories were recorded for the permissive transfers. The incoming students had to be especially motivated to rise before dawn for the long trips by bus and L, some traveling nearly the entire length of the city from past 110th Street all the way to the far North Side, fairly close to the northern city limits. One destination was Sullivan High School in Rogers Park, smallest in the city with just 1,100 students in 1970. It had plenty of room to accept the newcomers.

Young Sullivan football coach Mike Pols, a popular chap around campus, was an immediate beneficiary of the transfer students. The first were Sam Brady and Albert Conerly, who played football. They were good enough to earn full athletic scholarships to the University of Minnesota. Another early transfer student became senior class president at Sullivan. Unlike some Northwest and Southwest side schools where parental opposition to integration added to the conflicts triggered by integration, the transfer students were welcomed at Sullivan.

"It snowballed with the publicity," Pols said. "Kids wanted to get out of their local (crowded) schools and go a winning program. The word of mouth spread.

Kids were taking the L together to come here. They did their homework on the train. Some did not get home until 7 or 7:30 p.m."

The transfer students need extra energy to play football. After their long travels to make first bell in the morning, the football players also had to walk between one and two miles to Sullivan's practice fields at Chicago Park District property in West Rogers Park. One cold day, Brady and Conerly did not feel like changing into their football uniforms out on the field. They ducked into a nearby apartment building vestibule.

But just as they were stripped to their skivvies before putting on their pads, "a little ol' Jewish lady came down to get her mail," recalled Pols. "She saw these two big Black football guys, called the cops and six cars quickly showed up to see Sam and Albert in their underwear. I ran in there to explain what happened, and the cops left. I guess the little ol' lady felt bad, because she then brought cookies to practice."

The influx of talented, motivated athletes from the South Side enabled Sullivan and Pols to become the "little school that could." The Tigers won the Public League football championship in 1978.

Unfortunately, the transfer program did not make a big-enough dent in the quality of inner-city education. Frustration mounted, and only increased among Black voters after the assassination of Martin Luther King in 1968. Daley made his infamous "shoot to kill" comment, when responding to those looting and rioting after King's death on the city's predominantly African American West Side.

But the killing of Black Panthers Hampton and Clark created the most enmity against the Daley machine among Black voters. Under the leadership of Hampton, the Illinois chapter of the Black Panther Party had become a powerful, progressive political organization that attempted to incorporate a multi-cultural "Rainbow Coalition" of progressive groups — including the new Black street gangs, along with White groups like the Young Patriots and Latinx groups like the Young Lords. Some of the gangs were violent. The Black Panthers advocated the illegal open-carry of firearms. Those facts undermined the Panthers' progressive goals.

On Dec. 4, 1969, a big squad of Chicago police officers assigned to Cook County State's Attorney Edward Hanrahan's office staged a pre-dawn raid, ostensibly to find illegal weapons, in the West Side apartment of Hampton, the leader of the local Black Panther Party. Dozens of shots were fired, and Hampton and Clark were both killed. Despite guns found on the premises and police assertions that the Panthers had fired first, bullet-hole markings presented by police in support of their claim turned out to be nail heads. An investigation found that the police had fired between 82 and 99 shots during the raid, and the Panthers had fired only one.

The raid smelled very bad from the start. Hanrahan, a rising star in the Illinois Democratic Party and anointed as a possible successor to Daley, was indicted by a grand jury in August 1971 for obstructing justice and conspiracy to present false evidence. And although Daley renounced Hanrahan and would not endorse him in the 1972 Democratic primary in his re-election campaign for state's attorney, Black voters tied Hanrahan to Daley. Although Hanrahan beat Daley's substitute candidate in the primary, he lost to Republican Bernard Carey in the November general election thanks to mass defections by Black voters.

Police misconduct had long been a major issue in the Black community. White police had engendered suspicion in their interactions with inner-city residents an effect that, along with gangs' codes of silence, has interfered with the clearance of crimes that directly affect the Black community. But brutality even by Black cops assigned to their own neighborhoods was legendary. One of the Hampton raiders was a notoriously rough Black officer. Worst of all was detective Sylvester "Two Gun Pete" Washington, who in the pre-war period had a "shoot first, maybe ask questions later" style as he spread fear and loathing in the Wabash Avenue police district.

Black motorists endured nerve-wracking traffic stops by police. One fortunate high-profile Black resident of South Shore was future Cubs Hall of Famer Fergie Jenkins. He reported never being stopped in other cars, including his spanking new 1969 Thunderbird obtained from teammate Ernie Banks' Ford dealership on Stony Island Avenue. But one night, driving a Cadillac on an ice-cream run for his family, Jenkins was pulled over as the cops thought they had struck gold again, a man of color driving a luxury car. A stolen vehicle? Drugs? After a few moments, the officers realized they had detained the best pitcher in the National League. They sheepishly asked Jenkins for his autograph. Almost always affable, Jenkins declined.

The brutality that spread out over the decades may have been due to the culture shock of White cops from the ethnic enclaves of the Northwest and Southwest Sides being assigned to inner-city precincts.

"To us North Siders, the South Side was like a different city," said a 1972 graduate of the Chicago Police Academy who rose to a command position over the decades. Hitting the streets in the late summer of 1972, the native North Sider, who will remain anonymous, was just one of five with college degrees among the 250 academy graduates. Some incoming police rookies were fresh from combat duty in Vietnam with no de-compression period.

"We had no clue," said the retired officer, who said there "absolutely" would be automatic conflict with inner-city residents. "It came from a clash of cultures. A kid who grows up Catholic on the Northwest Side, you throw him into one of these districts where most are unemployed. He comes home to his young wife, and he asks how are these kids living like this? Or these poor people, little kids running around without clothes. It was tough taking a young kid who grew up on the Northwest Side of Chicago, take this kid right out of the Academy and throw him into the 11th District (West Side) or 7th District (Englewood).

"Not that cops were automatically born racist, but it was something they were never exposed to. In the academy back then, there was no diversity training. No bringing in guest speakers from African American or Muslim communities."

If rough treatment of detained suspects or during traffic stops was mitigated, it had to be by a fair-minded colleague of the cop who was lashing out. Otherwise, the "blue wall of silence," noted in a re-examination of policing as a result of the George Floyd murder in 2020, held firm.

"You can't beef on another cop," the retired officer said. Years after his 1972 rookie work, the officer, by then promoted to sergeant, warned a patrol officer he was mentoring in his precinct against ratting out two colleagues he had seen "whomping" on a suspect. The officer ignored his counsel and ended up a pariah – no one would work with him.

And if many encounters between White cops and Black residents in the inner city did not go well, racial profiling was endemic if Blacks were seen in White areas in situations that were not routine, like the workplace or a sports event. While residents of the South and West Sides felt hemmed in by employment discrimination and housing and educational opportunities, they surely could not walk any street of the city freely at any time as an American citizen.

The Sullivan High transfer students walking through the all-White neighborhood during the day to football practice did not ruffle feathers. They likely hiked in protective groups with White teammates. But if an unaccompanied, well-dressed Black man was spotted by the 1972 rookie cop and his partner walking down Devon Avenue on a Wednesday night after the retail stores closed, he would be stopped.

"It was a natural reaction to stop him to find out why he's there," the retired cop recalled. "He did not belong there (at that hour). The police instincts would have been to keep an eye on him. Is that our own built-in prejudice? Yes."

Given the tradition of police treatment of people of color in and outside the inner city, Black residents caught between the gangs' "snitches wear stitches" code of silence warning about testifying against them, and police trying to clear violent crimes, they were not likely to become witnesses. One retired Chicago police detective, who wrote a Facebook ode to the Daley machine reprinted elsewhere in this book, was repeatedly asked if an enhanced witness protection program, backed by the federal government, might impact gang violence if citizens could safely testify. The former detective had no response to the concept of re-locating witnesses to safety.

The killings of Hampton and Clark provided the seeds for the transformation of politics on the South and West Sides. More progressive African American pols, like Illinois State Senator Richard Newhouse and State Representative Harold Washington, were using the Hanrahan-led raid as platforms in their re-election campaigns. Washington, a former machine politician, would become more and more independent and progressive throughout the 1970s and, as a result, gained popularity in the African American community.

Washington — a lifelong White Sox fan — would eventually use this political momentum to engineer a stunning election as Chicago's mayor in 1983. He narrowly defeated Daley's son, Richard M. Daley, and incumbent Mayor Jane Byrne in the Democratic primary, then overcame Hyde Park attorney Bernard Epton in a contentious, racially charged general election. Both men had connections to the Sox. During his first term as mayor, Washington introduced and supported a plan to replace Comiskey Park with a new stadium across the street. Years earlier, in 1961, Epton — another lifelong fan — made an unsuccessful bid to buy the team from Bill Veeck.

Among experienced politicians Ralph Metcalfe did not limit his newly-independent streak to police brutality issues. He knew the South Side as an insider. Metcalfe was a Tilden Tech graduate who participated in the 1932 and 1936 Olympics, winning a gold medal in the latter's 100-meter relay event. He started his career as a political protege of Dawson and became a Chicago alderman in 1958.

Metcalfe was one of the "Silent Six" Black aldermen who blindly supported Daley in the City Council during the 1960s. But the Hampton/Clark raid and an incident where a close friend died in police custody after being held for six hours on a drunk driving charge, led to Metcalfe's transformation. He succeeded William Dawson as a congressman in the 1st Congressional District in 1970, co-founded the Congressional Black Caucus and became a leading advocate against police brutality.

"I realized (Daley) didn't care about Blacks, that he courted our votes, got them, then turned his back on us," Metcalfe would say later in the 1970s. "He was the only enemy I've ever had in politics."

South Sider Daley's 21 years in office as mayor and political kingmaker with almost dictatorial power is now perceived as perhaps the greatest missed opportunity to right many of the wrongs in Chicago history.

Daley was a faithful attendee at Mass every morning on his way to City Hall. But if he applied many of the original teachings of his church to dealing with his fellow man, they were well-hidden.

Even as unskilled-labor jobs dried up at the Chicago Stockyards and the big steel plants on the Far South Side began to wobble, Daley still had the raw clout to crusade against discrimination in a variety of still-booming industries and unions thriving before the Ronald Reagan-led rollback of labor rights of the 1980s. Even in the mid-1960s, those in the know realized welfare benefits and public housing were not conducive to nuclear families and the far-reaching positive benefits such structure brought in a still-patriarchal society. Employed male breadwinners were the surest path to families achieving at least working-class, if not middle-class status, and not creating successive generations of single-parent poverty with the crime and hopelessness it breeds.

One particularly booming industry under Daley was construction. From the single-family homes of Marynook and Washington Heights on the South Side to the three 100-story towers and lesser downtown and lakefront skyscrapers erected under Hizzoner's watch, the assorted trades involved had plenty of work. Discrimination was rampant in the union-dominated construction industry. In addition to fearing the "other," White ethnics wearing hard hats or carrying electrician's tools desired a near-closed system of placing sons, brothers and other tribal members into apprentice programs. They wanted no one encroaching on their good deal.

The Nixon Administration, of all public institutions, and not Daley's City Hall, opted in 1969 to look into the rampant discrimination, at least in projects supported by federal funds. The Labor Department, represented by Arthur Fletcher, a rare Black Republican activist and an assistant secretary of labor, scheduled a hearing on discrimination in construction trades for Sept. 24, 1969, at Chicago's LaSalle Hotel. But 500 hard-hatted tradesmen jammed and disrupted the hearing room, forcing Fletcher to postpone the hearing.

The next day, some 2,000 tradesmen provided an inadvertent — or maybe not — sneak preview of a far-in-the-future (January 6, 2021) assault on government. Fletcher scheduled another hearing at the U.S. Customhouse at Canal and Harrison streets, southwest of the Loop and north of Comiskey Park. But the mob surrounded the building, blocking all entrances. When several Black witnesses tried to enter, the hard hats accosted them and police moved in.

Suddenly, White blue-collar workers fought White cops, likely many from their own parishes and corner taverns. Five police officers were injured in a sneak preview of that future Capitol insurrection. However, the majority of those arrested were Black bystanders, several of whom were accused of firing guns into the air.

In another eerie preview of a 2021, which no one could remotely foresee in 1969, two construction workers were linked with a "disabling" chemical, just as bear spray and anti-personnel concoctions were used against Capitol and Washington, D.C. police on Jan. 6, 2021. Charles R. Johnson of Portage, Ind., was arrested near the Federal Building, to which the hard hats had later marched, carrying a can of "disabling spray." Ironworker Edward Ivy was treated at Presbyterian-St. Luke's Hospital, having been injured by what officials described as "disabling chemical spray." *Chicago Tribune* reporter William Jones, covering the melee, was kicked in the groin. The injury did not prevent Jones from writing the story of this hard hats-cops clash or winning a Pulitzer Prize for local reporting two years later.

The memory of the Customhouse riot was obscured in the long run by the blizzard of concurrent anti-war demonstrations and Days of Rage rampages by the Weathermen radicals. In addition, the Chicago 7 trial was about to start, with all its fracases in and out of the court. Few could yet conceive that "middle Americans" — Richard Nixon's "silent majority" — could so blatantly disrupt government. Far less favorable descriptions of rioters were applied a half-century later.

If Daley was shocked by the "hard hat" riot, he did not express dismay in the same manner as his "shoot to kill" order of a year earlier. He depended on the construction workers for votes, for sure, at the expense of those they tried to block from employment. All the problems Daley could have headed off at the pass, or made an earnest attempt to solve, were instead kicked way down the road. All the sorrow of mass hopelessness, of inner-city children shot in the streets or in their bedrooms, and violence bursting out from the inner city into Daley's gleaming downtown, represented the end of that road.

But in the wake of Daley's death at 74 on Dec. 20, 1976, master pundit Mike Royko explained why the power broker he so expertly covered in the *Chicago Daily News* and *Boss,* his best-selling book, could not play above his breeding and wield his uncommon power for the common good:

"As he proved over and over again, he didn't trust outsiders, whether they were long-hairs against war, black preachers against segregation, reformers against his machine or community groups against his policies. This was his neighborhood-ward-city-county, and nobody could come in and make noise. He'd call the cops. Which he did.

"There are those who believed Daley could have risen beyond politics to statesmanship had he embraced the idealistic causes of the 1960s rather than obstructing them. Had he used his unique power to lead us toward brotherhood and understanding, they say, he could have achieved greatness.

"Sure he would have. But to have expected that response from Daley was as realistic as asking Cragin, Bridgeport, Marquette Park or any other Chicago neighborhood to celebrate Brotherhood Week by having Jeff Fort (the city's top black gang leader at that time) to dinner. If Daley was reactionary and stubborn, he was in perfect harmony with his town."

So amid the turmoil of 1972, Daley plowed ahead in his Boss-hood, not desiring to alter his lifelong course. His one respite from this drama was his boyhood team, the Chicago White Sox, who would be a source of hope for both White and Black South Siders in 1972. "He likes the White Sox, parades and fishing," Royko would write about Daley. Bill Veeck said Daley always felt that supporting the Sox was important, because he felt the team was vital to the community.

"He was tremendously supportive," Veeck told filmmakers Tom Weinberg and Jamie Caesar when they interviewed him for their 1985 documentary "A Man For All Seasons."

"We didn't agree philosophically on everything, but we had a mutual respect," Veeck recalled. "He was a great baseball fan and knowledgeable. And I think he was a splendid mayor. He held the city together and got things done. He had historically been a White Sox fan, a paying White Sox fan. Every Sunday during the summer, you'd see them coming up from Bridgeport to go to the games. He was the only mayor I've known who paid for his tickets. He didn't have to, but he felt that…part of what's being a baseball fan is supporting the team."

In the center of a changing, sometimes roiling South Side, Comiskey Park was a model of relative consistency. And like the Stockyards and Wisconsin Steel, the park employed many native South Siders. The high-school-aged batboys and clubhouse attendants, for instance, were representative of the wide variety of communities that the South Side offers.

Rory Clark, one of the batboys, lived in the African American Oakland neighborhood just east and south of Sox Park. He went to St. Ignatius High School. Clubhouse attendant Jim O'Keefe lived in Irish-dominated Bridgeport;

he went to De La Salle Institute. Jim Riley, a batboy and clubhouse attendant, lived in Evergreen Park, the southwestern suburb just outside of city limits and attended Mt. Carmel High in the Woodlawn neighborhood.

Clark, who grew up only a few blocks away from Comiskey at 37th and Michigan, had been an Andy Frain usher before using ingenuity to get hired by the team in 1972.

"I was an usher and I used to see Stu Holcomb, who was the general manager, walking through the park on a regular basis," Clark recalled. "And I had talked to the other batboys and I knew that two of them were leaving next year. So there were going to be two openings. So one day I just walked up to Stu Holcomb and I introduced myself.

"I said you're going to be losing two batboys next year, and I'd like to be one of their replacements. And he said, well, I don't hire the batboys. I said yeah, I figured that, but you run the team, right? He said yeah. I said well, if you introduce me to the person who hires batboys, that will get me the job instantly. He said, well, why would I do that? I said well, you used to be the athletic director at Northwestern University, right? He said, yeah. I said well, I'm going to Northwestern next year so we're practically brothers.

"So, he got this little uncomfortable laugh, and he said OK. Come and see me when the team is out of town. So, as soon as the team bus was pulling off, I walked into his office. He took me down and introduced me to (Sox equipment manager) Larry Licklider, and I got hired on the spot."

O'Keefe, who played on the De La Salle baseball team, got his gig as a Sox clubhouse attendant in 1971 in the fine, time-honored Chicago tradition of "knowing someone" — his older brother Mike, who had been one of the team's batboys since 1968.

"The *Chicago Daily News* ran a contest every year — 'Why you want to be a White Sox bat boy?'" O'Keefe remembered. "My brother Mike finished in the top two in that contest and got the job. I'd visit Mike at the park and I was just probably pestering the living daylights out of Larry Licklider. They hired me in '71 as a batboy, but two weeks before Opening Day, I broke my ankle playing baseball for De La Salle. So I was on the shelf for 10 weeks.

"By the time I was able to start getting around, Larry had already had hired another bat boy. So they gave me a job in the clubhouse. In the long run, I enjoyed it more, 'cause there was a different perspective than being out on the field. For the most part I spent most of the '71 season and all the way through '74 in the clubhouse."

Jim Riley got his job, first as ball boy and batboy in 1972, through his uncle, who was an electrician at the park. Later on, he would become a clubhouse attendant for the team. "I would run errands for the players if they asked me," Riley said. "I did everything from getting birth control pills for a guy's wife to taking another player's kid biking.

But the jobs of these three — and all the other staff personnel at White Sox Park — were on hold as the season approached April 1, 1972. On that day, the history-making work stoppage began. In the long run, though, the strike was just a footnote delaying the start of what would be one of the most incredible seasons in White Sox history during a year in which the status quo both inside and outside Comiskey Park was upended.

Mayor Richard J. Daley (right) with Bill Veeck (left of Daley) at Daley's final White Sox home opener in 1976.

Photo credit: Leo Bauby Collection

Chicago's racial divisions were made clear on Sept. 25, 1969, when thousands of protesting White construction workers blocked access to a U.S. Labor Dept. hearing on racial discrimination in the building trades, fighting with police in the process. A portion of the crowd then marched to Civic Center Plaza, where a group of protestors climbed the then two-year-old Picasso statue (pictured here). Chicago in the late 1960s and early 1970s was roiled with political and racial conflict, with Mayor Richard J. Daley's political machine suffering losses.

Photo credit: the Associated Press/Edward Kitch

CHAPTER 5

April 6, 1972: John Allyn
-The Reluctant Owner

Comiskey Park was supposed to be the center of attention on the South Side on April 6, 1972. The game was scheduled to be the 61st Opening Day at the old ballpark designed by Zachary Taylor Davis.

But instead of having a full house for a new team headed by superstar Dick Allen, the ballpark was closed to fans. Instead, Day 6 of the players union job action had commenced, and the White Sox organization was contending with how to handle the cancellation of a much-anticipated Opening Day.

The trade for Dick Allen had energized the fan base. But with the strike, the cash-starved team was missing out on much-needed revenue.

"With the good weather expected and the urgency many fans feel to see the new club, we expected about 50,000," said Tom Maloney, the Sox ticket manager.

"This weekend we stand to lose about $200,000," added team Executive Vice President Stu Holcomb. "There are not indications now when the strike will be settled, and I would say it looks uncertain for our weekend games."

This was a historic moment. The Association's Executive Director, Marvin Miller, had successfully unified the players over the issue of increasing players pensions to match three years' worth of inflation. And now, most owners were hoping that they could break the union and Miller's hold over the players.

While this drama played out on the sports pages, the front page of the *Chicago Tribune* on April 6 detailed the uncomfortable changes taking place for many on the South and Southwest sides of the city, represented by an emotional, raw battle between two aldermen.

One side was represented by the recently elected 16th Ward Anna Langford, an African American civil rights activist and attorney who had worked with Martin Luther King. She was one of the first two female aldermen in city history, both of whom were elected in 1971. And she was the very first Black female alderman.

The other side was represented by Rev. Francis Lawlor, who was first elected in 1971, representing the 15th Ward, the ward adjacent to Langford's. Lawlor, a Roman Catholic priest, had taught for more than 20 years at one of the city's most prominent Catholic schools, St. Rita High School.

The two new aldermen came to verbal blows over a subject which was sensitive to many Chicagoans in 1972, especially those on the South and Southwest Sides: White flight.

Lawlor had been actively organizing a coalition of block clubs with Irish, Polish and Lithuanian residents in the Chicago Lawn, West Englewood and Marquette Park neighborhoods, all communities in Lawlor's ward. The goal of these block clubs was "racial stability" — Lawlor wanted to keep integration to a bare minimum in his ward, as more Black families began to move to the

Southwest Side.

At this City Council meeting, Lawlor began ranting about Board of Education desegregation plans for schools in his ward. He then accused Langford of attempting to help Black families move into formerly White homes. "The Black people…are coming in and taking over every part of our community," Lawlor told his colleagues.

This set off Langford. "That man (Lawlor) has a one-track mind that all Blacks should be shipped back east of Ashland Avenue," she said.

The impolite conversation carried on in that public setting, but the conversation reflected an urgent reality. Seemingly overnight, in neighborhoods throughout the South and Southwest sides, White ethnic families were moving out and Black families were moving in.

This change took place in the heart of White Sox country, the home base for the team's fan base. It was happening in Auburn Gresham — the longtime home of Buck Weaver, the disgraced, brilliant third baseman for the 1919 Black Sox, who maintained his innocence up until he was found dead on the sidewalk of 71st street near Wolcott Avenue after suffering a heart attack near his apartment. And the changes swept through West Englewood, Chicago Lawn, Chatham, Avalon Park, Marynook, Greater Grand Crossing, Brainerd, Washington Heights, South Shore, Pill Hill and other communities.

While this human drama continued in neighborhoods surrounding Comiskey Park, the strike was forcing most owners to turn their backs on their players. Teams were making sure players had no access to their facilities, either at spring training sites in Florida and Arizona, or at major league stadiums throughout the country. In the Chicago area, Wrigley Field was off-limits to Cub players. Instead, a group of them practiced at the Holy Cross High School field in River Grove.

One exception stood out among Major League teams. At White Sox Park, perhaps half the team was practicing for an uncertain season. Player representatives Jay Johnstone and Rick Reichardt were there. So were fellow outfielders Carlos May and Walt Williams. Rookie Jorge Orta and veteran Mike Andrews were among the players representing the infield, while veteran Stan Bahnsen joined four other pitchers, including second-year fireballer Bart Johnson and rookie Rich Gossage.

The Sox were the first of the 24 clubs to offer striking players the use of their home stadium for practice,

"We offered to let them use the park on a day-to-day basis for the benefit of the players and the fans," Holcomb said. "[White Sox owner] John [Allyn] made the offer with no strings attached."

The reaction from the league and other owners was immediate and severe. American League President Joe Cronin warned the team that the league was discouraging teams from allowing players access to ballparks. And Kansas City Royals owner Ewing Kauffman threatened to protest future games against the Sox when the strike ended, due to their cooperation with the players.

But Holcomb —speaking for Allyn— said that the team would allow players to use White Sox Park to practice for as long as the walkout continued.

"(The league) asked us to close the ballpark, but there was never anything to prohibit players from practicing," Holcomb said. "The boys are here and as long as they want to work out, it will be open to them."

Allyn presented a unique stance from a man considered to be one of the more low-key owners in the league. But Allyn proved his independence in other ways during the labor crisis, even blaming fellow owners for their role in the labor rift. "This thing (the strike) never should have happened in the first place if common sense was used and the (owners') pension committee had done its job," he said.

"Marvin Miller is the one man who is going to decide when this strike is over — he is the voice of the players and whatever he says, the players will fall in 99 percent. In the owners' meeting, you just get 24 different opinions.

"Now I've had my say. And that should really get me hung."

"It was John Allyn's determination, really selflessness, that saved the White Sox for the city of Chicago. Every White Sox fan owes him a debt of gratitude for his untiring efforts to keep the team in Chicago."
– Then-White Sox owner Bill Veeck after John Allyn's death in April 1979

In the White Sox organization's 120-year history, the team has had only four ownership groups. Three of those groups are well-documented in major league history and well known to even casual fans. The "Old Roman," Charles A. Comiskey, established the organization in 1901, and his heirs would continue to be majority owners of the organization through 1958, winning two World Series and presiding over another infamous World Series team, popularly known as the Black Sox — the team forever tarnished by throwing the 1919 Fall Classic.

Veeck would own the team in two different periods (1959-1961 and 1975-1980), playing in one World Series (1959) in the process and forever becoming identified with offbeat, innovative ways to attract fans to the ballpark. And Jerry Reinsdorf (1981 to present) led an ownership group which enjoyed a 2005 World Series title and presided over a consistently profitable franchise now worth almost $1.7 billion. Reinsdorf was able to prosper, partially due to a publicly financed 1988 stadium deal which allowed the Sox to enjoy nearly all revenue generated from the ballpark.

The fourth ownership group is often forgotten by history. But the two Allyn brothers, Arthur, Jr., and John, who owned the team in the period between 1961 and 1975, were important transitional stewards of White Sox history. And it could be argued that John Allyn was the most important figure in team annals, most notably for his role in saving the team from moving — not once, but twice.

John Allyn was an unlikely champion for this South Side organization. He lived with his wife and four children in the privileged environment of Winnetka, one of the wealthiest towns on Chicago's North Shore. A self-described "sportsman" and "country club guy," Allyn did like baseball, but he grew up a Cubs fan.

It was John Allyn who purchased full ownership of the Sox from his brother in late September 1969, saving the team from an almost certain move to Milwaukee. It was John Allyn who shook up the front office in 1970, hiring Stu Holcomb, who in turn hired all the major pieces for successful early 1970s Sox teams, including Roland Hemond, Chuck Tanner, Harry Caray and Nancy Faust. It was John Allyn who green-lit the most important acquisition in the early 70s, Dick Allen. And it was John Allyn who again saved the Sox from another almost certain move in 1975, when a wealthy group led by entertainer Danny Kaye offered to buy the franchise and move it to Seattle.

"John Allyn is an unsung hero in White Sox history because he kept holding on to the club, and gave us support as best he could at all times," said Hemond. "He kept the club going in Chicago, despite what he could have received from buyers that might want to move the club."

The Allyns' involvement with the South Side baseball club began with Veeck, who always had deep connections with Chicago's business community. These were cultivated by his father, William L. Veeck Sr., the former sportswriter who, as team president, helped build the Cubs powerhouse teams of the 1920s and 1930s.

One crucial Veeck connection was with Arthur Allyn Sr., one of the city's most notable investment bankers and the owner of the powerful LaSalle Street brokerage firm A.C. Allyn & Co. Through his company, Allyn Sr. also had relationships with major figures in Chicago business. So Veeck leaned on Allyn Sr. when he bought his first major league team — the Cleveland Indians, which he purchased in 1946 for $1.5 million. Allyn Sr. was a main investor in the Indians, along with other powerful Chicagoans like Phil Clarke and Lester Armour of the City National Bank and attorney Newton Frye Sr. Comedian Bob Hope was also in the ownership group — he grew up in Cleveland. Veeck, establishing his tradition of flipping a team soon after purchasing it, sold the Indians in November 1949 for $2.2 million.

This same group of minority investors, headed by Allyn Sr., went along with Veeck when he purchased the St. Louis Browns in 1951. Veeck sold the team for $2.4 million two years later to a group of Baltimore investors who moved the team to Maryland for the 1954 season, netting Veeck and his investors a 38 percent profit.

Next up was the White Sox. In 1958, the sibling drama between Dorothy and Charles (Chuck) Comiskey II had reached its climax. Their father, J. Louis Comiskey, the son of the "Old Roman," died in 1939, and left the team to his widow Grace and their three children. But when Grace Comiskey died in 1956, her will left Dorothy with a controlling, 54 percent interest in the White Sox.

Chuck Comiskey had been hands-on with the team going back to 1948, working with General Manager Frank Lane to build the competitive "Go-Go Sox" of that era. Chuck had been considered the heir apparent to take over the team as the team's principal owner. Indeed, after Lane resigned in 1955 and joined the St. Louis Cardinals, Chuck served as co-general manager and team vice-president with John Rigney, Dorothy's husband, who pitched for the team in the late 1930s and early 1940s. Through the consistent strengthening of a strong farm system, judicious trades and the hiring of manager Al Lopez, this duo continued creating a constantly contending team which would eventually win the 1959 AL pennant.

But the White Sox would capture that flag under a new majority owner. Dorothy began secret negotiations to sell her majority stock in the summer of 1958 to either Veeck or Chicago insurance magnate Charles O. Finley. She would eventually choose Veeck and his usual group of investors, headed by Allyn Sr., in the winter of 1958. Veeck would also bring along Hall of Fame slugger Hank Greenberg as a minority owner and team GM. Greenberg had previously served as Veeck's top baseball executive in Cleveland.

Finley, meanwhile, wound up purchasing the Kansas City Athletics in 1961, move that team to Oakland in 1968 and preside over a dynasty that won three consecutive World Series in the early 1970s. That team would be the chief nemesis to a revived White Sox team in the AL Western Division.

The Veeck group would enjoy some of the fruits of the success that had been built during the 1950s. In 1960, the team broke a Chicago baseball attendance record and lead the American League with 1,644,460 turning out to Comiskey Park in the joyous afterglow of 1959. But health issues with both Allyn Sr. and Veeck would dramatically change the direction of the franchise within the next year.

In October 1960, shortly after the end of the season, Allyn Sr. died of a heart attack. In his will, his holdings through the Artnell Corp. (a hybrid of the first names of Arthur Sr. and his wife, Nellie) were split evenly between his two sons, Arthur, Jr. and John. Those holdings, of course, included the White Sox.

Then Veeck shocked Chicagoans by checking into the Mayo Clinic in April 1961. Veeck said he "ran out of gas." But he was actually suffering from a variety of issues, including trauma from a right leg that was first partially amputated during his time in the South Pacific during World War II. Veeck had a seventh amputation procedure on the leg in June 1960. His health was also jeopardized by a five-pack-a-day cigarette habit and a round-the-clock schedule, where he would occasionally report to work at the start of regular business hours in the morning after a long night on the town.

Greenberg ran all aspects of the team during Veeck's absence, and there were rumors that the Jewish baseball icon would buy out Veeck and take over as principal owner — an action that probably would have changed the course of Chicago baseball history. But Greenberg later told writer Lawrence Ritter that he was concerned about prejudice among other AL owners impeding his ability as the Sox majority owner.

"I recognized then that there was a lot of prejudice against me," Greenberg told Ritter. "I'd have had my life savings tied up in the club, and I realized that if I ever needed any help, I sure wouldn't get it from my fellow owners. It would be closed ranks against me. Strangely enough, that was the first time anti-Semitism really affected me adversely in baseball."

Instead, Veeck and Greenberg decided to sell their stock in the team. A syndicate headed by entertainer Danny Thomas and 39-year-old LaSalle Street attorney Bernard Epton offered $4.8 million for the 54 percent owned by Veeck's group. Thomas, the television star and producer, got his start in Chicago, performing as an MC at the 5100 club at 5100 N. Broadway Ave. Epton would later become a household name with his 1983 run for mayor. Epton, a moderate Jewish Republican from Hyde Park, almost beat Washington by running a divisive racial campaign in an attempt to get the White ethnic vote in the city — a campaign that would tarnish Epton's reputation in his remaining years.

But Veeck's group accepted less from the colleagues they knew: The Allyns, who paid $3.5 million for the Veeck/Greenberg shares. The announcement was made at a press conference at Comiskey Park on June 10, 1961.

"I am going to keep this ball club," Art Allyn told the media. "I have no plans to negotiate the sale of the White Sox. I plan to keep them here. I definitely am not putting them on the block. We would listen to offers, but there is no intention of selling."

A bitter Chuck Comiskey still owned 46 percent of the team and attempted to acquire the majority stock from the Allyns immediately after they made the deal with Veeck. But Allyn wouldn't listen to Comiskey. "They (Comiskey) called and asked for a meeting, but there is no meeting planned," he said.

Comiskey finally sold his 46% share for around $4 million to a syndicate of prominent Chicagoans, headed by businessman William Bartholomay and powerful attorney Thomas Reynolds in December 1961. "This brings to a close 61 years in baseball for the Comiskeys," Chuck Comiskey said, with a trace of emotion, during his farewell press conference at the Sheraton Hotel downtown.

Only six months later, in May 1962, the syndicate headed by Reynolds and Bartholomay sold its 46 percent share of the team to the Allyns. Reynolds and Bartholomay then led an ownership group that purchased the Milwaukee Braves later in 1962. Their tenure in County Stadium proved fractious. The pair eventually moved the team amid litigation to Atlanta in 1966, opening the South to major league baseball and leaving a void in Milwaukee that would affect the Allyns and the Sox later in the decade.

Reynolds later became the head of Winston and Strawn, one of the nation's most powerful law firms, which would employ future Illinois Governor James R. Thompson. Reynolds again became connected to the White Sox in the mid-1980s as chairman of the Illinois Sports Facilities Authority, which oversaw construction of the new Comiskey Park.

Arthur Allyn, Jr was presented to the public as the team's majority owner, while brother John was in the background, listed as a minority investor. But in fact, each had 50% equity in the White Sox. When the brothers' ownership began, Art Allyn had only attended two baseball games in his life. His real interests were his brokerage business and a unique hobby — collecting butterflies.

The Allyns inherited a club which, as a gate attraction, had been revived by Veeck through his innovative promotions.

After the deal to purchase Comiskey's share of the team, Art Allyn would sever all ties to the team's founding ownership group, including that name change of Comiskey Park to White Sox Park.

Veeck also gutted the farm system that had been developed in the 1950s by Lane, Chuck Comiskey and Rigney. A quintet of homegrown future All-Stars — Norm Cash, Earl Battey, Johnny Callison, Don Mincher and John "Honey" Romano — were traded for veterans in Veeck's attempt to reclaim the AL title in 1960. Battey and Mincher ended up starters on a 1965 Minnesota Twins team that beat out the 95-victory Sox for the AL pennant. Greenberg continued for a few months in 1961 as General Manager before leaving the organization for good in September.

Arthur Allyn hired an unlikely replacement as GM — team publicity director Ed Short— while retaining the Sox longtime on-the-field brain trust of manager Al Lopez and pitching coach Ray Berres. They still had a strong pitching staff, led by Comiskey holdovers Joel Horlen and Gary Peters. Also, a series of judicious trades — in which talent like Tommy John, Tommie Agee, Wilbur Wood, Hoyt Wilhelm, Pete Ward, Juan Pizarro and Don Buford were acquired — helped maintain the Sox as a competitive team which consistently finished in the first division through the mid-1960s.

Allyn — a stern, somewhat humorless-looking figure who wore black horn-rimmed glasses and sported a crewcut — belied his conservative image with some groundbreaking moves as owner. In 1962, he purchased the Sarasota Motor Hotel near the team's spring training facility in that Florida city, so his Black and White players could be housed together in what was still a segregated South. And he was one of the first owners to buy a private jetliner for his team. Allyn was also active in attempting to land a second professional football team to play in Comiskey Park, vacated by the Cardinals after the 1958 season. The *Chicago Sun-Times* reported in March 1964 that Allyn was planning to purchase the American Football League's Denver Broncos and move them to the South Side for the 1965 season, a report he wouldn't confirm. However, Allyn did tell the Denver Post that he had made an offer for the AFL's Oakland Raiders and was turned down.

Allyn was first and foremost a businessman who saw the Chicago White Sox organization as a convenient tax write-off. That attitude would get him in trouble with the IRS in 1967, when the Artnell Corporation was cited by the IRS for not paying more than $560,000 in back taxes on gross income of more than $1.5 million from ticket sales and radio and TV rights from several earlier years.

Some of Allyn's ideas for running a ball club were ahead of their time. By the mid-1960s, the team was advertising White Sox Park in newspapers and in their media guides as "Chicago's Downtown Ballpark." And in an effort to attract those "downtown" fans, Allyn made plans to build Major League Baseball's first private club for fans. The "Coach and Nine" would be directly across the street from the main entrance to White Sox Park — essentially the location of the entrance to the present Guaranteed Rate Field. The facility would have had room for about 600 patrons. But the idea never got off the ground; the location was instead used for a parking lot.

More importantly, Allyn was the first White Sox owner to begin lobbying for the team to move from its longtime home at 35th Street and Shields Avenue. By 1966 through a feature in the Sox game program, he asked fans if they would attend games in a domed stadium. In June 1967, as his team was in the middle of a four-team race with Boston, Detroit and Minnesota for the pennant, Allyn picked that time to announce perhaps the most ambitious of the city's plans for a new stadium. It would be part of a $50 million privately-financed sports complex at Dearborn Station in the city's South Loop — a 50-acre area bounded by State, Polk, Clark and 15th streets. The plan involved leasing the air rights to the still-active train Station, the primary depot for private Santa Fe cross-country passenger lines including the El Capitan and the Super Chief.

The grand project would be a three-stadium complex to house all the professional sports teams in the city — the Bears, Sox, Cubs, Bulls and Blackhawks, along with the Chicago Mustangs, the professional soccer team owned by the Allyns, which played at White Sox Park in the new United Soccer Association. The plans called for a 46,000-seat baseball stadium, a 60,000-seat football and soccer venue and a 15,000-seat stadium for hockey and basketball. Completion was expected by 1972.

But Allyn didn't get any buy-in from the other sports organizations. Mayor Richard J. Daley also ignored the plan, preferring his own public-private multi-purpose sports stadium that was first proposed in a 1964 mayoral commission report.

The 1967 season was the 16th consecutive year that the White Sox finished above .500 and in the first division in the American League. During that time, the Sox outpaced the crosstown Cubs in home attendance in 15 of those 16 years — the exception being the recession year of 1958. Even in 1967, when the resurgent Cubs began attracting fans back during a competitive season which saw them in first place in July, the White Sox (985,634 attendance) still slightly outdrew the Cubs (977,226).

But the fan response was tepid for the Sox during a 1967 season where the pennant race continued until the last days of the season. Boston would end up winning the AL that year, with the Sox finishing fourth, three games out. They had a great chance to clinch the pennant and change the fortunes of the organization but lost their last five games to lowly Kansas City and Washington, allowing the Red Sox to snare their "Impossible Dream" flag. This collapse followed a disappointing 1966 season which also saw an attendance decline at Sox Park. Further, the Allyns were also losing money on the Mustangs, who sold the second-fewest tickets in the United Soccer Association in 1967. The Mustangs folded after their inaugural season.

Faced with a situation where he needed more revenue from his sports organization, Allyn turned to the city 90 miles north of Chicago: Milwaukee. On July 24, 1967, the White Sox and Minnesota Twins took a break from the tight pennant race and played an exhibition game at County Stadium. More than 51,000 fans attended — the largest turnout in County Stadium history there.

The exhibition was the first major league game in Milwaukee since the end of the 1965 season, the Braves' final campaign in Wisconsin. The sponsoring organization was Milwaukee Brewers Inc., a group of local businessmen trying to land a major league team. They were headed by Milwaukee car leasing executive Bud Selig, who had become the Braves largest public stockholder in 1963, before angrily divesting himself of those shares when the team announced it was moving to Atlanta.

The packed County Stadium proved Milwaukee was ready to host another major league team. "These fans are dying for baseball," said Sox manager Eddie Stanky. "I'm not in the higher echelons, but baseball certainly should come back to Milwaukee after this."

Milwaukee's warm welcome influenced Art Allyn's shocking announcement before the media at Chicago's Sherman House on Oct. 30, 1967 — the White Sox would play 10 home games in Milwaukee during the 1968 season. Each AL team would play the Sox for one night game during the week in Milwaukee, while the Cubs would also play one of their two pre-season exhibition games against the Sox at County Stadium. Allyn developed the plan with Selig, who from the start was interested in the White Sox playing *more* than just ten games at County Stadium.

"I had gotten to know Art, not well, but we talked on occasion," Selig recalled more than 50 years later, from his Commissioner Emeritus office in Milwaukee. "After the season in 1967, we got together and I told him 'Number one, we'd like to buy the team.' Well, he wasn't interested in that then, but that's when I proposed playing the ten games in Milwaukee, and he was interested in that. And that was a big thing for us in those days. So Art and I actually developed a nice relationship after that."

"It's our attempt to develop Milwaukee for our television market," Allyn said of the deal at the time. The Sox were moving on television from WGN-TV to WFLD-TV, a UHF station, starting in 1968. And many of those games would be broadcast on a separate Milwaukee UHF station planned by WFLD's corporate owner, Chicago's Field Enterprises, Allyn explained. He also denied a report by Al Hirshberg, a Boston sportswriter, who wrote that the Sox were eventually moving to Milwaukee. "There's no truth to it," Allyn said.

But in 1968, the Milwaukee games would be the only well-attended home dates on the White Sox schedule. The team drew 805,775 at home, and 265,552 of that (one-third) was at County Stadium, as Chicago fans stayed away from the first below-.500 Sox team since 1950. In the last season before each league expanded by two teams and moved to two six-team divisions, the Sox finished in a distant eighth place.

The abysmal 67-95 record was only part of the problem. Amid 1968's civil unrest, the team's location in what some considered to be an "unsafe" area didn't help matters. And the Cubs had begun to capture Chicago's imagination with another above .500 finish and their first season with more than one million in attendance since 1952.

Allyn re-upped with Selig on a deal to play another 11 regular season games in Milwaukee in 1969. And this time, the attendance at County Stadium (196,784) accounted for *more* than one-third of the home season attendance (589,546).

Behind the scenes, as the team's fortunes cratered, Arthur Allyn was actively looking to sell it. Not surprisingly, his most-interested suitor was Selig, who wanted to move the White Sox to Milwaukee for the 1970 season. And it almost happened. By late August 1969, Selig had offered Allyn $13 million for the franchise, which he immediately accepted with a handshake.

"The deal was done," Selig would tell *Chicago Tribune* baseball columnist Jerome Holtzman in 1998.

But the day after Labor Day, that handshake deal was nullified. "I remember it like it was yesterday," Selig said. "Art called me and said, 'My brother John wants to buy the team, and I have to sell it to him.'

"I was shocked. It was disappointing, because we had a deal."

In his heart, Selig knew that the American League didn't want to abandon Chicago, so approval would have been difficult.

"Would the league have approved it?" he said. "Well, we never got that far. I have my doubts. I'm sure (Commissioner) Bowie (Kuhn) would have been against the deal. I was heartbroken."

But Selig's dalliance with the White Sox soon became moot, when he learned about Seattle Pilots owner Derey Soriano's financial issues. Soriano would end up in bankruptcy court, leaving the team available for sale.

"The whole Seattle thing started the same day Art Allyn told me he was selling to his brother," Selig said. "And it later led to us getting the Pilots and bringing them to Milwaukee."

> **"Isn't life funny? All these years you'd go out to White Sox Park and Art Allyn would be glad-handing the visitors while over in a corner, speaking only when he was spoken to, would be the man who owned 50 percent of the White Sox. That was Art's brother, John…"**
> – *Robert Markus, Chicago Tribune, Sept. 26, 1969*

For most of the 1960s, John Allyn was a consistent, quiet presence at White Sox Park. He could be seen in the Bards Room or at Art Allyn's press conferences, usually in the back of the room, smoking a pipe. He definitely looked the part of a 1960s LaSalle Street businessman — horn-rimmed glasses, thinning hair which was gray at the temples.

John Allyn also was what newspapermen of the era called a "sportsman." He was a Bears fan and even cheered on the pennant-chasing 1969 Cubs along with his teenage daughter, a rabid Cubs fan. He was an expert marksman, with more than 40 muzzle-loading rifles located in his home. And he was an avid golfer, with memberships at two exclusive Chicago-area country clubs and Augusta National in Georgia. Whenever sportswriters approached him at the ballpark, they were usually subjected to conversations about either golf or baseball.

In short, John Allyn seemed a better fit than his brother to run the White Sox. But despite inheriting 50% of the club from his father, John Allyn was instead involved with other divisions of the Artnell Co., established during the financial crisis of 1929 as a holding company for various Allyn-owned businesses. By 1969, Artnell had at least a dozen different subsidiaries "with tentacles currently reaching from the United States to Canada to West Germany to Australia to South Africa," according to the Tribune's David Condon. Those divisions included an Ohio firm that manufactured bus, rail and truck seats, Chicago's Rosner-Hixson Laboratories, a Houston maker of oil field tools and a tool-factory in South Africa.

John Allyn had been tapped to run the doomed Chicago Mustangs soccer team. He said he learned much about running a sports operation with the Mustangs, even traveling to Europe to sign players. To assist him in the Mustangs front office, Allyn hired Stu Holcomb, the longtime college football coach and administrator, who most recently was the athletic director at Northwestern University.

Holcomb would play a key role in John Allyn's next mission — to take over the White Sox.

When John Allyn first heard of Arthur Allyn's plan to sell the team to Selig in August 1969, he immediately thought the move was a bad decision. John believed abandoning what was still the second-largest city in the country in 1970 and the third-largest broadcast market for the 12th largest city was unthinkable. And he believed that leaving a stadium that the team owned for a situation where the White Sox would be leasing County Stadium was bad from a business perspective.

"If you owned your own baseball park, would you switch to Milwaukee and give all that rent and other benefits to the county," John Allyn asked the Tribune's David Condon. "We've found it much easier to negotiate with ourselves as landlords."

So John Allyn gave his brother, Arthur, an ultimatum. "I felt the team had to remain in Chicago, (so) I suggested to my brother…that he take up the Milwaukee offer with the Artnell company board of directors. He did not choose to do so."

Instead, the brothers concocted a deal where the assets of the Artnell Company were split — John would take over the White Sox and three of the Artnell subsidiaries (including the Sarasota motel) and assume all liabilities, while Arthur withdrew from the company, taking a few subsidiaries with him, along with cash.

John Allyn was introduced as the Chicago White Sox new principal owner and CEO on Sept. 24, 1969, the same day the New York Mets clinched the NL East over the Cubs. But when talking with media, the then 52-year-old Allyn first talked about family commitments. He was then raising four children with wife Margaret in Winnetka. "I'll have to talk fast, I have to get home for a birthday party," he said.

He then pledged to keep the White Sox at Comiskey. His brother's plans to build a multi-purpose facility was on hold, due to the city's reluctance. And he did not want a publicly-funded stadium managed by the city. "I don't believe a tax-supported stadium is completely ethical," he said.

Instead, John Allyn liked the idea of remaining at Comiskey — his main goal was to once again draw more than one million fans, an attendance level not reached since 1965. He said that, despite living on the North Shore, his family loved going to Sox games on the South Side. "(We) only saw about 40 games this year, not as many as our family wanted to see," he said. "You know, I've been bringing my family to this park for years and we've never seen an unpleasant incident."

John would proceed to overhaul the organization, getting rid of GM Ed Short and manager Don Gutteridge (a holdover from the Comiskey-Lane era) and naming Holcomb and Leo Breen as team executives. He would later oversee the most important hires for the White Sox in the early 1970s— from Roland Hemond and Chuck Tanner to Nancy Faust and Harry Caray.

His boldest move provided a tremendous return-on-investment: Adding the six-figure salary of Dick Allen to his modest payroll.

"He gave his blessing because he showed respect for Chuck (Tanner) and myself," Roland Hemond recalled 40 years later. "He knew that we weren't trying to throw the money away; that we solidly felt this is a special player."

John Allyn remained a low-key but consistent presence as Sox owner in the early '70s. At spring training in Sarasota, Fla., he would show up in a personalized White Sox uniform, filming the team with a handheld home movie camera. And during the season, he was a regular at the home games, making appearances in Chuck Tanner's office after victories with a cigar for his manager. "He'd mingle with the guys," outfielder Carlos May would recall. "He was a fun guy, easy to play for. For me, (even in contract negotiations) it was easier to communicate with (Allyn) than it was with Roland (Hemond) and Stu (Holcomb) because he seemed like he was fair minded man."

But Allyn didn't allow himself to get too close to many employees. Faust rarely remembers talking to him. Her only real memory was playing for his daughter's debutante ball at a North Shore country club right after being hired in 1970. "That was kind of a privilege, 'cause I was new," Faust said. "And I was playing for the family of the owner of the ballpark. But, other than that, I don't remember a lot. I do know that he hired Stu (Holcomb). And then Stu went on, of course, to hire Harry (Caray). And Harry made a big difference, I believe, in my career because Harry became aware of my music."

John Allyn was also a photography buff, and his wealth allowed him to purchase some of the earliest home videotape technology available, including a video camera and videotape player. Allyn used this to tape players during batting practice. He would then show the video to the players, who would use it to study their techniques, an approach to technology in baseball that was years ahead of its time. Scott Rosenbaum, the son of batting practice pitcher (and future Sox traveling secretary) Glen Rosenbaum, would videotape players for Allyn.

"In (Sarasota, Fla.) in spring training of '74, John had bought a brand-new videotape system, which was like really, really wild," Rosenbaum recalled. "He said, 'I've got this equipment, do you know how to use it?' I said 'No, but I can figure it out.' So, he had one of those videotape recorders back then which were like the size of a suitcase, bigger and heavier and the videotape was on spools, and you had to run it like a reel-to-reel tape player.

"I'd set the camera up behind home plate and videotape the workouts. And once we got into the regular season, I'd do the same thing during batting practice. We'd even put the camera in one of the lockers, so we'd have easy access to it."

After Dick Allen's monster 1972 season, in which he won the American League MVP, Allyn signed the superstar first baseman to a three year, $675,000 contract that was the largest multiyear baseball salary of its time. The only problem was that Allyn started to have financial issues. A recession that gathered steam and hit full force in 1974 was wreaking havoc on Artnell's various businesses. And after 1972, WFLD-TV did not extend its five-year, $1 million contract to air White Sox games, a controversial deal signed by brother Arthur Allyn in 1966. Allyn had to buy time on a per-game basis on another low-profile UHF station, WSNS-TV, so they could televise Sox games with Caray working six innings each starting in 1973. The Sox sold their own ads for the broadcasts, but revenue from those ads was no profit center for Allyn.

"They owned all the advertising," then-WSNS boss Ed Morris recalled in 2002. "The problem is they didn't know how to sell it."

The White Sox were not helped by being slotted in the AL West, where they would play three away series each year in West Coast-based Anaheim and Oakland. This meant that they would be playing those games at the unfriendly TV times of 9:30 p.m. or 10 p.m. back in Chicago. Ironically…or perhaps not so ironically…Selig's Brewers were given the choice AL East spot, where the White Sox traditional rivals —the New York Yankees, the Detroit Tigers, the Boston Red Sox — were situated. Years later, Selig said that he would have preferred the AL West, and that the idea to put the Brewers in the AL East was decided by league officials.

"I wasn't too happy, 'cause we were in the same division with tough teams like the Yankees, the Red Sox, the (Baltimore) Orioles," he said. "But it would all turn out well after we moved to the National League (under Selig's watch as MLB Commissioner in 2001)."

With this financial pressure, and one-fourth of the payroll going to Dick Allen, John Allyn was forced to cut bait on players who would not agree to sign their 1973 contracts.

Reichardt and Andrews began the 1973 season without having signed new contracts and played under what is known as the renewal clause. These automatically-renewed contracts continued to bind a player to his club at the same salary as the year before, as if they had signed.

The two players never did re-sign with the White Sox and were given their unconditional releases which made them free agents. The Sox could have easily sold Reichardt and Andrews for the $20,000 waiver price each but instead asked for and received waivers on both players for the purpose of giving them their unconditional release. The club received only the formality of $1 per player.

It was believed that the Sox chose this route essentially in fear of a grievance filed by the Players Association, which may have been eager to test the validity of the renewal clause in a courtroom.

Said Allyn, "It was strictly a matter of principle. We had to decide just what we would do financially in each case and when that line was reached, that was it. There were varying opinions within our organization whether the release of either player would hurt us, but the opinion was absolutely unanimous in regards to the salaries we offered — everybody thought our offers were fair."

Those salary offers were $48,000 for Andrews and $40,000 for Reichardt; both of them would be taking the maximum 20% pay cut. That they were released came as a surprise to the writers and fans in Chicago, especially because, at the time, the White Sox were beset with injuries. Later, Manager Tanner conceded the team made a mistake in giving Reichardt and Andrews outright releases and that Stu Holcomb should have used them in waiver deals for other players in exchange.

And Stan Bahnsen, who won 21 games for the team in 1972, was also on the trading block in 1973, due to further difficulties with contract negotiations.

"I didn't know this until much later that John Allyn had told Stu Holcomb well, just go ahead and trade him, you know," Stan Bahnsen recalled 50 years later from his home in Florida. "He just didn't have the money, even though the team did draw, to pay the big salaries. And apparently (Holcomb) met with Chuck and Roland and told them that he wanted them to trade me. And Roland and Chuck then went to Mr. Allyn and said that if you trade Stan, then we'll quit."

Instead, Allyn fired Holcomb – sold to the public as a resignation in late July 1973 - and promoted Roland Hemond to the position of Vice President and General Manager in 1974.

Bahnsen signed a new contract with a small raise on June 13, 1973.

But Holcomb's departure didn't stop the financial bleeding. After Dick Allen left the team in late in 1974, the Sox in recession-battered 1975 dropped to 750,000 attendance, third-lowest since 1950. Revenue from the other Artnell businesses was negligible. By late summer in 1975, John Allyn's financial difficulties continued to compound. The IRS was demanding $400,000 in back taxes. Then his brother, Arthur, resurfaced with a lawsuit alleging that John had withheld money due him in the 1969 sale of the Sox.

With limited revenue at hand, Allyn would have problems paying out gate receipts to the visiting teams at White Sox Park during that season. So, once again, the Sox were on the selling block, first for $13.5 million before Allyn's price went down to $10 million as the season progressed.

The league had been looking for a replacement team in Seattle, which had filed a $32 million lawsuit against baseball after Selig bought the Seattle Pilots near the end of just their second spring training in 1970, then hurriedly moved them to Milwaukee to become the Brewers.

By September 1975, the league wanted John Allyn to sell his team to a Seattle-based syndicate led by entertainer Danny Kaye, who would then move the Sox to the Pacific Northwest. The American league offered Allyn a loan to meet payroll in return for a 90-day option to shift the Sox to Seattle. The American League promised a replacement team for Chicago, with Charles O. Finley proposing to move his Oakland A's to the South Side.

But Allyn was instead set on finding ownership that would keep the team in Chicago. He reached out to his former business associate, Bill Veeck. Working quickly, Veeck arranged for a $500,000 loan through the Continental Bank in which Allyn needed to cover payroll and other operational expenses. He then offered to pay Allyn the $10 million for the team, provided that Veeck could find investors to come up with the cash. Veeck had already set up shop at the Executive House, a hotel in downtown Chicago, where he proceeded to meet with potential investors. Jack Brickhouse and Fred Krehbiel, Veeck's nephew, assisted in finding capital.

Veeck would have high-powered help in landing ownership partners. Mayor Richard J. Daley provided a number of connections from the Chicago business community. Chicago Sting owner Lee Stern came through with $200,000. All told, 46 investors joined Veeck. The syndicate raised $4.8 million, while another $3.75 million was corralled through loans from Continental Bank. Veeck appeared to have the now-80% needed for the purchase.

But AL owners, who as a group despised Veeck from his previous colorful ownership stints, voted down the sale 8-3-1, with Kansas City abstaining. Selig was rumored to be one of the "no" votes, along with Finley and Cleveland's Ted Bonda. Owners told Veeck to raise another $1.2 million. A "Save Our Sox" committee was organized by WBBM-TV sports anchor Johnny Morris, urging all locals to donate to the cause. More than 55,000 donations were offered up, some for as little as 20 cents.

Longtime Cubs broadcaster Jack Brickhouse, who also broadcast the Sox on radio, then TV, for almost 25 years, came to the rescue with an angel investor — the Chicago-based Canteen Corp., which gave Veeck $250,000 to put him over the top. Canteen CEO Patrick O'Malley was a longtime confidante of Daley, and he considered this an opportunity to save baseball for the South Side.

"First of all, it appeared to be a sound investment, because Bill Veeck has always turned a handsome profit for those who invested in his previous baseball ventures," O'Malley said, when reached by the media at his suite at New York's Waldorf-Astoria Hotel. "Secondly, we wanted to do our part to save this franchise for Chicago. For a long time, I worked on the South Side and was always at White Sox Park. I wanted to help preserve our tradition, if possible."

On Dec. 10, 1975, owners voted 10-2 to accept Veeck's offer. Although the balloting was officially secret, California Angels owner Gene Autry revealed he was one of the "no" votes. "I have to vote against a fellow who runs down baseball, then re-enters it," Autry said.

"Actually (AL President) Lee MacPhail appointed (future Boston Red Sox president) John Harrington and me to study the deal, and report back to the league and recommend," Selig recalled. "There were a lot of problems, but we finally agreed to the deal because at that point, John Fetzer, who was my mentor and the owner of the Detroit Tigers said, 'Look, they've done everything that we've asked for. We don't like the deal, but I don't think there's anything we can do.' So we approved it, even though it was a deal with a lot of problems."

Allyn said he was thrilled with the decision and happy that the White Sox would remain in Chicago. For a second time in six years, he had saved the Sox for the South Side. And he retained 20% of the team, a share he would keep until his premature death on April 29, 1979.

Even though only four years had transpired since Allyn sold the team, reports of his death were buried in the sports pages. Veeck, however, didn't forget about his impact on sports in Chicago. Instead, the Sox owner offered a fitting epitaph for Allyn.

"John was absolutely determined that the club remain in the city," Veeck said. "We are going to miss him terribly. He was a very fine man — a great sportsman and a wonderful partner."

John Allyn must be remembered as the man responsible for maintaining an American League baseball team in his city. When the White Sox organization began faltering to a modern low in attendance for Chicago baseball, he refused to give up. He was determined to keep the Chicago White Sox in Chicago and in the hands of local owners.

John later severed partnerships with his brother in their company. That ended up causing a severe rift between them, which led to litigation. But none of that was known — or would even have mattered to — the fans. They had their beloved team right where they wanted it: Home.

Welcoming Dick Allen to the White Sox on April 1, 1972
were owner John Allyn (left) and manager Chuck Tanner,
who believed he could handle Allen well as a fellow
Western Pennsylvania native.

Photo credit: Leo Bauby Collection

The White Sox had a famed near-miss just before their three-year dark ages. GM Ed Short (left) shows off unused 1967 Sox World Series tickets to (from left) Manager Eddie Stanky, Milwaukee baseball promoter and future commissioner Bud Selig and recently-acquired Sox outfielder Tommy Davis at a press conference on Jan. 15, 1968 at Milwaukee's Pfister Hotel.

© *Milwaukee Journal-Sentinel –USA TODAY NETWORK*

White Sox fans proved they'd make the trip to Milwaukee to see their team. They announced their presence with this banner in the County Stadium bleachers for the first game the Sox played there, a 4-2 victory over the California Angels on May 15, 1968.

© *Milwaukee Journal-Sentinel –USA TODAY NETWORK*

(From left) Edmund Fitzgerald and Bud Selig, the top backers of a return of baseball to Milwaukee, show off their agreement for the White Sox to play another 11 games at County Stadium in the 1969 season. The Oct. 29, 1969 event at the Pfister Hotel in Milwaukee was also attended by Sox GM Ed Short (center) and team public relations chief Stu Holcomb (right).

Over many decades since, Fitzgerald's name has been best remembered for the Gordon Lightfoot song, "The Wreck of the Edmund Fitzgerald," about the bulk carrier ship which sunk in Lake Superior in November 1975. That vessel bore his name because its construction and operation were financed by Northwestern Mutual Life Insurance, of which Fitzgerald was a top executive.

© Milwaukee Journal-Sentinel –USA TODAY NETWORK

John Allyn (second from left, in suit) loved owning the White Sox. He would often show up in the dugout to hang out with his players, even sometimes in full uniform. Pitcher Steve Kealey (far left) is with him in this photo, along with long-term White Sox promotions director Millie J. Johnson (right, standing on dugout steps), who planned the legendary Bat Day double-header against the Yankees that drew 51,904 fans to White Sox Park on June 4, 1972.

Photo credit: Leo Bauby Collection

CHAPTER 6

Opening Day/
Tanner and Sain

On April 15, 1972 —nine days after the White Sox were scheduled to open in Chicago — the team began its regular season, not as expected at home against the defending AL West champion Oakland A's, but in Kansas City.

The players' 13-day strike had been settled the day before, with the owners and players finally coming to an agreement to end the labor dispute, which would cancel regular season games and shorten the length of the season to 154 games for the White Sox.

The players' most impactful flexing of their collective bargaining muscles resulted in what, at first glance, would seem only a modest victory for the players — a $500,000 increase in owners payments into the players pension fund. But the united front staged by the players during the strike, led by Marvin Miller, would become a precursor to the union's successful challenge to the reserve clause a few years later, leading to free agency.

The owners won in their challenge to not play the missed games, and thus avoid paying the players their salaries for time missed during the strike. But that would be a pyrrhic victory for teams like the White Sox, who wound up playing an unbalanced schedule against division rivals, including Oakland, against whom they would play 15 games, instead of the normal 19.

"The actual settlement was a little more than the players asked, but not a substantial amount," White Sox owner John Allyn told the media at the time. "It was a fair settlement. As for whether the fewer games will help or hurt anyone, that's academic. We would need a close race, a very close race, for that to be a factor. We lose four games with Minnesota and three with Oakland and maybe that will help us, but that's the rub of the green."

"Both the owners and players are now aware of each others' strengths," said outfielder Rick Reichardt, who attended earlier meetings in Dallas, after former Sox player rep Joel Horlen was released from the team during spring training. "The strike was more of an issue of principle than money. I'm gratified to know so many athletes have the best interests of the players at heart."

Owners and the players' union squared off at what was now becoming the standard meeting place for the game's labor talks — the Marriott Hotel adjacent to Chicago's O'Hare Airport. By this time, O'Hare was the jewel in Mayor Richard J. Daley's crown of Chicago public works accomplishments. The modest former Orchard Field, which had been expanded in the late 1950s and early 1960s under Daley, was now the "World's Busiest Airport" — a symbol of Chicago's refusal to go the route of other Rust Belt cities. O'Hare indeed proved that Chicago was "the city that works," the main attribute backers of Daley crowed to the outside world.

But as the owners and players came to an agreement to resume baseball,

Daley was at City Hall downtown, dealing with challenges that he never had to deal with before in his time as mayor.

Youthful, normally simpatico machine Democrats Ed Burke and Ed Vrdolyak, the so-called "Young Turks," were battling Daley from within City Council, chafing over his control.

But Daley's much bigger challenge came from independent Democrats like state gubernatorial candidate Dan Walker.

Walker was outraged by Daley's initial support of indicted Democratic State's Attorney Edward Hanrahan, who was up for reelection later in the year. Hanrahan would face a trial in June.

"I'm unequivocally opposed to the reelection of Ed Hanrahan as state's attorney, "Walker said.

Walker —a former corporate attorney— had just won the Democratic gubernatorial primary in March. He upset Daley's hand-picked choice for governor, Paul Simon, the state's Lieutenant Governor. Simon had served under Republican Gov. Richard Ogilvie, in the years before he would become a national presence as the socially liberal but fiscally conservative U.S. Senator representing Illinois in the 1980s and '90s.

Now the dynamic gubernatorial candidate was casting aspersions on Daley — accusing him of patronage politics when he appointed three high-profile Democratic proteges as ward committeemen. And Walker shocked many when he seemed dismissive of Daley's expected traditional support of the primary winner's campaign.

"He's the mayor of the biggest city in Illinois," Walker said in a press conference at the Sherman House on the Friday before Opening Day. "I just expect that somehow or other we'll be getting together."

As galling as Walker was to Daley, the 70-year-old mayor was even more aghast at recent threats to unseat 59 Democratic delegates endorsed by Daley to represent Illinois at the summer's Democratic National Convention in Miami. A diverse, young group calling themselves the Chicago Credential Challengers were behind the threat to unseat the delegates. The group included Chicago alderman William Singer, a young Jewish attorney; African American aldermen Anna Langford and Williams Cousins and the Rev. Jesse Jackson, head of Operation PUSH.

At the root of the delegate challenge was a call for more diversity within the party. The Daley-endorsed delegates were almost all White males.

Daley had been elected with a majority of African American support in 1955, 1959 and 1963. But at a City Hall press conference in reaction to the Chicago Credential Challengers, Daley revealed a reactionary side when asked about diversity in the Illinois delegation.

"Where are the rights of the people to elect who they want as delegates?" Daley asked. "How can they be told they must have so many delegates who are women, who are Black and who are Spanish-speaking?"

But in Daley's own backyard, his cherished White Sox were a shining example of the diversity that Daley openly questioned.

Three of the team's top players were African American: Outfielders Carlos May, Pat Kelly and Dick Allen, the just-acquired superstar at first base. Four other starters were White and from Southern California (Ed Hermann, Bill Melton, Mike Andrews) or Wisconsin (Rick Reichardt). Their top rookie was infielder Jorge Orta, born in Mexico to Cuban parents, who was a Roland Hemond discovery from the Mexican Baseball League. And on the bench in platoon roles, the Sox featured a host of diverse talents: African Americans in fan-favorite Walt "No-Neck" Williams (an outfield leftover from the late '60s), speedy shortstop Lee "Bee-Bee" Richard, outfielders Buddy Bradford and Dick's brother, Hank Allen (who also played in the infield). Also, Latino infielders Rich Morales and Luis Alvarado and Whites like eccentric outfielder Jay Johnstone and backup catcher Tom Egan.

This diversity would be reflected in the stands at White Sox Park, where players like Dick were always pleasantly surprised by the high numbers of minorities in the stands when compared to other stadiums in the majors.

"We drew a lot of Afro-Americans and Latinos to Sox Park," Allen would recall 40 years later when he returned to Chicago to commemorate the 1972 season. "It's the most minorities I've ever seen in the stands in my whole career… and that includes LA, St. Louis and Philly."

This group of diverse ballplayers would congregate at their South Side home for their first organized workout on the day before Opening Day. Dick engaged in his first official White Sox workout. And despite the cold weather and frigid northeast winds blowing off Lake Michigan, Allen reeled off six homers in the spacious park during batting practice.

The next day, they gathered at Kansas City's Municipal Stadium, the ballpark where the Royals would play for one more year before moving to Royals Stadium in 1973.

So, Municipal Stadium would be the site of Dick's American League debut. Fittingly, as the Sox' first African American superstar, the Allen arrival would take place on the 25th anniversary of a milestone event in not just Major League Baseball History, but also in United States history. Later saluted as a highlight of each baseball season, Jackie Robinson's debut as the first African American player in the majors took place on this date in 1947 for the Brooklyn Dodgers when they opposed pitcher Johnny Sain and the Boston Braves.

Sain was also present at Municipal Stadium on this day in the visitors' dugout. He was starting his second full year as Chicago's innovative pitching coach, monitoring his ace knuckleballer, Wilbur Wood — the anchor of Sain's unique three-man rotation. Before a mere 8,749 at the damp, windy ballpark, Wood was masterful, shutting out the Royals over the first eight innings.

But Dick Allen wasted no time stealing the show. He was a dominant presence in his inaugural White Sox appearance with his trademark mutton-chop sideburns, a red batting helmet framing his Afro, giant aviator glasses, the ever-present red long-sleeve sweatshirt, a 40-ounce piece of lumber that he used for a bat and the large No. 15 affixed to the back of his powder-blue road uniform.

In the ninth inning, Dick blasted a two-out, 415-foot rocket to left center off Royals starter Dick Drago to break the scoreless tie.

Wood allowed his own run in the bottom of the ninth to tie the game, and reliever Bart Johnson lost it in the 10th, giving up a single to Royals slugger John Mayberry which scored Paul Schaal.

Dick was visibly upset by the loss. The *Chicago Tribune's* George Langford reported that he "sat in front of his locker with head in his hands for several minutes, then retired to the whirlpool in the trainer's room without comment."

During the game, the Sox were told of a protest filed by Royals owner Ewing Kaufman, who cited Chicago and owner John Allyn for staging team workouts at White Sox Park during the strike. "This created an unfair competitive advantage for Chicago during the first few games of the schedule," Kaufman wrote in a letter to the league.

In the manager's office, Chuck Tanner noted that he could also file a protest with the league, since the Royals had used their club equipment in workouts at the University of Kansas. But with typical equanimity, Tanner said that, unlike Kaufman, he wouldn't follow through with a protest.

"There's been enough trouble-making," Tanner said with a wry smile. "I just want to play baseball now."

"Mgr. Tanner soft-spoken yet volub. skipper. Young, bronzed face, snowy sideburns. Credits many for Chisox rise, incl. famed pitching coach J. Sain, known for unorth. methods. Much-traveled Sain the grand guru of 20-game winners. Tanner emphs. defense, shows tactical charges kept of every opp. AL hitter. Charts color-coded accord. to Chi. pitchers, show site of every fair base hit in season, suggest defense shifts. No wonder modern bat. aves. so low!"

– Roger Angell, Excerpt from notes in his book, "Five Seasons", 1972

The White Sox in-uniform brain trust included one man who was a journeyman outfielder toiling in the minors for almost 10 years before a modest major league career of only 396 games that took him through Wrigley Field as a sometimes-starting center fielder. The other was a three-time All Star pitcher who pitched in four World Series and was name-checked in one of the most popular rhymes in 20th century baseball culture: "Spahn and Sain and pray for rain."

But when Tanner and Sain worked together in the Sox dugout beginning in 1971, they were considered among the most effective, innovative manager/pitching coach tandems in baseball.

Tanner was the avuncular, eternally optimistic, super-aggressive first-time major league skipper, who used a sort of "tough love" on his team and also pioneered the use of analytics and video to help his players. Sain was a quiet, almost folksy pitching coach who had already successfully imparted his methods to three different World Series-winning teams. He repeated a mantra of keeping hitters off balance by changing speeds and deliveries, along with a unique (for baseball) mental approach where he touted the virtues of positive thought on the mound.

With few exceptions, players on the 1972 White Sox squad worshipped this duo. Goose Gossage went as far as crediting them — along with Dick Allen — for being the ultimate influences on his 22-year Hall of Fame career.

"In my career, I never wasted pitches because Chuck Tanner and Johnny Sain told me not to waste pitches," Gossage said of his rookie year manager and pitching coach, 50 years later.

"Johnny Sain and Chuck Tanner said, 'We will never second-guess you if you give up a hit on an 0-2 pitch, all we're going to jump you on is if you didn't throw that pitch as hard or commit to what you were trying to throw.'"

Gossage viewed the duo much more favorably than his future New York Yankees manager/pitching coach tandem of Billy Martin and Art Fowler.

"Billy Martin was from the school of don't give up an 0-2 base hit," Gossage remembered. "That's bullshit. I hated that mentality. It makes you become defensive. Johnny Sain and Chuck Tanner said 'You stay aggressive'. And that's just common sense.

"Looking back at these first formative years in my career and having Chuck Tanner, Johnny Sain and Dick Allen in charge of my life, it was incredible. I was so fortunate."

Tanner was born in New Castle, Penn. on July 4, 1928. One of three sons of Charles Tanner, Sr., he had a modest upbringing.

"We didn't have electricity until I was in tenth grade," Tanner would recall later. "No bathroom. We were better off than some because we had a two-holer out back; some people only had one hole. We had a pot-bellied stove, but there were days I'd wake up with snow in my pockets."

Because the Tanner family grew up only 10 miles from Wampum, Pa., the home of the Allen family. And Hank Allen remembers his older brothers competing against Tanner.

"Chuck played basketball against my brother Coy in high school," Hank Allen recalled. "And when I was in high school, Tanner used to work in the off-season as a photographer. He came down and took my high school picture in an off-season."

Tanner, Sain and Roland Hemond all had one thing in common: In their early careers, they all spent extensive time in the Boston Braves organization. In Tanner's case, he was signed by the Braves out of Shenango High School in New Castle in 1946, and then proceeded to spend the next nine years rising up in the team's minor-league system. He met and married his wife, Barbara "Babs" Weiss while still in the minors and they would eventually have four sons, including Bruce, a future major-league player and scout.

When Tanner was finally called up to the parent team in 1955, the Braves had already moved from Braves Field on Commonwealth Avenue next to the Boston University campus to County Stadium on the west side of Milwaukee. A fourth outfielder, he saw scant playing time there and was claimed by the Cubs off waivers in 1957. He'd have the finest moment of his playing career with the Cubs in Pittsburgh (50 miles from New Castle), and the city where he had his greatest triumphs as a manager, more than 20 years later. Both Tanner and Ernie Banks hit inside-the-park home runs in the July 18, 1957 game at Pittsburgh's spacious Forbes Field.

In 1962, Tanner finished his playing days with the California Angels and launched his second career as a manager with that organization. He rose through the ranks in the next eight years, managing the Quad Cities Angels (1963-1964),

El Paso Sun Kings (1965-1966, 1968), Seattle Angels (1967) and Hawaii Island-ers (1969-1970). Tanner had a cumulative record of 561-537 (.511) and he won minor-league Manager of the Year honors in 1968 and 1970 while in the Angels system.

In the minors, Tanner developed his player-friendly, yet "hands-on" man-aging style.

"He was a super nice guy off the field, but a really tough individual," Bruce Tanner said. "His style in the minor leagues back then — it wouldn't fly today — if he wanted to get a point across, he picked a guy up by the shirt and he'd put them up against the locker, you know, and that obviously that couldn't happen today. But that's how he kind of got his point across."

Tanner met Roland Hemond and Johnny Sain while both also worked in the Angels minor-league system. All three were brought in and introduced to the Chicago media by White Sox executive vice president Stu Holcomb on Sept. 14, 1970,

"I'm here to make the White Sox 'go' again — as they did 10 years ago," Tan-ner told the press in his introductory press conference at Chicago's downtown Executive House.

Tanner's and Hemond's hirings would actually play second fiddle in the me-dia coverage to Sain's hiring. Sain was already a baseball celebrity — a star pitch-er and transcendent coach who had been in the public eye for the last 25 years.

"We all went to the Executive House to see the new manager, Chuck Tanner, and the director of player personnel Roland Hemond, and found Johnny Sain there, too, as a sort of dessert course to the luncheon program," the Tribune Robert Markus wrote on that day.

Sain was born in 1917 in Havana, Ark. to an auto mechanic father also named John, who had success as a left-handed semi-pro pitcher. John Sain, Sr. taught his son how to throw a curve with varying motions and speeds, a skill which would become a major teaching point for the younger Sain in the future.

But, like Tanner, Sain spent years toiling in the minors, bouncing from the Red Sox organization to those of Tigers and Braves, who at last brought the right-hander up to the big leagues in 1942. Sain spent his rookie season as the team's main relief specialist under manager Casey Stengel, using his breaking pitches and guile to make up for a less-than-impressive fastball.

He then spent three years with the U.S. Navy's flight team during World War II, and credited this experience for improving him as a player and eventually a coach. "I think learning to fly an airplane helped me as much as anything," Sain said. "I was twenty-five years old. Learning to fly helped me to concentrate and re-stimulated my ability to learn."

When he came back to the Braves in 1946, Sain had full control of his variety of breaking pitches and became an ace on the team's staff. His lefty teammate Warren Spahn would become a top pitcher the following year, and by 1948 this duo was leading the Braves to a National League pennant.

Sain was clearly the staff leader, going 24-15, while Spahn was a solid No. 2 at 15-12. Even though the Braves had two other capable starters in Bill Voiselle and Vern Bickford, Spahn and Sain were dominant during the pennant stretch and became forever cemented in baseball lore, due to a poem written by Boston Post sports editor Gerald V. Hern during an extended bout of rain in early September 1948 in Boston:

First, we'll use Spahn,
Then we'll use Sain,
Then an off day,
Followed by rain.
Back will come Spahn
Followed by Sain
And followed,
We Hope,
By two days of rain.

Sain won 20 games in four of five seasons with the Braves between 1946 and 1950. He was traded to the New York Yankees for Lew Burdette in 1951. While it would turn out to be a lopsided deal in favor of the Braves, for whom Burdette was a top-line starter for the next decade, Sain was able to reinvent himself as an effective spot-starter for the dominant Yankees. Pitching again for Casey Stengel, Sain was able to appear in three more World Series with the Yankees in 1951, 1952 and 1953. He took the mound for the last time in 1955 with the Kansas City Athletics, ending with a career record of 139-116.

Like Dick Allen, Sain was a player who knew his value and wouldn't hesitate to dicker with owners and general managers on a fair salary. He held out in spring training 1948 for a $30,000 salary and coined the term "Climb the Golden Stairs" to describe salary negotiations — a term which referred to the second-floor executive offices at Braves Field. "Either I make money in baseball or I was in the wrong business," Sain would later tell author Danny Peary.

But as impressive as he was as a player, Johnny Sain was even more so as a pitching guru. After one year coaching for the Kansas City Athletics in 1959, he was a dominant figure in the 1960s, acting as the transformational pitching coach for three different World Series teams: The New York Yankees (1961-1963), Minnesota Twins (1965) and Detroit Tigers (1968).

Pitchers ranging from Whitey Ford and Jim Bouton with the Yankees to Mudcat Grant with the Twins to Denny McLain and Mickey Lolich with the Tigers all credited Sain with revitalizing their careers. All told, Sain would coach sixteen 20-game winners in 17 seasons — and he would mentor and heavily influence the last 30-game pitcher in the majors, McLain.

"He's the greatest pitching coach who ever lived," said Bouton.

"If I were hired as a manager, the first thing I'd do is make Johnny Sain my pitching coach," added Grant.

But Sain's disagreements with managers always ended up with him either resigning or getting fired. Sain's iconoclastic approach to pitching — he encouraged all pitchers to throw many curve balls and had an aversion to pitchers running for exercise — would clash with insecure managers. He was forced to resign from the Yankees under Yogi Berra; the Twins' Sam Mele and the Tigers' Mayo Smith both fired him. Sain had been relegated to coaching in the Angels minor league system when the Sox hired him in 1971.

"I get along with ballplayers and I especially get along with pitchers," Sain told the media at the Executive House when he was introduced to Chicago.

Tanner and Sain turned out to be a perfect match; both men appreciated players, and Tanner admired Sain's abilities. "Herein lies the way Chuck was," said Goose Gossage. "He bought into what Johnny was saying and selling, and so did we as pitchers. It took a manager with progressive thinking to let him do it."

The new leadership duo's first mission with the Chicago White Sox was to move knuckleball veteran Wood from the bullpen to the starting rotation in 1971, despite Wood's success as a reliever. "Chuck didn't like so-called 'shit-ballers' in the pen," Wood recalled with a laugh 50 years later. "He wanted live arms out there."

For the White Sox, those live arms would be Bart Johnson and Terry Forster in 1971, with Gossage added in 1972.

Placing Wood in the starting rotation turned out to be a brilliant move, as the baffling knuckle specialist would rack up 20-plus wins in his first four seasons under Tanner and Sain.

On offense, Tanner would preach aggressive play.

"He loved to put pressure on the pitching staff — not so much the hit-and-run, but he loved to steal," said Bruce Tanner. "You saw it later on when my dad managed the [1979 World Champion] Pittsburgh Pirates and he'd have [center fielder and base-stealing threat] Omar Moreno always taking big leads off first and threatening to run. Dad just didn't want the stolen base, he wanted to make sure the guys behind him like Dave Parker and Willie Stargell were getting good fastballs to hit.

"Dad started that with the '72 Sox, where Pat Kelly would lead off and was always a threat to steal. He did that so Dick Allen could get good pitches to hit."

Tanner was a relatively young manager for the time — he was 42 when hired by the Sox. With 17 years of experience as a professional baseball player, Tanner had empathy for his players.

"Chuck was a player's manager — he let you play the game," Wood said. "He didn't have a bunch of rules and regulations. And a bunch of B.S. You know, it was, 'Don't embarrass yourself. Don't embarrass the ball club. Don't embarrass me. If you got anything to say, come into my office and say it. You don't have to talk to other people.' And what more do you want?"

"I never got the sense when I talked to them that it was a situation of a boss talking to a worker," added Walt Williams. "Chuck was a real motivator."

While he could be tough with players behind the scenes, Tanner always projected a positive representation of his players to the media. A Tanner quote criticizing one of his players in the newspapers was rare. Dick Allen was, of course, protected by Tanner, who would routinely cover for his consistent absences from batting practice. But he would also shield other players from any exterior distractions.

"His main goal was to protect his players," Bruce Tanner said. "He was able to connect with them individually, but also bring them together as a group. The goal was to get them to play beyond what they were capable of and stay positive."

In 1972, the median salary for a major leaguer was slightly more than $34,000, and ballplayers were considered secondary to front office, ownership and even certain members of the media. Tanner, however, tried to emphasize the player first — even opening up the hotel bar, a long-barred area for players on the road.

"Traditionally, ballplayers were not allowed to drink in the hotel bar," Wood recalled. "That was for the manager and the press and the 'upper echelon,' we'll say. Chuck opened it up. People ask, 'Why did he do that?' Well, stop and think about it. After a ball game, yeah, we'd like to have a few cocktails or whatever. So, yeah, we can go to the hotel bar. We don't have to go down three or four blocks away from the hotel. You didn't get in trouble, I didn't get in trouble. The ball club didn't get in trouble. Everybody was happy. And it worked out well. You know. The writers, they would drink with us. But, there was, at that time, there was a rule, an understanding what you see here, what you say here, it stays here."

With players, Tanner seemed to understand how to motivate each individual differently. At times, he could be an old-school manager, especially to the younger players.

"He could be a disciplinarian who would say 'Boy, you better act like a big leaguer or I'm going to pinch your fucking head off,'" Gossage recalled. "One day he grabbed me and slammed me into a locker with all this power and controlled force, and he goes, 'Let me tell you something, you make them tear this uniform off and you take care of those fans, you got that?' I said, 'Yes sir!'"

"Chuck stuck up for the guys — he was like your father," Carlos May said. "He would kick your butt if you did wrong and pat you on the back when you did good. I always played good ball for him. I even played hurt, and he appreciated that. I'd go out and give it my best. He earned respect and we gave him respect. He was the best manager I ever had."

"He had a personality where he was really good to the players, but he knew how to reprimand you. He knew how to talk to you," added Bill Melton. "That's pretty important for a young club trying to come up."

Second baseman Mike Andrews obviously anticipated a culture shock coming over in 1971 from the Boston Red Sox, for whom he played in their "Impossible Dream" World Series run in 1967 and who remained borderline contenders the next three seasons. He had trepidations playing for a team that had lost a franchise-record 106 games in 1970, yet Tanner and front office partner Roland Hemond changed his mindset.

"It had to change," Andrews said. "I loved both of those guys. If you couldn't play for Chuck Tanner, you couldn't play for anybody. I saw what those guys were trying to do and when I went to spring training, I looked around and saw a lot of talent, especially those young kids in the bullpen, Terry Forster and Goose Gossage. I said 'This isn't so bad.' Those guys, Hemond and Tanner, made it happen."

Tanner also knew how to be flexible with rules, most notably with Dick. But others like Bill Melton could also dictate policy to this reasonable manager.

"I remember I was going really bad with one of my typical slumps," Melton recalled. "We went into Kansas City and Chuck was hitting me ninth. I said what? That's the only time I went to Chuck, said how can you do that? I said 'Chuck, it's embarrassing enough that I have to go out there, but man, I'm not going to wait that long to go out there at night.' He started laughing. So I said, "Here's what I'll do. You're the manager. You run the show. I'll hit ninth tonight. But I don't want to see me there tomorrow. I think I went four-for-four. So, he'd laugh. That's the kind of conversation you were allowed to have back and forth with him."

But Tanner also had an innovative side. Most notably, he was an early adopter of analytics. By 1972, he had longtime Sox batting practice pitcher Glen Rosenbaum keep charts on every hitter in the American League, using unique color coordinated markings to show how batters hit different Sox pitchers.

"I had a separate sheet for each one of the hitters on opposing rosters and for us I had a different color pen for every one of our pitchers, and every game I sat back of home plate and kept track of pitches," Rosenbaum recalled.

"So, if that day Wilbur Wood would be pitching, I'd get his color pen out and for every hitter he pitched that day I'd show exactly where the ball went, whether it was a line drive or a ground ball and that's how we kept track. Every day before the game I laid the charts out on the table in the clubhouse and all our position players could see where each hitter that they were going to be facing that night, where they hit the ball. So, I did this on charts all year long."

Tanner was also a master at stealing signs. "He knew every single third-base coach's signs for a bunt, a hit-and-run or a steal," said Rosenbaum. "And it was amazing, even later on when he was out of baseball, I would sit with him in the stands and he goes, 'They're running right here.' And all of a sudden the guy would take off. I'm like, how did you know that? And he'd always say that the third-base coach would give it away."

As pitching coach, Sain emphasized the mental side of the game, an approach that he said he developed during his time in military service.

"Johnny Sain was the best pitching coach that I've ever known." Roland Hemond said in 2014. "He could make a good pitcher better. He could make a bad pitcher better. I mean, he just had the ability to instruct. He'd have players walk around with a baseball, try different grips. He says everybody's fingers are different. They might try a different grip.

"Right before he died, he told me 'I was a Navy pilot during World War II, and…I had to concentrate so much on the instruments.' And he said when I came back, I didn't get upset with the umpire on any call. It didn't bother me if somebody bobbled the ball on the infield. He said 'my concentration had improved so much.'"

"He was a very quiet, guy, very unassuming, but he had a presence about him that you listened when he talked," said Glen Rosenbaum.

"Johnny worked with pitchers strictly by talking. He didn't do any of the pitcher drills or anything like that. I did all of those in spring training, all the pitching drills, the pickoff plays. John had nothing to do with that and turned it all over to me. When he was talking with pitchers, he always emphasized having a plan for each batter. I wished I had him when I was a professional player because he believed in taking what you had and making it better. He never tried to make you do something that wasn't you. He said 'None of you guys in this whole group are alike. I'm going to accent the positive.' I loved his approach," Rosenbaum added.

That approach included pitchers throwing in some manner on a daily basis. Wilbur Wood was the workhorse in this regard — in his four seasons of 20-plus victories (1971 through 1974) under Sain, he started an amazing 181 games.

"He believed that you had to throw the ball," Wood said. "You start a ball game, you don't just take off and rest for five days, six days and then pitch again. And he believed in a four-day rotation, pitch every four days. And I think that's one of the biggest faults in today that the guys don't throw enough."

With the 1972 White Sox, Tanner and Sain experimented with a three-man rotation of Wood, No. 2 pitcher Stan Bahnsen and Tom Bradley as No. 3.

"That was because they wanted Wilbur to go out there as often as he could go," Bahnsen recalled. "Wilbur said, 'I can pitch 47, 50 games, I'm going to win 20 games.' I said, 'Well, yeah, but the rest of us can't do that.'"

As for Sain's notorious disdain for pitchers running on a semi-regular basis, something that alienated him from previous managers like Mayo Smith in Detroit, Tanner wholeheartedly accepted this philosophy.

"His thing was if you're pitching seven and eight or nine innings one day and you're exerting your body like that, why are you going out the very next day and exerting your body again?," Bruce Tanner said. "He felt like over the long run that that would break you down."

Sain's mantra for his pitchers included learning a breaking pitch. Just 20 years old starting the season, Gossage spent 1972 under Sain's tutelage, learning how to throw curves.

"After I made the club Johnny goes, 'You're going to be at my hip every day, and we're going to that bullpen every day and we're going to spin breaking balls,'" Gossage said. "And that's exactly what we did, every day. And after games, he'd say 'Hey, instead of watching movies on TV tonight and sitting in your bed and doing nothing, get at the foot of your bed, prop your pillow at the head of your bed and spin some balls into the pillow. Take three or four balls back to the room with you and spin them into the pillow. Work on that spin I'm showing you.' And I did, every night."

"I'm a fastball pitcher and already had a pretty good curve," said Bahnsen. "But John completely changed my breaking pitches. He improved me. With Johnny, you used an entirely different grip and spin rate. And he taught me how to change speeds with it, although it took awhile to get used to his way. I know I lost a couple of games, at first, throwing his curve ball."

In addition to throwing breaking pitches, Sain also encouraged the mental approach on the mound.

"He was big on deception," Wood said. "He'd say, 'Yeah, you can throw a fastball by the hitter once. And you can do a fastball by the hitter a second time.

But the third time is more difficult. And this is where you can do something different.' And he was right 100 percent of the time."

"He influenced how I threw the knuckleball. You changed speeds with that, too. Johnny had a lot of good theories in pitching. And you didn't have to be a scientist to understand. It was very simple."

Like Tanner, Sain also used innovative approaches for teaching. One such approach was his patented "Baseball Spinner," a baseball attached to a wooden handle on a rotating metal axis. The ball was used to teach pitchers how to spin the baseball in their delivery.

"It was a baseball, and he had a hole drilled through the center and it had a rod through it and then a handle." Rosenbaum said. "He would hold that and then he would hold it and demonstrate to each pitcher, how to grip the ball and how to rotate and get the spin. He'd hold it at an angle, like where your arm is going to be coming from. He'd use it during spring training."

Tanner and Sain would last through the 1975 season with the Sox, becoming the '70s version of the two constants in the home dugout during the glory "Go-Go Sox" years of the 1950 and 1960s, — manager Al Lopez and pitching coach Ray Berres.

But when Bill Veeck bought the club in December 1975, he named 67-year-old Paul Richards to manage the team. Veeck asked Tanner to take a front-office position for a year, before returning as manager in the 1977 season, replacing Richards. Tanner declined and moved on to Oakland for a season, before joining the Pirates in 1977.

"I knew one thing," Tanner told *Chicago Tribune* sports editor Bob Vanderberg in 1980. "I had to be on the field. He (Veeck) said he didn't want me to leave, but that Paul Richards was like a security blanket for him, which I understood. There was no animosity — but I have to make my own decision and do my own thing and I'm a manager and I want to manage."

Tanner would continue his aggressive style with the Oakland A's, where he signed a three-year contract with owner Charlie Finley in 1976. That team had lost key players like Reggie Jackson and Catfish Hunter to trades and the new free agency era. But it was still a star-studded roster with Gene Tenace, Phil Garner, Bert Campaneris, Sal Bando, Joe Rudi, Bill North, Claudell Washington, Billy Williams and Don Baylor on offense and Vida Blue, Mike Torrez, Rollie Fingers and Bahnsen leading the pitching staff. These A's stole an AL-record 341 bases in 464 attempts, with North (75 steals) and Baylor (52) leading the way. They finished second in the AL West with an 87-74 record.

But after the season, Tanner was part of a unique baseball *trade*. He was swapped to the Pirates for catcher Manny Sanguillen — a transaction only Finley could make.

The 1979 World Series Championship over the Baltimore Orioles was Tanner's best time in Pittsburgh. He led a colorfully-garbed team to 98 wins, a sweep of the National League Championship Series vs. Cincinnati, and a thrilling comeback from down 3-games-to-1 in the Fall Classic. This aggressively exciting group— which famously adopted the Sister Sledge song "We Are Family" as its team song — featured future Hall of Famers Willie Stargell and Bert Blyleven, fearsome line-drive hitters like Dave Parker and Bill Madlock, and sidearm-throwing closer Kent Tekulve.

"They do everything with abandon, because that's the way Chuck Tanner wants it," Hall of Fame manager Sparky Anderson wrote of the 1979 Pirates in a scouting report prepared for the New York Times. "He's an aggressive manager, a manager who doesn't go by the book. That's why Pittsburgh is such an exciting team."

But Tanner would mostly field losing teams for the remainder of his career, which included the drug-plagued Pirates teams of the mid-1980s. He was fired from Pittsburgh after the 1985 season and hired by Atlanta, where he managed the team to second-division finishes in 1986 and 1987, before he was fired by GM Bobby Cox after 39 games in 1988.

While in Atlanta, Tanner was re-united with Sain, who had been working as a coach in the Braves farm system during the late 1970s and early 1980s. Sain was again promoted to the majors by Tanner, and once more left his influence on future Hall of Fame pitchers. Sain's Braves assistant and protegé was Leo Mazzone, who went on to become the pitching coach for Braves teams that reached the postseason 14 consecutive times in the 1990s and early 2000s.

Sain continued to preach his gospel points of pitchers throwing often and adding a breaking pitch to their arsenal. He personally coached future Hall of Famer Tom Glavine, who was drafted by the Braves in 1984. And Mazzone taught future Hall of Famer John Smoltz how to spin his curves, a la Sain.

During spring trainings, Sain would invite Mazzone to his makeshift home on the road, an RV, to have dinner and talk shop. "He'd fix a little cornbread, barbecue some ribs or whatever, we'd sip on some vodka and we'd talk pitching all night," Mazzone said to the Atlanta Journal-Constitution in 2001. "He had the most brilliant pitching mind of anybody I met in my entire life."

Sain's RV time was strictly for February and March. His permanent home became Chicago; he planted roots in the city in the magical year of 1972. On July 3, a Monday when the team was off, Sain — a divorced father of four (John II, Sharyl, Ronda and Randy) — was introduced to Mary Ann Zaremba, the 35-year-old widow of a slain Chicago police officer. "He called me the next day and said 'You have to marry me,'" Zaremba said. He invited her to White Sox Park for the Fourth of July night game against Baltimore. A month later, the two were, indeed, married.

Sain would stay in Chicago with Zaremba and their stepson, Richard Zaremba, for the rest of his life. He died at a nursing home in west suburban Downers Grove in 2006.

Tanner would move back to New Castle and take a job with the Pirates as a senior adviser to the general manager, which he held until his death in 2011.

He always told his son that he had two favorite teams during his career. "Besides his '79 (Pirates) team, Dad talked more about that '72 Chicago White Sox team than any other," said Bruce Tanner. "He was amazed at how close they got to the Oakland A's — one of the greatest three-year teams in that era. It was quite a feat."

As so many Sox fans remember so well.

Manager Chuck Tanner (right) talks with (from left)
Wilbur Wood, Bill Melton and Rick Reichardt during
a mid-winter White Sox promotional tour.

Photo credit: Leo Bauby Collection

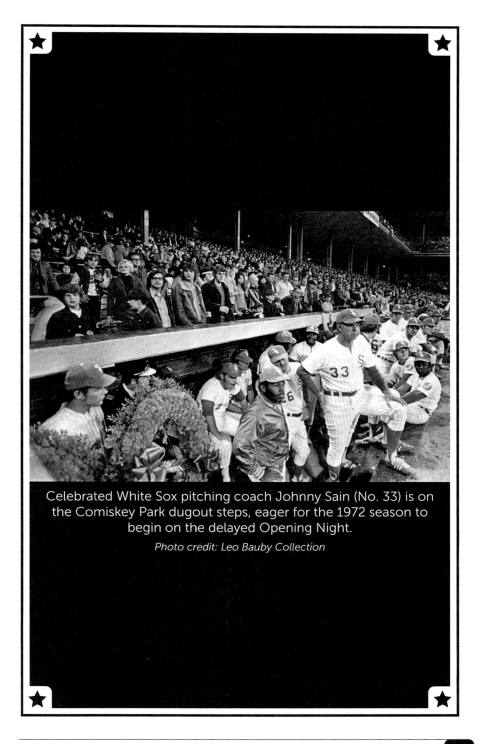

Celebrated White Sox pitching coach Johnny Sain (No. 33) is on the Comiskey Park dugout steps, eager for the 1972 season to begin on the delayed Opening Night.

Photo credit: Leo Bauby Collection

Chuck Tanner, Bill Melton and Wilbur Wood in the Comiskey Park Bards Room for a pre-season promotional event where the '71 HR crown winner Melton shows off his personalized Louisville Sluggers.

Photo credit: Leo Bauby Collection

CHAPTER 7

Roland Hemond
– The Crafty Operator

"We were doing more with enthusiasm than with experience and we began to enjoy having success together. We became tighter than pantyhose two sizes too small..."
–Dick Allen in 2012, reflecting on the 1972 White Sox.

The man who selected the pantyhose two sizes too small in 1972 was 42-year-old Roland Hemond, a slightly-built man and native New Englander, who would have a seven-decade-plus career in major league baseball. A story-teller par excellence, Hemond could hold fans or sportswriters in the palm of his hands for hours, even into his late 80s.

As the architect of this White Sox team which turned around the fortunes for the organization in only his second year in Chicago, Hemond thus began a long run as General Manager. He spent 15 seasons as GM, working for three different Sox ownerships — John Allyn, Bill Veeck and Jerry Reinsdorf. His masterful work in bringing the franchise oh-so-close in 1972 earned Hemond the *Sporting News* MLB Major League Executive of the Year Award, the first of three lifetime major league awards for excellence in baseball. His work assembling the '72 Sox would help define his career and rank as a personal favorite in his later years.

Wherever he went, Hemond was like a baseball Yoda, wise and wizened, witness to so many impactful events and players. Never stamped out of a baseball casting call, with an elfish diminutive look and the accent of his native Rhode Island, Hemond was a man who literally worked his way up from the most modest of roots.

Armed with decades of baseball experience and an engaging, approachable personality, he would be sought out as a banquet speaker at events all around the county.

Some 42 years later, the 84-year-old Hemond was getting ready for his June 14, 2014, oral history appearance about his storied baseball career for the members of Green Diamond Gallery, a private baseball museum on the northern outskirts of Cincinnati. After spending several hours touring the exhibits, all the indefatigable Hemond needed to get going was a short pre-speech nap on a gallery couch. He then regaled the audience with recollections and sports philosophy.

Looking back on his professional baseball career which began in the very early 1950s at Hartford of the Eastern League, Hemond talked about how he had gotten a break from someone who helped him get into the game and how that act of kindness shaped his entire career:

"How lucky can I have been to have had a break myself and then to give back to others who aspire to get into the game. Today, I find a little bit that some of them [baseball executives] have great college degrees, great credentials and that impresses owners. However, they think they know more than they really should and there's so much to learn. You should have respect for your scouts, your farm system people, your secretary, everybody that helps the organization succeed, and some of them I find they're a little bit aloof and they're a heck of a lot smarter than I am, too, but it's a people game. You're dealing with human flesh.

"I always say a player wears his uniform, but there's a human being in that uniform, so if you treat the players like you do your own children then you're going to get better results. So, you give them every chance to succeed and sometimes you have to scold them a little bit or have somebody shake them up."

Even in this 2014 career retrospective, all roads in his storytelling led back to 1972 and his franchise-saving swap of pitcher Tommy John for slugger Dick Allen at the winter meetings in December 1971.

Sometime in the future, there has to be a permanent enshrinement in the Hall of Fame for Hemond's long and meritorious service to baseball. His 2011 honor as the second recipient of the Buck O'Neil Lifetime Achievement Award (for extraordinary efforts to enhance baseball's positive impact on society) does not adequately recognize his eras-spanning career and how he revolutionized front-office management and trade strategy.

When baseball's Hall of Famers reconvene in late July each year in Cooperstown for the induction of new members, the spacious veranda behind the Otesaga Resort Hotel becomes the most exclusive space in baseball, especially right after the ceremony. Then, the Hall members huddle, gossip and schmooze sitting in two long rows of white rocking chairs that line nearly the full length of the porch.

In July 2012, Hemond relaxed beside the baseball legends on the veranda hideaway that affords a wide view of Otsego Lake, the "Glimmerglass" of James Fenimore Cooper's Leatherstocking Tales, with sailboats a quiet presence on the beautiful water.

"I got in the side door," he half-jokingly said, recognizing that while he had received the O'Neil Award, Hemond still had not been elected a *member* of the Hall. His career had overlapped every Hall of Fame member present on that veranda, and he could tell a story about each, including key 1972 rookie and pupil Goose Gossage.

The only aspect of baseball on which Hemond traditionally was closed-mouthed was forthcoming trades during his GM days. He was no leaker, even in the cozier days of baseball honcho-beat writer relationships. He excelled in the art of the deal, and any advance publicity could kill a transaction. So he became an expert in divulging nothing confidential — despite always being accessible, polite and unfailingly returning phone calls of print and broadcast reporters.

"Roland was brilliant," said longtime Chicago television and radio sportscaster Tom Shaer. "He helped and informed us without betraying confidences or his obligation to the White Sox. He understood so well our jobs and his as GM."

Otherwise, there was no better front-office recanter of persons, places and things in baseball than Hemond. He became known as the guy who never forgot a name or failed to return a call while working hard to improve his ball club.

He would start many lunches by telling a friend, "Let me just make one phone call." An idea about a trade had, at that moment, developed in his head and he simply wanted to "throw out a flare." He ended many meals the same way: "Hold on, this guy may be back from lunch." An early 1980s team publicity photo showed Hemond posing with phones at each ear.

Hemond was called old-school. He *was* the school, knowing everyone in baseball in this country and points beyond, and helped start the careers of baseball brass like Phillies President Dave Dombrowski. It was Hemond who promoted Tony LaRussa from Triple-A to be Sox manager in August 1979.

His best work, of course, came in Chicago from 1970 to 1985. Hemond helped save the Sox for Chicago under team bossman John Allyn, with a series of good trades. Most impactful was the John-for-Allen deal. It was a highlight of his career, and he took pride in turning around the franchise.

Despite the success Hemond had with the '72 team, injuries to key players in 1973, including Dick's freakish left lower leg fracture on June 28, crippled the team's chances. The Sox were favored to beat out the Oakland A's for the '73 AL West division flag and were one game out of the division lead at the time of the Allen injury.

The White Sox had begun to capture hearts of Chicago again as the Cubs floundered in 1973 and drew 1,351,705 with crowds dipping below expectations on prime-drawing weekends in August in the middle of one of the North Siders' all-time collapses. Good advance sales enabled the White Sox to attract 1,302,527 fans (up from 1,177,318 in 1972), most since 1960 and then the fourth-highest in franchise history. And the team's broadcasts had moved back to clear-channel, NBC-owned WMAQ (AM 670) after two years in the radio wilderness.

On Dec. 13, 1973, Hemond traded for 14-year Cubs third baseman Ron Santo, who had refused a trade the previous week to the California Angels. Santo became the first major-league player to invoke a new rule permitting veterans of 10 years in the majors and five years with the same club to refuse to be traded. Pundits nicknamed the rule the "Santo Clause."

Hemond planned to alternate Santo and Bill Melton at third and considered moving Santo to first base on occasion. "Of course, he will also be a designated hitter," Hemond said. His calculation was way off-target. The 34-year-old Santo could find no real spot on the 1974 team. His perennial All-Star production had declined since age 30 due to the ravages of Type 1 diabetes. Santo ended up feuding with Dick over who would be the veteran player leading the team. All the while, Dick played hurt most of the '74 season. With the Sox waffling around .500, Allen — nursing a bad right shoulder and right ankle — abruptly quit the team in mid-September while still leading the AL with 32 homers.

Shorn of power, the Sox declined further in the 1975 season, winning just 75 games. Their financial decline with lower attendance sent John Allyn's finances into the tank, too. He almost missed his final payroll. Earlier in '75, the franchise's money troubles forced Hemond to sell popular catcher Ed Herrmann to the New York Yankees to settle the Sox' spring training hotel bill in Sarasota.

Suddenly, the Chicago White Sox were again for sale — possibly headed to Seattle, which was owed a franchise by Major League Baseball. Allyn also fired Caray live on Johnny Morris' WBBM-TV sportscast.

Then, Bill Veeck entered the picture with his desire to return to ownership. After Allyn sold the team back to Veeck in the fall of 1975, Roland stayed on during a time of tremendous change in the business structure of the game with the dawn of free agency coming fast.

Finally approved to reacquire the Sox a second time, Veeck got to work immediately, with Hemond's assistance, by setting up a table adorned with the sign, "Open For Business," in the hotel lobby at the 1975 winter meetings.

Veeck and Hemond hit it off, but it came with a physical price for the latter. The night-crawling Veeck wore out Hemond, who was 47 at the time. Mandated to tag along with the sleepless owner on his post-game rounds to the Millers' Pub rib joint in Chicago's Loop, Hemond found himself frequently bleary-eyed. But he had to keep up with his boss in showing up for work at 9 a.m. at Comiskey Park.

Actually, being out with Veeck cut into some of Hemond's burn-the-midnight-oil work efficiency. He was spotted at times in the same clothes he wore the previous day; he had slept in his office, making dozens of additional phone calls or going over more scouting reports, trying to get an edge.

As a result of his years with Veeck from 1975-1980, Hemond confessed he became accustomed to working with little sleep and became a master in finding places to sneak away and take a nap.

"I was amazed that this 80-year-old plus guy could stay out until 2 to 3 in the morning and regale the audience in the Lobby of the Palmer House with stories at SoxFest conventions," recounted one Sox fan, who marveled at Hemond's energy level.

After a disastrous first season with Veeck in 1976 (97 losses despite a 27-22 start), Hemond assembled with limited funds the beloved "South Side Hit Men" of 1977, perhaps the most beloved third-place team ever in baseball. Armed with Veeck's "rent-a-player" strategy, Hemond would pick up talent like sluggers Richie Zisk and Oscar Gamble in the final year of their contracts and squeeze out every last bit of production before losing them in free agency. Zisk and Gamble produced, with 30 and 31 homers, respectively. Combined with the likes of Eric Soderholm, Jim Spencer, Lamar Johnson, Jorge Orta (who had been a rookie on the '72 team) and Chet Lemon, the '77 White Sox produced a team-record 192 homers and held onto first place until August 19. The Sox attracted a record 1,657,000 to Comiskey Park and outdrew the surprising Cubs, who also held first place until August 6.

"The era with Bill was a lot of fun even though the financial situation was limited," revealed Hemond. "Bill wasn't financed for (the then-new) free agency era. But he did come up with ideas that led to the 1977 season. He knew that we wouldn't be able to retain players like Goose Gossage, Terry Forster and Bucky Dent, so he said we'll rent players for a year."

Working with Veeck would have an indelible impact on Hemond, who would often reflect back about his time with him: "He was the most memorable person I've encountered for many reasons. First of all, he decided to keep me with the team when he bought the White Sox from John Allyn.

"Veeck taught you about life. He was injured in World War II and lost a leg. Yet he always said that you might have physical problems or whatever, but don't burden other people with your problems.

"He said to let your imagination run rampant and propose anything. Any time you came up with an idea his ordinary response was, 'Well, get it done.' He didn't shoot down ideas; he wanted you to try new things and be confident about it. He would like to challenge you to get things done. He would say, 'You don't work for me; you work with me,' and I found that philosophy [helped] to the greatest extent.

"People want to go the extra mile to get it done if you feel confidence in them. If you dampen their enthusiasm, you squelch their creative juices. He helped form my own style from then on.

"Bill would say, 'It's a great game by itself, Roland, but you're providing a game for all sorts of people, so you should make sure they have a good time coming to the ballpark. You can't guarantee the team will play well or win the game, but if they have a good time, they will want to come back.' That was us; that was his philosophy."

More importantly, the 1977 season bought time for Veeck's low-budget ownership. Even though the 90-win Sox didn't finish close to the AL West title in the end, there was an afterglow moving forward. That was necessary as the Sox declined over the next three seasons, the highlight being the wildly gone-wrong "Disco Demolition Night" on July 12, 1979.

Hemond did the best he could with the financial strictures. He promoted La Russa, just 34, from Triple-A to his first managerial job in 1979. He also acquired Dodgers discard Ron Kittle and drafted — on Veeck's recommendation — future Hall of Famer Harold Baines.

Veeck began shopping around for a buyer in 1980, and hints of interest from Denver mogul Marvin Davis surfaced since Seattle got a new team in 1977. Davis planned to move the team to the Mile High City and pay Veeck as a consultant, separate from the purchase price. Eventually, an agreement was reached to sell to Ohio racetrack titan Edward DeBartolo, Sr. But the American League, never cutting Veeck any slack, rejected the deal. To the rescue came Chicago real estate syndicator Jerry Reinsdorf and TV sports impresario Eddie Einhorn.

Veeck literally handed over the keys to the ballpark in an early 1981 press conference. Despite the Sox' sagging fortunes, Hemond's reputation was positive enough that the new owners retained him.

Hemond finally had the decent-enough budget he had lacked since the middle of the Allyn ownership days. Mandated to quickly upgrade the Sox, he landed the likes of Carlton Fisk and Greg Luzinski to turn the White Sox into an instant contender in '81. More talent acquisitions along with Gary, Ind. native Kittle's emergence as a power threat and the development of young starters such as LaMarr Hoyt and Britt Burns under La Russa and pitching coach Dave Duncan rounded the Sox into a strong club by the 1983 season.

Given the unflattering nickname of "Winning Ugly" from then-Texas manager Doug Rader, the 99-victory Sox won the AL West by an astounding 20 games and became the first Chicago baseball team since 1959 to finish in first place. Some of the more than 45,000 Comiskey Park fans stormed the field to celebrate after the Sox clinched the division on Saturday night, September 17, against the Seattle Mariners.

Unfortunately, the South Siders stumbled in the AL Championship Series against the experienced Baltimore Orioles, who went on to win the World Series. The pratfall did not diminish Hemond's achievements as he garnered his second MLB Executive of the Year award, this from United Press International (UPI).

The Sox could not repeat their '83 magic over the next two seasons. Then, a restless Reinsdorf and Einhorn shuffled the deck, pushing out Hemond and elevating broadcaster Hawk Harrelson to General Manager for the 1986 season.

Decades later, the change was obviously still upsetting to Hemond, who refused comment at the time.

In a private moment at his Green Diamond Gallery career retrospective, Hemond uncharacteristically revealed that getting fired in 1985 still stung.

"I had expected that I would stay in Chicago for life," admitted a half teary-eyed Roland, who normally would not share his personal feelings, always remaining very positive about people and the good fortune in his career.

But being shown the gate in Chicago was hardly Hemond's last chapter. After an interim stint working in the commissioner's office, he landed as Orioles GM late in 1987. He became associated with one of baseball's most infamous streaks as his Birds lost their first 21 games in 1988, becoming a national sensation for all the wrong reasons. Baltimore lost 107, overall. But as Hemond knew, baseball cannot bottle success or failure from season to season. The Orioles were baseball's surprise contender with 87 wins in 1989, earning Hemond his third and final Executive of the Year Award.

Hemond lasted as Orioles GM until 1995 and transitioned into a senior executive and "Special Advisor to everyone" role as he helped out in both Chicago and Arizona, including nurturing White Sox GM Ken Williams, leading to the South Siders finally ending their 88-year drought in winning the World Series in 2005.

Seeing his beloved Sox finally snare a championship was "one of the highlights of my career when we beat the opposing club (Astros) in extra innings (on his 76th birthday)," he often said.

Midnight already had passed, but Hemond, wide awake at Minute Maid Park, recalled, "So when Jeff Blum hit the home run at the top of the 14th, Margo (his wife since 1958) turns around says, 'Happy birthday Lovey,' because now the game had gone on to October 26 on my birthday. And one of the young ladies in the commissioner's office was in the television part of it and she said, 'Put the camera on Roland to see how he reacts to that home run.' So, then I get embarrassed when I went upstairs. Ken Williams the general manager, says, 'Gee, you and Margo were smooching down there with that home run.' So, the next day I was getting calls from around the country from people asking who the young blonde was that I was kissing. So, I said, 'It's Margo. Please.'"

Later on the day of his birthday, the White Sox captured Game 4 and swept the Astros, giving Hemond two World Series wins and a world championship on his 76th birthday.

"So, here's the ring to prove that." he said, showing off the jewelry. "I have one more ring, but if I wear one more ring, they'll think I'm Liberace, and I don't play the piano."

But none of Roland Hemond's rings are from the 1972 World Series that he dreamed about as the Sox battled the A's for the AL West flag that summer, 50 years ago. He would confess over and over again "If only Bill Melton and Bart Johnson had not gotten hurt...we would have won it all in '72..."

Despite his life-long regret about finishing second that year, Hemond would always say: "All I know is I'm the luckiest guy I know to have been in baseball during this period of time."

The early years

Hemond got his start in baseball after giving up his dreams of studying journalism at Providence College and becoming a sportswriter. He had served four years in the Coast Guard after consuming a steady diet of bananas to bulk up, barely meeting the required minimum weight of 115 pounds.

Roland Hemond was born in 1929 in the French-Canadian textile mill town of Central Falls, located near Pawtucket, R.I. He did not speak English until he started grade school. Young Roland grew up as a rabid Red Sox fan and attended Game 4 of the 1946 World Series against the Cardinals just before his 17th birthday.

The two-century journey through baseball began via a chance meeting in 1951 while Hemond was finishing a four-year hitch in the Coast Guard, where he learned to type.

"There was an advertisement in the *Sporting News* that they were going to have a baseball administrative course at Florida Southern in the fall of that year, which was when I was coming out of the service," Hemond said. "I hitchhiked to Lakeland, figuring that I probably would go to that course after my discharge, because I wanted to see a cousin of mine who was in the Pittsburgh Pirates farm system. He was supposed to arrive in Deland, Fla. on a particular day.

"So, after I get to Deland, I hitchhiked to the training camp and a lady came by and said, 'Is Mr. Rickey in?' They said, 'No, he won't be until Monday.' So, I figured, boy, I'm going to stick around here, maybe meet Branch Rickey, who was the Pirates GM then, and they had also changed the time for my cousin to arrive. So, I asked the lady if she could take me to the bus station to go see some major league teams practice in spring training in St. Petersburg. I would come back on Monday.

"Anyway, Mr. Rickey never did show up but the lady I met, Mrs. McMahon, introduced me to her husband, Sgt. Leo McMahon. He was wounded in the Canadian army in France during the war and lost his sight, so he was always booked as "The Lucky Sergeant" at the minor-league teams they would go to. He'd sing the national anthem with his old Army uniform on. He kind of took a liking to me."

McMahon recommended two baseball people whom Roland should talk to about a job in baseball. The first was Fresco Thompson, the Farm and Scouting Director of the Brooklyn Dodgers. The second one was Charlie Blossfield, the General Manager of the Hartford Chiefs, a farm club of the Boston Braves.

McMahon put together a letter of recommendation for Hemond to deliver to both men. Thompson said he had no openings but encouraged Roland to see Charlie Blossfield.

"So, I go there," Hemond recalled, "and Mr. Blossfield said, 'When can you get out of the service?' I said, 'Well, I could get to my job on July 5, and I'd have to go one day back to New York to get my discharge.'"

Nearly 75 years later Hemond still has the letter of recommendation written for him by McMahon to Blossfield. It reads in part:

> *"This will serve to introduce Roland Hemond, the boy I wrote you about. Charles, here is a fine, upstanding, clean-cut young man who has been visiting with us on his furlough. He's ambitious and a very willing young man to make his way in the work he wishes to follow, which is baseball executive work."*

Hemond kept this letter in his briefcase throughout his career to remind himself of his humble beginnings in baseball.

"I've been extremely fortunate," he said. "It's not that easy to get into the game anymore. Now if you have a college degree you stand a better chance. Human Resources won't accept you unless you have a college degree."

Long before anyone conceived of sabermetrics and hiring young business analysts into front offices, Hemond broke into the game the old-fashioned way, starting at the bottom and doing a little bit of everything, including cleaning toilets, earning $28 a week at Hartford.

He soon impressed the parent Braves club and got a two-week tryout in Boston. He was an intern for John Mullen, the Braves' farm director, who worked under a member of a baseball multi-generational family, GM John Jacob Quinn, whose father Bob Quinn, owned the Red Sox from 1923 to 1933.

When the Braves moved to Milwaukee in 1953, Hemond became Assistant Farm Director. One of his charges, Hank Aaron, would go on to baseball immortality.

Hemond picked up two pieces of important jewelry with the Braves. He acquired a World Series ring in 1957 after Aaron hit the pennant-clinching homer against the Cardinals before the Braves beat the dynastic Yankees in seven games in the Fall Classic. He also bought a wedding ring, marrying 18-year-old

Margo Quinn, daughter of John Quinn. Hemond had first met Margo in 1952, when she was 11.

"Pretty good scouting, though. Pretty good deal. I didn't know what I was getting into in that regard," said the veteran married man.

"Margo would come with her parents to the Sunday games at Braves Field and she was a little brat, that's what I called her. She would take Hank Aaron's name and put him on the Boston Braves roster while he was playing at Jacksonville, like we're dummies here. So, I told Mr. Quinn the next day, she's a sweet little girl in some respects, but she messes my board every Sunday when we're home. She said, 'How else could you be aware of me if I didn't do something like this?' So, later on I married Margo, when she was 18."

Typical of Hemond, he combined his 1958 honeymoon with a scouting trip to the Dominican Republic.

Roland and Margo would have five children: Robert, Susan, Tere, Jay, and Ryan. Robert and Jay followed in their father's footsteps and had careers in baseball. The Hemond family had an old-fashioned baseball arrangement. Many players of the era had to leave their families behind for part of the season due to finances and children's schooling. Mickey Mantle and Roger Maris had a bachelor-type roommate arrangement in New York in their famous summer of 1961. Even in the modern free-agent era, some players delay having kids until late in their careers so as to not take them out of school and move them around the country.

So Margo and the kids stayed behind in their home in California when Roland ran the White Sox' baseball operations, and the troop came to Chicago for the summer. The Hemonds stayed in a suite in the downtown Executive House, at a Holiday Inn or in Roland's apartment. All the children made the trek to the Windy City through 1977. Jay Hemond said he continued coming to Chicago until he started college in 1984. One reason why they stayed behind may have been a clear lack of job security, giving this husband and father pause about uprooting the family cross-country. Until Bill Veeck's arrival, Hemond *did not have a contract* with the White Sox.

Overhauling the White Sox

Hemond's first Chicago employer, Sox owner John Allyn, looked to clean house near the end of his franchise's disastrous season that drew just those 495,000 fans to old Comiskey Park.

Soon, GM Short, Manager Gutteridge, and other holdovers of losing baseball would be gone.

Hemond arrived on the scene in September 1970, hired by new Executive

Vice President Stu Holcomb. Holcomb had first joined the Sox in October 1968 at the request of Arthur Allyn to repair the badly damaged image of the ballclub, which began taking serious hits in the 1967 season.

The Sox played before a sea of empty seats, and Holcomb was hired then to fill those seats for 1969. Holcomb had already worked for Arthur and John Allyn for the past two years running their pro soccer franchise. Holcomb had resigned his athletic director's job at Northwestern University in August 1966 to start up the soccer team. After its league folded in September 1968, Arthur Allyn transferred Holcomb to do PR for the Sox, where he did public relations and marketing.

When John Allyn took over sole ownership of the Sox in September 1969, the 61-year-old Holcomb was promoted to replace Ed Short and run baseball operations. With John's blessing, Holcomb began to stop the bleeding. He flew out to Oakland to inform Gutteridge his contract would not be renewed for 1971. Gutteridge resigned immediately, on Sept. 2.

Tribune sports columnist David Condon wrote on Sept. 16, 1970, two days after the new manager and top front office man were hired: "The White Sox shakeup was inevitable. You could see it coming in spring training...one observer commented this may be scouting the most inept team ever to play in the major leagues. Those were the days when they had more people in the press box than in the stands. But I have confidence in the new regime to change all that. I gave a world of confidence to owner John Allyn, who has a lot of guts, as his father before him.

"I was surprised, however, once Holcomb, onetime soccer executive, emerged as the top cat. Perhaps as a former football coach, Holcomb had a better instinct for survival. But I prefer to believe that John Allyn is convinced, as I am, that Stu Holcomb as the man to lead the White Sox from the wilderness. My faith is in Holcomb, though I reserve judgment on lieutenants he acquired: (Manager) Chuck Tanner and what's his name, the personnel boss...but happy that things will be better at 35th and Shields."

In that tumultuous final month of the 1970 season, the Sox pried "what's his name" away from the California Angels, for whom Hemond worked after "Singing Cowboy" Gene Autry tapped him in January 1961 to serve as the farm and scouting director for the new American League expansion team. Working under GM Fred Haney, Hemond built a solid scouting team that blanketed North America, developing the "Angel Way of Doing Things" while cultivating strong ties to the Mexican Leagues.

Hemond already knew Tanner from his time as a Braves outfielder and had forged a decade-long relationship with the baseball lifer when he was the Angels' farm director. That would serve both well in Chicago. Tanner had played for the Angels in 1961-1962 before starting his managerial career in the team's minor league system the next year. In 1970, Tanner was manager of the Angels' Triple-A affiliate Hawaii when the Sox came calling.

"Stu Holcomb got in touch with me to see if I could join him in Tucson or Phoenix, when the Triple-A club will be playing there," Hemond said. "He had already talked to Chuck about managing the team. And then Glen Miller, who was the farm director of the White Sox, and his assistant, C.V. Davis, had strongly recommended that the Sox try to get Chuck and me to join the organization. As I entered the room, someone opened another door and Chuck Tanner came out. And I said, 'My God.' They knew that if I were the general manager, that he would have been my choice of managers anyway. So, the sequence of who they hired first or second didn't make any difference, and that was the start of preparing for the 1971 season."

The Sox, with Tanner's blessing, then hired Sain, who had been the pitching coach for five of the last 10 AL pennant winners. After being fired by the Tigers in August 1969, Sain became the Angels' roving minor league instructor, where he befriended Tanner.

Roland was excited to have Sain join the White Sox. "I knew that Sain was a great pitcher, but I believe he's the one man who could reach the Hall of Fame just as a coach," predicted Hemond right after the Sain was hired.

Immediately, the new regime went to work to revive the moribund franchise. Right out of the gate, Hemond began to earn a reputation for being a wheeler dealer, a latter-day version of Trader Frank Lane, as he poured himself into his new job. He spent long days working to improve the fortunes of his new team. If not on the telephone, he was reading press guides or scouting reports. If not discussing a trade, he was thinking about one.

Hemond's style when making trades was to be direct during the call or meeting. He wasn't one to beat around the bush with other teams and back into the purpose of the call.

Come contract time, Hemond would be honest in his dealings with his players. Terry Forster recalled that in 1976 after he was tendered a contract for the '77 season, he asked if he should sign the contract especially because of the White Sox' shaky finances. Roland told him no and ended up engineering the trade that sent the lefty and Goose Gossage to Pittsburgh.

Between the end of the 1970 campaign and the opening of the 1971 season, Hemond made five key deals and shook up the roster. He was not trying to stay a bottom feeder to get top draft positions or acquire even more young players beyond the small core of Bill Melton, Wilbur Wood, Carlos May, and Walt "No-

Neck" Williams.

Hemond later recalled that his first trade call with the Sox went to Bing Devine, St. Louis General Manager. He tried to get Dick Allen in a swap for shortstop Luis Aparicio, but the Cardinals instead traded Allen to the Dodgers for second baseman Ted Sizemore and catcher Bob Stinson. Devine later regretted not doing the deal to get Aparicio in exchange for Dick, who had hurt his right hamstring in August 1970 while having a monster year for the Cardinals.

However, after that first rebuff to obtain the Wampum Slugger for the '71 Sox, Hemond really got rolling. During the 1970 World Series, he sent first basemen Gail Hopkins and John Matias to Kansas City for outfielder Pat Kelly and pitcher Don O'Riley.

Two months later, on Nov. 30, 1970, at the winter meetings in Los Angeles, Hemond swapped center fielder Ken Berry, infielder Syd O'Brien and pitcher Billy Wynne to the Angels for pitcher Tom Bradley, outfielder Jay Johnstone and catcher Tom Egan.

Johnstone was not pleased to be traded to the White Sox.

"They wanted to rebuild with young players and the first thing they did was swing a deal for some of the kids they had with the Angels," top baseball funnyman Johnstone later recalled. "I was one of those kids. I was also upset even though Hemond and I lived in the same town (San Marino, Calif.) and he had signed me on high school graduation day (in June 1963). Tanner phoned me up after he first got the job and said, 'Jay, we're thinking about making a deal for you. Would you like to play center field in Chicago? What do you think?'

"'Gee, Chuck, that's real flattering but I'd rather stay in California (where) my family and friends are,'" responded Johnstone.

Then two weeks later Hemond called and gave him the same pitch.

"'Love to have you,' Johnstone recalled of Hemond's pitch. "'Sorry, Roland, I'd rather stay and play with the Angels. I told Chuck that two weeks ago.' Hemond said, 'Okay. We understand.'"

"About a week later they made the deal -- so much for asking me in the first place."

The very next day on Dec. 1, 1970, Hemond traded Aparicio to Boston for infielders Mike Andrews and Luis Alvarado.

Hemond went after another Angels player, Reichardt, whom he had scouted when he was playing for the University of Wisconsin. On Feb. 5, 1971, this former can't-miss prospect was picked up in a trade with the Senators for pitcher Gerry Janeski.

A month later, in spring training, catcher Duane Josephson was sent to the Red Sox for pitcher Vicente Romo and first baseman Tony Muser.

Hemond purchased another Angel, reliever Steve Kealey, on March 15, 1971.

Within a few months, Hemond had revitalized the Chicago White Sox. He had added a starting pitcher in Bradley, a regular second baseman with some power in Andrews, an adequate shortstop in Alvarado to replace Aparicio, some badly-needed speed in right fielder Kelly, an outfielder with power in Reichardt and a fill-in center fielder in Johnstone, who had occasional punch.

Going into 1971, the Sox couldn't get any worse than they were in '70, anyway. But Hemond simply tried to make the team better to play competitive baseball.

Hemond's overhaul did not disappoint. The series of deals — nine, involving 31 players prior to Opening Day — restored competitiveness on the South Side, as the win total increased from 56 to 79.

"We decided to trade value, not just change things around. After you lose 106 games, you need new personnel – you need new faces," said Hemond, looking back at the building blocks for the team.

Hemond completed his share of great trades, but also admits he made some stinkers, as any general manager will do in an unforgiving sport where failure is just around the corner.

Decades before Twitter and cell phones, Hemond was innovative in his trade methods. "I had brought some walkie-talkies that they used in a ballpark," he said. "And so I brought them to the convention in Hawaii (1972 winter meetings) and then I would have scouts look around the lobby, who was down there that maybe I could try to reach before he makes a deal with somebody else. Except that in a meeting the sound was too high and some guy's cussing me out for having invented the use of communicating by walkie-talkie and he says, 'You get an unfair advantage: You're talking to more people than we are.' And I could hear the voices of the other general managers, and everybody laughed."

In addition to all the player moves in 1971, the new regime converted closer Wilbur Wood to a starter in 1971. He would go 22-13 with 1.91 ERA to start those four consecutive 20-win seasons. But prior to the 1971 season Hemond almost traded Wood.

"I almost dealt him for a left-hand pitcher, Darold Knowles, with the Washington Senators," Hemond said. "I got lucky that Joe Burke, the general manager, backed off. I thought we were going to pull it off. But I hadn't seen that much on Wilbur Wood the previous year because I just arrived on the scene, basically. Well, sometimes the best trades are the ones you don't make. I thank my lucky stars that I was fortunate enough not to have consummated the trade."

Meanwhile, radio play-by-play voice Harry Caray lured fans in for the '71 season with his brash style on the jerry-built network of low-watt suburban radio stations. But the Sox still trailed in publicity, controversy and media carriage in comparison to the crosstown Cubs, who enjoyed the bully pulpit on WGN-TV and radio, and drew more than 1.6 million fans three consecutive seasons.

The fans responded immediately. After a shocking sweep of a rare Opening Day doubleheader in Oakland, the 1971 home opener drew a raucous, overflow crowd of 43,253 to old Comiskey Park. Previous Sox lid-lifters had trouble attracting 10,000.

"Initially, we thought we would have about 17,000 people at the ballpark," Hemond said. "Turned out, there was 40,000-plus. By the fourth inning we ran out of hot dogs and beer and what-have-you because management had not prepared for a big crowd, because the previous season we had drawn so poorly."

So, the shock treatment worked. Despite the network of limited-coverage suburban AM stations and one metro-covering FM outlet in an era when few cars had FM receivers, the Caray-fronted broadcasts sold the Sox. Attendance dramatically increased by 335,000 and Caray pocketed a nice bonus, based on that jump at the gate.

Still, despite the significant on-field improvements, overall attendance increase to 833,891 and Caray's broadcast sales job, whispers about a franchise relocation still remained audible in the background. The Sox still needed yet another boost to keep the wolf from the door.

The biggest trade of Hemond's career

A man on a mission, Hemond then made perhaps the greatest blockbuster trade in White Sox history, landing Dick at the '71 winter meetings to vault the Sox into serious contention in 1972.

Despite being rebuffed in this first attempt to broker an Allen deal with the Cardinals, Hemond again went to work to land the slugger in November 1971. A blizzard of activity erupted in Arizona Biltmore Hotel, where the Meetings were in session. Few, if any, baseball executives welcomed the buzz more than Hemond, and he had arrived with the wish list to prove it.

While encouraged by his previous progress, Hemond knew the next step would be more difficult. The team lacked depth, not to mention star power. Specifically, there was an urgent need for an established run-producer who would allow Melton to have more and better opportunities in the cleanup spot. In the final weeks of the previous season, in which Melton totaled 33 home runs to become the first home run champion in Sox history, opponents began to pitch around him more frequently.

"I believed the franchise was headed in the right direction at the time," Hemond recalled in 2012. "But when you consider how far back we started, we still had a long way to go to become a competitive ballclub, let alone a contender. There was a lot of work to be done."

At the 1971 winter meetings, Hemond had come to the right place. In a span of five days, no fewer than 53 major-league players would change uniforms. Still, Hemond could never have dreamed that two telephone calls only minutes apart would so drastically change the fortunes of a franchise.

The first voice on the other end of the line was that of Al Campanis, the Los Angeles Dodgers' General Manager. He was in search of an established pitcher to fill out their rotation. When the name Dick Allen was mentioned, Hemond's ears perked up considerably. Not only had the veteran totaled 23 home runs and 90 RBI the previous season, he also had much of the damage at Dodger Stadium which, like White Sox Park, was one of the most pitcher-friendly stadiums in the game. Not yet 30, Dick was in his prime.

If only a blockbuster trade was that easy. Also, as Hemond didn't have to be reminded, controversy followed Dick wherever he had been in his star-crossed career. His many critics considered him to be a slacker or worse. Dick maintained that the reputation was a media creation and grossly unfair, but his late arrivals and occasional no-shows at the ballpark did little to change minds. The Dodgers were his third team in three years.

What's more, Dick was paid a reported $95,000 the previous season, which put him in line to become the highest-paid player in White Sox history. But the Sox had one of lowest payrolls in the major leagues.

Could the organization afford Dick Allen? And if so, how would he be accepted in the clubhouse?

Immediately, Hemond sought out the opinion of his own manager. Dick didn't have many fans among those in authority positions, but with Tanner, he had no bigger one.

"Get him!" Tanner said.

The ringing endorsement was based on personal experience, not hope or hearsay.

Tanner's own reputation played no small role in the decision. In his one full season as a major league manager, his most obvious asset was the ability to get the most out of his players regardless of their talent levels.

"Chuck had a lot of respect for Dick as a person and a player," Hemond recalled. "When he conveyed that message, it was good enough for me. I knew that, if anybody could get the most out of Dick, he would be the one."

Moments later, Hemond called Campanis to confirm his interest. The Dodgers already had three solid starters in Sutton, Osteen and Downing, but there was concern about the health of Bill Singer as the fourth member of the rotation.

What would it take to make the deal? Pitchers Tommy John and Terry Forster, Campanis answered. In Forster, a 19-year-old with a golden left arm, Campanis had visions of another Sandy Koufax, the Dodgers great who had retired five years earlier.

Trouble was, Hemond thought much the same thing.

"You may get John," he replied, "but you won't get Forster."

Because the demand for Dick wasn't great at the time, Hemond wielded some leverage. Finally, after a few more names were bandied about, the two sides settled on John and Steve Huntz, a journeyman infielder.

Next, Hemond had to sell owner John Allyn on the idea.

"I told John that Dick would make us a much better team," Hemond said. "I stressed that his salary would be worth it because of all the fans that he brought to the ballpark. No team would have a better combination than Dick and Bill in the three-four spots, and that would create a lot of excitement among our fans. I must have done a good job to sell it, because John Allyn liked the idea after a while."

Certainly, Allyn would like the bold move better than general manager Stu Holcomb, the former college football coach and Northwestern University athletic director who was in charge of the business side. Because Holcomb was chained to the bottom line, Hemond made sure that he would be the last person in the front office to know about it.

"While Chuck and I discussed strategy in the hotel lobby one day, we saw Stu at the top of the escalator," Hemond said. "We were afraid that he might get wind of it. So, I told Chuck to hurry up there and keep him occupied for a while."

The Dodgers stipulated that before any such deal was consummated, they would have to replace Dick in the middle of the batting order. When the Baltimore Orioles agreed to trade veteran outfielder Frank Robinson in return for four prospects, the final piece was in place.

Barely 15 minutes later, Hemond received another phone call. This time it was Lee MacPhail, the New York Yankees general manager. His team was in search of a third baseman, and MacPhail wanted to know if Rich McKinney could handle the position on a regular basis. McKinney made an impression on the Yankees the previous season when he hit .379 against them. He was drafted as a shortstop but had experience at three infield spots.

"I said that third base was Rich's best position, but because we had an All-Star in Bill Melton already, there was no place for him there," Hemond said.

The Yankees had five starting pitchers for four spots, and the veteran Bahnsen, who had won the AL Rookie of The Year award in 1968, was the odd man out. When they agreed to part with the right-hander in return for McKinney straight up, the White Sox filled a big hole in their rotation.

Many observers were surprised that the Yankees didn't hold out for more in a trade that drew the ire of their fans. In four seasons with fairly average teams, Bahnsen averaged 13-plus victories and 34 starts. Boston Red Sox outfielder Carl Yastrzemski once remarked that no pitcher threw harder in the American League than the 27-year-old Bahnsen.

On Dec. 2, 1971, when the double-barreled moves became official, no one was sure whether Dick would play left field or first base, which was his best position. All that mattered was that Melton had a tag-team partner and the Chicago White Sox had another gate attraction.

"We've got a bomber!" gushed Tanner, even more excited than usual.

John and Bahnsen were receptive to the change of venues, and Bahnsen welcomed the chance to play for Tanner and Johnny Sain.

"I didn't know Sain when he was with the Yankees, but I've heard a lot about him," said Bahnsen. "All the pitchers I've talked to tell me he's helped them. I know Tom Bradley looked a lot better last year when he was with Chicago. He looked like twice the pitcher he'd been the year before."

The arrivals of Bahnsen and, especially, Dick paid dividends before a pitch was even thrown. Throughout their history, White Sox teams had been built to the dimensions of their spacious ballpark, which placed a premium on speed, defense and pitching. Suddenly, fans had a rare vision of not one but two legitimate thumpers in the middle of the batting order. Immediately, there was talk that Allen and Melton could become the most lethal one-two combination in team history. The *Chicago Tribune* labeled the twosome "Murderers Row." The buzz translated into a noticeable spike in ticket sales. By mid-January, WFLD-TV, in its last season of a five-year deal as the Sox' flagship station, already had sold full sponsorship of pregame shows and 60 percent of its airtime for regular-season in-game commercials, a 36% increase from the previous year.

Now Dick had to sell himself to his teammates, namely those who had been asked to accept only token pay raises. That is, if they received bumps at all. With the Dick Allen contract taking up nearly 25% of all player salaries, others found the feeding trough less nourishing. So, Holcomb began to cut corners elsewhere.

Other key pieces of the 1972 team included Hemond picking up Jorge Orta and Cy Acosta from his connections to the Mexican Leagues.

"With Jorge Orta, I saw him, along with our scout, Jorge Noga, in Mexico," Hemond said. "And he was playing for the rookie club of the Mexican League. Just like if we were using one of our players in the rookie league. And he came up, and boy, quick bat. And not tall, but husky kid. It was a rainy day, and the town that we were in, there was a delay for the game to start. But the manager there ran him for us. And you could see that he was quick and could run. Then when the game started, he hit some vicious line drives. Then he dropped a bunt. He wanted to show us what he could do. And lo and behold, I called the gentleman, Dr. Labraia of the Guadalajara club who owned that farm team as well.

"And when I was with the Angels, we acquired Aurelio Rodriguez, outstanding third baseman. And now Labraia figured, well, maybe it's a possibility to pitch us his contract. And the doc invited me to go down to Guadalajara. His daughter was getting married that day. We had an early breakfast and we worked out a deal. He says you're getting one of my gems again, Roland. Rodriguez, and now Orta."

Hemond purchased Orta's contract on Nov. 30, 1971. He was invited to spring training as a non-roster invitee.

"And he had such a good spring in '72, and Dick Allen was helpful to him, too," Hemond said. "He says I'll play off the line more, Jorge, I'll help you out. And he hit a home run off Jim Kaat, who was in his prime. Anyway, they were having trouble getting him out. And Chuck said well, we might as well bring him up north. And I couldn't believe that you see a player in August in the lowest league of Mexico, and all of a sudden, he's in your lineup."

"First time up he hits a line drive base hit to left field. And had a fine career. So those are the miraculous things that when you're lucky, people like that who provide more than you could expect at any given time."

Acosta, a native of El Sabino, Mexico, was also purchased from the Jalisco club in 1971 of the recommendation of Noga and assigned to the Sox' Triple A-affiliate in Tucson.

Hemond recalled picking up the right-handed Acosta at O'Hare on Sunday, June 4, 1972 to be ready to pitch in the Bat Day doubleheader that afternoon after bringing him up from Tucson. Acosta was promoted to replace Bart Johnson, who been sent down to Triple-A after his 18-10 extra-inning Saturday loss to the Yankees. Hemond believed part of his job was to do menial tasks like ferrying players to and from the airport.

"Anything to get to know these players," he said. "I was walking out to the bullpen, I know it was cold. And I said doggone it, get him a jacket. I went down to the clubhouse and got him a jacket." His first appearance was later that afternoon in the "Chili Dog" second game of the twinbill, and he got the win when he pitched the ninth inning before Dick's blast. Pitching in just the last four months of the season, Acosta went 3-0 in 26 games over 34⅔ innings with a 1.54 ERA.

Hemond's moves during the '72 season

A players' strike pushed the start of the regular season back 10 days, and the White Sox players were front and center in the walkout even if they hadn't planned it that way. The players union sought a 17% increase in fixed retirement benefits as well as a boost in medical and health care premiums.

In what was expected to be a routine visit to their training camp in Sarasota, Fla., union chief Marvin Miller informed the players that the team owners had made what he considered to be a lowball offer and refused to negotiate in good faith. White Sox players voted unanimously to authorize a strike, if necessary, a result that player representative Joel Horlen announced somewhat reluctantly. The veteran pitcher was released less than four weeks later on April 2, 1972. Horlen ended up pitching for Oakland, which snakebit the Sox. The team never had more than three full-time starters for the '72 season because Bart Johnson was pitching hurt.

Before the work stoppage ended on March 25, Hemond traded for Bradford, then with the Reds, for a player to be named later. Bradford had been signed by the South Siders as an amateur free agent in 1962 and was traded away in 1970. Now, he returned.

Once Dick's '72 contract was secured, Hemond sent first-baseman Roe Skidmore, who in 1971 hit .299 with 20 home runs and 77 RBI in Triple-A, to the Reds to complete the deal.

After the sweep in Kansas City began the strike-delayed season, the Sox went on a seven-game winning streak, giving the team an undefeated home schedule in April. Allen slammed a two-run in the 10th inning to power a 7–5 win over Cleveland on Wednesday afternoon, April 26.

The White Sox were gaining notice with their fast start as they took their half-game division lead into a road series against the Tigers.

Later, beginning Wednesday, May 10, the team won 12 of 13 and soared into first place in the AL West by 1½ games.

In mid-to-late May the revitalized squad swept the Angels at home. After winning the first two games in Detroit 3–1 and 8–0, the Sox squeaked through the final game of the series, winning 9–8 on Carlos May's two-out, three-run, ninth-inning home run. May, playing with a gimpy leg, hammered a 1-0 fastball, barely fair, into the right field seats.

Bat boy Jim Riley was so excited about May's walk-off home run that he knocked himself out hitting his head on the ceiling of the dugout.

May's heroics pushed the Sox to an 18–10 overall record and an amazing 16–2 start at Comiskey Park. The Sox were now in first place, the latest they'd been in the lead in five years. "It's May Day! Sox Are in First," blared the headlines.

On June 1, Tanner and Hemond went to Wrigley Field to watch the Cubs, especially relief pitcher Phil Regan. The veteran right-hander, long accused of applying Vaseline to baseballs to make them sink, had sunk into Manager Leo Durocher's doghouse, due in no small part to Durocher's overworking of Regan in 1968-70. Cubs GM John Holland ended up selling Regan to the White Sox for a sum in excess of the $20,000 waiver price.

In 2021, Regan recalled how he went to the crosstown franchise: "I wasn't pitching much for Leo at the end. He and I weren't getting along really well. One day I threw a bullpen, and I saw Tanner sitting at the game. After the game, we went to the airport, they called me over and said I was sold to the Sox. The GM (Stu Holcomb) was in the hospital, and Roland (Hemond) and Chuck made the deal without his approval."

"Chuck was great. You could go in and talk to him. He had great sayings. He was very easy to play for. He was easy-going. Players got along with him. There weren't a lot of rules and stuff."

Yet, Regan did not pitch much for the Sox. He got into 10 games and threw only 13⅓ innings with a 4.05 ERA with 0-1 record. He was released just a month later on July 20, 1972, which was his final stop in his 13-year career. "Holcomb got mad if I didn't get a guy out," Regan said. "Holcomb called when they released me, said I was great on the club and offered a connection to play in Japan."

As the Sox remained competitive and battled for the division crown, fans knew that the team had problems at shortstop, center field, back-up catcher and fourth starter. There was a clamor to get Luis Aparicio back from the Red Sox.

Bart Johnson's absence due to improperly-cared-for injuries really thinned the pitching depth. His arrival in late 1969 as a 19-year-old provided hope. Johnson was followed to the majors by fellow home-grown hard throwers Forster and Gossage.

Johnson was touted as a future Nolan Ryan. For two seasons (1971 and 1974), he was a budding star, but injuries shortened his promising career.

Before he had signed with the Sox after being scouted by Jorge Norga and Doc Bennet, Johnson had considered a career in basketball, as he was named to several high school All-America teams.

"I decided on baseball because I honestly thought I had the talent to become a Cy Young Award winner. In basketball, though, I wasn't going to dominate, I'd just be a piece of the puzzle on a team in the NBA," Johnson said in a 2006 interview with Sox historian Mark Liptak.

His basketball athletic talent was such that UCLA head coach John Wooden recruited him. Johnson even thought he could play both pro baseball and basketball at the same time. In fact, he tried out twice for the Seattle SuperSonics.

After a solid 1971 campaign in which he went 12-10 with a 2.93 ERA (10th best in the American League) and had back-to-back games with 12 strikeouts in September, Johnson sustained a knee injury in an off-season basketball game. He was limited to nine appearances in 1972.

In June 2012, Johnson recalled: "That year was very frustrating for me especially after my great year in 1971 and expectations were high with Goose making the team that year and Terry having pitched well in his rookie year (1971).

"We lost the entire opening series of the 1972 strike season. Two games went extra innings and I suffered two losses in relief, including the opener, where we lost 2-1 in 11 innings.

"In less than 18 hours, I was 0-2 and was worried that I would be shipped down to the minors, as I had hurt my right knee in the off-season playing basketball. I immediately told the Sox about it and they examined me and said the knee was basically OK, but I did tear some cartilage. When I went out to pitch, I just couldn't push off it. They wound up operating on my knee that September after I was sent down to the minors, following my third loss to the Yankees in June."

Fans and the media were unaware that Johnson was pitching hurt. "Bart Johnson, the perplexing fastball expert who for unexplained reasons can no longer zip a fastball, surrendered eight runs in the 13th inning," wrote *Chicago Tribune* beat writer George Langford to open his June 4, 1972, story "Johnson Shelled, Sent Down."

Speculation about Johnson surfaced that he was afraid to hit batters after three close pitches by him in 1971 ignited brawls. The incidents earned Johnson some notoriety, upsetting the young pitcher who was one of the "Fighting White Sox" featured in 1972 Sox publicity material.

At first, the 22-year-old Johnson resisted going down to the Sox Triple-A team in Tucson. Instead, he ended up back with the Class-A Midwest League Appleton Foxes, where in 1969 he went a stellar 16-4 with a 2.17 ERA and league-leading 200 strikeouts.

In 1973, coming back from surgery, Johnson worked in just 22 games for the Sox. He amassed 80 innings, striking out 56, showing some signs of regaining his old form.

"I certainly wish I could have contributed more to that '72 club," was Johnson's admission. "I had a knee operation and I forget what my record was, but I had a horrible year. I felt all along if I'd have had an average season or a good season, we would have won it. So, there's some frustration there and that's part of the game."

Melton goes down, Hemond must fill the hole at third

After Johnson got shelled in the Saturday contest of the four-game series against the Yankees at Comiskey Park, the White Sox went on a tear after Dick's Superman heroics the next day with his Chili Dog pinch-hit, walk-off shot off Sparky Lyle. The Sox won six of seven, mostly due to Carlos May's hot bat. Oakland kept winning, too, but by the trading deadline, the Sox sat just 2½ games behind the A's with the American League's second-best record. Hemond failed to pull off any deals by the trading deadline, not knowing that a week later he would need a new third baseman. He passed on acquiring 35-year-old slugger Frank Howard from the Rangers, focusing instead on his first-year player draft selections on June 6. Sadly, none of the 1972 draftees panned out.

Just after the trading deadline passed, the United States Supreme Court on June 19th issued its 5–3 decision upholding the reserve clause that Curt Flood had challenged after being traded to Philadelphia for Dick in October 1969.

With hopes high and tickets selling, Roland and Sox management felt they had a legitimate shot to win the AL West.

All was not right with the team, however. Bill Melton, the defending American League home run king, still hadn't recovered from a lower back injury suffered the previous November, when he fell off a ladder at his California home.

Melton was placed on the disabled list on June 23rd and would remain out for the season— having produced just seven homers. Dick lost his protection in the lineup.

The Sox, meanwhile, limped home from a 14-game, five-city tour that left them six games behind the Oakland A's, who were about to invade Comiskey Park for a four-game set.

The White Sox took three out of four from the A's to cut the deficit to four games, closing out June with a 39-27 record.

By July 9, the word came down that Melton would not return until the next season.

That day, Hemond acquired third baseman Ed Spiezio, a native of Morris, Ill. — 55 miles southwest of Chicago — from the Padres to plug the hole left by Melton. Spiezio proved to be a capable replacement in the field, but the Sox missed Melton's bat. Spiezio gamely tried to help, contributing with a seventh-inning home run in a 4-3 victory in Cleveland on July 11.

Forty-two years later, Hemond told how he scrambled to get Spiezio. "We got him on waivers," he said. "It was hard to acquire another third baseman. As a matter of fact, he did a real good job. He didn't possess the power of Melton. So, Melton was still missed. But as a fill-in job, I was really proud of him. I found out later after he was through playing how he played with a broken rib the rest of that year, but he never let on that he had a problem. And I was indebted to him as a player just coming here in a difficult position. He got some big hits for us, but he was more a singles and doubles hitter.

Spiezio proved a good find as the Sox erased Oakland's eight-and-a-half-game lead, built seemingly quickly in mid-July and August. They finally tied for first place on August 12th and later exclusively held the top spot for a week. But the savvy A's owner Finley knew where to find talent to bolster his core roster as the grind continued.

Finley picked up five players late in the season, including outfielder Matty Alou and shortstop Dal Maxvill, to eventually push his club over the top. In contrast, the White Sox only made token late-season additions.

Hemond signed reliever Moe Drabowsky as a free agent after the Cardinals released him on Aug. 15. Highland Park resident Drabowsky, a colorful character, had started out with the Cubs as a ballyhooed prospect in 1956. The Sox GM was well aware of Drabowsky's postseason resumé in relief in Game 1 of the 1966 World Series for the Orioles, going 6⅔ innings and striking out 11 Dodgers. But after pitching in just seven games, Drabowsky was released on October 1, concluding his lengthy career.

On August 17, Hemond traded for knuckleball pitcher Eddie Fisher from the Angels for player to named later. Catcher Bruce Kimm, a future Cubs player and manager, would eventually go to the Angels to complete the deal in early September. In his second Sox stint after teaming with Hoyt Wilhelm as flutterball specialists in the mid-1960s, Fisher went 0-1 in 22⅓ innings over six appearances. He returned for the first part of the 1973 season.

No pitcher picked up Johnson's 178 innings from 1971, which forced the Sox to go with a three-man rotation for most of the year. Spiezio's two home runs could not make up for the loss of Melton. The Sox failed to acquire a right-handed slugger to provide protection for Dick when Melton went down and the left-handed-hitting Carlos May slumped. One veteran bat available was that of Tommy Davis, in his second stint with the Cubs in 1972.

The Braves were shopping Rico Carty, who had recently been reactivated after being on the disabled list for six weeks for a hamstring injury. Hemond passed. He also did not sign left-handed pinch-hitter Bob Burda, released by Boston.

"You can give up too much, and that's all right if you win the pennant, but if you don't, it can hurt you for the future," warned Hemond.

Still, Dick wondered aloud why the Sox had not gone out and acquired an extra couple of bats in August as the A's had. He knew that the fans swarmed

Comiskey Park to watch him swing the bat, pouring money into the team's coffers.

Before the Friday, September 1 game in New York, Hemond announced the signing of Allen's 32-year-old brother Hank as a free agent, which caused some controversy, because the "other" Allen needed 112 days of active service to become vested for his MLB pension. Hank did get into nine games with 21 at-bats, collecting just three singles, during the month of September 1972.

Hemond defended the signing because Dick's older brother could help deal with all of the incredible attention Dick had gained, especially on the road, during his monster 1972 season.

The budding Holcomb-Tanner-Hemond feud

Dick Allen did not know the behind-the-scenes drama in the front office over the club's precarious finances. With the White Sox' five-year TV contract with WFLD expiring after the season and nothing in place yet for video rights 1973, management had to cut corners.

There were rumblings about conflicts between Hemond and Tanner in one corner and Sox general manager Stu Holcomb in the other. Holcomb, who handled the hiring of Hemond and Tanner two years earlier, basically had the authority that a half-century later is bestowed on team presidents acting on behalf of owners. Hemond admitted he had hidden his efforts about trading for Dick and went over his boss' head by explaining to John Allyn how much value Dick would bring to the Sox. The Allen machinations proved to be the first crack in the relationship between baseball lifers Tanner and Hemond, and converted football man Holcomb.

Tanner and Hemond had acquired Regan in June 1972 without Holcomb's blessing, while he recovered from a hernia operation. Holcomb was none too pleased to process the Regan arrival when he came back on duty.

Roger Wallenstein, who hosted and produced "Instant Replay," a post-game White Sox show for WEAW-FM for the 1971 season, had an interesting perspective on Holcomb and Hemond when interviewed in 2021: "Hemond was just terrific," Wallenstein said. Hemond even appeared live on "Instant Replay" with the countdown ticking down to the trade deadline, explaining he might be interrupted by incoming calls.

"He never said he didn't have time to talk to us," Wallenstein said. "He was never too busy. Just always very, very nice. And he was a great general manager for the ballclub. The deals he made. Just as the face of the front office, Roland was absolutely outstanding."

Meanwhile, Wallenstein said Holcomb "was an interesting guy, but he was much more serious, though. I always thought Tanner and Hemond were supportive of me. They were making my so-called job easier, whereas Holcomb had no interest in that at all. It was like going through the motions and 'Yes, I'll do this (interview), but I'm not going to enjoy it.' He was very kind of stoic. I think we only interviewed him once and went to the office and did the interview and thanked him and that was the end of it."

By late in the 1972 season, the feud started coming out in the open. Holcomb dumped the club's Florida Instructional League team in early September 1972 as a cost-saving measure. Hemond was openly upset about the decision.

"You put me in a ticklish spot," said an exasperated Hemond when asked about the Sox being the only team not to field a fall instructional program to help develop its prospects. "I would be lying if I said I was approving of what we're doing."

Chicago Tribune beat writer Richard Dozer wrote: "It frightens you to see a club draw 1,200,000 fans and suddenly retrench to effect an immediate savings of perhaps $50,000."

Holcomb's penny-wise, pound-foolish decision flew in the face of the attendance resurgence that put the now-consistently contending A's, who struggled to draw at home in Oakland, to shame.

Jerome Holtzman wrote in the *Sporting News* on Nov. 18, 1972: "I see where Stu Holcomb, the General Manager, is trying to blame the Chicago writers for the September rift between him and the manager Chuck Tanner and Hemond, the club's personnel director. Holcomb insists: 'There was no such rift and the writers were trying to cut me up because I didn't give them their way in the press box.'

"Sorry, Stu, but Chicago writers who broke the story weren't involved in the press box feud. Anyway, it's gonna be interesting to see if Holcomb continues to defy the Baseball Writers Association of America rules and insists on having the first and last say in who can and cannot enter the White Sox Park press box. Frankly, I wish Holcomb would find a seat elsewhere — on owner John Allyn's lap, if necessary."

Holcomb indeed played macho man in deciding on press box admissions. Although Nancy Faust recalled Holcomb as supportive of her as team organist and a woman of talent, Holcomb tried to bar Waukegan sportswriter Linda Morstadt from entering the upstairs media work area. Holtzman, as Chicago Chapter Chairman of the Baseball Writers Association of America, called the issue of Morstadt's admission to a vote. The four traveling beat writers deadlocked at 2-2. Holcomb butted in and claimed he voted "no" as the tiebreaker. Holtzman told Holcomb he did not have a vote. Eventually, Morstadt was admitted, Holtzman using an elitist rationalization that she had formerly worked for *Chicago Today*, the Tribune-owned afternoon tabloid, which traveled with Chicago teams.

After the 1972 season and his MLB *Sporting News* Executive of the Year Award, Hemond seized on his higher profile and sought to increase his executive authority to have the Sox poised to take the next step for 1973.

In 1973, the front office knew Melton would likely return from his back troubles. Hemond got glowing medical reports on the off-season rehab progress of both Melton and Johnson as Edgar Munzel wrote in the *Sporting News* on Nov. 25, 1972: "Hemond could cull his Mexico connections to help arrange rehab workouts for Melton. Johnson, after his right knee surgery by Dr. Gerald Loftus, began running on beaches in Southern California."

Counting on Johnson to return to the pitching staff for '73, Hemond traded starter Tom Bradley to the San Francisco Giants for center fielder Ken Henderson. Melton returned healthy, albeit a bit diminished in power, to third base.

The Sox zoomed to a 27-15 start with attendance still increasing. Back-to-back mid-May dates with the Minnesota Twins drew 43,000 and an astounding 55,555 for a Bat Day Sunday doubleheader. Many box seat ticket holders found their seats already occupied by bat-wielding youths when they arrived. The Sox were favored and roared out of the gate, building up a four-and-a-half-game lead by late May.

But after just 72 games played, Dick was lost for the season with a broken left leg. Starting pitching depth suddenly became an issue because Hemond misjudged the subtraction of Bradley. Wood and Bahnsen had to work on two days' rest, at times. Wood started both ends of a doubleheader and made 48 starts overall, the reasoning being his knuckleball provided less strain on the arm. Hemond's mid-August acquisition of lefty Jim Kaat came too late to save the season. Without Dick, the Sox crumbled, falling out of the race by August. But major issues arose behind the scenes regarding player contracts and the future of the organization.

Hemond and the penny-pinching Holcomb argued over player compensation. When a Sox player couldn't or wouldn't agree to terms, Holcomb ordered Hemond to release him.

Open dissension about Holcomb broke out among the players. So, there was roster-wide sigh of relief when Holcomb was finally pushed out. He ended up formally resigning on July 26, 1973, believing a coup had been engineered by Hemond and Tanner. He was right.

Holcomb did not want to give raises to Mike Andrews, Jay Johnstone, Ed Spiezio and Rick Reichardt for 1973. They ended up being released when they did not sign the new contracts offered to them.

"The job hasn't been just making trades or bringing in player personnel," Holcomb said at the time. "I brought in Harry Caray as a sportscaster. We improved the park. There are thousands of things that did not meet the eye."

Hemond gave owner Allyn a "him or me" warning after Holcomb ordered him to release 21-game-winner Bahnsen because of the pitcher's contract dispute. Director of Player Personnel Hemond went to owner Allyn and basically offered to resign. He had enough of the meddling of Holcomb, a non-baseball man who interfered in baseball matters. Holcomb was an inadvertent role model for baseball honcho-wannabe Tribune Company executives meddling 15 years later with the Cubs, and former Harvard professor Michael McCaskey calling roster shots in the same era with the Chicago Bears.

Instead, Holcomb resigned due to the pressure applied to owner Allyn from Tanner and Hemond, who was then promoted to General Manager. Most baseball people thought Hemond already had that job title.

The *Chicago Tribune's* David Condon reprinted most of Holcomb's resignation letter to Allyn in a July 28, 1973, story. It read more like a plea than a resignation message:

> *"You want to know what happened? Around July 1, I had this talk with Tanner, and he said he was quitting (because Tanner disagreed with Holcomb on personnel moves). I couldn't have that. However, I can say a couple of things in justification for taking the heat. Hemond and Tanner were my choices originally." I could have hired 'name' people instead and protected myself. Then, if they'd failed, I'd be off the spot because I'd gone with proven baseball men.*

> *"But if I'd hired men from the minor league and they'd failed, the mistake would have been charged to me for not going with experience.*

> *"I liked Tanner and Hemond because they were eager, hungry, determined, and knowledgeable. They should have been happy to see players come up from the minors and make good as they made good. But I realize that Chuck Tanner is a positive personality. He has a great future. John Allyn spent lots of money giving Tanner what he wants.*

> *"When I told Tanner I wasn't giving Reichardt more than $40,000, Chuck said I was being fair. When Reichardt left, Chuck told us that Rick had quit on him – but he didn't say it to you fellows (sportswriters).*

> *"Those are some of the things that Chuck hasn't said. Of course, Chuck reminded me that if we released (Mike) Andrews, we'd have to pay him."*

"The problem was Stu Holcomb," second baseman Andrews told Sox historian Mark Liptak, decades later. "He was supposed to run the owner's soccer team but when that folded, they had to find something for him and made him the GM. He didn't handle things well at all. I know Stan (Bahnsen) said he wasn't going to pitch unless he got a new contract. Because of his stellar number of wins, the Sox finally agreed with what he wanted. Reichardt was flat waived.

"I was talking with the Sox about a new deal. The Sox weren't going to cut my salary and we were almost ready to sign it when Holcomb went to the papers and said something like 'Andrews obviously hasn't lived up to what we thought we were going to be getting.' I was having problems especially with my throwing. I wasn't playing much and it was a bad situation. I went to Chuck (Tanner) and said: 'This isn't good, can I just be released?' Chuck said to me, 'Mike, I don't blame you, let me see what I can do.' Chuck was able to get me released and I wound up signing with Oakland."

Holcomb said when informed by Tanner that Andrews wanted to be released: "I asked Chuck if he wanted to do it and Chuck said sure, as long as Andrews did not want to play for us."

Tanner's reaction was: "Hell, I knew it in the ('73) spring that this stuff was going to go on. I told John Allyn the same thing when I talked with him. As a manager all you can do is the best you can. I don't know, maybe the Sox had money troubles at that time, I don't know if they had the money to pay these guys. It hurt us because we didn't have anybody left after the injuries. One other thing about this. I remember Jay Johnstone just looking shocked about it all…'How could they just release me?'"

Johnstone had been released by Holcomb on March 7, after he refused to sign his '73 contract.

"Holcomb sent me a contract with 20% pay cut," he recalled years later in "*Temporary Insanity*," his autobiography. "I didn't believe that I was only going to be blamed for that .188 batting average all during the previous season. The Sox jacked around with Rick Reichardt in center field ahead of me. I felt they stuck it to me all season and, frankly, I believe it had to do with me being a Player Representative and all the problems the Players Association and owners had in 1972.

"I met Holcomb down in Sarasota before spring training…he handed me the same contract for the same 20% cut from $25,000 to $20,000…I said what's this? You asked me to fly me all night so you can give me the same contract as the best you can do."

"Well, I can't take it," responded Johnstone.

Holcomb countered: "We can always trade you."

"OK, trade me," shot back Johnstone.

"Or we could release you," said Holcomb.

"Fine release me. I'm not signing that contract," replied Johnstone.

The next day, the White Sox released not only Johnstone, but also Spiezio. Further, they sent letters to five other players who were holding out and said, in effect, the same thing happened to Johnstone and Spiezio can happen to you."

Johnstone later landed with the Oakland A's and, in 1985, finished a 20-year career with a .267 batting average.

Tribune columnist Robert Markus, an occasional Dick Allen critic, defended Holcomb on July 30, 1973: Holcomb "just performed his most important duty as GM" when he hired virtual unknowns in Tanner and Roland Hemond in September 1970. "He did so well that there was no longer need for Holcomb himself in the front office. The day Holcomb hired Tanner and Hemond he set the White Sox on the road to recovery. He took a sick franchise and made it well."

Career highlights and honors

The '72 *Sporting News* Executive of the Year Award would be the first of many in Hemond's career. Winning the Buck O'Neil Lifetime Achievement Award in 2011 also meant a lot to Hemond, though he still wished for full admittance to the Hall. Roland was recognized for "the profound impact he has had on the game, for his baseball intelligence as a keen talent evaluator and in building winning teams, to the universal respect he has earned for mentoring generations of baseball executives, past and present."

While accepting the O'Neil award, he spoke about how much scouting was a key to the game.

"The biggest reward for a scout comes because of his love of the game, primarily," he said. "When the player reaches the major leagues and has his first at-bat or pitching appearance, that's a stimulant that's hard to describe for anybody outside the game. You have to show up every day and give it your best as a scout. Try to find a sleeper here and there. Never leave the park early. And know that failure is a part of the business, just as it is inherent in the game of baseball."

In 1992, Hemond created the Arizona Fall League as a graduate "finishing school" for ballplayers to create an environment closer to home compared to Caribbean winter-league experience in a foreign culture. MLB organizations could get their top prospects off-season games against fellow top talent following the regular minor-league schedules. He envisioned a league where teams could not only develop their talent, but also showcase that talent and where scouts could compare a talent pool in a close location instead of far-flung locales.

Three annual awards exist in Hemond's honor:

1. The Roland Hemond Award, created in 2003 by the White Sox in honor of those who are dedicated to bettering the lives of others through extraordinary personal sacrifice,

2. The Baseball America Award, presented to the person who has made major contributions to scouting and player development.

3. The Society for American Baseball Research (SABR) Award, given to the executive who has displayed great respect for scouts.

Hemond also received an honorary degree in Humane Letters from the University of Phoenix, was named an honorary member of the Princeton University Class of 1954 and was the 2003 recipient of the Branch Ricky Award for "contributions to the community."

Until 2019, Hemond was still active as an executive for the Arizona Diamondbacks. In 2021, he was retired at age 92 and living with his son, Jay, in Colorado until he died in his sleep December 12, 2021. His death led to an outpouring of remembrance by the baseball community.

Until his retirement, he continued to be involved in the Association of Professional Baseball Players of America, an organization that helps former and current players and baseball personnel in need. He had helped establish that organization in 1986. The Baseball Assistance Team (BAT) in December 2020 absorbed of Roland's other pet projects, the Professional Baseball Scouts Foundation, which he served as co-founder. The foundation was established in 2003 to aid longtime scouts who need special support.

Reflecting on his crown jewel achievement

In June 2012, Hemond was reunited with Dick Allen for the 40th year 1972 White Sox team reunion at Guaranteed Rate Field. Staking out the lobby of the Palmer House, Roland waited for the slugger to show up to begin the day's festivities.

Around Roland's neck were a pair of worn red baseball spikes still caked with mud. He had tied the laces of both shoes together to drape the spikes over his neck.

Dick showed up with his brother, Hank. He spotted Hemond and went over to give the diminutive man a warm hug.

During the embrace, Hemond told Dick, "Hey, you left these spikes on the field that Saturday night (Sept. 14, 1974) when you told the team that you were retiring…I thought you would need them again."

Hemond handed Allen the spikes, who broke down in tears. "I am sorry, Roland, I know I let the Sox down, but I was playing hurt and didn't deserve to take money away from John Allyn when I could not contribute to the team," he said.

After a few minutes, Allen composed himself and both men spoke about how important the '72 team was to their lives.

The next night, Monday, June 26, Hemond addressed the packed Stadium Club which gathered to honor Allen and '72 team. "We were disappointed not to play in the postseason, which was our goal," he said.

"But when you look at the big picture, we did something even more important. We put the franchise on solid ground again. It was a great time for all of us, and anyone who was there won't forget it. I can't tell you how many people have told me that they became White Sox fans that season, and they still are to this day."

Hemond was deeply moved and talked about how the '72 season was a turning point for the organization and how much pleasure this ballclub gave him. He then addressed Allen, sitting with his family, and said, "Without you, this would never have happened, and the team would not be in Chicago."

Hemond spoke about acquiring starting pitcher Stan Bahnsen on the heels of the Allen deal. And how Chicago media began hyping a "Murderers' row" of Allen and defending AL home run champion Bill Melton in the Sox lineup.

With Wood established as a 20-game winner in '71 and Forster taking over as closer, teamed in the bullpen with rookie Goose Gossage, the Sox zoomed into contention with Allen leading the way.

Finally, the Sox grabbed their fair share of attention and attendance climbed over the magic 1 million mark.

"There was great camaraderie, said Hemond. "And I think winning ball clubs most of the time are cohesion; give the extra effort, break up a double play, score runs. Manufacture runs. Playing with not with the name on your back...it's the shirt in front of you; Chicago, whatever. And we had that. It was a great atmosphere. I didn't feel left out, for instance, when the guys are doing well because they were happy that we had acquired them to be in this type of atmosphere.

"So, I'm sure many of the players that were in that '72 club, they're still talking about it later to their grandchildren or whoever they want to listen because it was a magical year.

"Wilbur Wood was one of the unsung heroes. He pitched like 370 innings. He pitched on two days of rest 25 times. We had traded for Tom Bradley, he gave us over 200 innings. And so, it was a combination of things happening well. So, the White Sox then became a contending club."

Of everything Hemond ever did in baseball since his entry-level job sweeping the stands in 1951, nothing had greater impact than the stunning trade for Dick Allen at those 1971 winter meetings. He revitalized a Sox franchise like few other players have ever done for any team — and won the American League Most Valuable Player award, to boot.

"Acquiring Dick was a daring move," Hemond said in 2014. "I felt though that Chuck Tanner would be the right manager for him. Chuck is from New Castle, Pa. and Allen was from (nearby) Wampum. Chuck had known Dick and Dick's mom for years. Allen was one of the most talented players to have ever played the game. We felt he could help us.

"And Dick had a tremendous year in '72 as one of the finest baseball seasons a player could put together. Clutch hits. He could steal bases. Great athlete. He'd cut bases. Score from first on a double because he diminished the turns and some other guys can't cut the bases like him.

"But anyway, he certainly played a major, major role in keeping the franchise of the White Sox in Chicago 'cuz at that time it very well could have happened that they would have ended up in Seattle or Toronto or Denver. And evidently, I still feel to this day that without Allen, maybe the franchise would not have survived.

"If Bill Melton hadn't suffered a herniated disk in the '71 off-season, I believe we would have won the pennant in 1972." Hemond became misty-eyed with that statement, coming straight from his heart.

The many millions who care about Chicago's charter franchise in the American League perhaps get equally emotional when they think of the gratitude which fills their hearts for all that Roland Hemond has given to their team — and to them.

Owner John Allyn (left) never regretted hiring Roland Hemond (right) as his top personnel man. Hemond's trades, paced by Dick Allen, turned the White Sox around in two years.

Photo credit: Leo Bauby Collection

In June 2012, Roland Hemond finally received his 1972 Sporting News MLB Executive of the Year plaque – 40 years later – with Goose Gossage and Dick Allen at his side.

Photo credit: Mike Gustafson, Owner Gustafson Photography
MikeGustafsonPhotography.com

CHAPTER 8

April 18, 1972: Harry Caray's
Outsized Personality Brings
Back the Fans

"The White Sox are coming, tra-la-la-la!"

– Harry Caray on the White Sox Radio Network, 1972

April 18, 1972 — On Opening Day at home in 1972, the Chicago White Sox broke from tradition, albeit inadvertently.

Even decades after installing lights in 1939, the team always held its home opener in the daytime, as did most every other team in the majors. But this year, the season's first pitch took place under the lights at 8:05 p.m., on a balmy early spring evening with temperatures that topped out earlier in the day at 80 degrees.

It wasn't supposed to be this way. The Sox were supposed to open at home on the afternoon of April 6 against the defending AL West champion Oakland A's. But the 13-day players strike, the first ever in pro baseball, obliterated all games before that date. Instead, the opponents were the Texas Rangers, who were starting their inaugural season after spending the last 11 years in Washington as the Senators.

Still, despite the potential fan bitterness after the strike, and even though the Sox lost their first three games to open the season in Kansas City, there was excitement on the South Side for this young team.

Only two years earlier, the Sox drew a measly 11,473 for their Opening Day. But on the Monday before this impromptu Opening Night at Sox Park, window sales were brisk. The team was expecting 20,000 fans — more than the 17,401 who turned up for the strike-delayed Opening Day on a Saturday at Wrigley Field a few days earlier.

Credit Dick Allen and his dynamic first three games in KC — five hits, a couple of key home runs, two spectacular fielding plays and a .417 batting average — as the main reason for the fan interest. The enthusiasm was still somewhat surprising, considering the White Sox lost all three contests, albeit by one run in each.

"We had a fairly good window sale today and most of the talk was about Allen," Tom Maloney, the Sox ticket manager, said. "It's hard to say how many we would have had if we had won those three in Kansas City, as spectacular as Allen was. It would have been terrific."

In the media, teammates prepared White Sox fans for their new superstar.

"(Allen) is very aggressive, he's a very good fielder and he's got the quickest bat I've ever seen," Bill Melton told the *Chicago Tribune's* George Langford on the eve of Opening Day. "He takes the ball right out of the catcher's glove and he's swinging a big (40) ounce bat. His timing is still not there but he's hitting the ball anyway.

"What surprised me was the way he yelled on the bench, encouraging guys, cheering them. Usually some guy who comes over from another ball club isn't like that at first, especially a superstar. There's no doubt in my mind he is for this team first."

For decades, Opening Day at White Sox Park usually was an event where Mayor Richard J. Daley would show up in a box seat with one or two of his sons — sometimes throwing out the first pitch, other times just enjoying the spring return of his cherished team that he had followed since boyhood.

On this night, however, Daley was nowhere to be seen. He had a good excuse. Daley's son, Richard M. Daley (the future mayor of Chicago), was celebrating his upcoming 30th birthday that evening with his father and family at the downtown Tavern Club.

But Daley was also occupied with turmoil and in this election year — a campaign season that would be the Mayor's most challenging of his political career.

During this week in April, Dan Walker — the charismatic independent Democratic nominee for governor -- announced that he would not endorse fellow Democrat Edward Hanrahan in his re-election bid for the Cook County State's Attorney's office. Walker cited Hanrahan's indictment for obstruction of justice in connection with the 1969 law enforcement raid in which the two Illinois Black Panthers were shot and killed.

Walker's decision enraged Daley, who continued to support Hanrahan. "It's unfortunate — you'd think that the Democratic Party would support all their candidates," Daley would say at the time. "The people spoke in an open primary and in positive terms when they nominated Mr. Hanrahan."

Meanwhile, the local media, independent Democrats and conservationists were throwing cold water on Daley's most ambitious public works proposals. One was a superhighway called the Crosstown Expressway which would wrap around and connect the city's south and western edges and bring some economic development. But it would level thousands of homes and businesses in the process. The other was a regional airport, which would be actually built *on* Lake Michigan in the lake, five miles offshore.

Daley was becoming increasingly frustrated with the press. "In your field do you always have to condemn the city?" he asked during a press conference that April week, when he commemorated the 17th anniversary of his election as mayor. "You should start a booster club, and talk about the great things in our city."

The mayor would find refuge on AM radio, where on the Monday before Opening Night he visited conservative radio talk show host Howard Miller.

On his various broadcast pulpits, Miller became even more identified with conservative issues, including raising funds for the police under the command of Hanrahan, who were also indicted for their involvement in the Black Panther killings.

"I don't agree (that) there's a civil war in this country between blacks and whites," Miller would intone on the air. "I think there's a great civil war between the lawbreakers and the law abiders.

"Let the Black woman that covets my school come live next door to my school," was another one of Miller's hot radio takes, this time on school busing.

Daley was a regular listener of Miller's. In fact, Time Magazine called him Miller's "No. 1 fan." So, of course, Daley would make an appearance over the phone on the debut of Miller's WMAQ show before the Sox home opener in 1972. He gave Miller support:

Daley: My family is a constant listener (and) really happy to see you on the air and back giving the information to the people of Chicago and giving it in a very courageous way and in the very kind way that you've always handled yourself on the media.

Miller: Thank you, Mr. Mayor. It's a great honor to hear from you. How is Mrs. Daley and all the children?

Daley: Fine, Howard

Miller: Of course, they're not children anymore, are they?

Daley: Not, they're all getting pretty big and we had another one of them married - Richard - so they're leaving us pretty fast.

WMAQ had recently broadcast the White Sox as well. It was the last home for Sox announcer Bob Elson (aka "The Commander"), the pioneering radio broadcaster for the team going back to 1929. Elson finished his stint on the South Side broadcasting the games on WMAQ from 1967 to 1970, when the station dropped the Sox after low ratings for the bottoming-out season in which the team finished *42 games* out of first place.

Elson, long criticized for a deliberate, almost sonorous outdated style, spent the 1971 season exiled to working Oakland A's games with partner Red Rush. He in effect traded jobs with his dynamic replacement, who by 1972 was starting his second year broadcasting the White Sox on radio. He already had proved a hit with fans in a way Elson never was.

Harry Caray was already respected as one of the great regional sports broadcasters, through his 25-year stint as the St. Louis Cardinals broadcaster on KMOX-Radio, which reached 44 states at night. KMOX's 50,000-watt signal also was augmented by one of the largest team networks in sports with more than

100 affiliates throughout the Midwest, South and Southwest.

But Caray's first-pitch call on this Opening Night between the Sox and Rangers was broadcast on a much smaller scale. Caray and his radio partner, Ralph Faucher, a WTAQ executive, were now on an ad-hoc network of five suburban Chicago stations and nine downstate and Indiana stations, headed by WEAW-FM in Evanston and WTAQ-AM in LaGrange. Sox management had tried to find a downtown successor to WMAQ after 1970. But only WIND, which just had assumed the Chicago Bulls' radio rights, evoked even mild interest.

Caray would have the privilege of calling the first Sox victory of the year. Dick Allen, giving hints of being a more complete player than advertised, received a warm welcome at first and a standing ovation after going 2-for-3 with three runs scored and two RBI. "I think I'm going to like it here… I think I've found a home," he said after the game. Left fielder Carlos May had a stellar night by driving in six runs, while Bill Melton (two singles, two RBI), Pat Kelly (two triples and a double) and Jorge Orta (a double and two singles) also shined. On the mound, Wilbur Wood started and gave up only three hits. The Sox would go on to thrash Texas, 14-0, kicking off a seven-game winning streak.

In his first home broadcast of the year, Caray would gush about Allen:

> *"You know what one of his greatest abilities is? The way he cuts that angle so sharply when he's rounding third base. A lot of other runners take a wide curve and lose time. Richie cuts it off tight and heads for home. He probably saves two or three steps that way."*

But Caray also dealt with one of his early White Sox controversies on this night. With one out left in the game, which was witnessed by 20,944, a fan climbed onto the field to shake hands with Sox outfielders. Soon that one fan became 100, who spilled from the outfield into the Astroturf-covered infield. The game could have been forfeited, but the mostly docile violators left the field once umpire Jim Honochick had public address announcer Bud Kelly ask them to return to their seats.

In the radio booth in the upper deck above home plate, Caray found nothing wrong with the scene.

"All I did was say that (the first fan who walked on the field) looked like a nice young guy who wanted to shake hands with his heroes," Caray testily said to *Chicago Tribune* columnist Robert Markus the next day. "I didn't see anything wrong with that."

But Markus would criticize Caray: "Not only is the White Sox outfield patrolled by pacifists, radio announcer Harry Caray may have given unwitting impetus to the scene that followed."

In a way, it was an early symbol of Caray's unique identification with fans on the South Side which, along with Allen's arrival, was a key factor of resurgence of interest in the White Sox in 1972.

"Everything good that has happened to me has happened as a direct result of something bad."

– Harry Caray from his 1989 autobiography "Holy Cow"

The legend of Caray is now well known, due to his time as a Chicago Cubs broadcaster from 1982 through 1997 on WGN-TV, an early cable television "superstation." Caray's catch phrase "Holy Cow" and his very likeness are now trademarked. He could very well be the most identifiable American sports broadcaster of all time — even now, more than two decades after his death. The broadcaster became so much a part of pop culture that Will Ferrell used his soon-to-be-popular Caray imitation in his successful audition for NBC's "Saturday Night Live" in 1995.

But when Caray started with the White Sox in 1971, he was at a low point in his career.

Born in 1914 as Harry Carabina, he had a deprived childhood in St. Louis, where his father abandoned him and his mother died young: "I never had talked much about my childhood...The human mind has a mechanism that forces you — or enables you, as the case may be — to forget unpleasant experiences. In some sense, it's fortunate — I was not particularly happy then," Caray would later say in his 1989 biography.

After a few years in Joliet, Illinois, and Kalamazoo, Michigan, Carey returned to his native city, starting his 25-year run broadcasting Cardinals games, first on WIL, and eventually on KMOX, where he led a booth which at different times also consisted of first-tier broadcasters like Jack Buck, Joe Garagiola and Milo Hamilton.

"When my dad started, Harry Caray was the main man, and he kind of let my dad know in no uncertain terms that he was the main man," recalled Fox Sports broadcaster Joe Buck in *Sports Illustrated* in 2014. "If there was something big going on in a Cardinals game, he'd tap my dad on the shoulder, and Harry would sit down and (call) it."

Caray would develop his unique, fan-based style in St. Louis — an honest, critical approach which took no prisoners. He was a homer, unafraid of both overwhelming praise for a player and withering critiques. This approach would rankle players and their families.

Rumors about an affair with Susan Busch, wife of Augie Busch, the son of owner Gussie Busch, in 1969 were major distractions. Cardinals management grew tired of Caray and fired him after the 1969 season.

He spent 1970 broadcasting the soon-to-be-dynasty that was the Oakland A's. But Caray — who kept his home in St Louis and refused to move to the Bay Area— wasn't a good match with Charlie Finley. The mercurial, autocratic Finley tried — and failed — to get Harry to change his catch phrase from "Holy Cow" to "Holy Mule," in honor of the team's mascot.

Jack Brickhouse — WGN-TV's longtime Cubs (1947-1981), Bears (1953-1976) and Bulls (1966-1973) announcer — also broadcast the White Sox for 20 seasons (1948-1967). And he remained wired into the front office on the South Side. So "Brick" had heard about the house-cleaning after the 1970 season.

Owner John Allyn tasked recently-promoted Executive Vice President Stu Holcomb to spearhead a top-to-bottom overhaul of the team's off-the-field operations. After directing his attention at the front office with hires of Roland Hemond, Chuck Tanner and others, the radio broadcast booth was next on Holcomb's agenda.

When Caray decided not to return to Oakland for 1971, Holcomb immediately went after him, while also considering other candidates. Newly-hired manager Chuck Tanner and player personnel director Roland Hemond had recommended Hawaii Islanders announcer Al Michaels. then just 26. But owner John Allyn refused to bite, citing Michaels' youth.

Brickhouse, a friend of Harry's, encouraged him to take the White Sox gig.

"He said 'Yes, I know about it. I'm negotiating with them. We're not too close on money," Brickhouse wrote in 1998. "I said to him, 'Harry, lower you sights and come on in. Ordinarily, I don't like your kind of competition. But Chicago is your kind of town."

The cash-strapped Sox could offer Caray only $50,000 to move to Chicago — a $30,000 cut from what he got in Oakland in 1970. So Caray — an inveterate salesman — crafted a deal. For every 100,000 in paid attendance above the 600,000 level, he would get a $10,000 bonus on his base pay of $50,000.

He was hired on Jan. 8, 1971, the same day that Allyn introduced Tanner and Hemond to the Chicago media during its annual midwinter press luncheon at the Bismarck Hotel, and the same day that the team introduced its' vibrant new red-themed uniform, with red pinstripes, red shoes, powder blue road uniforms and bright red numbers on the back.

"Caray is a real pro at the mike, and after 27 years still reflects a fan's enthusiasm," wrote The *Tribune's* David Condon on that winter's day in 1971. "He's more enthusiastic than Elson, probably because Caray had more to be enthusiastic about at St. Louis and Oakland."

But Caray initially had to deal with a broadcast media landscape where the Sox were inconsequential.

On television, the White Sox were in the middle of a five-year deal with WFLD-TV (Channel 32), which had been launched in 1966 by Field Enterprises, with the station paying the Sox $1 million a year in rights fees. But WFLD was a UHF station, which *Broadcasting Magazine* estimated reached only around 42 percent of homes in the metropolitan Chicago when Art Allyn signed the deal in November 1966.

They had left WGN after the 1967 season, after spending nearly 20 years on that powerful Tribune Broadcasting station. The White Sox were tired of playing second fiddle to the Cubs, who routinely had more games broadcast on the station; in 1966, for instance, WGN televised 85 Cubs games to 65 for the Sox.

But that move backfired. As the team continued to slide in the standings, their ratings on WFLD with announcers Jack Drees and successive color analyst partners Dave Martin, Mel Parnell, ex-Sox lefty ace Billy Pierce and Bud Kelly continued to slide, even though the UHF market penetration increased during that time with the purchase of new UHF-equipped sets – particularly homes' first color receivers — and UHF converters acquired for old sets.

On radio, where Caray would be heard exclusively in 1971 and 1972, the situation was even worse.

Even before Elson and Rush left, and after WMAQ abandoned the Sox, no other mainstream radio station wanted to pick them up. For the first time in two decades, the Sox would not have a downtown station beam its games to every part of the area. WCFL-AM had been the team's radio home on AM 1000 from 1952 to 1966, but stopped the broadcasts after it converted to a Top 40 format in mid-1965.

But even that significant drawback did not compare to the on-field problems the White Sox faced going into 1971. The resulting general disinterest forced the team to create its own suburban network of stations. In addition to WEAW-FM in Evanston and WTAQ in LaGrange, the network included WJOL in Joliet (the station where Caray launched his career in the early 1940s), WVFV-FM in Dundee, Ill. and WLNR-FM in Lansing. The network was augmented by nine small stations in downstate Illinois and two Indiana cities which long were bastions for the Sox: Michigan City and South Bend. But the vast majority of the outlets were still on the then-only-emerging FM band, limiting the potential audience. The majority of car radios, on which so much radio listening was done, were still AM-only. FM remained a mere option, selected nowhere near as often as air conditioning or power windows. Plus, many of the Sox' AM affiliates transmitted with low power and partial-direction signals at night, when 65% of their games were played.

Simply put, listeners had to be creative dial-twiddlers to receive Sox broadcasts from the jerry-built network.

In southwest suburban Worth, in the middle of traditional Sox country, then-teenager Tim Cronin had to coordinate his ears and hands. Later a renaissance man as a hockey and golf writer and author, Cronin already had a passion for tuning in distant or weak stations, as a "DXer." So he was not daunted tuning in the Sox.

"WTAQ in La Grange was 5,000 watts nondirectional daytime, 500 watts directional nights," Cronin said. Nights, the signal was decent enough to listen to talk – it was an annual occasion to listen to, and I was happy to hear Ralph Faucher pronounce the names correctly. But a few miles more to the southeast and I'd guess it was gobbled up in the 1300 frequency by a station in Grand Rapids, Michigan.

"I'd listen to the Sox on WTAQ, or WEAW-FM, or WLNR-FM, or WJOL-FM. Or WJOL-AM on weekends. I'd imagine if you were driving through the city and wanted to listen to the game, you had to change several times."

A future award-winning *Chicago Tribune* columnist, Bob Verdi was similarly challenged driving to work in the early 1970s as a young *Tribune* sportswriter.

"I lived about 25 miles north of Chicago," said Verdi, who later worked with Caray on his 1989 autobiography, "Holy Cow." "If I was driving downtown from my home to the office, I would literally have to change stations two or three times to find the White Sox. I could pick up maybe WTAQ, but then it would fade out and I would have to find one of these other little stations that carried the game…which is a crime because this was Harry Caray.

"I remember that one of the sponsors on Harry's pregame show on WTAQ was Zenith. Harry had interviewed a guest, and afterward he thanked the person and then said, for being our guest you'll get this wonderful Zenith radio. I'm not sure you'll be able to pick up one of our games on this radio, but…"

One of the advantages of carriage on the Sox network was cheap airtime. The team paid each outlet $25 per game while retaining the ad revenue. For the "Instant Replay" radio postgame show, Tom Weinberg teamed Roger Wallenstein. "We paid the station around $1 a minute for the airtime," Weinberg recalled. "We didn't make any money at all, because we didn't know anything about selling ads for radio. But on WEAW, we didn't have any listeners anyway."

Weinberg and Wallenstein eventually ran out of money and thus were not fortunate enough to stay on the air for Dick Allen's MVP season in 1972. But while they had access to the microphone, they had the good fortunate of creativity and access. Sox Personnel Director Hemond, Manager Tanner and the majority of players were cooperative, with Hemond taking Wallenstein's post-game call just minutes before the June 15, 1971 trade deadline.

"Instant Replay" was ground-breaking in one respect in the Chicago market. The program had the luxury of time, lasting up to an hour. On WGN, the Cubs' post-game "Scoreboard" show hosted by Vince Lloyd simply recapped the game, aired several audio highlights, ran down other scores and then signed off after 15 minutes in favor of the No. 1-rated station's music programming.

One "Instant Replay" interview generated the only static Weinberg and Wallenstein encountered. Sox executive Leo Breen was angry after hearing a Bob Elson interview critical of his former team. Breen threatened to pull Wallenstein's credentials, but then cooled down. Wallenstein also failed to land Caray himself as an interview. Harry liked to do the pointed questioning, not be the subject of same.

Caray broadcast far above his composite wattage. His style motivated listeners to go to great lengths to hear him loudly and clearly. His mere appearance at White Sox Park immediately energized fans and staff alike.

"When Harry was hired there was excitement in my house because at the time I was married to a fellow who was a huge Cardinals fan," Nancy Faust recalled. "We used to late at night try to tune in his broadcast in St. Louis."

Faust was so excited about Harry's hire that she wrote him a letter welcoming him to the White Sox. His written reply, which was typed on stationery with the letterhead "Harry Caray School of Broadcasting", had this prophetic reply:

March 25, 1971

Dear Ms. Faust:

Thanks for your letter of the 9th. I will look forward to seeing you at the park this summer. You can bet the summer will be anything but dull!

Thanks again.

Sincerely,

Harry

The Harry effect would be seen at the first home game of the 1971 season against Minnesota. The Sox drew just 11,000 fans for their 1970 opener and had five crowds under 1,500. But their paid attendance for Harry's first home game in 1971 was 43,253, the largest Opening Day crowd for the Sox at that time.

Caray's first game-winning call came that day, when the Sox won 3-2 on a Rich McKinney single off Twins reliever Ron Perranoski:

"Perranoski from the belt…the pitch…here it is…Base hit! Left field!
Sox win! Sox win! Holy Cow! The White Sox win!

By the end of 1971, Caray had become a fixture at 35th and Shields. The team, which finished with a 79-83 record, went from 495,355 in attendance to 833,891. And Caray's attendance bonus kicked in — he earned an extra $20,000.

Despite the challenges of broadcasting on an ad-hoc suburban network, by 1972 Caray had established himself as the face of White Sox baseball by embedding himself with the fans, both figuratively and literally. His broadcasts were filled with announcements about who was attending the game, although he reportedly once was duped by a phony note about three well-known attendees:

"Leon Russell, Stephen Stills and Jethro Tull
are here drinking Falstaff."

After 15 years of promoting Budweiser on the St. Louis broadcast, he was now touting the beer served at Sox Park, Falstaff. So his radio broadcasts were filled with shout-outs to Falstaff and the other sponsor, the '70s-era Midwest fast food chain, Chicken Unlimited (*"Crisp on the outside, moist on the inside, marinated with an old family recipe — need I tell you, it tastes delicious"*). Chicken Unlimited was served at the ballpark, giving fans a "dinner option" they did not possess at daytime-only, concessions-short Wrigley Field.

He also resurrected his occasional shirtless broadcasts from the center field bleachers in 1972, a long-ago staple of tropical afternoons at Sportsman's Park in St. Louis. In these faraway cheap seats, he would use his massive butterfly net for 440-foot home runs and mingle endlessly with the fans on-air. Sometimes he'd bring a cooler filled with Falstaff, and hand bottles out to fans.

"Harry was pure show and had a fans' point of view, so he would go through extremes," Weinberg said. "There was no in between with Harry, which is appealing to fans in a way because baseball's not the most important thing in the world, right? So, if you spend a few hours a day or night listening to Harry, it's more relatable than if it's Bob who's just telling you baseball stuff forever."

After home games, Caray would continue courting and networking with fans, celebrities, athletes, business colleagues and just about anybody else who would spot him on Rush Street, the Near North Side thoroughfare which was the capital of Chicago nightlife.

Caray kept a "drinking diary" during 1972, which he used for tax purposes, back when the IRS was more permissive with deductions for "business entertainment," as long as those deductions were documented. The diary lists his daily bar stops along with the names of the people who he presumably would entertain.

The diary shows Harry visiting multiple bars every night — all told, he documented 1,242 bar stops that year. Sully's was his favorite spot (70 visits), while The Key Club (52), Butch McGuire's (32), O'Leary's (29) and Back Room (26) rounded out the top five.

But there were other favorite haunts as well, most of which were on or near Rush Street, then the busiest nightlife strip outside of Las Vegas. Gene & Georgetti's. Eli's. Adolph's. Le Bastille. The Buttery. Sasha's. The Barclay Club. The Four Torches. The Playboy Club. Eugene's. Mon Petit. Tommie O'Leary's Original Key Club. The Acorn On Oak. The Domino. Singapore. Faces. Pepitone's (Part-owned by Cubs first baseman Joe Pepitone).

And Harry's drinking guests were a cross-section of Sox players and coaches, athletes from other teams and sports, announcers and mainstream celebrities. Ted Williams, Wilt Chamberlain, Dick Allen, Bill Melton, Jack Dempsey, Frank Gifford, Dick Enberg, Jack Brickhouse, Gale Sayers, Jack Benny, Don Drysdale — they're all listed in Harry's "drinking diary."

Every day of 1972 lists bar-related activities up to Christmas Day, when he went on a vacation to Acapulco. The endless drinking and networking showcased a diverse group being entertained by Harry:

Tuesday, Jan. 11, 1972 —Butch McGuire's ($9.95), Pub 23 ($8.20), Singapore ($11.80), The Store ($9.10).
Guests: [Broadcasters] Red Rush and Bob Elson; [Comedian] Jack Benny; [Chicago Sun-Times columnist] Irv Kupcinet.
Meals: $18.90. Cabs: $9.95. Tips: $5.75.

Tuesday, April 18, 1972 (Opening Night at Sox Park) - Visits to Millers Pub ($20.00). Palmer House ($10.35). Riccardo's ($9.20).
Guests: [Chicago Sun-Times columnist] Bill Gleason. [Texas Rangers manager] Ted Williams. [Hall of Fame pitcher] Don Drysdale.
Meals: $18.20. Cabs: $7.40. Tips: $6.00.

Wednesday, April 26, 1972 - Signal Key, The Basement ($4.80). The Backroom ($7.75)
Guests: [White Sox players, coaches and front office reps] Dick Allen, Bill Melton, Joe Lonnett, Stu Holcomb.
Meals: $18.25. Cabs: $8.10. Tips: $6.00.

Wednesday, July 5 1972 - Schaller's Pump ($9.20). McCuddy's ($10.05). O'Brien's ($9.85). Key Club ($6.70). Sully's ($9.30)
Guests: [Baltimore Orioles manager] Earl Weaver; [Chicago Tribune

columnist] Dave Condon; [Chicago Bears quarterback] Bobby Douglass.
Meals: $17.77. Cabs: $8.10; Tips: $6.00.

Thursday, August 17, 1972 - Eli's. Faces ($16.80). O'Leary's ($10:75).
Guests: [NBA players] Wilt Chamberlain and Chet Walker.
Meals: $19:45. Cabs: $9.20. Tips: $7.75.

Caray would continue this grueling nighttime ritual for years, often meeting up with surprising characters. Like in 1975, when Sox broadcasters past and present met up at one of Harry's favorite Rush Street spots, Adolph's. *Chicago Tribune Magazine* writer Clifford Terry spotted Caray with none other than Ken "Hawk" Harrelson. Harrelson, the former Red Sox slugger then in his first year in Boston's broadcast booth, was resplendent in a pink sport coat and sunglasses when Harry caught up with him sitting in one of Adolph's booths. "At least you know the right places," Caray joked with Harrelson, as he ordered his trademark hot toddy with J&B, which he used to "soothe his throat."

Bill Sullivan, the former Notre Dame basketball player who owned Sully's, said that Caray was always a gracious guest.

"(One night at Sully's) he was with about four or five guys and I picked up the check," Sullivan recalled in 1998. "The men's room was downstairs at that time and I went to the bathroom and right behind me comes Harry."

"He said, 'Sully, you seem like a nice guy, but I want to tell you something. Don't ever pick up my check or I'll never come back. You can buy me a drink every now and then, but don't pick up my whole check.' So I said, 'Wow, do I love this guy already.' For a sports guy to say that is unbelievable."

Caray also began connecting professionally with Faust in 1972 — a partnership which would create a timeless baseball tradition later in the decade. Harry took an immediate interest in working with Nancy, starting by suggesting the front office move her organ perch from the center field bleachers to the upper deck below the broadcast booth behind home plate before the start of the '72 season.

"Once he knew who I was, he would say, 'They oughta bring her in where she can be with some people, because there weren't many fans out there (in center field)," Faust remembered 50 years later.

Soon, they began playing off each other during the games.

"I had the advantage of having visual contact with Harry," she recalled. "If the timing was right in the middle of the game and things were going right for the White Sox, I'd catch his eye and go into something like 'Rock Around the Clock' or 'Jailhouse Rock'. He'd start dancing."

Faust would also listen to Harry's broadcast via transistor radio and make sly musical comments about what Caray had just said on the broadcast.

"I remember once (during a slow game) he said, 'This game is a drag and they're going to have to carry me out of here'. When I heard him say 'carry', I played 'Carry Me Back to Old Virginny'. And he made it a point to say 'Well, even the organist agrees!'"

This connection would eventually lead to the two of them performing a sing-along version of "Take Me Out To the Ballgame." Legend has it that Bill Veeck heard Harry privately singing along with Nancy's playing of the song during the seventh-inning stretch at games in 1976. Hearing this, Veeck surreptitiously installed a public address microphone in the booth and turned it on when Caray began singing the song. When Caray asked Veeck about this, the maverick owner is said to have replied:

"Harry, I've been looking for 45 years for the right man to sing this song. Everybody, no matter where they were sitting, as soon as they heard you, they knew they could sing better than you, so they'd join in."

By 1977, the song became a staple at Comiskey Park — and it would continue as a treasured tradition after Caray took it with him to Wrigley Field in 1982.

At Comiskey, he would always begin the song with a shout-out to Faust: "Alright, Nancy!" For years at Wrigley Field, it was "Alright, Gary (Pressey)!"

"Harry made a big difference, I believe, in my career because he became aware of my music," Faust said.

Caray would often ask her to drive him to Rush Street or the Ambassador East — the hotel where he resided when in Chicago.

"Harry couldn't drive," Faust recalled. "But he'd say, 'Hey, can I have a lift?' A few times, we'd go out for an after-game dinner before I dropped him off. He liked to go to Gene and Georgetti's (a famous Chicago steak house which opened in 1941). I remember him being very fussy about food. And I knew nothing. I'm happy with McDonalds, you know. But he wanted his tomatoes just so on a plate with cream cheese on the side. He was quite a food connoisseur. And he'd share his feelings about the game and management."

Caray also made a connection with Dick Allen in 1972. His fever-pitch calls to go with Dick's heroics were unmatched. Caray provided the soundtrack to perhaps the season's thrilling moments, such as Aug. 23, in a Wednesday afternoon home game against the Yankees, which would lift the Sox into first place, a half-game in front of the Oakland A's.

With the Sox up 3–2 in the seventh inning, Allen stepped to the plate against veteran reliever Lindy McDaniel, a forkballer who had toiled for the Cubs a decade earlier. Caray was broadcasting shirtless from the bleachers with his butterfly net located to his right:

"… Two balls. No strikes. Now the pitch. Here it is. THERE IS A LONG DRIVE…DEEP CENTER…WAY BACK… IT MIGHT BE … COULD BE… ALMOST INTO THE NET. Hol-l-ly Cow! Richie Allen hit it into the center field stands. I almost got it with my net. It hit a fan's hands right in front of me. Never has a ball been hit any further. Hol-l-ly Cow! A home run with a man on. The White Sox now lead 5-2!"

But Caray also could be hyper-critical of even the best players. Former *Tribune* assistant sports editor Bob Vanderberg wrote of this moment from 1972, when Dick was going through one of his rare mini-slumps and tapped out weakly to the pitcher, prompting this response from Caray:

"Little tap, easy out. And it's none of my business, but it sure looks to me like Richie Allen could use a little batting practice. And he didn't set any speed records running down to first base either."

Other stars like Wilbur Wood weren't shielded from Caray's withering criticism, either. Late in September of '72, after Wood had already won 24 games, he had a meltdown in a game against the division-leading A's in Oakland. Harry wasn't having it:

"Biggest game of the year and our best pitcher doesn't have a THING out there."

Third baseman Bill Melton was a main target of Caray's ire. The power hitter could be prone to slumps — and when he was in a slump and was fooled at the plate on a bad pitch, then Caray could be merciless: *"Struck him out and made him look HORR-ible."*

"Looking back, he was very hypercritical of all of the players," Melton recalled 50 years later. "Sometimes I couldn't leave the parking lot because people would be out there calling me every name in the book and stuff like that. And that (negativity) came from Harry."

Caray's criticisms of Melton continued to the end of the latter's Sox career, culminating with a shouting match between the two in a Milwaukee hotel lobby in 1975. The announcer also was tough on young manager Tony La Russa in 1979-81, so much so that La Russa declined a request for remembrances of Caray on his death in 1998. La Russa remembered he was struggling to establish himself as a manager, and Caray was cruelly judgmental under the circumstances.

Clubhouse attendant Jim O' Keefe remembers a basic rule that Chuck Tanner had for him. "Back in '72, there was one radio in the whole clubhouse," O'Toole said. "After a loss, we had to shut the radio off because Harry Caray was one of the announcers back then and if there's a loss you just had to turn it off. There was one time after a loss, when I turned off the radio. (Centerfielder) Rick Reichardt came in and said, "Turn the radio on." And (reserve outfielder) Jay Johnstone was like, "Leave the radio off," because it was Harry Caray ripping the team. That was their little spat, and Tanner diffused that really quick, and the radio stayed off."

While Caray was always critical of players, he never backed down from those athletes he criticized. "If he ever said anything about you, and he heard you were looking for him, he was right there for you," former Cardinals catcher and longtime Milwaukee Brewers broadcaster Bob Uecker said in 1998. "He'd come walking into the clubhouse, he'd stick his face right in your face. He was not embarrassed to put his face in your face and say, 'You got a problem with something I said?'"

He was singularly identified with White Sox baseball by the mid-1970s and Caray eventually came to be seen by some as bigger than the team. But Dick Allen's sudden departure near the end of the 1974 season and declining Sox performance (with plummeting attendance) in 1975 set a negative tone around the franchise. Bob Waller, Caray's partner on new (UHF) rightsholder WSNS in 1973-74 was a little too candid for the Sox' tastes. His replacement for 1975, former Sox and Cubs catcher J.C. Martin, was too cornpone.

Caray and the Sox seemed ready for a divorce as owner John Allyn had trouble making the final player payroll as 1975 concluded. But even getting fired by the team didn't stick. Allyn announced on Oct. 1, 1975 that Harry would not be back the following season if he still owned the team. Allyn had heard one complaint too many from Tanner and players about his caustic style.

But Bill Veeck announced his intention to buy back the Sox two days after Allyn's announcement, and Harry was just the man to helm the Baseball Barnum Veeck's bread-and-circuses game presentation. By 1977, he was paired with outspoken former outfielder Jimmy Piersall on radio and TV — a teaming which would produce some of the most unfiltered, outrageous baseball broadcasts of the time. Caray and Piersall produced guerilla theater on the air.

Despite the sometimes-outlandish work with Piersall, Caray always maintained his ability to describe the game with alacrity, drama and color.

"Harry fits in with our group," Veeck told *Sports Illustrated* in 1978. "He fits in with our philosophy and style, which is casual, even raucous. Our audience is not at all like the Cubs', which is mostly youngsters and people over 50. Ours comes from the 16-to-40 age bracket. They are as exuberant as any I've ever seen, and a great part of that is Harry. Can you envision Dodger fans standing up in the middle of a game to cheer Vin Scully the way they cheer Harry here? He says what he believes on the air, and the fans identify directly with him.

"Frankly, I hate to listen to him when we're losing because he can put the greatest degree of contempt in what he's saying. It's more than popularity. It's a matter of texture. Harry is basically one of the fans. He drinks beer with them or whatever else is available. He talks to them in saloons, which is good. But he's also a professional who does his homework. He's not merely flamboyant."

Caray even managed to get into a feud with future Major League baseball commissioner Bud Selig. The then-Brewers owner refused to allow him to sing "Take Me Out To The Ballgame" during a White Sox visit to County Stadium in 1978, a series which was routinely popular with Chicago fans. Of course, Selig welcomed the cash flow generated by the visiting boosters.

"It just shows you how petty Mr. Selig is," Caray would tell the Milwaukee Journal. "We bring up 10,000 fans here and they won't let us use the P.A." Selig would respond to the Journal: "All Harry Caray cares about is Harry Caray … we've been here nine years and, the Lord willing, we'll be here many years after Harry Caray has left the Chicago scene."

As it turns out, Caray would never leave Chicago. But eventually, he would move on from the South Side…and soften his style in the process.

After serving one year under new Sox owners Jerry Reinsdorf and Eddie Einhorn in 1981 — a year when the Sox would return to WGN-TV — Caray decided to move on. He didn't want to be part of a new pay-TV operation for the majority of games starting in 1982. Behind the scenes, he never established a rapport with Reinsdorf. So he cut a deal with Tribune Broadcasting CEO Jim Dowdle to broadcast the Cubs. Both Dowdle and new Cubs general manager Dallas Green laid down a law with Caray — that he tone down his criticisms of the team and its players.

Caray joined the Cubs in 1982 and became a broadcasting legend, using many of his staples that he developed during his time with the White Sox, including the singing of "Take Me Out To The Ballgame" during the seventh inning stretch. He became bigger than ever in his dotage via the WGN superstation's worldwide reach, eventually broadcasting the games like everyone's slightly-rambunctious great-uncle, through age 83. One day on the road, fans massed to clamor for autographs while Andre Dawson, Ryne Sandberg and Mark Grace posed for a photo. Suddenly, Caray appeared nearby. The gaggle of fans all rushed away from the star players toward the Pied Piper of Wrigley Field.

Caray's play-by-play prime was long past, but his presence carried the day and kept Middle America tuned in – and singing along in the seventh inning. A series of guest announcers, including Bill Murray and Jack Buck, filled in while Caray was sidelined from a stroke in 1987. Near the end of the 1988 season, President Ronald Reagan dropped by for a guest stint in the booth with Caray.

He almost overpowered the broadcasts themselves. To kids, he was almost a ubiquitous cartoon character. When a toddler saw Caray partner Steve Stone do his standup on a telecast circa 1985, she cried, "That's a Harry Caray!"

How much was the sometimes-doddering Caray the centerpiece in his final years? On July 13, 1995, with the game time 7 p.m. temperature 104 degrees at Wrigley Field amid Chicago's infamous killer heat wave, the upstairs press box lunchroom was out of ice. The heat had not melted the ice. Rather, all was collected to cool towels to place around Caray's neck in the stifling TV booth. The show had to go on with an octogenarian as its star.

At Caray's funeral in 1998, Dowdle said he and Caray negotiated Caray's salary every year at a table in the Pump Room of the Ambassador East Hotel. "No lawyers, no written contract, just a handshake."

"He led more fans to the ballpark than any other announcer in the history of baseball," Dowdle said.

Caray, honored with the Ford C. Frick Award at the Baseball Hall of Fame in 1989, may have done his most important work leading fans back to the ballpark in his earliest days with the White Sox by helping to engender more fan interest in a team which had been dangerously close to moving out of town.

Don Zminda, who authored *The Legendary Harry Caray* biography in 2019, quoted baseball broadcasting bard Bob Costas expertly analyzing Harry's modus operandi while meeting him after hours in the mid-1980s:

"God knows how many Budweisers he'd had, and I'm just a guy in my early 30s and I couldn't remotely keep up with him. And at one point I said to him, half-jokingly, kind of surveying this scene and all this adoration, 'So Harry, what's this all about?' And he goes, 'What's it all about, kid? I'll tell you what it's all about; booze, broads, baseball and bullshit. That pretty much sums it up.' Well, that…and saving a franchise along the way."

Bill Melton — who became a pre- and post-game broadcaster for the White Sox after his career ended — just wishes that he could have experienced the kinder, gentler Harry who broadcast the Cubs.

"He was a great announcer, no question about it," Melton said. "But he became beloved at Wrigley Field because he changed his attitude. He talked more about the goodness of a player, even when he was going bad. His attitude changed, and he wasn't ripping organizations or players."

"To me, that's when he became a Hall of Fame broadcaster."

Harry Caray had begun his shirtless broadcasts from the bleachers in tropical St. Louis. But Harry became even more a cult figure stripped to the waist in center field at Comiskey Park, waving his fishnet at a Dick Allen homer landing nearby on Aug. 23, 1972.

Photo courtesy of the Chicago Tribune/TCA

Harry Caray (left) and 1971-72 broadcast partner Ralph Faucher in their Comiskey Park radio booth. A WEAW sign was likely used because the Evanston FM station was the only one whose signal reached the entire Chicago market.

Photo credit: Leo Bauby Collection

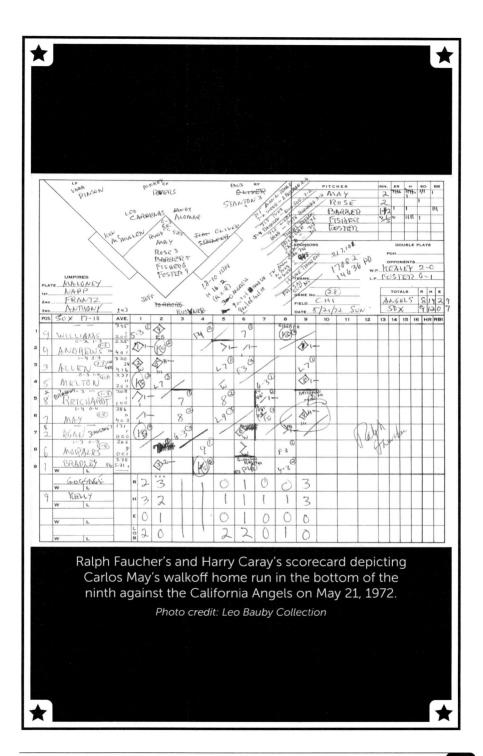

Ralph Faucher's and Harry Caray's scorecard depicting Carlos May's walkoff home run in the bottom of the ninth against the California Angels on May 21, 1972.

Photo credit: Leo Bauby Collection

In 1972, Harry Caray became a powerful beacon in his second year in Chicago. Harry attracted listeners despite a low-wattage radio network that challenged fans seeking to tune in.

Photo credit: Leo Bauby Collection

CHAPTER 9

A Century-Long Battle to Get 'Above the Fold'

Dick Allen's broad shoulders did far more than just power the under-manned White Sox into a stirring race against the would-be dynastic Oakland Athletics.

Through his ICBM-range home run feats and team-player personality that belied all the controversies of his past, Dick was banner headline news in 1972. He single-handedly boosted the White Sox narrative to "above the fold," getting top billing in Chicago's newspaper sports sections, the lead story on TV and radio sportscasts and even one of the all-time most memorable covers of *Sports Illustrated*.

By taking over the media flow from the crosstown Cubs, established in their raucous Leo Durocher Era, Dick blasted past structural disadvantages relating to the North Siders and Sox ownership blunders. He staked out the high ground in Chicago's consciousness. Had Allen's and other Sox injuries not sidetracked 1972's momentum in subsequent years, the Sox could have achieved parity with a Cubs franchise that went into eclipse in mid-summer 1973.

The Sox defied experts in Allen's MVP season and defied the ingrained deficits in the Chicago baseball marketplace that originally were out of their control.

The South Side team founded at the turn of the century operated in the only two-team market in which one franchise played all its home games during the day, while the other steadily increased its night schedule from the 1940s to the 1970s. A team easier on both print and broadcast deadlines will get more than its fair share of coverage, no matter its won-lost record.

But successive financially-strapped Sox ownerships were also competing against a true corporate kingpin in Philip K. Wrigley ("P.K."), chairman of the Wrigley Gum Company. Personally writing many of his Spearmint and Doublemint advertising pieces, Wrigley was a firm advocate of free promotion for the baseball team and cozy ballpark he inherited from father William Wrigley, Jr. Remembering the blanket radio coverage at no cost to stations permitted by the elder Wrigley and team president William L. Veeck, Sr., P.K. Wrigley opened the doors wide to TV exposure for the Cubs at the dawn of the medium in 1946, at first with no official rights fees and then below-market rates for the televising outlets.

The Chicago White Sox had no comparable broadcast policy, though they shared the bully pulpit of Chicago broadcast sports — WGN-TV — for 20 years. And yet, in a move which sacrificed exposure for dollars, owner Arthur Allyn jumped his WGN deal to snare $1 million in annual rights fees from UHF outlet WFLD-TV. The fledgling station reached only half the TV households as WGN and never lived up to its initial ambitious programming promises.

Even while still on sometimes snowy UHF TV and that cobbled-together radio network of only small suburban stations, Dick Allen's accomplishments resounded like a big boom in the market. He was promoted by a voluble Harry Caray playing way above the wattage of his radio outlets and backed up by owner John Allyn, who saved the Sox at the beginning and end of his tenure.

If Charles Comiskey's banishment of the scandalous Black Sox in late 1920 — sealed for all time the following year by new commissioner Kenesaw Mountain Landis — was the franchise's low point, then the sorry narratives of 1968-70 and the ownership bungling leading up to the multiyear disaster were a close second.

At old Comiskey Park, the largest crowd in 1969 was 33,000 for the Boys Benefit game against the hyper-popular Cubs. For an American League game? Some 15,000 and change for a doubleheader against the front-running Baltimore Orioles in June. Successive home openers in 1968-69 drew just under 8,000 and 11,000, respectively. Season attendance plunged to near bottom-of-the-Great Depression levels.

The White Sox were breaking Arthur Allyn parent company's (Artnell) bank, in the wrong way. The future "dean" of Chicago baseball writers, Jerome Holtzman, reported in late 1969 the Sox had lost $500,000 in 1968 and perhaps $1 million in 1969, with the WFLD rights payouts saving them from an even deeper hole. As a comparison, the 1969 Cubs showed a nearly $1 million profit, a requirement for Wrigley to put money back into the ballpark and team operations. If Wrigley had poured his *personal* fortune into the Cubs, the Sox' status in Chicago might have become truly untenable in this environment.

Much, but not all, was cured by Dick Allen's strongman baseball feats. He boosted the Sox' popularity, thus moving them forward several logical preliminary steps to regain some pre-eminence in Chicago. And yet a slew of locked-in factors, most established long before any of the 1972 principals had reached maturity, would continue to present challenges for the Sox in decades to come. Allen simply moved the South Side bar higher and kept the wolf farther away from the door.

The story of how the Sox got to their dire situation, requiring Allen's rescue operation, dates back almost to the Black Sox. The franchise, a two-time World Series entrant in 1917 and 1919, was considered the strongest in the American League when Shoeless Joe Jackson headlined a platoon of talent banished to baseball's blacklist for fixing the 1919 Series. No team can easily recover from such a purge.

So for decades after 1920, the Sox wandered in the American League netherworld of also-rans. In the 30 seasons following 1920, the Sox finished under .500 21 times, got as a high as third just twice and had a peak season of 86 wins. The almost-unbroken dynasty of the New York Yankees might as well have existed on Mars, that lofty level was so far off in the distant standings.

The Sox simply did not possess the financial and player-procurement ability to match the Bronx Bombers, man-for-man. Three generations of the Comiskey family did their duty to keep the franchise going, but not much more beyond the addition of lights at Comiskey Park in 1939. The ballpark began to suffer from wear and tear due to ownership's financial negligence or shortchanging of annual maintenance and upkeep.

Eight miles north at Wrigley Field, dynamic team president Veeck assembled a powerful contender led by Hack Wilson and Rogers Hornsby that established a major league attendance record of nearly 1.5 million in 1929. Ladies Days pioneered by the Cubs packed as many as 51,000 into 36,000-seat Wrigley Field. The Cubs never won it all during this period, but they booked a Fall Classic berth like clockwork every three years from 1929 to 1938 before falling into a 1940s rut. Their decline was due in no small part to Veeck's premature death from leukemia at age 56 in 1933 and the inability of Philip Wrigley to replace his day-to-day leadership.

Despite the two Chicago baseball franchises' unequal financial and artistic standings, they shared equality in media profiles of the era.

All local daily newspapers staffed both teams for coverage, home and road. The baseball writer's job was considered the most elite, as he rode the rails with the team from Boston to St. Louis, sharing drinks and card games with the players. Print accounts of games, allowing fans to peruse daily box scores and the Sunday averages with a fine-tooth comb, was the primary way of following the Chicago Cubs and White Sox.

Wielding a ruler to measure column inches, Bill Veeck complained loudly in the late 1970s that the Cubs generated more ink than the Sox in the daily papers. But the Baseball Barnum realized exactly what he was doing. He'd generate Sox publicity simply by opening his mouth. And Veeck knew that the winning team in town would get more coverage — "above the fold" of the *Chicago Tribune* and other broadsheet papers or "on the back page" of the *Sun-Times*, along with the *Chicago Today* tabloids. He also comprehended that the Cubs had the built-in coverage advantage playing all home games during the day — which left more time before newspaper and broadcast deadlines.

Time to prepare print stories and produce sportscasts was much tighter off an 8 p.m. White Sox night game when morning papers scrambled to get game accounts into the home-delivered editions and TV stations wound down for the night.

If both Chicago teams were winning or interesting, newspapers would devote roughly the same resources, depending on their game times' relationship to the deadlines of that day. Conversely, both teams would receive less coverage if they were out of the race in the final month. The downtown papers would pull their writers off the road, while deploying backup scribes to cover some of the remaining home games.

The *Tribune*, in particular, prided itself on covering every Big Ten football game, dispatching their baseball writers to all parts of the Midwest to complete the blanket of correspondents, and shorting baseball of first-string journalistic talent. The sight of Bob "Lefty" Logan covering a Cubs-Padres twi-night doubleheader in San Diego off *Tribune* sports editor Cooper Rollow's office TV set on Aug. 30, 1974, could not be forgotten by a stunned witness getting his start in journalism. Logan's Page Two story in the sports section revealed a common fib from newspapers to their readers in these good ol' days: A San Diego dateline with "*Special to the Tribune*" credit.

But the Sox in mid-century were never shortchanged by the city's sports *columnists*. Pro-Sox opinionists always had a clear plurality in the market.

Depicted with a big stogie in his column photo, adopted South Sider Condon, a New Mexico native and former Notre Dame tennis player, was wired into the city's sports elite. He broke stories of ownership changes and resignations, such as John Allyn's elevation in Sox ownership in 1969 and Stu Holcomb's forced departure in mid-1973. But in the process of huddling with the rich and powerful, Condon rarely criticized his subjects, most jarringly during a Wrigley Building lunch in August 1968. Boothmate Phil Wrigley astoundingly said sometimes an owner would prefer to finish second due to the stresses of winning, among other nonsensical proclamations. No skeptical or questioning words came from Condon in the resulting column.

Condon also injected himself into the stories, such as posing for handshakes with John Allyn at his ownership announcement in a lead *Tribune Sports* front page photo. After hoisting a few the night before with Charlie Finley, another confidant, Condon donned a blond wig and draped a pantsuit over his 260-pound frame. He mimicked Morganna the Kissing Bandit, to buss the A's Joe Rudi at first base (generating a five-photo sequence on the *Tribune Sports* front page) July 2, 1970 at Comiskey Park. Ethics and professionalism were far different a half-century ago.

Native South Sider Bill Gleason, a Parker High School alum, confined his whimsy to columns in the afternoon *Chicago's American* and the morning tabloid *Sun-Times* before finishing his career with the suburban *Daily Southtown* in the 1990s. In 1974, Gleason founded the well-remembered "Sportswriters" on WGN Radio, later syndicated on TV. He positioned himself as the advocate of the beer-drinking South Side fans. He'd write that "all Cubs fans come from Peoria because that's where their broadcasters come from" while excusing the team's stumblebum baseball-operations mismanagement as Phil Wrigley playing jokes on fans and media.

The sainted afternoon *Daily News*, a "writers' paper", was led by White Sox-friendly John P. Carmichael with his Barber Shop column and John Justin Smith. Carmichael went to work for the Sox after his retirement from newspapering. Jerome Holtzman, Chicago's most famous beat writer for the *Sun-Times* and *Tribune* who'd eventually serve as Major League Baseball's official historian, grew up as a Sox fan on Chicago's West Side in the 1930s.

Only Rick Talley, hailing from far downstate Pinckneyville in Whitey Herzog country, was an avowed Cubs fan. Talley did not arrive in town until 1968 to become lead sports columnist of the American, then its successor tabloid, *Chicago Today*.

The work of Mike Royko, the greatest Chicago columnist of them all, did not appear on the sports pages. But he was local journalism's biggest professed Cubs fan. Royko sometimes played the Cubs for laughs with alter ego Slats Grobnik and his team quizzes. Yet in his Page 3 role in the *Daily News*, and later in the *Sun-Times* and *Tribune*, Royko mostly wrote about Major Richard J. Daley's Democratic machine and the absurdities of politics and society. He could not focus on sports.

Royko was the one journalist in Chicago who'd have been immune to top editors' pressure if he decided to rain holy hell upon the meddlesome Phil Wrigley and his incompetent baseball operation. The fact that Royko simply settled for "wait 'til next year" Cubs-fan suffering, humor and combining with Condon to create the billy-goat curse was a gigantic missed opportunity. After Royko died in 1997, his columnist role was handed to native South Sider John Kass, a dyed-in-the-wool Sox fan who occasionally wrote about the team.

Complementing the era's primacy of print were words wafting through the ether – radio play-by-play. One of the few booming businesses in the Great Depression, giving 1932 college graduate Ronald Reagan immediate employment, radio provided blanket coverage of both the Cubs and White Sox in an era before either team's ballpark had lights. The all-daytime schedules were perfect, not pre-empting any network prime-time dramas or comedy shows. In the first two decades of baseball on radio, both Chicago teams' broadcast exposure was equal.

Veeck, Sr., William Wrigley Jr., and Phil Wrigley were particular advocates of the free promotion radio afforded, noting the license plates of out-of-state cars parked around Wrigley Field. No rights fees were charged, and by 1931, as many as seven stations carried the Cubs simultaneously. Road games were covered only via Western Union ticker studio re-creations.

WGN, WMAQ and WCFL, which became exclusive White Sox outlets at various times from 1952 onward, carried the South Siders in radio's golden age. Also setting up microphones at Comiskey Park were WBBM, WIND and WJJD, all of which would be exclusive Sox radio outlets later in the 20th and earlier in the 21st centuries. Bob Elson began his four-decade Sox announcing career on WGN in 1930. A decade later, Elson summoned Peoria's Jack Brickhouse to a WGN announcing job. Brickhouse immediately began covering the Sox.

When WGN-Radio dropped out of baseball broadcasts after 1943 due to commitments to late-afternoon network children's programming on the Mutual Network, Brickhouse switched to WJJD, in its first full year in 1945 as the Sox' main radio outlet for day games. He spent the '45 season filling in for Elson (absent due to U.S. Navy service) before moving on for one season of broadcasting the baseball Giants in New York.

With wartime restrictions on materials lifted and veterans returning in 1946, Chicago's first commercial TV station, WBKB (Channel 4) began dabbling in new programming. Station chief Capt. William Eddy, a technical wizard for the times, pushed the boundaries of his primitive equipment and experimenting small staff. The most attractive local sports programming was the defending National League champion Cubs from Wrigley Field.

Eddy sent his mobile unit to Wrigley Field for a hoped-for inaugural telecast of the Cubs' home opener against Musial and the Cardinals on April 20, 1946. But electrical interference from elevators in the station's 190 N. State St. headquarters interfered with the remote signal, and the game never aired. Working out the bugs and employing two cameras, Eddy's crew finally transmitted the July 13, 1946 game against the Dodgers to the small number of sets in offices, homes and bars. He would have no trepidation from Phil Wrigley, a mechanical tinkerer who likely was fascinated by the new video technology.

Eddy pushed the envelope even further in 1947. He televised a full home schedule of Cubs games with announcers "Whispering Joe" Wilson and Brickhouse, working for $35 a game in his return to Chicago. The games televised included Jackie Robinson's Chicago debut on Sunday, May 18, 1947, drawing a record Wrigley Field paid crowd of more than 47,000. The Robinson game was the only scheduled telecast for WBKB that day.

WBKB also televised the home games of the defending NFL champion Bears from Wrigley Field and soon-to-be champion Cardinals from Comiskey Park. Complete Blackhawks games from Chicago Stadium, in the years before the home TV-averse Arthur and Bill Wirtz, also signed on for first puck drops at 8:30 p.m. Eddy also rigged up a microwave relay system, using his property in

Michigan City for the last leg across Lake Michigan to the Chicago studio, to televise Frank Leahy's powerful Notre Dame Fighting Irish team.

Through all the innovations and curiosities from sports operators, the one significant absentee from WBKB was the Sox. WBKB televised no games from the South Side in 1947. Any conversations between the parties have been lost to history. But the likely narrative was a Comiskey ownership not yet receptive to TV. If Eddy could have gotten the Sox' approval, he might have sent his mobile unit to 35th and Shields despite any technical challenges.

Brickhouse apparently had better luck with the Sox when he helped sign on WGN-TV as Chicago's second station in April 1948. As sports director of his station, he corralled the Cubs for a full home schedule of telecasts to compete with WBKB, while persuading the Sox to air both day and night games, the latter usually once or twice per homestand. Baseball games were a perfect attraction for male-demographic sponsors like beer, gasoline and cigarettes, and filled airtime during the day when the stations normally were off the air. But the matinee games had the added benefit of women at home and watching, too.

After production costs were cleared, Cubs games promised profits for WBKB, WGN and ABC-owned WENR, making live Wrigley Field telecasts a threesome for 1949. The *Sporting News* reported Phil Wrigley did not charge any of the stations a formal rights fee. Instead, he levied a $100,000 "construction cost" for the new ballpark. Wrigley thus laid the foundation for medium and long-term media success.

The Cubs dropped into the second division in 1947 after a third-place finish the previous season, the first year of televised baseball. They were an embarrassing 64-win last-place team in 1948 and even worse with 61 cellar-dwelling victories in '49. But in the post-war attendance boom, with returning veterans having not yet made their exodus to the suburbs further from urban ballparks, the drooping Cubs drew more than 1.3 million per season in 1946-47 and more than 1.2 million in the disastrous 1948 campaign. Broadcast exposure likely helped build interest in the Cubs. In contrast, the Sox had yet to produce a one million season gate, and wouldn't until 1951, when Minnie Minoso's arrival helped touch off the fabled Go-Go Era.

The healthy Cubs attendance for the post-war times no doubt was the final nail in the coffin for any Phil Wrigley plans to install lights. Wrigley originally planned to light up his ballpark for the 1942 season, likely in response to the White Sox having installed their own light towers in 1939 and outdrawing the Cubs with first-division teams in 1940 and 1941. Cubs home attendance plummeted almost 40% from 1938 to 1941. But soon after Pearl Harbor on Dec. 7, 1941, Wrigley donated the steel for his towers to the war effort.

With the all-daytime home schedule, Wrigley thus set up the Cubs as a destination for female fans and kids, arriving on public transportation at Clark and Addison and not needing a male escort, as might be needed to attend at night. Meanwhile, the entire televised homestands offered bloc counter-programming for the usual daytime diet of soap operas, game shows and old movies that would develop through the 1950s.

WBKB and WENR did not pick up any White Sox games with WGN remaining the sole video outlet. And the lure of the Cubs' post-1945 ballpark attraction was strongest enough for WGN, which maintained a substantial newsreel operation. Throughout 1949, the station ran a nightly 15-minute show, using film shot each game day at Wrigley Field and narrated by Brickhouse. WGN promoted the show with large ads in *TV Forecast*, the forerunner of TV Guide. Watching filmed highlights after dinner from that day's game must have seemed like a Buck Rogers-type innovation for TV set owners in 1949.

And yet, with the same day-game first-pitch times as the Cubs and distance and deadlines for editing film from Comiskey Park the same as Wrigley Field, no similar newsreel WGN program was televised for the many Sox day games. The footprint for the Sox' broadcast-coverage disadvantage compared to the Cubs was being established. The Cubs highlights show was dropped for 1950, when NBC-owned WNBQ (Channel 5) aired "Today's Ballgame" with film at 10:30 p.m. weeknights.

In 1950, Chicago White Sox night games disappeared from WGN's schedule after two years of faithfully televised late-starting (8:30 p.m.) games. Radio was also Sox-dark, with WJJD signing off at Mountain Time sunset due to its 1160 AM frequency also being used by full-time, 50,000-watt KSL Radio in Salt Lake City. All Sox day games continued on WGN in 1950.

In the immediate post-war era, throughout baseball, teams staged a limited schedule of night games, specifically to boost a gate that was often skimpy for weekday contests. In 1949, when the Sox drew 937,000 at home — second-highest total in franchise history — night games against the Yankees, Indians and Red Sox attracted respectable crowds. But others involving tail-enders like the Browns, Senators and Athletics sometimes drew private gatherings as low as 2,000. The mindset of management, now led by general manager Frank "Trader" Lane, obviously centered on protecting the gate.

Sure enough, as the 1950s progressed, Friday night games at Comiskey Park often were the top draws of homestands, sometimes passing 40,000 as working fans liberated from factories and offices looked at the 8 p.m. starts as their "TGIF" outing.

Mid-20th century baseball's view of night games, starting at 8 p.m. or later compared to as early as 6 or 6:30 p.m. today, centered around a common concept: The average working man would go home, eat dinner and then go back to the ballpark. As late as 1968, the *Chicago Tribune's* George Langford wrote of poor attendance at Athletics games in their first season at Oakland from that same standpoint — fans were unwilling to battle traffic on freeways to go to the newly-built Coliseum after first going home. Owners and their adjutants obviously did not want potential ticket-buyers to leave their dinner tables and then put their feet up on the ottoman to watch the game free on TV instead going back out to spin the turnstiles.

For those not dashing home before a night out at the ballpark, the Sox connected with nearby restaurants to encourage the "dinner and a ballgame" routine.

"Their marketing told them, we cater to businessmen (for night games)," recalled four-decade veteran Chicago baseball reporter Bruce Levine of WSCR-Radio, who grew up in the middle-class South Shore neighborhood in the 1950s. "Allow them time to have dinner, come to the ballpark, it's an 8 p.m. game which is over in less than 2½ hours. The Sox had relationships with restaurants (such as Mama Batts on Cermak Road) on the South Side – some advertised in team publications. They supplied interest and bought tickets. They were quasi-partners."

When Comiskey Park was ready to stage its final game on Sept. 30, 1990, *Tribune* sportswriter/editor Steve Nidetz recalled attending his first Sox game in 1959 after having dinner at Mama Batt's, spying Bob Elson by the bar.

Another Mama Batt's memory came from Mark Schultz, an uncommon Sox fan hailing from Chicago's Far North Side Rogers Park neighborhood. With his mother and sister in tow, Mark's father Sol Schultz took the group to the eatery before the younger Schultz's first Sox game, a night contest against Cleveland, in 1965.

Night games were indeed outings as the Fifties settled in. Thus, Chicago baseball on TV was a daytime-only production by 1952, when the local TV market had been winnowed down to just WGN. With a horribly-miscast Rogers Hornsby as lead announcer, WENR-TV had also dropped the Cubs after one season, mindful of its cash-strapped ABC parent in New York. "Whispering" Joe Wilson and WBKB televised the Cubs through 1951, then dropped baseball as CBS, for whom WBKB had become the primary Chicago affiliate, expanded its daytime programming.

As Brickhouse's "Hey Hey" home run call became a staple over the years, thanks to his crew originally bringing the unconscious outcry to his attention, the Tribune Company-owned WGN-TV baseball schedule differed from the majority of big-league franchises.

Among notable exceptions was New York, which had extensive televised baseball from the medium's beginning. The Dodgers locked up WOR-TV (Channel 9) for themselves, airing all home games and a considerable road game schedule. The Yankees and Giants shared WPIX-TV, Channel 11 (also owned by Tribune Company), for home games. After the Dodgers and Giants fled to the West Coast, the expansion Mets took over WOR for most home games and the majority of road games. The Yankees then had WPIX exclusively, with most home games and a now higher road-game count.

In contrast, in Los Angeles, the Dodgers for many years televised only games from rival San Francisco on KTTV (Channel 11) while the expansion Angels aired a greater number of road games on owner Gene Autry's KTLA (Channel 5). Both New York and Los Angeles benefitted from early FCC allotment of extra VHF channels beyond that of those cities' typical trio of network owned-and-operated stations. Both giant markets had *four* additional commercial VHF channels other than the network-run Channels 2, 4 and 7. This gave baseball teams a choice in selecting their flagship TV stations. As a side note, New York gobbling up so many VHF channels ensured Philadelphia, relatively close at 90 miles away and with 2 million residents by mid-century, had only three VHF outlets assigned, with another doled out to nearby Wilmington, Del.

In other, smaller big-league markets, baseball owners tended to cut the number of home telecasts after the initial late 1940s burst, compensating with more road games. Concerns about televised games' effect on attendance – which cratered in 1952 – were a big factor in Boston Braves owner Lou Perini's decision to move to Milwaukee, where he barred all games, home and road, from TV. Spinning the County Stadium turnstiles to more than 2 million, the avid new Braves fans saw their team on TV only during the 1957 and 1958 World Series – the NBC contract superseding any owner's policies – during Perini's tenure.

Meanwhile, no new VHF commercial channel was assigned to Chicago. Its only unused frequency was Channel 11 – reserved for educational broadcasting purposes – to which WTTW signed on in September 1955.

Channel shuffling in 1953 meant WGN had a monopoly on local sports rights as WBBM, WNBQ and WBKB were committed to programming from their network masters. If the White Sox had decided to dramatically increase their video footprint, they had nowhere to go other than WGN. The Chicago TV market would remain essentially static for more than a decade.

By the early 1950s, the NFL had an outright ban on telecasts of games in their originating markets. Not only would the Bears and Cardinals home contests be banned on Chicago TV, but no road-game telecasts would be permitted for one team at the same time the other was playing at home, to protect the latter's gate. As a result, less than a handful of Bears and Cardinals games would be televised throughout the 1950s. Meanwhile, hockey's Chicago Blackhawks went from third-periods-only to no telecasts at all. Pro basketball was not yet a factor.

So, WGN became known as a baseball station. But with the Sox not allowing any home night games on TV, the Cubs got the lion's share of that exposure. In 1960, *all 77* Cubs home games were televised to just 43 for the Sox. The Cubs had fallen into a perpetual on-field rut thanks to an unproductive farm system, an incompetent front office and a meddling owner who would not spend his own fortune on the team. Without night games at Clark and Addison, attendance had dipped well below one million, to small-market-like totals while the South-Siders enjoyed historic box-office success due to their "Go Go" contenders.

But here was the cut. Moving through life's pipeline from the 1950s onward was a bulge of potential young fans – the Baby Boomers. With *entire* Cubs homestands on WGN and weekday Sox telecasts sporadic, a habit unique to Chicago developed. When the final school bell rang at 3:15 p.m. in the city's public schools, and similar times in parochial institutions and the suburbs, a mad dash for home and the TV set would begin.

"The Sox were the dominant team (in attendance) in Chicago 'til the late Sixties," said Levine, a Yankees fan growing up in the 1950s and 1960s among a slew of Sox rooters on the South Side. "But the Cubs had better exposure because of day games.

"The momentum from women and young children watching during the day was building. It was the first generation of TV viewers. Running home from school to watch the last few innings or even more in a rain-delayed game became an art form for me and a lot of friends, even the Sox fans. We'd watch baseball after school.

"As it turned out, it was a huge (informal) marketing campaign. I don't know if (Phil) Wrigley understood the momentum he was creating with only day games — and all of them televised."

Cubs telecasts gained another boost in 1961 when "Bozo's Circus" made its debut from WGN's new color studios on Bradley Place, two miles west of Wrigley Field.

The live, hour-long Noon show became so popular that its waiting list for tickets stretched for years with even pregnant mothers reserving tickets to assure their future offspring admission. "Bozo" ended up as a prime lead-in for Cubs telecasts for the kiddie corps, who could chomp on their baloney or peanut butter-and-jelly "sammiches" before deep-voiced John Mallow came on for

15 minutes of news at 1 p.m. Then the kids could watch "The Leadoff Man" with Vince Lloyd, later Lloyd Pettit, at 1:15 p.m. for a live interview from the field with the biggest names in baseball.

Recalling watching both teams on WGN, Levine believed WGN had a Cubs orientation. And 40 years later, Vince Lloyd remembered the Cubs drew higher ratings even though the White Sox consistently had better records. But the Sox still had an ace in the hole – Jack Brickhouse – whose major commitment to the South Siders despite his Cubs connections has been underappreciated through the decades. Still, it had limits.

"Brickhouse gave it his all, but was not as at home in Comiskey as Wrigley," said Levine.

Such observations, voiced over the decades, started with the late WGN Sports Editor Jack Rosenberg. "Rosey" was Brickhouse's trusted right-hand man noted for clacking away at his typewriter, a sounds-of-summer background noise in the broadcast booth. He worked with Brickhouse at Comiskey Park from 1954 to 1967.

"He did them (Cubs and Sox) with equal sincerity and flair," Rosenberg said in 2013. "We were asked that a lot. We looked at (the Sox) the same as we did the Cubs. We had an obligation to both and we carried it out. He was a professional all the way. He treated them both as his assignment and did them both."

Mark Liptak and Rich Lindberg, the top two Sox historians, give copious credit to Brickhouse for his broadcasts and support of Bill Veeck in his Sox purchase from John Allyn in late 1975.

"A lot of Sox fans of a certain generation feel that Jack was simply just another shill-announcer for the Cubs because they actually never heard him broadcast a White Sox game," Liptak said. "Nothing could be further from the truth. Jack was, in fact, as big a Sox fan as he was for the Cubs.

"All you have to do to dispel any notions of Jack not caring for the Sox is to listen to the excitement in his voice as he broadcast on WGN-TV the game from Cleveland on Sept. 22, 1959. When the Sox won the pennant, Jack was electric in his enthusiasm."

Liptak was particularly impressed by the empathy Brickhouse showed Sox pitcher Joel Horlen on the "Tenth Inning" post-game show on July 29, 1963 at what was later known as RFK Stadium in Washington, D.C. With a 1-0 lead and one out in the ninth, Horlen lost a no-hitter on a Chuck Hinton single. With two out, Don Lock slugged a walkoff homer to trigger what Brickhouse always called a "disastrous turn of events here at (pick your ballpark)." Horlen looked like he had lost his best friend, but Brickhouse deftly maneuvered his way through the tough interview like the consummate pro he was.

Lindberg, an author of Sox books whose historical research appeared in team publications for decades, also believed Brickhouse was even-handed: "What people don't realize about Jack Brickhouse, I believe, is that he loved the Cubs and White Sox on equal terms," he said.

In his Rosenberg-ghost-written Hall of Fame induction speech Brickhouse said it all:

> *It has been my privilege to broadcast the exploits of the Chicago Cubs and Chicago White Sox for 40 years or more. There, in Wrigley Field and Comiskey Park, I have experienced the joy and the heartbreak — probably more of the latter than the former – but Chicago and its beautifully loyal fans have had a resiliency which has kindled a perpetual flame of hope.*
>
> *In the fantasy of my dreams, I have imagined myself as the announcer of a Cubs-White Sox World Series, a Series that would last seven games, with the final game going into extra innings before being suspended of darkness at Wrigley Field.*

Brickhouse was always hustling to add sports rights to WGN's schedule. He was willing to handle marathon workdays to keep sports on the air himself. Twice in 1956, he broadcast a Cubs doubleheader from Wrigley Field on a Saturday, followed by his usual 2½-hour wrestling show starting at 8:30 p.m. from nearby Marigold Gardens. Brickhouse at one point had a national audience for the grapplers and grunters because the "Marigold" program was fed to the DuMont Network before it went dark in 1955.

As the 1960s began, Brickhouse added to the sports lineup where he could. After the Blackhawks' first Stanley Cup title in 23 years in 1961, selected road games became a WGN-TV staple with Lloyd Pettit's Hall-of-Fame calls. Soon all Hawks road contests aired on the station. When Dick Klein started the expansion Bulls in 1966, he and Brickhouse famously hammered out a 12-game TV deal on a cocktail napkin over a near-drunken contest of "stingers" at Matty's Wayside Inn in north suburban Glenview. So when the opportunity to televise a historic Chicago White Sox game presented itself in 1959, Brickhouse, backed by WGN brass, jumped on it.

The station had its first toe-dip into road baseball telecasts, a decade after other big-league markets, with a Cubs game at St. Louis' old Sportsman's Park on a 95-degree Saturday night, Aug. 30, 1958. A year later, as the Sox closed in on their first AL pennant in 40 seasons, WGN arranged for the Tuesday night, September 22, telecast from Cleveland, with the magic number at one. Brickhouse borrowed as his on-air partner Lou Boudreau from WGN Radio for the telecast from the Good Kid's familiar territory: Cavernous Cleveland Municipal Stadium. The game was not originally listed on the schedule released a few weeks previously.

Brickhouse made the call when Luis Aparicio fired to first to double up Cleveland's Vic Power, prompting the broadcaster to scream, "The 40-year wait has now ended," while encouraging viewers to set off any noisemakers they could find. Chicago Fire Commissioner Robert Quinn actually triggered the city's "air-raid" sirens, making half the Chicago-area populace fearful the Russians truly were coming – in the middle of Soviet Premier Nikita Krushchev's visit to the United States.

Boudreau did a live "dressing-room" show, joined later by Brickhouse. Hours later, as the Sox' chartered propeller plane wound its way home, Brickhouse interrupted Franklyn MacCormack's All-Night Showcase of music and poetry on WGN Radio with a live airborne broadcast of more partying Sox. The indefatigable broadcaster stayed on the air as the plane taxied up to the huge welcoming crowd at Midway Airport. In a scene unimaginable in the 21st century, Brickhouse stuck his microphone outside the cockpit window to capture the sounds of the cheering mob.

WGN's TV and radio broadcasts were priceless exposure for the White Sox by any measure.

One week later, Brickhouse – not warhorse Sox radio announcer Bob Elson – was rewarded with the World Series assignment to team with the Dodgers' Vin Scully on NBC-TV (until the 1970s, each participating team's main broadcasters typically split the Fall Classic video assignments). Elson apparently was not liked by NBC brass, while Brickhouse had previously handled several World Series on NBC, including the call of Willie Mays' famed catch at the Polo Grounds in 1954.

WGN staged another unique Sox road telecast on Opening Day, April 10, 1961 from Griffith Stadium in Washington, D.C. The savvy Jack Rosenberg, already well-connected in power circles, arranged for Vince Lloyd to slip into the Presidential Box to interview John F. Kennedy just before the first pitch. JFK ranked as the first president to appear on a WGN sports broadcast.

A wider audience recognized WGN's work for both Chicago teams. The covers of the *Tribune's* weekly TV Week supplement previewing the upcoming 1959 and 1960s seasons reflected that status. Brickhouse was flanked by Cubs manager Bob Scheffing and Sox manager Al Lopez in 1959. A year later, the 1959 NL and AL Most Valuable Players, Ernie Banks of the Cubs and Nellie Fox of the White Sox, posed in their uniforms with Brickhouse and a huge RCA TK-41 camera that would be used for WGN's first season of color telecasts from both Chicago ballparks.

And when it came Vince Lloyd's turn to be the cover boy for TV Week on Aug. 15, 1964, the backdrop of his posed shot in the broadcast booth was Comiskey Park. Rosenberg penned a glowing story on Lloyd with a photo of the broadcaster at home with his wife and son.

WGN began televising Chicago baseball road games with a degree of regularity in 1960. With White Sox home night games still blacked out, the station filled some of the gap with scattered prime-time Sox away contests. Brickhouse always went on the road with the Sox while Lloyd, and later Pettit, would stay behind to handle that day's Cubs home tilt. Up to 15 Sox road night games were televised annually, while only a handful of road night Cubs telecasts augmented with the full complement of home games.

By mid-1961, when former minority Sox investor Arthur C. Allyn assumed control of the team from an ailing Bill Veeck, the comment attributed to Allyn, that WGN would not want sports programming to interfere with its prime-time entertainment programming was, well, just plain wrong.

Long unplugged from a network connection, WGN's 7 to 10 p.m. schedule was loaded with one-off reruns. No show was scheduled in a "strip" five-days-a-week the way independent stations and network affiliates programmed reruns in later decades. WGN ran one-season-and-canceled recent network shows like "Stoney Burke" with Jack Lord, "The Greatest Show on Earth" with Jack Palance and "The Rogues" with David Niven and Charles Boyer in a hodge-podge all over prime time. Staging a ballgame might be more expensive with production costs, but it would be more attractive to viewers and offer extra exposure for the baseball TV advertisers. The later perception that Allyn saw the White Sox as a stepchild on WGN was somewhat off base, given the facts. But when he sought to televise more games, especially on weekends, his team would not have an equal presence.

Three years into Arthur Allyn's Sox ownership, he finally lifted the 14-year embargo against televising home night games, creating truly expanded coverage. The red lights of the cameras after dark at Comiskey Park came at just the right time: A heated three-team pennant race among the White Sox, Yankees at the end of their dynasty and an improving Baltimore Orioles team. A Monday-through-Wednesday, Aug. 17-19, 1964 trio of games against Mickey Mantle, Roger Maris and the Yogi Berra-managed Bronx Bombers were scheduled for Good Ol' Channel 9. The TV eye did not hurt the gate. The Sox drew 32,000, 35,000 and 37,000. Allyn also permitted the Friday night, Aug. 21, game against the Orioles to be on WGN. The TGIF crowd numbered 41,000.

The well-attended, well-watched Yankees series certainly boosted WGN's 1964 baseball advertisers, who had bought a season package for both teams. More home Sox night games also meant more eyes on the product and conceivably higher fees flowing into WGN. The station had big-name staples as sponsors: Hamm's beer with its popular cartoon bear, Phillips Petroleum, Allstate Insurance, Camel and other cigarette brands and Chicagoland Dodge dealers.

The healthy prime-time crowds in spite of TV obviously gave Allyn a mental green light to increase the schedule of home night games on WGN. A total of 10 under-the-lights contests, mostly Fridays, were booked for 1965. WGN added 13 Sox road night games compared to just five Cubs road night contests. Overall, 86 Cubs and 65 Sox games were televised. But with Cubs Saturday and Sunday home day games locked into WGN's schedule, Allyn could not get weekend Sox road games on TV, unlike the majority of other big-league teams.

Allyn started putting two and two together in his head and came out with the wrong number. He may have thought WGN was too loyal to a Cubs franchise that, through 1966, was the National League's losingest non-expansion team of the decade. Given subsequent decisions, he likely also was peeved by Cubs crowds dipping as low as 530 for a Sept. 21, 1966 game against the Cincinnati Reds. Soon the Cubs would complete their lost season with a record-tying 103 defeats and a third recent season of total attendance below 700,000.

Meanwhile, the White Sox had just barely missed an AL pennant with 98 wins in 1964, had three consecutive seasons of 94 or more wins from 1963-65 and drew more than one million annually. Allyn may have failed to understand the concept of the Baby Boomers running home from school to watch the game's top stars, of which the National League possessed the majority in the 1960s, contrasting with being sent to bed at comparable junctures in Sox night games on TV.

Restless and cash-hungry, Allyn would later make a decision that turned an imperfect Sox broadcast arrangement into a damaging one. It created tougher conditions for being "above the fold" in exposure on the Chicago sports scene.

The WGN crew of (from left) Vince Lloyd, Jack Rosenberg and Jack Brickhouse, shown at Comiskey Park in the early 1960s, was just as supportive of the White Sox as the Cubs.

Photo courtesy of Patricia Brickhouse

CHAPTER 10

May 21, 1972: From the
Outhouse to the Penthouse

After the White Sox' triumphant, rowdy 14-0 blowout of Texas on Opening Night at Comiskey Park, the team ripped off a seven-game winning streak at home against the Rangers, Kansas City Royals and Cleveland Indians. It culminated with a dramatic, come-from-behind 7-5 extra-inning victory against the Indians on April 26, the final game of the homestand. The Sox were down 4-0 in the seventh, came back and set up their new superstar, Dick Allen, to win the game with a two-run homer in the 10th.

"(The ball) splintered a chair in the 10th row of the left upper deck," the *Chicago Tribune's* George Langford wrote after the game. "I just knew he was going to hit the cash register for two!," chirped Pat Kelly, the Philadelphia-born right fielder who was perhaps Dick's closest friend on the team.

Dick enjoyed a dynamic start to the 1972 season. He had 14 hits in 31 at-bats over the first eight games — including two home runs of more than 400 feet — while scoring eight runs and driving in six. And the media had already started to compare him to past Sox greats. "In the Bard's Room, the cushy lounge beneath the stands where Sox management entertains its guests, Allen already is drawing hushed comparisons with Minnie Minoso — perhaps the greatest drawing card on the South Side in 30 years," the *Tribune's* John Husar exclaimed after the extra-inning victory against the Indians.

Harry Caray, talking with Husar after the game, raved about Dick's effect on his teammates. "I'm very close to the boys in St. Louis, you know, and to tell the truth the guys there loved Rich. In fact, so did the Dodgers and even the guys in Philly. This guy really relates to his teammates."

The new arrival, in turn, was warming up to Chicago, where he had some issues in his National League days, especially among the bleacher fans at Wrigley Field. "Those Bleacher Bums used to go after me," Dick told the press after the Indians game. "They threw change, papers, anything."

But he told the press he was impressed with the South Side.

"This is a different atmosphere. A good baseball town, a good pitching staff, a young team with lots of guys who are going to be around for awhile. I think I've found a home."

The White Sox would continue their surprising pursuit of first place in the American League West in May. Beginning on Wednesday, May 10, they went on a tear, winning 12 of 13 games. By the time they started a weekend series on May 19 at home against the California Angels, they were 2½ games behind division-leading Minnesota and only half-a-game behind second-place Oakland. They won their first two games against the Angels and had a chance to take sole possession of first place in the AL West in the final contest of the series on Sunday, May 21.

Temperatures were in the low 80s on this Sunday afternoon in late May. But a crowd of only 14,436 showed up at White Sox Park; despite the fast start, the team hadn't completely caught on yet with the South Side faithful.

While the fans entered the white washed old ballpark at 35th and Shields, about two miles south and west of Comiskey, thousands of people were rallying against one of Mayor Richard J. Daley's pet public works projects — the Crosstown Expressway.

The Crosstown would have been the crowning achievement among the group of expressways built in Chicago under the 1956 Federal-Aid Highway Act — the Congress (Eisenhower), the Northwest (Kennedy), the Southwest (Stevenson) and the Dan Ryan. This ambitious, billion-dollar Crosstown project would have linked all four of the city's interstate expressways in "the way the rim of a wheel links the spokes," wrote the *Chicago Tribune's* Jerry Crimmins.

This eight-lane, 22-mile urban superhighway would cut across the western and southern outskirts of the city, starting near Cicero Avenue and the Kennedy Expressway on the North Side and miles later connect with the Dan Ryan. Daley had been pushing for the Crosstown since the mid-1960s. "It'll be the most modern and beautiful expressway in the nation," he told a Kiwanis Club group in 1967. And he had federal support, with more than $1 billion pledged for the Crosstown.

But the construction of the expressway would have decimated neighborhoods along its route — especially on the South and Southwest Sides, in the neighborhoods where the White Sox were the chosen team. Little Village, Garfield Ridge, Clearing, Marquette Park — all would have seen thousands of homes demolished by eminent domain to make way for the expressway. And the bungalows and frame houses that remained in these bedroom communities along the route would have been subjected to noise and air pollution from tens of thousands of vehicles on a daily basis. If the Crosstown were expanded as far south as 99th Street, then neighborhoods like Beverly and Longwood Manor would also be dramatically affected.

So on this warm Sunday afternoon, as the Sox-Angels game was going on in Armour Square, the anti-Crosstown crowd numbering into the thousands converged at 55th Street and Kostner Avenue, in the heart of the Gage Park neighborhood, then proceeded to march west down 55th Street to Laramie Avenue in the heart of Garfield Ridge, adjacent to Midway Airport. "Today we walk again in an effort to put people ahead of concrete," said Dan Walker, the charismatic anti-Daley attorney who was now the Democratic candidate for governor.

Walker's opposition to Daley's plans for the Crosstown Expressway was a key platform in his gubernatorial campaign, as the powerful mayor continued to be challenged by younger people within his own party. Walker was joined by U.S. Rep. Roman Pucinski, who was running for Senate against popular Republican Chuck Percy. Pucinski was a lifelong machine politician who needed Daley's support in his Senate campaign. But even he had to defy Daley on his Crosstown plans, because his constituents in his largely Polish-American 11th Congressional District were opposed to the expressway.

"This is just Mayor Daley's way of rerouting trucks from downtown and destroying our neighborhoods, our churches and our schools," said Michael Wilczynski, one of the protestors. "We have seen what happened to people near the Kennedy and Congress (Eisenhower) Expressways, and it's clear this would only benefit people living in the suburbs."

"This is a people's rally, saying we don't want the Crosstown Expressway, to alert politicians to our feelings," added James Heffernan with the Anti-Crosstown Coalition. It was a message heard loud and clear by Daley — and Illinois Gov. Richard Ogilvie, a Republican who shared Daley's interest in the highway.

Black voters were already starting to ditch Daley, after largely supporting him for his first five terms as mayor. A variety of issues, from segregated housing to police brutality to overcrowded, underperforming schools, was exhausting his support among a majority of Blacks in Chicago. So Daley could ill afford alienating the White ethnics who would be adversely affected by a Crosstown Expressway. While still supporting the idea, he and Ogilvie tamped down on plans for the highway. The idea would basically die with Daley in 1976.

Like the city's racial and political issues of 1972, the Crosstown controversy had significant effects for decades to come. Most notably, the $2 billion in federal funds for the expressway were reallocated to expanding essential public rail transportation to both O'Hare and Midway airports under Mayor Jane Byrne and Illinois Governor Jim Thompson in 1979 and continuing into the 1980s.

But while saving large swaths of neighborhoods, some attributed the failure to build the Crosstown as the source of traffic bottlenecks as the number of cars outgrew the 1950s-era network of expressways. With no bypass of the downtown area, all expressway traffic from the north and west had to feed into the city's center on a thoroughly jammed wheel spoke. Three lanes of the Kennedy and three more from the Edens Expressway merged into four inbound lanes of the Kennedy on the Northwest Side when the two reversible lanes in the middle were either closed or flipped outbound. Drivers desiring to get to the South Side or beyond without needing to turn off into the city's center had to hit their brakes, use the Tri-State (I-94) Tollway father west or otherwise commute at odd hours.

The "reverse commute" became predominant at rush hour by the end of the

20th century as many jobs relocated to the suburbs. Twenty-five-mile-long inbound backups, from Lake-Cook Road all the way downtown on the Edens and Kennedy often occurred on Friday afternoons.

Some media observers would later say that the massive jams also impeded any latter-day White Sox efforts to significantly expand their fan base north and northwest, beyond their traditional South and Southwest Sides strongholds. More than a few fans would not be in the mood to creep along at 20 mph for more than 90 minutes to travel 20 miles to a ballgame.

The traffic snarls of the future were out of mind at 35th and Shields on that warm Sunday in 1972. The White Sox would complete their sweep of the Angels after beating them in an exciting, come-from-behind 9-8 victory. Led by Allen, the Sox took over first place in the AL West that day. And it would be a milestone for the long-moribund organization — for the first time since the 1967 pennant race, the Sox were in first place in mid-May.

The headline in the *Chicago Tribune* was "It's May Day! Sox Are In First," playing off the month and the surnames of two of protagonists in this high-scoring game. In the fifth, Dick Allen blasted a majestic 440-foot three-run homer to straightaway center off of Angels starter Rudy May, which gave the Sox a 5-0 advantage. And then, after the Angels came back to take an 8-6 lead, homegrown White Sox outfielder Carlos May belted a three-run, game-winning homer near the foul pole in the lower right field seats off Alan Foster to give the Sox the win.

For May, the moment was sweet because of an incident a few years before. "I knew Foster from spring training because he was with the Dodgers for a few years," he told the media after the game. "One time in the spring he jammed me with a pitch and broke my bat. Then he said to me, 'Did you get all of that?' I didn't say anything to him but swore that I'd get him someday."

May had been suffering from a leg injury and was not expected to play in the series. But the 25-year-old from Birmingham, who had been drafted by the Sox back in 1966, had dealt with adversity before — his career was severely threatened after he lost his right thumb in an accident while serving with the Marines Reverses in 1969. "This May is some kid," manager Chuck Tanner told the media after the game in his office. "I wanted to give him a rest today because of his injured leg. I asked him about it after the game Saturday night but he said he wants to play. Other players might have sat out the last four days with the injury he has. But that's the little bit extra these guys give."

"In 1964 when I was with the Phillies we had a team a lot like this one," Dick told the media who had assembled around his locker a few days later, after May's heroics. "There weren't many established players. But that's how we played 'em, grinding 'em out day after day…"

"Are we going to the outhouse or the penthouse?"

– White Sox outfielder Rick Reichardt during spring training, March 1972

Dick was fairly spot-on in his description of the '72 White Sox, although there were quite a few "established" players on the team…or, at least, they would be established in the coming years. May would be a two-time All-Star in his career, including an appearance with Dick in that season's Midsummer Classic. Infielders Bill Melton and Mike Andrews, along with outfielder Pat Kelly, appeared in at least one All-Star Game. And among pitchers, Wilbur Wood made three of the games and rookie phenom Rich "Goose" Gossage would eventually beat all of his 1972 Sox teammates, including Dick, with *nine* All-Star appearances.

But for the most part, this was an unspectacular group — not unlike the 1971 White Sox team which finished third with a 79-83 record. Even with the addition of the big bat, they weren't highly regarded going into the season. *Chicago Tribune* writers Richard Dozer picked the Sox fourth in the AL West and George Langford thought the Sox would finish second. The big question mark was defense. Who was going to catch the ball? In 1971, the South Siders were last in defense. The pundits also perceived the three-man rotation advocated by pitching coach Johnny Sain as a weakness. The team had lacked a consistent fourth starter since Joel Horlen was released, and Bart Johnson suffered a knee injury playing basketball in the off-season.

Even the players were realistic about their capabilities. Reichardt, acknowledging the hit-or-miss nature of this team, coined the team's slogan "Outhouse or the Penthouse" during spring training as a comment on the team's unpredictability. With Dick and Wilbur Wood leading the way, they could compete…or maybe not.

Still, the team with Dick Allen had instant chemistry. Fifty years later, almost to a man, the members of that '72 squad would name it as a favorite.

Some of these players came from the White Sox once-vaunted farm system that had been in decline in by the early '70s. Others came from shrewd transactions concocted by Roland Hemond. And while Dick and Wood were primarily responsible for carrying this over-achieving group, the supporting cast, led by May and Kelly on offense and Forster and Bahnsen on the mound, made its own contributions. The sum total had the Sox staying competitive until the end of the year and being remembered as one of Chicago's most exciting sports teams in recent memory.

Outside of Allen, May had the best year among offensive players with the Sox in '72. He'd end up with 12 homers, 68 RBI, a .308 batting average, a .405 on-base percentage and an 843 OPS. His WAR, just above 4, was the fourth-best on the team, behind Dick, Wood and third starter Tom Bradley. May finished 21st in MVP voting and made the All-Star team, enjoying a breakout season.

Not surprisingly, May considered 1972 to be the highlight of his nine-year career in the majors, which was spent mostly on the South Side. May, a younger veteran who was first brought up by the Sox in 1968, said the teams prior to 1972 were friendly, but not close. That changed, partly due to Dick, but mostly on account of Tanner.

"That '72 team was a great team," May recalled while talking on the phone from his home in suburban Chicago. "Great bunch of guys. I hung out more that year than the other three or four years I was there prior to Dick coming in. Guys, they wouldn't hang out when I first got to the Sox. That's because management wouldn't let players drink in the hotel bar — that was reserved for coaches and managers. The players would have to go out and find a bar. But when Chuck came, he said we could drink in the hotel, so after the ball games a bunch of guys would be in the bar drinking. Dick was there. It was a great year."

May was born in 1948 in Birmingham, Ala., where he was a high school baseball star along with his older brother Lee, who also would have a fine major league career with the Reds, Astros, Orioles and Royals. In 1966, Carlos May was one of the most sought-after amateur baseball players in the country. And at that time, the Chicago White Sox still had one of the most effective networks of scouts in the majors — a group that had been assembled starting in the 1950s with the Go-Go Sox front office of Frank Lane and Chuck Comiskey. By 1966, there were eight full-time Black scouts in the majors — and the Sox had two of them, Sam Hairston and Chicagoan Charles Gault.

Hairston — a former Negro League All-Star — was a catcher who in 1951 became the first African American player on a White Sox roster. Hairston was signed by the majors' first Black scout, former Negro League legend John Donaldson, who was hired by the team in 1949. Hairston joined the Sox three months after they fielded Chicago's first Black major leaguer, Minnie Minoso, who lent Hairston his bat after a White player refused to do so. Hairston remained on the major league roster for only five weeks and was buried in the farm system for the next decade, after the big club acquired their catcher of the 1950s, Sherm Lollar.

He retired in 1960, after which the Sox hired him as a full-time scout in Alabama. Competing in the region for talent with another Negro League star-turned-scout, the Cubs' legendary Buck O'Neil, Hairston suggested a number of future major league talents whom the Sox passed on, including Lee Maye, who signed with the Braves and Lee May (Carlos' brother), who signed with the Reds. The organization finally agreed to draft Carlos after he was scouted by Hairston. "You missed his older brother, you better not miss this one," Hairston said about the younger May, who was the 18th pick in the First Round of the 1966 Major League Amateur Draft, which had been instituted just one year earlier.

At the same time, Sam's son, Jerry Hairston, was aspiring to an MLB career that would last 14 years. Grandsons Jerry, Jr. and Scott (27 seasons, combined) made the Hairstons a rare three-generation Major League family.

May rose through the Sox system quickly, exhibiting great patience at the plate (striking out only 24 times while drawing 45 walks in the Midwest League in 1967) and, eventually, power (13 homers in Single-A Lynchburg). His first appearance on the South Side came in late 1968, under legendary Sox manager Al Lopez, who agreed to come back to the team after Eddie Stanky's firing. After a torrid spring training in 1969, May stayed on the White Sox roster for good, earning the starting left fielder's position while batting second behind future Hall of Famer Luis Aparicio. But Lopez rarely talked to May. Instead, then-coach Don Gutteridge told him he had made the team in '69. Wearing No. 17 for the Sox, Carlos May would be the only baseball player in history to wear his birthday on the back of his uniform — he was born on May 17.

Gutteridge, who started as a minor league manager in the White Sox system in 1952 after being hired by Frank Lane, took over as skipper from a retiring Lopez in May 1969. And Carlos May quickly became one of the team's best players. By the start of August, he was a leading Rookie of the Year candidate, with a .281 batting average, 18 homers and an .873 OPS. "He really loves to hit," Gutteridge told the Christian Science Monitor. "In that respect, he reminds me of Ted Williams. May even made the All-Star team that year, held at RFK Stadium in Washington, D.C., striking out in a single pinch-hitting appearance.

But his career would be threatened in late August, while serving a stint in the military reserves, as many draft-age men — particularly athletes — did during the Vietnam War. May spent two weeks training with the U.S. Marines at Camp Pendleton, where he was assigned to the mortar unit. As part of his training, he had to swab out his mortar gun with a ramrod.

"When I went to clean the gun with the long swab, my round, it didn't go down because the barrel was dirty," May said. "When I put the swab in to clean it, I pushed on the firing pin and it came out and took half my right thumb with it."

May had to have part of that right thumb amputated and several skin grafts. But while in the VA hospital, he vowed to play baseball again with the 1970 season.

"I was picking up bats when they had me down in Long Beach at the VA hospital," May recalled. "They flew a guy from Texas, Dr. Stark, he came in and did an abdominal skin graft and I was able to hold a bat. This happened in August, so November/December, I was holding a bat and trying to throw balls. I came back the next year."

The comeback of Carlos May was the talk of the American League in the spring of 1970. Even American League President Joe Cronin showed up at the White Sox spring training complex in Sarasota, Fla., where he marveled at May's ability to play after an injury that the Marines had described as a "50 percent disability," a designation which meant that May wasn't physically able to remain in the military. "He looks good," Cronin told the Associated Press. "Honestly, I never thought he would be back, but he looks as if he's going to make it."

May would indeed make it back for Opening Day at White Sox Park in 1970, where he received a standing ovation from a small crowd of 11,473 during his first at-bat. May finished 1-for-4 in the game. He impressed the intimate ball-game gatherings of Sox fans, earning the nickname "King Carlos."

May amassed 543 at-bats during the 1970 season. He hit 12 homers, drove in 68 runs, batted .285 and led the team with 12 steals – all despite continued issues with the thumb. "The problem was it kept busting open," May said. "So (long-time Sox trainer) Charlie Saad, the best trainer I ever had, he put tape on it and I could throw without it breaking open again. I always used two gloves anyway, so I had a special glove with the thumb out. All that helped me to stay in the game."

The awful 1970 season brought the third-worst winning percentage in White Sox history (.346) to go along with terrible attendance. But for May, the thrill of being back in the majors after a potentially career-ending injury took precedence over Sox attendance concerns. "There were probably days (in 1970) when we played (at Comiskey Park) in front of a hundred people, but I didn't care," May said. "I was smiling everyday just to be in the big leagues. Nowadays guys make so much money, they don't appreciate it like we did, just being there. But I really appreciated it."

During these lean economic times for the franchise, the White Sox were often lacking in staff support — such as a permanent hitting coach. "All the other teams had one, but we never did," May recalled. Instead, he relied on teammates like Tommy McCraw for advice. The only team-sanctioned hitting coach May had was Deacon Jones, the team's roving minor-league instructor. Jones, a life-long White Sox organization man who had cups of coffee with the major-league team in 1962 and 1963, set a still-standing Midwest League record by hitting .409 in 1956. He later became only the second African American manager in the Midwest League, helming the White Sox' Appleton, Wis. club in 1973.

"He couldn't throw, but he could hit with the best of them," May said of Jones. And, after Chuck Tanner arrived, new third-base coach Joe Lonnett helped May with hitting. "He would tell me if I was lunging and stuff like that. If I get in trouble, it's my feet," May recalled. "He'd tell me to just stay back. Keep my weight evenly distributed and just stay back. Basically, that was it. I just don't remember having a hitting coach, ever."

May had his best years in the majors when Tanner was manager and Dick Allen was a teammate. In Tanner's first full year at the helm in 1971, he played May at first base. As Carlos recalled: "I went to Puerto Rico and played first base down there and I came back and played it for the entire '71 season, but I really didn't like first base. So, when Dick (Allen) came, that took a whole lot of load off me."

In his All-Star season of 1972 and also in 1973 and 1974, May would hit behind Dick and Bill Melton, and would see good pitches, as the opposition frequently pitched around the sluggers. A natural line-drive hitter, May began producing more power in '73, smashing 20 homers and driving in 96 runs. May credited Dick for teaching him to be more aggressive at the plate. "I used to take a lot of pitches, 2-0 pitches, 3-1 pitches and he asked why I was doing that," May said. "We talked about it and he tried to get in my mind when you got a pitcher in that situation, you've got to take advantage of it.

"We had a lot of fun together. In 1972, we had me, Dick and Pat (Kelly) and Bill Melton driving the offense, at least until Melton got hurt (in June). Then it got a little tougher for us and we came short of beating out the A's (for the AL West divisional titles in 1972, 1973 and 1974). But we did the best we could with what we had."

While May had a strong relationship with his teammates, he didn't have a good rapport with any of the front office representatives with the team — from Ed Short, the former radio sales rep who spent much of the 1960s as Sox GM; to Stu Holcomb to Roland Hemond. In those waning days of the reserve clause, before the advent of free agency, May remembers with distaste the losing salary negotiations he had with both Holcomb and Hemond, where he ultimately lost arbitration battles with the team, and was paid only $70,000 for the 1973 and 1974 seasons. "They were hard guys to deal with because I didn't have an agent," May recalled.

Dick would leave the team in September 1974 in a controversial retirement that led some to accuse the superstar of quitting on the team. May was shocked at the time.

"I knew how he felt about the game," he said. "He loved playing baseball. When he got to Chicago, he was bitter, but he still loved the game. To me it seemed like he had some baseball left in him."

May's production declined with the White Sox in 1975, and on May 18, 1976 new owner Bill Veeck and Hemond traded him to the New York Yankees for pitcher Ken Brett. May had a slight rebound with the Yankees as they began their mid-1970s renaissance, making it to the World Series in 1976 for the first time in 12 years. May played in the Fall Classic for the only time in his career, going 0-for-9 as the Yankees were swept by the powerful Cincinnati Reds. May also endured tragedy. He lost his three-year-old daughter Elizabeth, who died after suffering from brain damage since birth.

In 1977, May returned to the Yankees, but could not get along with mercurial manager Billy Martin. These Yankees were again bound for the World Series. But May, who batted only .227 in a part-time DH role, was sold to the bottom-feeding California Angels only a few weeks before the end of the season. May said Martin engineered the deal to spite him.

"Billy Martin got mad at me and put me on waivers," he recalled. "Because something happened on the back of the bus where Mickey (Rivers) and me and some other guys were laughing and Billy didn't want any laughing. The bus pulled into somewhere, I don't remember where. Billy was sitting on the bus and when I passed by him, he smirked at me and I knew something was wrong. Sure enough, right after that, I got a call that he put me on waivers. Still, when they got to the playoffs, they had no left-handed pitch hitters, so he just did it to spite me. I was going to confront him and get him to hit me, and it was going to be me and him, but it's a good thing I didn't. My wife talked me out of it."

May spent the next four years of his professional baseball career in Japan, playing for the Nankai Hawks, making more money there than he ever made in the U.S. "It was a culture shock," he said. "We enjoyed the food, and my wife liked the shopping, but baseball was inferior. I made decent money over there and I had to make a buck."

After retiring from baseball, May returned to Chicago, where he worked for more than 20 years for the U.S. Post Office. He also stayed in the game as a hitting coach for the Cook County Cheetahs and the Schaumburg Boomers, two independent minor league teams in the Chicago area. In 2001, he returned to the White Sox as a team ambassador, a position he still holds.

All told, it was a successful career for someone who suffered a potentially career-crippling injury in his rookie year. And although he never made the big money that would come from free agency that began right after he retired, May has no regrets about his career — especially his time with the White Sox during their short renaissance.

"You want to make the big money, but my last year was the year the big money started," May said. "I'm not bitter about it. I was just happy to be there."

They were celebrated on the cover of Baseball Digest as "Baseball's New Murderer's Row:" Dick Allen, Carlos May and Bill Melton who acquired the well-deserved nickname "Beltin' Bill Melton." The three men all had the ability to hit 20-plus homers — a real accomplishment in the early 70s, especially in spacious Comiskey Park. Unfortunately, this trio in 1972 was intact only through June 19. That's when Melton — the easygoing third baseman from Southern California — was shelved for the year, due to a recurring, debilitating back injury he had suffered the previous November in that ladder incident at his California home.

"I was putting shingles on top of a patio roof," he said. "It wasn't that high off the ground. It was kind of slanted down. I had a ladder. Went up on the ladder, and I was going to tap just some shingles down a little bit. And my son at that time was about five or six years old. And I brought him up on the roof and sat him there. While I was doing this, he got up and slipped. He came towards me. I caught him and went backwards and landed on my tailbone. And just went kind of numb, you know. It was like a tooth would go numb. Then I realized I had a ruptured disk."

Melton did not know the true ramifications at the time. "I flew to Chicago and got some epidural shots and the doctors let me go," he said. "I was able to go back to California and work out again and regain some strength."

He tried everything, including injections made from papaya extract, to relieve the pain. Nothing worked. He was put on the disabled list on June 23, two weeks after clubbing a game-winning homer against the Brewers, into a 25 mph wind.

"About 30 games into the (1972) season I started feeling my hamstrings pull. The discs were cutting into the sciatic nerve," Melton recalled. "I was in the on-deck circle and the pain was so bad it dropped me to my knees. They brought me back to the hospital and wanted to operate, but back then it wasn't a 'scope.' They cut through your muscles and your spine and you were done. That was your career."

Melton was in the hospital when he read about an experimental Chymopapain injection procedure, which he underwent. The injection seemed to help, but the FDA back then allowed a person to have the new therapy only once.

With Melton in traction at Mercy Hospital, and later pronounced out for the year, Allen lost crucial protection in the lineup. After showing his prodigious power through four losing seasons prior to 1972, Melton experienced a disheartening finish amid the otherwise-breakthrough season for the franchise. Like May, he was one of the standout White Sox home-grown products of the time, having come up in the team's strong farm system of the 1960s.

Melton was born in 1945 in Gulfport, Miss. and raised in Duarte, Calif.

Much like Dick Allen, Melton excelled in all sports and was better known for his basketball and football abilities in high school. Unlike Dick, he didn't play high school baseball. But his athletic abilities were good enough to get him a baseball scholarship to San Diego State. That stint wouldn't last long, however.

"I got kicked off the baseball team after six games for smoking in the student union," Melton recalled with a laugh, while talking over the phone from his Mission Viejo, Calif. home.

He would transfer to tiny Citrus College in southern California, where he hit .300 with nine home runs, and began attracting professional interest. Keenly watching was the White Sox longtime area scout, Hollis "Sloppy" Thurston. He had been hired by Frank Lane in 1951 and covered talent-rich Southern California from the "Go-Go Sox" era through 1967. Thurston, a former pitcher who spent 10 years in major leagues in the 1920s and early '30s, was a connection to the Old Roman's White Sox. He spent four years (1923 to 1926) on the South Side, winning 20 games in 1924. The "Sloppy" nickname was, in fact, ironic — he was always immaculately dressed.

"Hollis Thurston called me over after watching me play," Melton said. "He said, 'I can give you $8,000 to sign with the White Sox.' I was floored. I took the $8,000, gave it to my mom and dad and started playing for the Sox in the Sarasota Rookie League."

Like May, Melton would rise quickly in the system. And like May, he made his debut with the White Sox during the 1968 season. The team released former St. Louis Cardinals great Ken Boyer to make room for Melton. He had played primarily in right field in the minors. But Al Lopez, in his last season as manager, converted Melton to third base.

"Lopez said I was in right field because I had a good arm," Melton said. "But he said, 'Someday soon, you're gonna have to be at third base.'" The position was still new to him when he made it to the majors with a debut at Yankee Stadium. "Mickey Mantle was my idol and this was his last year," Melton recalled. "So I'm out there at a new position…third base…and Mantle comes to the plate and hits a two-hopper to me. And I kind of hesitated. Even though Mantle had notoriously bad knees, when I hesitated, he was already by the bag when I threw the ball."

Melton's ability to handle third was a real question in 1970. At one point, a pop foul hit him in the face and broke his nose, leading to his temporary re-assignment to right field as utilityman Syd O'Brien took over.

At third, Melton lined up next to Hall of Fame shortstop Luis Aparicio, the last real connection to the 1959 World Series team. "Luis would direct me and move me around in the infield, because I didn't know the hitters," Melton said.

"So, if he'd move to the left, I'd slide over to the left to fill part of the hole. He was a great asset to just watch him play. I even went down to South America and played for Luis' team in Maracaibo (Venezuela)."

Melton was a natural fastball hitter who had trouble with the curve. So the long-term plan for him was to improve as a breaking-ball hitter. "As a matter of fact, what they made me do my first year as a professional, was I wasn't allowed to swing at any fastballs," Melton said. "Regardless if men were in scoring positions, bases loaded or whatever, I had to hit curve balls. And I didn't know how to hit a curve ball. They spent time in the hitting cage with me, and off those machines. And finally I became a pretty good breaking-ball hitter."

By 1970, he was a premier power hitter in the American League. Despite the challenges of playing at Comiskey Park, he hit 33 home runs and drove in 96 during the year in which the White Sox occupied the absolute cellar of both leagues. And the next year, he became the first Sox player in the team's 71-year history to lead the league in homers, when he once again hit 33. He had an AL-leading 25 long balls by the end of July, prompting a *Sports Illustrated* write-up by Larry Keith, a rarity for a Sox player at the time. Melton clinched that title on the last day of the season, beating Reggie Jackson of the A's and Norm Cash of the Tigers, who were tied with him going into the finale. Both Jackson and Cash were off to the playoffs that season, so they rested. But Melton played for a below-.500 Sox team, so he was in the lineup.

"On the last day of the season, when your team's not in it, most of us live down towards Rush Street, so we had a pretty good time there the night before," Melton remembered. "So I went out to the ballpark, and sure enough, I'm leading off 'cuz Reggie Jackson was done. Norm Cash was done. And I had 32. We all had 32. So Chuck (Tanner) led me off. Second pitch off of (Brewers pitcher) Bill Parsons, I hit a line drive to the left field bleachers for 33. I came around third, and two fans were there, cheering and stuff like that. I came back out in the field and after the first pitch, there was a time out, Chuck Tanner pulled me off the field so I could get a standing ovation from the fans. That was a nice gesture."

Melton's heroics in 1971 helped set the stage for 1972 and the resurgence of the team after Dick Allen's arrival. Melton followed Allen in the batting order throughout Dick's tenure with the Sox. "I was the protection for him," he said. "He made that statement after a couple years because he used to walk. They would have walked him left and right. But, because I was behind him, he used to sit and talk to me, say you got more pitches to hit."

Melton remembers the 1972 team as being a unified group without cliques. "I got along with all of 'em," he said. "I sat next to Pat Kelly and Carlos May. I was in the middle so they'd beat me up every day, whether I'd strike out three times in a row or whatever. So, there was more laughter down there than anything. I basically felt very comfortable with everybody. I didn't chum with anybody. Or have to go out to dinner with anybody special. We'd play all night games so we never had that many opportunities to go out to dinner anyway.

"The funniest guys were Dick Allen and Pat Kelly. Night after night after night. It was hilarious. They'd call each other all sort of names back and forth, it was funnier than hell. The clubhouse would break up in laughter. They'd do their little shadow-boxing routine in the middle of the clubhouse, like ten minutes before the game, so we'd all be laughing when we ran out on the field."

Melton returned from his back injury with a strong 1973: A career-best .277 batting average to go with 20 homers and 87 RBI. But he was also involved in a play which would eventually end Dick Allen's 1973 season and lead to the end of Dick's White Sox career. On the road against the Angels in late June, Dick stretched for a wild throw from Melton. The batter/runner, Mike Epstein -all 250 pounds of him- crashed into Dick, breaking his lower left leg and ending his season.

"It was a shame," Melton said. "We would have had a good shot at winning the division in 1972, except I was out. And then we had a good chance to win in 1973, except Dick was out."

Late in 1973, the Sox traded young starter Steve Stone to the crosstown Cubs in a deal which brought future Hall of Famer Ron Santo. Melton saw his position being usurped after a good season.

"I was given a tag as a bad third baseman," Melton told United Press International during spring training in 1974. "The fact is I was never a third baseman until I got to the big leagues. "I lived through two years of (the press) telling me how bad I was. I can live through this, too." But as it turns out, Santo in his final big-league season was an ineffective utility player in 1974, and his presence negatively affected Dick more than it did Melton.

Melton still hit 20 homers that year, but his offense was in decline, and he was becoming a target for Sox broadcaster Harry Caray. "I remember I was really in a slump that year — it was tough," Melton recalled.

Fortunately, recently acquired pitcher Jim Kaat, who won 20 games in '74, helped him out. "Thank goodness for Jim — he really stepped up when I was in that slump," Melton said. "He knew Harry Caray was really beating me up on the broadcasts and took me out to dinner to talk me down."

Despite Kaat's help, Melton had a loud confrontation with Caray in the lobby of a Milwaukee hotel. After Dick walked away from the White Sox in September, the team started a precipitous decline into the second division which continued into 1975. Melton's numbers mirrored that decline with just 15 home runs.

Bill Melton was traded to his hometown California Angels in 1976, but his skills had eroded — he hit only six homers, hit .208 and feuded with a manager, former A's boss Dick Williams, for the first time in his career. In spring training, Melton said that Williams promised he would only DH for the Angels, so Melton didn't take any reps at third. When the Angels started the season in Chicago, Williams suddenly penciled in Melton at third base. "You know why?" he recalled. "It's because Dick wanted Harry Caray to rip me. He actually got pleasure from that. Players told me that every time I went up to the plate when we played the Sox at Comiskey, Williams would run up into the clubhouse to listen to Harry rip me!"

After a brief stint in Cleveland, Melton retired in 1977 and spent much of his retirement in southern California, working as a real estate agent. But Melton returned to Chicago to become a staple on White Sox pre-game and post-game shows on television, starting in the early 2000s. With Hollywood good looks and a delivery described decades earlier by SI's Keith as a "pleasing, resonant broadcaster's voice," Melton was a natural in front of the camera. He also offered a decidedly different approach from Caray.

"The last thing I wanted to do was be critical of any player," Melton said. "Not so much because of Harry Caray, but the reason is...even though they fail, (they) put so much work in, it's unbelievable. And for me to sit up there and criticize somebody because — I made a ton of mistakes, there's no question about it. I deserved a lot of the booing and that's fine. No player wants to be booed and go in the clubhouse and hear a guy talk about how bad he is."

The most notable 1972 acquisition outside of Allen would be Stan Bahnsen, the New York Yankees right-hander who was Rookie of the Year in 1968. On the same December day in 1971 that the White Sox acquired Allen for left-hander John, Hemond traded infielder Rich McKinney for right-hander Bahnsen.

Bahnsen remembers exactly where he was when the trade went down. "I was in New York City working with a promotional company," said Bahnsen from his home in Florida. "(Sports broadcaster) Marv Albert called me there, 'cuz he knew I was there a lot. And he says -- he would always call me and ask me about a trade. He called me, he said what do you think about the trade? I said which one? Oh, you don't know? You were just traded to Chicago. I said really? He said yeah, but he said they got Richie Allen the same day. I said, oh great. That was exciting for me because I was going to be there with a superstar, even though I had never met him or played against him."

The Bahnsen deal would turn out to be one of the steals of the 70s. The

Yankees hadn't had a decent third baseman since Clete Boyer. McKinney was supposed to be that replacement. But McKinney was so bad for the Yanks that he was farmed out to Syracuse by late May, then was traded to Oakland at the end of the season. Meanwhile, Bahnsen had an excellent season. "I was 21 and 16 that year, and I had some good games," Bahnsen said. "But I pitched quite a few innings, too."

Born in Council Bluffs, Iowa in 1944, Bahnsen was a two-sport star in high school, excelling in both basketball and baseball. After a year on scholarship at the University of Nebraska, the Yankees chose him in the fourth round of the draft in 1965.

"When I was a kid there was one game a week on TV," he said. "That was on Saturday. And it was usually the Yankees, especially when Roger and Mickey were in the home run race to break Ruth's record. So, when I was drafted by the Yankees I was totally shocked 'cuz I had pitched just one year at Nebraska. I jumped at the chance to pitch for a major league team."

Bahnsen progressed through the Yankees minor-league system quickly and by 1966 he was in Triple-A Toledo, where he threw a no-hitter on July 13, and earned an expanded roster call from the Yankees. On Sept. 9, 1966 he made an electric major league debut, pitching two perfect innings in relief against the Boston Red Sox, striking out Joe Foy, Carl Yastrzemski, Tony Conigliaro and Rico Petrocelli while picking up a save.

"After my first game in the big leagues, [Yankees Manager] Ralph Houk wanted me to be a closer," Bahnsen said. "I'd gone to spring training in 1967 and was told that I made the team if I agreed to be a closer. They said, 'Our starting rotation is set. We want you to be our closer'. I said, 'I can't do it.' It was hard to turn down a job in the big leagues. But I was convinced I was a starter. So they sent me to Triple-A as a starter and then they brought me up again at the end of 1967."

Bahnsen established himself early for a mediocre Yankees team in 1968 and used his power fastball-curve combination to amass a 17-12 record with a 2.05 ERA in 267 innings pitched. He accomplished this despite missing starts, working on weekends only during a segment of the season while fulfilling Army Reserve duty. He had a work schedule like the Cubs' Ken Holtzman, who also pitched only on weekends for part of the 1967 season while on leave from week-day reservist's duty.

Bahnsen dipped to 9-16 in 1969. The lowered mound that year, mandated by Major League Baseball to help hitters, hurt Bahnsen. But he rebounded with 14-11 and 14-12 records in 1970 and 1971. "I had four pretty good years as a starter in New York even though that team was without Mickey and Roger and

Clete Boyer and Bobby Richardson," he said. "That whole era had just retired right when I got to New York. So we had really young players and struggled, but we had a good pitching staff."

Although he played on a competitive Yankee team — their 1970 team went 93-69 and finished second in the AL East — Bahnsen was impressed with the White Sox talent. "I thought we were loaded. At the corners we had two power hitters in Bill Melton and Richie Allen," Bahnsen said. "Ed Hermann was a pretty good catcher and he threw a lot of runners out. We had Pat Kelly in right who had great speed, and he was (NFL Hall of Fame running back) Leroy Kelly's brother. We had Carlos May, who was a nice left-handed bat. We had Jorge Orta, who was a good left-handed hitter, a young kid. And we had Terry Forster and Goose Gossage in relief, which was an unbelievable bullpen."

The Sox also had Johnny Sain, baseball's best pitching coach. Sain continued to teach variations on the curveball and revitalized pitchers' careers.

"John was really — well, I guess he's not underrated; he had more 20-game winners than any coach ever in the big leagues," Bahnsen said. "He just had a really good kind of a country way of teaching you and getting you to do things."

Bahnsen enjoyed the best season of his career in 1972 with the White Sox. Bahnsen's 21 wins stood out as his career high. He threw 241 innings to get those wins. He took the ball for an amazing 41 starts as part of Sain's "iron man" rotation. Wood, Bahnsen and Bradley started 130 of the team's 154 games in 1972.

"I knew I was not going to have my fastball all the time," Bahnsen said. "In fact, by the end of the season I ended up being a breaking-ball pitcher."

Bahnsen, more than any other starter, benefitted from the Sox' strong bullpen combo. "Gossage and Forster were just unbelievable when they were in that bullpen. If we had a lead after seven it was probably going to be a win 'cuz nobody wanted to hit off those two guys," Bahnsen said. "It worked out. If I got five or six innings, that's about all I could go. And some days I knew I didn't have good stuff because I needed that extra day's rest. But it worked out for us. We had a good ball club. We didn't have an established fourth starter."

Off the field, Bahnsen became one of the team's most-polished practical jokers, an art he learned from Yankees greats Mickey Mantle and Whitey Ford, who prided themselves on pranks.

"Stan would do the old-school pranks, like nailing guys' shower shoes into the floor of their locker," Bat Boy Jim Riley remembered.

"The other thing he specialized in was the 'While You Were Out' calls," Riley continued. "Stan would get a bunch of empty 'While You Were Out' memos from the Sox Park switchboard operator. Then he'd fill them out with phony information.

"One time, he filled out a message from a 'Mr. Lyon at the Brookfield Zoo' and left it at Carlos May's locker. Carlos called the zoo and said, 'Is Mr. Lyon there?' And everybody's listening because there's a phone in the back of the clubhouse toward the field and then there was one in the trainer's room, and so we're all around the corner while Carlos is on the phone, and he said, 'This is Carlos May, Chicago White Sox, I got a message here to call Mr. Lyon about a speaking engagement.' So, the person must have said there's no Mr. Lyon here. He goes, 'Well I got this message. Is this the number?' And he reads it. They said, 'Yeah, sir, I think someone's playing a practical joke on you. This is the zoo; you're asking for Mr. Lyon.' Carlos goes, 'Oh fuck.' He slams the phone down and says, 'Where's that motherfucker Bahnsen?'"

After all the positives of that year, 1973 was a letdown for Bahnsen, along with the entire team. Still pitching in the team's three-man rotation, this time with San Francisco Giants acquisition Stone as the third pitcher, Bahnsen logged a career-record 282 innings. But his arm was tired by the end of the season. He ended up throwing sidearm.

"It's twice as hard for me as it is for Wilbur. He throws the knuckler, and of course, that's not wearing on the arm. I'm essentially a power pitcher. It's a big difference that should be considered," Bahnsen told Chicago sportswriter Jerome Holtzman. His one highlight was a near-perfect game on Aug. 21, when, facing the Cleveland Indians, Bahnsen got two outs in the ninth inning before former teammate Walt "No-Neck" Williams slashed a single under third base-man Melton's glove. As the team fell out of the pennant race in 1973 and sunk to fifth place in the AL West, Bahnsen began to wilt. He finished with an 18-21 record. "I was going for 20 wins, but instead I wound up with 20 the other way," he told Holtzman.

The disappointing season was also difficult in other ways for Bahnsen. His father died midway through the season. And, along with teammates Reichardt and Andrews, Bahnsen encountered difficulties in settling on a contract with GM Holcomb and owner Allyn, who was beginning to contend with the ex-treme financial difficulties that would force him to sell the White Sox two years later. After Reichardt and Andrews were released and Bahnsen was put on the trading block by Holcomb, Tanner and Hemond interceded. That's when Hol-comb was fired.

By 1974, Bahnsen had become one of Harry Caray's whipping boys, merci-lessly criticized by the broadcaster for his high pitch count and struggles on the mound. The man known in New York as the "Bahnsen Burner" became known in Chicago as "Stanley Struggle". He finished 12-15 in 1974, and when Dick Al-len walked away from the team in September, Bahnsen knew the team that had succeeded beyond belief in '72 was finished.

He also served as the White Sox' player representative in 1975, right before the beginning of the free agent era. "They wanted a starting pitcher to do that, since presumably a starting pitcher had more time on his hands," Bahnsen said. "I would take reports from Marvin Miller, and I remember just before we got free agency I had a meeting with the team. I'd have a 10-minute meeting whenever Marvin would send paperwork to me, which was only a couple times a month. I told them, somebody is going to make a million dollars in this game. And the players said, no way. They'll never pay anybody a million dollars in this game. Now I laugh at it, 'cuz you've got guys now making $30 or $40 million a year."

Bahnsen would be traded by the Sox to Oakland in 1975, with the White Sox receiving Chet Lemon in return — an outfielder who would start for the Sox into the early 1980s. "I wanted to stay in Chicago, but I could see the writing was on the wall for John Allyn — he was broke," he said.

Bahnsen pitched another seven years for Oakland, Montreal, the Angels and the Phillies. Bahnsen went on to book and promote sports-related cruises in Florida with well-known baseball players for Norwegian and MSC Cruise Lines. "We used to have like five or six guys do a different cruise every day for baseball fans," he said. "I know players in both leagues 'cuz I played in both leagues. That was a lot of fun. But I never called Richie (Allen). I knew he wouldn't do it."

Bahnsen still has fond memories of the 1972 Chicago White Sox. "It was the most fun I had in one season," he said.

———————————

Twenty-four-year-old Tom Bradley walked out to the mound at Comiskey Park to face the Twins on April 9, 1971. He had never seen a crowd this huge in his life. Enthused by the Opening Day road doubleheader sweep of the Oakland A's, the White Sox faithful showed up to the support their team.

That then-record Opening Day gathering of 43,253 at the South Side ballpark saw a season lid-lifter held on a Good Friday for the first time. The fans were eager to see a fresh and exciting baseball team wearing new and distinctive red pinstriped uniforms. They were not disappointed as the White Sox had a 3-2 walk-off win in the bottom of the ninth thanks to Rich McKinney's pinch RBI single. This game would later become known as "The Miracle on 35th Street" because the large crowd was a surprise, after the Sox averaged only 7,505 per date the year before.

Bradley went 8⅓ innings in his first start for the Sox, leaving the game in the ninth tied 2-2. He lasted longer in the game than the ballpark's supply of hot dogs, which ran out by the fourth inning. While he did not get the win, he earned a ton of praise for his first outing, considering he had only 74 major league innings under his belt.

"I'd never pitched in front of that many people," Bradley remembered a half-century later. "And it was against Minnesota, it was pretty cool day. I pitched very well, but then I got a little tired in the seventh and Rich Reese got a two-run single to tie the game up in the eighth inning. I was pretty well overwhelmed. I kept my composure pretty well. I was able to do a good job, keep us in the game. We eventually won the game."

Bradley was one of 18 new faces on the '71 White Sox. He had been acquired in November 1970 as part of the Ken Berry deal engineered by Hemond that re-united Bradley with his Hawaii Triple-A manager Tanner and pitching coach, Sain.

"I had known him from the Angels days. So, I'd sometimes try to get a player that I've known, and he was a solid individual," recalled Hemond.

Bradley's home opener performance began two of the most all-time dominant pitching years for a White Sox hurler.

The bespectacled young right-hander with distinctive thick eyeglasses that corrected his severe 20/450 nearsightedness, struck out more than 200 hitters in 1971 and 1972 while posting a sub-3.00 ERA in both seasons.

Bradley ate up a lot of innings in 1971 with 285⅔, sixth in the American League. His performance was better than his 15-15 record. He tied for fourth in AL shutouts with six, became known for his control and struck out 206. Only Gary Peters, Ed Walsh and Wilbur Wood had struck out more hitters in the seven-decade history of the Sox.

Chicago Daily News writer Dave Nightingale wrote a piece on Bradley in the November 1971 *Baseball Digest* story, *Tom Bradley-New Hope for The White Sox.*

Nightingale heralded him as being destined for major-league stardom. The article was prophetic because Bradley was already planning his post-baseball career at age 24: "I'd like to coach college baseball someday and wouldn't it be something if I could go back to the University of Maryland" (where he had earned a baseball scholarship in 1965).

He was drafted by the California Angels in the seventh round of the June 1968 major-league draft at the recommendation of Al Monchak, who joined Tanner as part of the White Sox coaching staff in 1971.

Bradley grew up in Northern Virginia. His father, Claude, worked for the U.S. Commerce Department. He attracted a lot of major league scouts who watched him pitch for Falls Church High School, where he was 11-3 his senior year. He decided to wait on a pro career and pursued his education at Maryland.

In fact, young Tom promised his parents that he would complete his degree before he began his professional baseball career.

"My Dad was obviously very instrumental in my career, and he pitched in the Washington, D.C. amateur leagues," Bradley said. "My dad played down on the ellipse by the White House back in the thirties and early forties for the Packer team. So, I had a very good coach, at a very young age, who taught me an awful lot. I started playing when I was six, seven years old. And going to the University of Maryland really is when I blossomed. I grew and gained some weight and gained strength. I made all-ACC First Team two years in a row."

Fulfilling the promise to his parents, he went back to Maryland after the 1971 season and graduated cum laude in 1972 in Classical Studies (Latin and Greek).

Going into spring training, Bradley knew the White Sox could contend, especially since the team had acquired Dick Allen in exchange for his 1971 roommate Tommy John.

With John shipped off to Los Angeles, the frugal Bradley, who still had not spent his bonus money from the Angels, needed someone to share living expenses with during the season.

He approached a 20-year-old kid named Rich Gossage, who had made the '72 squad as a non-roster invitee, to live with him in an apartment in Hinsdale, Ill. It would be Bradley who would forever change Rich Gossage's image, when he came up with the nickname "Goose."

"In '72 he made a club out of spring training, and he came in to pitch one night and he kind of craned his neck a little bit," Bradley recalled. "And also those gangly arms and legs when he delivered the pitch, I can visualize his motion right now. He just looked like a Goose to me.

"And also, I made the comment, look at all those goose eggs up on the board. He came in against Oakland, I think he was throwing aspirin tablets. I think he had pitched two or three scoreless innings. I said, 'Look at all those goose eggs.' I knew that there had been some Gooses, Goose Goslin, who played many years ago and the name just stuck from that point on. We didn't want to call him Richard, Rich or Rick, so the name stuck to him."

Bradley combined with Wilbur Wood and Stan Bahnsen to start 130 of the team's 154 games in 1972. For the season, he went 15-14 with a 2.98 ERA.

He struck out 209 batters (fifth in the American League) with 7.235 strikeouts per nine innings (fourth best in the AL). He became only the third pitcher in White Sox history, besides Ed Walsh and Gary Peters, to record two seasons with more than 200 strikeouts.

Bradley made 40 starts. "I had seven starts with two days' rest," he said. "I had a 2-4 record, even though my ERA was respectable at 3.19."

As in the '71 season, his 15-14 record concealed how valuable he was for the White Sox. He had a WAR of 4.9, eighth best among 1972 American League pitchers.

Tom Bradley's most heartbreaking loss of the season was a 1-0, 11-inning loss to the Angels on September 15th when the Sox were just three games behind the A's. Bradley had pitched his heart out but lost when, with two outs in the bottom of the 11th, Leo Cardenas singled home Curt Motton.

In the top of the 11th inning, Bradley had doubled, but was cut down trying to reach third base on an attempted Walt Williams sacrifice bunt. Bradley's record fell to 14–14 despite fanning nine and walking just one.

He was amazed at the incredible year that Dick Allen had in 1972. "I think some players may have been a little bit offended that he was given special treatment," Bradley said. "It didn't bother me, as long as he came to the ballpark and did his job. He didn't take that much batting practice, but that shows you how great a hitter he was. He didn't need to.

"He had a heck of a season. I'm sure there were people who were, I don't want to say, jealous of him.

"They probably resented the fact that, why doesn't he have to be here and be on the field for batting practice? But if we hadn't have had him, we wouldn't have finished second that year. So, it didn't bother me. And I don't remember Chuck ever talking about it to the rest of the team."

On a personal level, 1972 also was a very significant year for Bradley because Mike Morris, the White Sox equipment manager, set him up on a date with a Delta Airlines flight attendant named Kathy Duff, the cousin of Morris' wife. In 1974, Bradley married Kathy; they had two children and now live in West Virginia.

With his degree at Maryland completed, Bradley was excited for the upcoming 1973 White Sox season. He even took an off-season job with the team in October 1972, selling season tickets.

But Bradley was shocked when Roland Hemond traded him to the Giants a month later as part of the deal that brought Steve Stone and Ken Henderson to Chicago, making the Sox the early season favorites for '73.

"I was heartbroken that I got traded," he said. "To have the two good years that I had, to get traded to San Francisco. I was devastated. But it's a business and you move on and do the best you can do.

"I hadn't even put cream in my coffee sitting at Comiskey Park selling tickets when Roland called me. Like a good soldier I continued to sell White Sox tickets even after being traded."

In 2014, Hemond recalled the contribution Bradley made to the success of the '72 team.

"He did a good job for us. He pitched over 200 innings two years in a row. So, he held his own very well. He won 15 games for us and stuff like that. Bradley kept us in the race. He would give you that kind of support with the innings he pitched."

Former roommate Tommy John never thought Bradley was the same pitcher after his two years in Chicago because of the effects of the three-man rotation in 1972. Bart Johnson was not part of the rotation due to injury, and Joel Horlen had been released on April 1, right before the 1972 strike began. Hemond agreed.

"It was pretty difficult for him as opposed to Wilbur Wood because he was more of an effort pitcher, fastball, curveball. And Wilbur could throw that knuckleball morning, noon and night," said Hemond.

Bradley's post-White Sox pitching record also seems to support John's criticism. After starting 40 games in 1972, he started only 61 more over the remainder of his career, going 23–26 with a 4.56 ERA. In May 1974, he entered during the ninth inning in relief for the Giants and heard a pop in his right shoulder. An injured rotator cuff, overworked by throwing more than $545\frac{2}{3}$ innings over two years for the Sox, would cut short his promising career.

He threw his last major-league pitch at age 28 and began to coach baseball at the college level. In 1990, Bradley fulfilled the fantasy he had told Dave Nightingale about 20 years earlier when he became the baseball coach at Maryland, staying on the job for 10 years.

Bradley attended the 1972 team 40-year reunion. In the lobby of the Palmer House after the celebration, he told Hemond: "If you had only gotten us one more pitcher, the Sox would have beaten out Oakland in '72."

Other distinctive players contributed to the 1972 White Sox.

Pat Kelly was the flashy dressing, Rush Street regular who, as the mainstay right fielder, stole 32 bases that year. Kelly was perhaps Dick Allen's closest friend on the team — a Philadelphia native who, in later years, became a born-again Christian and minister with the Evangelical Baptist Church in Baltimore. He passed away in 2005.

Colorful co-player rep Jay Johnstone, who was a part-time outfielder for the team. He later became known as one of the great characters and pranksters in baseball while playing with World Series teams with the Yankees (1978) and Dodgers (1981). Johnstone also served as a backup on the National League East-winning 1984 Cubs. He would die of complications from Covid-19 in 2020.

Rick Reichardt was the team's main centerfielder and the other player rep. A former college football star who started for Wisconsin at fullback in the 1963 Rose Bowl, Reichardt got $205,000 to sign with the Angels in 1964 — then the largest bonus ever offered to an amateur player. The payout helped prompt Major League Baseball to blow up the free-for-all system for acquiring talent and create the amateur draft.

After a lengthy 1973 contract dispute with Holcomb where he temporarily played under that 20% pay cut, Reichardt walked away from the Sox in June and was unconditionally released. He hooked up with Kansas City for the rest of the 1973 season before being released by the Royals in 1974. Reichardt's once-promising major league career where he was touted as the next Mickey Mantle was over.

Jorge Orta was the quiet son of a Cuban baseball legend who grew up in Mexico, where Roland Hemond's organization signed him. He was a rookie in 1972 and mentored by Dick. Orta became an established major-league player with a 15-year-career, most notably on the 1985 World Series champion Kansas City Royals.

Ed Herrmann, who was with the White Sox from 1967-1974, was the sure-handed, plate-blocking catcher who, somewhat surprisingly, led the American League in intentional walks in 1972, since he often batted in front of the light-hitting shortstop tandem of Luis Alvarado and Rich Morales. Herrmann went on to a long career as a scout for Kansas City before passing away in 2013.

Walt Williams is forever known as a charter member of the Harry Caray "No Outfield" he had uttered on the air in 1972 in various combinations of "No Outfield" lineups: "No Thumb" (Carlos May) in left, "No-Neck" (Williams) in center and "No Arm" (Pat Kelly) in right!" A changeup included "No Arm" in center (Rick Reichardt) and "No Brains" Jay Johnstone.

In 2016, Walt "No-Neck" Williams died at age 73 from a heart attack.

Before Dick Allen arrived in 1972, the Chicago White Sox were a team of characters and iconoclasts who would struggle just to get near .500. But with Allen, they were something else entirely — they became the team with enough charisma to save an organization.

Carlos May became a steady ballplayer even after an accident in the Marine Corps Reserves threatened his career.

Photo credit: Leo Bauby Collection

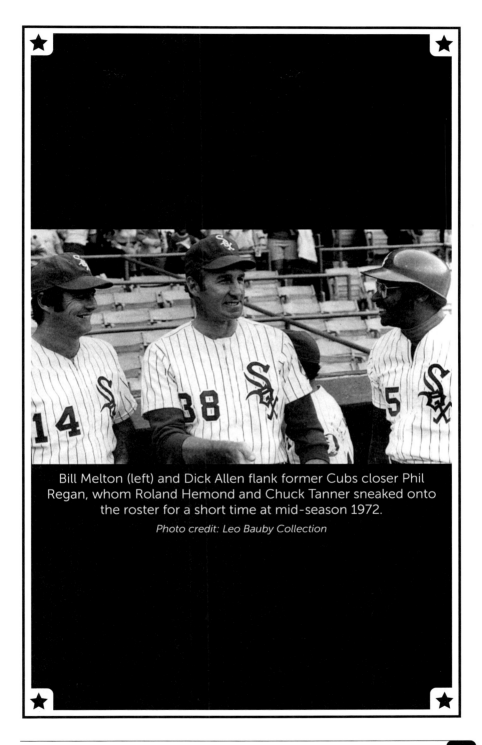

Bill Melton (left) and Dick Allen flank former Cubs closer Phil Regan, whom Roland Hemond and Chuck Tanner sneaked onto the roster for a short time at mid-season 1972.

Photo credit: Leo Bauby Collection

The wives of White Sox players donned matching hot pants and team jerseys with go-go boots for a promotion at Comiskey Park in 1972.

Photo credit: Leo Bauby Collection

CHAPTER 11

Nancy Faust:
The Soundtrack of the Sox

"She's Nancy Faust, the pixie-ish blonde organist at the Chicago White Sox Ball Park, whose quick wit and impromptu style have made her the darling of thousands of baseball fans."
– Chicago Tribune Sunday Magazine cover story on White Sox organist Nancy Faust, published on June 4, 1972

On June 4, 1972 — the same day when Dick Allen hit his dramatic, ninth-inning game-winning home run against the New York Yankees to propel the White Sox into second place in the AL West — the front page of the Sunday *Chicago Tribune* was unflatteringly devoted to a group of dynamic personalities with South Side connections.

Below the fold on page 1 of the *Sunday Tribune*, a headline warned of a potential rift between Chicago Mayor Richard J. Daley, his 58 Machine-backed Illinois delegates at the upcoming Democratic National Convention and a group of independent, diverse Democrats trying to unseat the Daley delegates.

"Daley Split Could Cost Race" was the headline for the article by the *Tribune's* William Jones. The story revealed national Democrats' concern over a simmering rift between the longtime Chicago mayor — who controlled Illinois politics from his Bridgeport home at 3528 S. Lowe Ave. — and a diverse coalition of Black, White and female politicians and activists.

In the article, Democratic presidential candidate Sen. Hubert Humphrey warned that this group of young reformers who were looking to oust Daley's hand-picked delegation at the convention — to be held five weeks later in Miami Beach — could end up costing the Democrats the White House in November.

Those reformers were led by two men with South Side roots. Youthful Jewish attorney Bill Singer grew up in the South Shore neighborhood before being elected alderman of the 43rd Ward on the North Side. African American civil rights activist Jesse Jackson had been a fixture on the South Side since 1965, when Dr. Martin Luther King selected him to lead the Chicago branch of the Southern Christian Leadership Conference's economic coalition of Black ministers and entrepreneurs, Operation Breadbasket.

On the left "rail" of the Sunday *Tribune*, where the newspaper promoted its numerous inside sections was the headline "She Makes Music at Sox Park."

Meriting this page 1 promotion was the cover story in the *Tribune's Sunday Magazine* about the 25-year-old woman just beginning her reign as a South Side institution — Nancy Faust. Although born on the North Side in the Ravenswood neighborhood, Faust would arrive as the White Sox innovative organist in 1970. She remained at 35th and Shields in that role for the next 40 seasons.

In time, Faust would be recognized on her own terms as an artist who innovated and influenced her peers in professional sports, just as quintessential Chicago author Nelson Algren influenced numerous important writers who followed him.

But on the magazine cover page, Faust was portrayed as a sex symbol, posing provocatively with Sox players Bill Melton and Wilbur Wood. In the color photo, Faust wore a black mat jersey gown with a revealing neckline and pearls. Melton stood to her right, clutching her waist while she mussed his hair, while Wood crouched below Faust on her left side, clutching her knees.

The inside "double-truck" (two-page) story featured another provocative photo of Faust with Melton and Wood — this time, the two players carried her in a sideways position, while she modeled summer attire: an orange crinkled cotton shirt with a yellow sweater and pleated cotton skirt. ("The players suits are winners too: Snappy red and white White Sox uniforms," said the photo's caption.)

As it turns out, the clothes she was modeling for the cover shoot were the raison d'être for the magazine feature on Faust. The editors even hired noted fashion photographer Victor Skrebneski for the shoot.

"I get this call from (then-*Tribune* fashion editor) Genevieve Buck, (who said) we're going to do a feature about clothing and styles," Faust recalled. "I showed up and saw the two players there to do the shoot with me. And I had no idea it was going to be anything like that. I don't know what I thought it was. I just was excited that they wanted to use me to put their designs on."

"They fixed my hair and they had the wind blowing on me," Faust recalled. "It was very unlike anything I had ever experienced."

The supporting prose to accompany the photos, courtesy of Evelyn Livingstone, had dated language like: "Nancy admits that Women's Lib hasn't been an issue in her own career since being a girl has definitely been an asset but thinks there is much to be said for some of its tenets."

But there are moments of clarity in the article, the hint at Faust's unique, inventive style that would influence the stadium entertainment experience in the years to come.

"During a game, she becomes all involved and chats with the fans who surround her, meanwhile keeping the crowd's enthusiasm at a high pitch with music that's distinctly of the moment," Livingstone wrote. "She dreams up something special for each batter as he comes to the box."

There were creative organists before Faust, such as Gladys Gooding, the one-time silent movie organist who played at Brooklyn's Ebbets Field for Dodgers games in the 1940s and 1950s; or Jane Jarvis, the Muzak executive who performed at Milwaukee Braves and New York Mets contests for almost a quarter of a century.

But Faust would revolutionize the stadium organ style with her ability to musically comment on the game, using improvisational skills not unlike a performer at Chicago's famed Second City, which began on the South Side (in Hyde Park in 1955). This included incessant musical designations for various players, both home and away. Faust also improvised off game action, playing witty musical excerpts of well-known pop titles to comment on what was going on down on the field. She was the person who virtually invented "walk up music" for players. And she was doing this almost from the time she started with the White Sox, playing the organ first located in the center field.

"As a 23-year-old in 1970, she was the first to incorporate rock and soul songs into sports music repertoire, and she did it flawlessly; the importance of this development can't be overstated," wrote Boston Red Sox organist Josh Kantor in 2014. "She drew on the traditions of live music at sporting events to establish the modern musical cues that became standards for celebrating the home team's players and lightly poking fun at the visiting team's players and at the umpires. She inspired Hall of Fame broadcaster Harry Caray's much-celebrated 'Take Me Out To The Ballgame' sing-along tradition, which he later took to Wrigley Field upon joining the Cubs and which still thrives there today...She invented what we now call 'walk-up music': The theme songs that today's home-team batters request the DJ to play when they walk up to the plate. Her style provided a perfect amount of whimsy to the baseball soundtrack, and her playing technique always brought the strength of the melody to the forefront so that her songs would be easily recognizable."

"(She is)...the greatest sports organist of all time," he concluded.

"I was young and cute at the time, but I also had talent," Nancy remembered. "I definitely could play anything. So whatever was popular, I always knew what the Top Ten songs were and you would always hear me playing something that was popular."

Much of this musical talent came from her mother, Jackie. She was a professional musician who played throughout the Chicago-area in the 1940s and 1950s, most notably on the nationally-syndicated "WLS National Barn Dance" on radio, where she provided background accompaniment.

"Every Saturday night, she'd perform live on the show, (which was broadcast from) the 8th Street Theater in Chicago," Faust said. "My mother didn't play organ, she played violin and accordion. She was really talented. Not only does she have a great ear, but she had the ability to read music just like in her sleep. She accompanied all kinds of entertainers through her life, from vaudeville-type entertainers that needed background music.

"I was fortunate to inherit her good ears."

When she was four, the family bought Nancy an organ. She quickly began playing the instrument by ear, and by the time she was a teenager, Nancy was filling in with her mother on occasion. At that time, in the mid-1960s, she attended her first major-league game at White Sox Park. Faust became enamored of the style of then-Sox organist Shay Torrent, who played on the South Side from the late 1950s through the mid-1960s before becoming the stadium organist at Anaheim Stadium (now Angels Stadium) in California for more than 20 years.

Torrent and Bill Veeck (in his first ownership period with the Sox) established the same organ perch in the center field bleachers at Sox Park, where Nancy would later play.

"We went to a game where the Sox were playing the Detroit Tigers — Rocky Colavito played for the Tigers then, and my cousin was a big Rocky Colavito fan," Nancy remembered. "I think I must have been about 12 years old. I remember that I knew that Shay Torrent was there, and I wanted to find him because I sort of knew him, because when I was young I performed at some Hammond organ recital to promote the organ and he was there. He was a real master."

By 1967, she was encouraged to entertain the idea of playing at Wrigley Field, and approached then-Cubs owner Phil Wrigley about the possibility of at least playing the National Anthem at games.

"My boyfriend at the time was a Cubs fan and wrote a letter [to Wrigley] on my behalf, because I really had no interest in doing it," Faust said. "But he wrote a letter saying, 'You need my services. You need me to play the national anthem at your games.'"

But Wrigley, who hired the first-ever stadium organist in 1941, politely declined her offer. The gum magnate had just installed Jack Kearney as the Cubs' first season-long organist. Wrigley explained in his responding letter he wanted to inject some organ-borne patriotism at his ballpark with the Vietnam War heating up.

However, in early 1970, she was approached by the White Sox.

"I was hired by (Sox Vice President/General Manager) Stu Holcomb," Faust said. "Stu heard me play at a function that he attended — he really liked an arrangement I made on (the Henry Mancini song) 'Moon River.' And I followed up with a letter after realizing that he was there, a letter of interest should he ever decide to make a change in terms of music. And he actually filed the letter, I guess, and called me about a month before the season started and hired me. I didn't have to audition."

"The center-field organ perch was a good place to cut my teeth, because I could grow and make mistakes, especially since no one was out in center field that year," Faust said of the 1970 season, when the Sox only drew 495,355 fans. "My very first year I think I was making $95 a game, which was comparable to a schoolteacher's salary. And I had no experience, really. I mean, I had plenty of experience as a musician but not as a ballpark organist, but not that much was required in terms of what I could do.

"So all I did was a little fanfare then as a batter approached the plate. And then I just provided the happy music in between each inning. Or if there was a pitching change. I also played for an hour as fans entered the park."

Holcomb, however, suggested that Faust be more involved in game action. "Stu gave me a roster of the players and their states," she said. "He'd say Bart Johnson was from California. And Ken Berry, Kansas City. And Rick Reichardt, Wisconsin. So he said if you could give a little fanfare when they walk up to the plate, wouldn't that be nice? I said sure, that's right up my alley. I can play anything. I knew all the state songs because I'd grown up playing the organ. My mother was a musician. I knew every song she ever knew. I played by ear. So it just came easy."

Soon, she was expanding her role to provide musical commentary on the game. "I think that I grew as I learned more about the team and more about each player and the terminology so that I could be more clever," Nancy said. "I'd see a player wearing number three, and my thought process was, I'll play (the theme to) 'My Three Sons.' I could give this a little more color. And I kind of just went from there."

While Holcomb was resented by players, Chuck Tanner and Roland Hemond, Faust credited him for much of her success.

"I worshipped Stu because he was a champion for me," Nancy said. "The year I was hired, I remember a petition being circulated because (some fans) didn't think a woman belonged here. But he ignored it and whatever he said gave me confidence."

Holcomb also went to bat for Faust when Detroit Tigers Manager Billy Martin complained about her music.

"(Martin) didn't like the music I was playing when his team was at bat, and he complained to the umpires, who told me to stop playing," Faust recalled. "And right away Stu called and said you keep doing what you're doing. Don't be intimidated.

"Stu just really liked me. He never gave me a problem about salary. He was very generous. I know from a player's standpoint that Stu wasn't well-loved. But he had to keep the purse strings in because of John Allyn, who was struggling, I guess."

1972 became a pivotal year for Faust.

"It was a big season for me personally, because that's the year they moved the organ from center field to the upper deck behind home plate," she recalled. "The team got a brand new (Hammond X66) organ for me and removed 10 seats to accommodate the organ. And now suddenly I was surrounded by fans. It was like a different park."

The move behind home plate enabled Faust to use fan requests, something that admirers like Kantor have given her credit for over the years.

"It was the first time I really had fans to interact with, which was not the case when I was in the center-field bleachers," Faust said. "It was easy for me because that's the one thing I could do is pat my head and rub my stomach at the same time. I could talk to people and still play."

Dick Allen's presence in 1972 not only energized the fans and his teammates. Faust also was motivated by his commanding presence on the White Sox.

"When they first acquired him, I probably thought of him as just another player," she said. "But then, all of the sudden you notice that the atmosphere is buzzing, and people plan bathroom trips around this guy. You just don't want to be in the john when the guy is up to bat. And he was doing wonderful things. And he had this certain kind of appearance that you recognized when he approached the plate. I think you could see that from any place in the park. He had that certain style which you associated with a great performance."

Faust struggled at first to find a "walk-up" song for Allen.

"When he got here, he was called Richie Allen, so I thought about 'If I Were a Rich Man,'" she said. "Although then I found out you don't call him Richie, you call him Dick. Then, I thought about him playing in Philadelphia. At the time, the only Philadelphia song I knew was a polka. 'Pennsylvania Polka,' that's what I would have played. But then [I thought] that's hokey, you can't play that for this guy. This guy is great. It would be like playing 'Winchester Cathedral' for the Queen. You don't make light of somebody that does something wonderful like that."

By then, "Superstar", the title song from "Jesus Christ Superstar," had been around for more than two years. The Andrew Lloyd Webber/Tim Rice-penned tune was first recorded as a single, then was added as part of a complete rock opera album in 1970, before it was launched as a Broadway stage musical in 1971.

"Superstar" had reached No. 14 in the Hot 100, so Faust — and the White Sox Park crowd — were familiar with the song. By June 1972, when Dick was dominating the American League, Faust began playing the song as his "walk-up" song.

"I probably had a gut instinct realizing this guy is a superstar, and everybody knew the song 'Jesus Christ Superstar,'" she said. "I think that's one of the first times I really played a song that reflected a guy's performance. It was almost like editorializing. Until then, it was more playing something clever that went with the name or the number or high hopes or whatever. But, this guy, he almost commanded a song that reflected his performance."

Her style coalesced in 1972, and Faust would expand on her creativity in the coming years, especially after Bill Veeck bought the team in December 1975. In 1977, Veeck helped create a tradition when he connected Caray to the Comiskey Park public address system, allowing the full crowd to hear him sing "Take Me Out To The Ballgame" with Faust and the fans.

And that same year, during a battle for first place in a four-game series in July against the AL West rival Kansas City Royals, Faust started another stadium tradition by playing the 1969 hit from the studio band Steam, "Na Na Hey Hey Kiss Him Goodbye" when one of the Royals' pitchers was pulled after getting shelled by the Sox' explosive offense.

The nearly 10-year-old song took off as a derisive farewell for vanquished White Sox opponents, and it became the talk of baseball. As a result of the new-found greater popularity of "Na Na Hey Hey Kiss Him Goodbye," Mercury Records rereleased it and presented Nancy with a gold record in a pregame cere-mony at Comiskey Park.

By this time, she was a wanted commodity in sports, especially on the North Side, where Cubs officials were actively recruiting her to move to Wrigley Field, as seen in this correspondence from April 23, 1979:

Dear Nancy:

Just a short note to remind you of our continuing interest in obtaining your services for our fans here at Wrigley Field.

Is this the last year of your contract with the Sox?

We would love to have you playing here at Wrigley Field.

Sincerely,

CHICAGO NATIONAL LEAGUE BALL CLUB

DENNIS BEYREUTHER

Assistant Director - Park Operations

Nancy's husband, Joe Jenkins, had pitched to her the idea of playing and working for both teams. "He had convinced me that, 'Oh, Jack Brickhouse used to broadcast both teams,'" she said with a laugh. "And all the vendors worked for both teams.''

But Bill Veeck squashed that idea immediately. Barnum Bill certainly wasn't about to share his star organist.

"This is what Bill Veeck said: 'Young lady, you pick one or the other,'" Faust said with a chuckle. "But at least he knew that somebody was interested, that the other side was interested."

She received another informal invitation to move her act to Wrigley Field in the early 1980s, courtesy of her old friend Caray, by then employed on the North Side.

"But I had no reason to go," Nancy said. "I guess I was happy. I had no reason. I would have been happy to do both. But I also felt that I was part -- well, by then the 'Nah, nah, nah, hey, hey, goodbye,' that's just how I was associated with the South Side."

"Jesus Christ Superstar" opened an entire new collection of walk-up songs and other themes Faust employed for nearly the next four decades at Comiskey Park.

Here is a partial list of notable names and attached theme songs from the 1970s to the 2000s with some of Faust's comments:

- Bill Melton: "Wedding Bell Blues," "Where Have You Been Charming Billy."
- Carlos May: "April Showers," Carlos Santana songs such as "Evil Ways" and "Black Magic Woman," "She Was Just Seventeen."
- *Mike Andrews: "Hotel Cal," "California Girls."
- *Ed Hermann: "Mr. Ed," "Munsters Theme."
- *Wilbur Wood: "Norwegian Wood," the Woody Woodpecker song, "Mr. Ed."
- Goose Gossage: "Free Bird."
- Richie Zisk: "You're a Rich Man," "If I Were A Rich Man," "Melody Of Love" (for his Polish background).
- Oscar Gamble: "Viva Las Vegas," the Odd Couple theme, "When You See A Chance Take It," " Sweet Home Alabama."
- Steve Stone: "Papa Was A Rolling Stone," "Like A Rolling Stone," "Every-body Let's Get Stoned," "Stoned Soul Picnic," "Hava Nagila," "Loves Me Like A Rock."
- Carlton Fisk: "Smoke On the Water," "Smoke Gets In Your Eyes," "My Guy ('he was so cute')".

- Ron Kittle: "Back Home Again In Indiana," "Do Ron Ron," "Chicken Dance."
- Frank Thomas: "Hit Me With Your Best Shot," "Hurts So Good," "Sledgehammer," "Big Time," "Iron Man," "U Can't Touch This," "All-Star."
- Robin Ventura: "Rockin Robin," "Ventura Highway," "Free Bird," "Fly Robin Fly," "Bat Man."

For umpire rhubarbs, Faust played: "Try To See It My Way," "Come Out and Play (Keep 'Em Separated)," "You Can't Always Get What You Want," "Why Can't We Be Friends," "[Can't Get No] Satisfaction."

When a tough opposing relief pitcher came in: "Mission Impossible," "The Heat Is On," "Fool on the Hill", "Don't Go Breaking My Heart," "Stop In The Name Of Love," "Don't Worry Be Happy," "You Gotta Have Faith," "Somebody's Gonna Hurt Someone (Heartache Tonight)," "Heartbreaker."

For the 2005 World Series, Faust played the team's theme — "Don't Stop Believing"—along with "Star Wars," "We Are The Champions" and "Sweet Home Chicago." Mark Buehrle tossed a perfect game and a no-hitter, providing Faust with grist like: "Hero Comes Along," "Nobody Does It Better" and "Vehicle."

She had many general favorites, as told to Armour and Co. in the *Chicago Tribune*:

"Margaritaville," "Here Comes the Sun," "Carry on Wayward Son" by Kansas ('Great song for the organ'), "Stairway to Heaven" by Led Zeppelin (played for a pop fly), "Classical Gas" by Mason Williams, "Smoke on the Water" by Deep Purple (Sox pitchers throwing smoke) and "Hash Pipe" by Weezer, a favorite of son Eric from its popularity at his college dorm.

Faust's growing playlist also was applied to organ gigs away from the South Side.

Veeck could not run Faust off her non-baseball sports engagements in Chicago, with one exception, as her popularity spread market-wide and beyond. She would go on to play for every team other than the Cubs and Bears, which did not have an organ at Soldier Field.

Nancy first expanded to the NBA's Bulls at Chicago Stadium in 1975. She enjoyed a long tenure through some lean years. Timing was everything. Faust departed the Bulls in the spring prior to Michael Jordan's arrival as franchise savior. With her Dick Allen experience, the imagination is stretched as to how she could have accompanied Jordan's other-worldly feats on and above the basketball floor.

Veeck extended his restraint-of-Nancy to a crucial Bulls-Portland Trailblazers first-round playoff game on April 15, 1977 at Chicago Stadium. The date conflicted with the Sox' first night game of the season against the expansion Toronto Blue Jays. Bulls official Mike McClure, a decade later the Sox' marketing chief under owners Reinsdorf and Einhorn, teamed with Lester Crown, an investor in both the Sox and Bulls, to pitch Veeck on allowing her to play for the sold-out crowd of more than 20,000.

As with the Cubs, Veeck said no, and the tug-of-war between the two teams became a sports page one story in the *Chicago Tribune* the day before the game.

Citing his own night game, Veeck told the *Tribune's* Richard Dozer, "She is under contract to us, and she is every bit as important to the White Sox as she is to the Bulls...I wish the Bulls every success, but not at our expense."

McClure figured, in the true Chicago Way, that the Sox owed the Bulls a favor. In May 1976, Charlie Saad had missed a week due to a death in his family, and the Bulls then loaned the team the services of Doug Atkinson, their trainer. "Being public relations conscious, we felt that Bill would see this as a chance to build some more goodwill," reasoned McClure, unsuccessfully.

Nancy's keyboarding had been a key part of the packed Stadium audiences' enthusiasm during a frantic 20-4 regular-season finish that elevated the Bulls from NBA irrelevance into the playoffs. The playoff game, a 107-104 Bulls win, went on without her.

While still playing for the Bulls, Faust drummed up college basketball work for DePaul at old Alumni Hall. "It was the Sam Manella years," she recalled. "I played 'Brylcream ... A Little Dab Will Do Ya'" for Sam's wild hair." Faust also enjoyed revving up the 5,200-seat cozy confines of the Lincoln Park gym for DePaul's Final Four team in 1979. She migrated to play at the Rosemont Horizon in 1980 when the Blue Demons outgrew their neighborhood home court.

Alumni Hall also hosted the Chicago Hustle, the city's first entry into women's pro basketball, so the financially-shaky franchise also took on Faust as organist for its short lifespan.

Faust had to engage in a post-graduate Organ 401 course when she landed the Blackhawks' organist job in 1984. Perched in the stadium's east balcony at a giant Barton pipe organ, Faust had to adjust to a sound delay. "I'd hit a key, and there was a delay with the sound going through the pipes," she recalled. "The thing that made it most difficult is I play by ear. I play by hearing the last note. It took a couple of years to adjust."

Work for that Chicago franchise networked Faust into even more assignments. For two seasons starting in 1987, she became a commuting organist playing for the Minnesota North Stars, a 1967 NHL expansion team which eventually moved to Dallas in 1993.

"I played every game that did not conflict with the Hawks," Faust said.

"American Airlines sponsored me. They flew me to the Twin Cities for games. Sometimes I'd stay over if they played several games close together. I don't know, that could have been the cause of my Hawks demise [in 1989]." Faust should not kick herself, though, as Arthur and Bill Wirtz also let the likes of Bobby Hull, Jeremy Roenick, Chris Chelios and Pat Foley go.

If Faust wasn't busy enough away from old Comiskey Park, she added even more play dates, for the indoor version of the Chicago Sting pro soccer club, owned by Sox investor Lee Stern, in the early 1980s. "Der Schting" drew as many as 19,000 to games at Chicago Stadium.

Faust became the most enduring baseball organist in history. She missed only five scheduled games in her career, around the birth of her son Eric on May 6, 1983. Interestingly, her longtime Cubs counterpart, Gary Pressy, beat her in sheer stamina at the keyboard. Over his 33 seasons from 1987 to 2019, Pressy never missed a game at Wrigley Field, proud of exceeding Cal Ripken, Jr.'s 2,632-game streak.

Nancy was on the job in time for the 50th anniversary All-Star Game in July 1983, a tune-up for her only Comiskey Park postseason performance, in October, for the "Winning Ugly" Sox. Moving across the street to new Comiskey Park in 1991, Faust was on hand for the 70th anniversary All-Star Game in 2003 and the long-awaited World Series championship team in 2005.

With a ring in hand, Faust opted to cut back to day games and her long commute from the Lake County, Ill. homestead where she kept a pair of affable donkeys. But to the very end of her White Sox keyboard tenure in 2010, she always tried to keep her act fresh and relatable.

"I was always able to adjust my style to the changing music," she said. "Of course I did a lot of disco when that came about, but before that I was playing Stones and the Beatles and just whatever was popular. I loved soul music. Anything with a lot of syncopation.

"I had the ability to adapt. And I think that's what kept me going. That's what enabled me to stick around."

But by the time the Sox moved into their new stadium, she wasn't the only show in the house. Faust had to incorporate her organ into a highly produced in-stadium entertainment experience, where recorded music, sound effects and scoreboard animation were also featured. Eventually, she was told to stop playing musical introductions for the home team. The players instead began choosing their own "walk-up" music. And she couldn't use her full improv skills to comment on the game when she wanted to make a musical statement.

"From my personal point of view it was frustrating to no longer be able to do that," Faust said. "There became a time when I was told only to play when I was told to play. I'd sit there really frustrated, realizing it's a great opportunity that I knew the fans would enjoy.

"And I have to say, when I played walk-up music it was to reflect the player coming up to bat. It was our home team player. There was always a connection. And it was for the enjoyment of the fans. But that changed. And then it became, what does the ball player want to hear, because he will perform better if he gets to hear the song that he loves.

"I had to reinvent myself. So then I played songs for the visiting players, which I welcomed because I had a new set of players every few games; every time a new team would come to town."

It was a far cry from her earlier days as an innovative young organist — especially in 1972, when she was the accompanist to the surprising, resurgent Sox led by their charismatic, iconoclastic star, Dick Allen.

Faust's entire body of work may not have been enough to gain entry to the Hall of Fame as a contributor. Plenty of worthy on-field luminaries, especially Dick, had their challenges in getting the required 75 percent of the vote from either the Baseball Writers Association of America or various incarnations of the Hall's Veterans Committee.

But the proprietor of the most impactful organ music in sports has garnered honors. In 2018, Faust was inducted into the Baseball Reliquary Shrine of the Eternals in Pasadena, Calif. And in a connection to her start in the game, she went in alongside pitcher Tommy John, one of the 1970 Sox for whom she played "Big Bad John" and the theme from "Tommy" from her center field perch.

Also, a 2021 ESPN feature went in-depth in crediting Faust for creating and touching off the "Na, Na, Na, Hey-Hey, Good-bye" chant now a staple at stadiums nationwide.

From such modest roots did a brand of sports entertainment emanate. "I provided the only soundtrack for the stadium at that time," Nancy recalled. "Just me and the PA guy, Bud Kelly. So, looking back I know what a privilege it was to have been able to play behind a star like Dick during his era. That I was able to be there and to have control of the music and pick a song like 'Jesus Christ Superstar' that was so fitting for him. He just made my job glorious."

Chicago's dissident doctors
page 18

Art from the U.S.S.R.
page 24

14

Nancy Faust, the White Sox music lady
page 52

Bill Melton (top) and Wilbur Wood (bottom) were two happy White Sox posing with a glammed-up organist Nancy Faust for the Chicago Tribune's Sunday Magazine cover on June 4, 1972. Hours after most readers saw the stylish photo, Dick Allen slugged his famed "Chili Dog Homer."

Photo credit: 1972/Chicago Tribune Magazine/TCA

As the decades passed, Nancy Faust kept on playing for millions in paid crowds at two South Side ballparks. She played Jesus Christ Superstar to introduce Dick Allen before his speech on June 26 2012.

Photo credit: Mike Gustafson, Owner Gustafson Photography
MikeGustafsonPhotography.com

Organist Nancy Faust in 1971, when she was stuck out in the outfield. In 1972, she moved above home plate with a new organ — and baseball entertainment was forever changed.

Photo courtesy of the Nancy Faust Archives

CHAPTER 12

July 24, 1972:
Dick Allen, All-Star

Due to the players strike in April, Major League baseball's annual three-day break for the All-Star Game came later than usual. In this abbreviated baseball season, All-Star week began on Monday, July 24,1972. And, during this time, both Chicago and its baseball teams were coping with change.

At City Hall, there was intriguing political drama, centered around the always-prominent Sox fan, Mayor Richard J. Daley.

Daley's Cook County Democratic organization was smarting from a national embarrassment. On July 11, at the Democratic National Convention, the party's credentials committee officially recognized that diverse group of 59 delegates to represent Illinois. They were chosen over Daley's hand-picked group of mostly White male delegates, endorsed by the mayor and his longtime political establishment.

The renegade group was led by two of Daley's most potent adversaries in Chicago: Bill Singer, the young attorney and liberal alderman, and Rev. Jesse Jackson, the dynamic 28-year-old onetime protégé of Dr. Martin Luther King. Jackson helped make Chicago's Operation PUSH a national civil rights organization. And the progressive delegates had the tacit support of the man who would become the Democratic Presidential nominee: George McGovern.

"It's nation time!" Jackson screamed at the Miami Beach Convention Center after "Singer 59" delegates were officially recognized. Meanwhile, Daley was forced to retreat to his summer home in Grand Beach, Mich. after being placed in the uncomfortable position of not being in control of the party he continued to lead, both in the state and nationally.

The rebellion was only momentarily successful. The convention was thrown into an uproar, and anti-war candidate McGovern had to give his acceptance speech in the wee hours of the morning after most television viewers had gone to bed. McGovern was further weakened against an incumbent President Richard M. Nixon, skillfully ensuring no more ground combat operations for U.S. troops in Vietnam as the summer of 1972 progressed and the stretch run of the campaign beckoned. Flag-draped coffins arriving home were a bad image for the slickly-packaged Nixon campaign. A bothersome minor scandal involving a break-in at Democratic headquarters in Washington, D.C. remained in the background, for now.

Some Chicago-area Democrats, normally inclined toward reform, sensed the insurgents would not be a benefit for the campaign.

"I was a suburban delegate to the 1972 Democratic convention," said former FCC Chairman Newton Minow, in '72 a power-broker in public broadcasting among his other high-profile political and legal pursuits. "I voted to seat the Daley delegates, along with my suburban colleagues Harold Katz, Aaron Jaffe and Dan Pierce — and we were right."

Still, the convention controversy proved that old-style, dictatorial machine politics was undergoing a slow transformation that would portend tumultuous events on the city's political landscape a decade later.

As his treasured White Sox returned to Comiskey Park for their final series before the All-Star break against the Cleveland Indians, Daley came back to City Hall after his extended vacation. He returned to a *Chicago Tribune* exposé of another recent embarrassment — his recent plans to build a third regional airport on a man-made landfill in Lake Michigan near the South Side. The landfill would have been about 8.5 miles due east of the Hyde Park neighborhood. But environmentalists were alarmed by the thought of pollutants being pumped into the lake brought on by the airport, while Hyde Parkers were alarmed by potentially increased traffic coursing through their storied neighborhood. So Daley was forced to abandon the plans. "It is time we eliminate the emotionalism and controversy about this issue," he said.

Despite the political losses in Miami Beach and major setback in his continued attempts to remake Chicago with ambitious public works projects, Daley remained popular where it counted — in the White ethnic wards that still predominated in Chicago, specifically to the south and west of White Sox Park. Chicago was a solidly Democratic city, but it was a city still filled with Daley Democrats, not McGovern Democrats. These sentiments were verbalized by Michael Howlett, a machine functionary who would later become Illinois' secretary of state. Howlett said: "I'd rather march in the St. Patrick's Day parade with Mayor Daley than march to the White House with George McGovern."

Nearly 50 years later, many of those White ethnics looked with fondness on Daley's heyday with what they perceived as a lost world where order was kept and everyone knew their place, especially people of color. Social media gave an additional platform to this nostalgia. One retired Chicago police detective, who grew up in an all-White Rogers Park in the middle of the 20th century, penned this 2021 Facebook ode to the machine underneath a vintage campaign poster for Daley:

The Good Old Days......

The Machine was well oiled .....

Patronage..... Cops were allowed to be Cops......sure there was

Corruption..... but Chicago had a reputation as a tough ....

take no prisoners city..... outsiders were kept in check ....

Neighborhoods and the kids living in them were watched over and kept safe by residents .... you knew not to cross over a certain Street or imaginary line on the edge of your turf which was the border between trouble and calm ....and I like it like that.....

Shitheads wouldn't venture into Italian ...Irish... Hispanic.... neighborhoods...your life and existence had tent posts that were strong and defined.....

I miss that time. The Neighborhoods were a great place to grow up. When I was born the first few years of my life I lived at Grand & Racine in my grandmothers home.... and I sowed my oats and learned the realities of life in Rogers Park on Howard Street..... at Saint Jerome school. It was full of Irish kids ....nuns and priests.... made us all tough.... you become the person you are yes by your parents .... but the surroundings you dwell in define you...

No matter what their surroundings or ethnic backgrounds, Chicagoans loved their pro sports. The city was never a "college town." Baseball in 1972 did not have the other sports encroach on it coming and going, pro basketball in the spring and football training camp in July, so gabbing about the summer game was supreme when the mercury was at its apex.

The conversation at the 1972 All-Star break swirled around a major change on the North Side, where Chicago Cubs manager Leo Durocher was dismissed after a stormy, sometimes successful but ultimately disappointing tenure. During his stint as manager from 1966 to 1972, Durocher restored the Cubs to relevancy, if not dominance, in the Chicago sports world.

At the gate, but not necessarily on TV with young Baby Boom viewers, the Cubs were the second team to the White Sox for most of the 1950s and 60s, finishing behind the Sox in attendance virtually every year. In several seasons the Sox nearly doubled the Cubs' ticket sales. But after a 10th-place finish in 1966, Durocher's Cub teams captivated the city. They finished above .500 from 1967 to 1971, culminating in a magical 1969 season where the team was in first place for 155 days, until mid-September when they lost 17 out of 25 games.

But despite his work reviving a team that finished in the second division every year from 1947 through 1966, Durocher couldn't finish first — even with a team that featured four future Hall of Famers (Ernie Banks, Billy Williams, Ron Santo, Ferguson Jenkins) and a solid supporting cast of multiple-year All-Stars.

Now, despite its prominence among Chicago media and fans through the team's presence on powerful WGN-TV and No. 1-rated WGN-AM, the Cubs were once again challenged by a rebounding Sox team, led by Dick. At the 1972 All-Star break, Durocher's aging Cubs team was in third place and a distant 10 games behind NL East division-leading Pittsburgh. The Cubs had gone 12-22 since peaking in late June. "[Durocher's firing] allows the players to find out for themselves if they can win," owner Phil Wrigley told the press on July 24, 1972. But Durocher's firing would presage another long decline for the North Side team, featuring no above-.500 seasons from 1973 to 1983.

Meanwhile, on the South Side, the legend of Dick Allen continued to grow.

By the time the White Sox approached the Midsummer Classic, the team was actually rebounding from a period where they could have fallen out of contention in the AL West.

The Sox had three All-Stars who were leading them — Dick, outfielder Carlos May and tireless knuckleballer Wilbur Wood. May, who had 10 home runs, 48 RBI and batted .287 going into the break, was the team's homegrown, budding star, who had a hot early June to help keep his team above .500. Wood, who had a 15-10 record with a 2.49 ERA on July 25, was clearly enjoying his still-somewhat-new change from former Fireman Of The Year to successful starter. And Dick, with 22 homers, 66 RBI and a .300 average going into the break, was preparing for his fifth All-Star Game appearance and first in the American League, where the former Phillies star was proving himself as perhaps its most dominant offensive threat.

But despite being an overwhelming presence at home — at one point in the spring, Tanner's team was an astounding 18-2 at White Sox Park — problems on the road kept them from putting the heat on the Oakland A's, the still-dominant team in the AL West. Those road struggles included a disastrous late May road trip to the West Coast, where the Athletics swept a three-game series and the Sox then dropped three out of four to the Angels. Then, after a resurgent June including the "Chili Dog Game" against the Yankees, the Sox began slumping again in early July. Perhaps the players suffered a kind of malaise after getting the news on July 9 that third baseman Bill Melton, the team's third-most potent offensive threat after Allen and May, would be out for the season.

When he heard the news about Melton, Dick closed his eyes, rubbed his forehead with both hands and tilted his chair back at a 45-degree angle.

"That's a blow, a helluva blow," muttered Dick at his locker while getting ready for a home game against the Detroit Tigers. He had carried the team offensively through July, playing in every game. The big man was getting fatigued — and was dealing with a bruised right big toe. "Lefty (manager Chuck Tanner) asked me…to rest, but I couldn't sit down with Melton out. But I'm going to need to rest soon whether Bill is gone or not. Sometimes I think I've had enough. Sometimes I think I've had about enough and can't see how many more seasons I can take."

Melton's injury left Dick with much less protection in the Sox lineup. Along with him and Melton, May was the main threat in the White Sox offense; *Baseball Digest* featured the trio on its cover with the suddenly-rekindled phrase "New Murderers Row." But May slumped along with the team in the weeks before the break, going 5-for-34 in the games leading up to it. His teammates were just as unimpressive: Walt Williams was 0-for-24, Mike Andrews 3-for-46, Jay Johnstone 4-for-28 and Ed Herrmann 1-for-28.

Dick later told *Sports Illustrated* writer Roy Blount, Jr. that playing for the 1972 White Sox was one of the greatest challenges of his career.

"People said we had a good team, I didn't think we had (bleep). I never had to play so hard in my life. I was completely exhausted, a nervous wreck. I'd been carrying the team for months. Nights I'd be hot one minute, cold the next, and wake up jumping. I didn't think I could play anymore. But this was the only place I'd felt I was liked. I didn't want to do anything to change it."

The Sox dropped six road games in a row in Baltimore and Detroit to fall a season-worst 8½ games behind Oakland on July 18. But right before the All-Star break, the Sox pulled off three straight wins over the Indians. On Saturday, July 22, Allen powered two home runs into the center field bullpen to boost his league-leading totals to 21 homers and 64 RBI.

And on the last day before the break, Chicago swept a doubleheader from Cleveland, 2–1 and 4–3, with both wins coming in walk-off fashion. Jay Johnstone's bases-loaded, pinch single decided Game One, and in the nightcap, May led off the ninth inning with a game-winning homer off Ed Farmer. The clout was a rude homecoming for Farmer, graduate of Chicago's St. Rita High school, who nearly a decade later became the Sox' closer. The beloved "Farmio" came home for good in 1991 as part of the Sox' radio team until he died in 2020.

May's homer was his second of the game, keeping the Sox within striking distance of Oakland at 6½ games out. But despite the heroics of his teammates, Dick was the man the crowd of 35,206 came to see on that sweltering afternoon. The *Chicago Tribune's* Bob Logan, who covered that game, noticed an almost rapturous Comiskey Park response to the mysterious slugger:

"To tell the truth…the impact of Dick Allen's superstar charisma on the crowd was the most striking event of the long afternoon. Visible tremors of excitement swept thru the place while the slugger homered off Gaylord Perry to tie the first game… And when he strode from the dugout to pinch hit in the after piece, the transformation of a hitherto dull affair was complete. The turned-on remnants of the throng stayed that way until May sent them home happy only moments later."

Dick started at first base in the '72 All-Star Game at Atlanta's Fulton County Stadium, after leading all American League players with 1,092,758 votes. And although his actual 0-for-3 appearance in the game was anti-climactic, it was proof of Allen's incredible popularity, especially in Chicago. He captured the city's imagination in a way no other athlete had in the recent past — especially an African American athlete. During the All-Star telecast, NBC replayed his "Chili Dog" homer, certainly the most dramatic clout in the American League at that point in the season.

Chicago's sports teams primarily featured non-controversial superstars, most of whom had long tenures with their organizations. The Cubs had media-friendly stars like Banks, Santo and Williams and, before them, popular sluggers like Hank Sauer and Andy Pafko. The National Football League's Chicago Bears had established stars like Gale Sayers, Dick Butkus and Mike Ditka. The National Hockey League's Chicago Blackhawks featured "Golden Jet" Bobby Hull's electricity on the ice and outwardly friendly demeanor on dry land, complementing multiple "Lady Byng" Trophy winner, durable Stan Mikita. The National Basketball Association's expansion team from 1966, the Chicago Bulls, had workmanlike stars like Jerry Sloan and Chet Walker. Even the Chicago Cardinals — Comiskey Park's NFL football team until it moved to St. Louis in 1960 — had relatively conservative stars like Ollie Matson and Dick "Night Train" Lane.

As for the Chicago White Sox, they had been known in the 1950s and 1960s for their first-rate pitching (Pierce, Peters, Horlen, Wynn, John, Wood and many others) and solid, bland everyday players who manufactured runs under managers Al Lopez and Eddie Stanky. The team's home run record of 33 was set by Melton in 1970 and matched the following season to lead the AL. Its flashiest offensive player in the last 20 years had been the exciting five-tool player Minnie Minoso, Chicago's first Black major league player. Minoso was never seen as controversial, and as a Cuban-born player who spoke limited English, he was often reduced to a crude stereotype in contemporary media coverage.

But this new star was different. On the field, he was instantly recognizable, wearing his batting helmet at all times and a long-sleeved red sweatshirt underneath his red-pinstriped uniform. He looked strong and forbidding.

"We had 8:00 games and like I said he would get there at 7:00 and put on his long draws and no matter how hot it was, he always had that long-sleeved sweatshirt on," May recalled.

When he was at the plate, Dick was a menacing presence, shifting his feet, set up in a slight crouch, with his 40-ounce bat twisted towards the pitcher, then uncoiling the heavy weapon as he swung at a pitch. When he connected, he often thrilled the crowd with line drives hit with authority.

"They announced Dick Allen, and you'd hear 'Oooh!' from everybody in the stadium," said future Sox star Ron Kittle, who went to many games in 1972 as a teenager. "I've never seen anyone hit balls as hard as him. It was either they catch it, or they get killed. That's how hard he used to hit the ball."

"Every time he came up, I don't care where anybody was, they were in the dugout," said Rory Clark, the batboy for the 1972 team. "Everybody was always looking when Dick Allen was up. He had so much respect from the other players. And they were like fans when he was up. They just wanted to see what he was going to do. He was just electric."

Off the field, the man seemed almost revolutionary, albeit in an unassuming way. He was quiet and, when he did talk to the media, he was articulate and soft-spoken. But he also had a style unlike any other major leaguer. He was decked out in the most daring early '70s fashions. *Sports Illustrated* writer Roy Blount, Jr., described Allen in 1973 as wearing a stunning "cinched-in waist" sports coat, flamboyant shirts with big collars and "yellow snakeskin boots." After arriving at the park, he'd "dress, maybe take a few grounders at shortstop, have a cigarette" and then take the field for the game, Blount wrote.

"He was the coolest of the cool," said Jim Riley, one of the bat boys at White Sox Park. "He was Superfly."

Despite that skipping of batting practice, he would sometimes show up, just to have fun with teammates. "One day Dick came for batting practice and I dropped my bat," teammate Bill Melton recalled 50 years later. "Everybody said what is this? We all kind of stared at him. He was laughing coming out of the dugout, 'cause we hadn't seen him for a month at BP. So he comes out and gets in the left-hand side of the batter's box and hits a couple out. We said, 'What in the hell is this?' He's a right-handed hitter and he just stepped in the batting cage and hit 'em out left-handed. I said, 'Jesus!' I mean, he was a mystery. And we were in awe. We were in awe of everything he did."

While Dick was respected by all Sox fans at that time, his presence had a special meaning for Black fans in the city, especially on the South Side. Kenny McReynolds lived in public housing less than a mile north of White Sox Park. McReynolds, who attended dozens of Sox games before Allen joined the team, was transfixed by the superstar, who would often be seen in the nearby Douglas-Oakland neighborhood before and after games.

"I remember him driving a huge red Cadillac — we'd see him over by Lawless Gardens (a high-rise building in the neighborhood) in his car — I think he'd hang out [with a friend] there," McReynolds said. "It was such a thrill to see him in the neighborhood. I'd see him and then, any sport I played, I had to be No. 15 like Dick Allen. Remember, Sox Park was in a Black neighborhood until you go west, when you're in (the predominantly White) Bridgeport (neighborhood). So to have Dick Allen performing for the Sox — it just gave a lot of African Americans in the neighborhoods something to get excited about."

"The kind of thing that he did for a young boy who grew up in the ghetto without a father, the kind of example he set is, you know, I credit that a lot with my own approach to being a man," added Clark, who, like McReynolds, grew up in the African American neighborhood adjacent to Sox Park. "I just really admired him as a man. More than I admired him as a ballplayer."

Dick, in turn, appreciated Chicago as a city unlike any other that he played in. "You know how I was in Philadelphia, I wanted to hide all the time," he said. "I never felt a part of anything, always an outsider. In Chicago, it's different. I'll even go out and talk at a speaking engagement here…I feel I'm able to come out and be myself."

"Unlike his baseball past, there were no missed busses, no missed planes, no late arrivals at ball parks, no suspensions, no fights with teammates, no squabbles with managers — nothing but brilliant, clutch baseball day after day," the *New York Times*' Murray Chass wrote of Allen in 1972.

By July, Dick's exploits were becoming legendary among fans. There was his incredible start to the season, when he recorded 14 hits in 31 at-bats in the first eight games — including two home runs of more than 400 feet. There was his 500-foot home run blast at White Sox Park that struck the back wall of the center field bleachers on May 21 against the California Angels' Rudy May, putting the Sox in first place. There was also, of course, the "Chili Dog Game." The slugger eating a chili dog before hitting that pinch-hit, three-run, game-winning homer awed many who later learned of the details.

The 40-ounce bat Mr. Allen wielded was probably the heaviest anyone was using in the majors at that time – but he was able to deftly control the prodigious lumber, routinely hitting the ball with power to all fields.

"His dozen bats were in the locker next to mine," Bill Melton said of his superstar teammate. "And I took one out. And I looked around, I said, My God, nobody can swing this. Forty ounces? Forty and three-quarters? Mine were 32, 33 ounces. I picked that bat up and I took it out to the batting cage just to see if I could swing it. And after about five or six swings, man, my arm started to swell up, you know, I was going, 'God almighty, this guy swings this thing around like a buggy whip.' He had big hands and powerful arms. He was a powerful man. As a matter of fact, he was kind of embarrassed of his hands. But they were powerful hands. And 40 ounces was unheard of in major league baseball."

Arguably, Dick hit the ball harder in his era than anyone else, and his exploits became almost mythical, even to the opposition, let alone to members of his own team.

"He is the closest thing to being a perfect ballplayer that I have ever seen," said the future White Sox Hall of Fame shortstop Luis Aparicio, who competed against Allen with Boston.

"I think Dick probably hits the ball harder than anyone in the world," said Baltimore's Boog Powell.

But almost as important were the little things that he would do during the season to help the Sox win games.

"In one game against the Yankees, for example, Dick averted a sure out in a rundown between third and home by diving back into third safely after putting a fake and a move on Hal Lanier (who had the ball) that would have made Julius Erving envious," Murray Chass wrote of Allen in 1972. "Then two innings later, in the eighth, with Chicago leading 4-1, he slid so hard into Gene Michael at second base that he broke up a double play just before Melton homered."

Dick's base-running abilities also astounded teammates. He stole 19 bases in 1972. But many teammates said he was the best *overall* baserunner that they had ever seen. "He cut the base paths just right, and he never over-turned a base. All his turns were right," Carlos May recalled.

"He could steal a base whenever he wanted, and he could read the outfielders as well as anyone," Melton recalled. "We'd be behind home plate watching him come around third to score, and he'd be looking at the center fielder or the left fielder who had the ball. As soon as he'd see the ball and he knew where it was, he would pick up speed or just go at the same speed home."

Goose Gossage, watching from the left field bullpen, noticed how Dick was even more productive in clutch situations. "I never saw a hitter set pitchers up like Dick Allen did," Gossage recalled 50 years later. "No ducks on the pond. Nobody on base. Dick comes up, strikes out, waves at three pitches, goes and sits down. Next time up, no ducks on the pond, strike three, go sit down. Next time up, no ducks on the pond, strike three, goodbye.

"Come up in the eighth inning, ducks on the pond, Dick's up. He taught me how to study people and hitters, and I studied him, and he was amazing. When he got up there with ducks on the pond, his whole demeanor was different. I watched it, it was methodical, boom, he'd drop that bat and unleash a goddamn line drive. It was not to be freaking believed. They talk about [Gossage's future Oakland A's teammates Jose] Canseco and [Mark] McGwire. Did they launch balls? Absolutely. Did they ever hit a ball like Dick Allen? I guarantee you they never hit a ball like Dick Allen!"

Gossage remembers Allen predicting many of his shots before they happened. "It'd be the third out in an inning, we're in Cleveland and Dick thinks there's three outs and there's two, and he turns around and tosses the ball to the umpire, the umpire jumps away, two runs scored and there's only two outs," he recalled of one such episode. "Dick comes in, he goes, 'Oh, my God, you guys, I can't believe I did that. I'm so sorry. I'll get them back.' So later in the game, he comes up, two men on, he hits a three-run bomb, and we win the game."

Allen preferred facing the best hard-throwing pitchers in the league, telling Roy Blount Jr.: "I don't use the strike zone much. I'm looking for something to hammer. I don't have time to argue whether the pitch was two inches either way. A man like Gibson, he says, 'All right, big guy, here it is. Pschoo!' He's challenging you. Pschoo! Why hold on to the ball? Why sneak it in? That's not what the good dudes do — Koufax, Gibson. 'Here's the heat,' they say. 'Here, you want me? Pschoo!'"

In fact, Dick partially credited his early success in the American League to inferior pitching in the Junior Circuit. He criticized AL pitchers for not challenging him enough, and not pitching him tight enough. Nolan Ryan, who became a star in the 1970s after being traded from the NL New York Mets to the AL California Angels, was one such pitcher he cited for not going with his strengths as a pitcher. Instead, Ryan tried to "hide" behind his breaking pitches, according to Dick. "Every time that sumbuck throws a curve I lose a little respect for him," the veteran batsman told Roy Blount in 1973. "He ought to go Smoke, Smoke, Smoke, Smoke; O.K. I got a good curve, here it is, ping; Smoke, Smoke, Smoke."

Gossage remembered that it was useless for a pitcher to try to intimidate Dick. "Every time I saw him knocked down, I saw him get up and unleash the darndest flying drive back at the pitcher." he said. "[Then Indians pitcher] Steve Busby told me he thought Dick Allen killed him when he hit a line drive back at him once."

"I remember [Dick batting against the Detroit Tigers'] Milt Wilcox," teammate Walt Williams recalled to White Sox historian Mark Liptak. "He was pitching against us and he threw one high and tight to Dick and he hit him. Dick picked up the baseball and sort of walked it out to Milt as he was heading down the line and quietly said to him, "I know you have to pitch inside but you better not hit me again."

Exploits like these led to the quiet man from Wampum, Pa. becoming a national media figure by June 1972, when he was featured on the famous *Sports Illustrated* cover. An insouciant Dick juggled three baseballs in the Sox Park home dugout while a lit cigarette dangled from his mouth. The full-color image became the most famous photo of Dick ever taken, cementing his reputation as baseball's ultimate iconoclast. And yet, years later, he would express disdain for the photo.

"When I interviewed him years later, he told me he hated that photo because of the cigarette dangling from his mouth," Kenny McReynolds said. "He didn't want kids to get the impression that it was OK to smoke." Shortly before his 2020 death, Dick still regretted that he was shown smoking on a magazine cover seen by millions.

Allen's resurgent first half of the season also brought the Chicago White Sox back to national prominence. The Go-Go Sox of 1950s and 1960s had a modicum of widespread public acclaim, especially with the 1959 pennant. But much of that fame was derived from the team's maverick owner, Bill Veeck. As impressive as players like Nellie Fox and Luis Aparicio were, they didn't necessarily move the needle nationally. Dick Allen was a different story.

"You'd notice more energy in the stands after Dick got here," Melton recalled. "And although you didn't have the media then like you do today — we only had (four) beat reporters covering the team, not 15 like they do today — we noticed more national reporters paying attention to us when Dick got here."

In the clubhouse, the oft-misunderstood public figure established a special relationship with his team. Dick had always been considered a "good teammate" by his peers but now became a quiet leader on the South Side.

"He's a very positive influence on the club," teammate Rick Reichardt said to Chass of the *Times*. "It's not just his hitting. He's probably the best baserunner on the club. He doesn't make mistakes. He's never down. He always points to the positive effort as far as winning is concerned. He helps out when another guy is down.

"I was not without my prejudices (about Dick). But I was surprised to find out how great a guy he is. He's been terrific to everyone on the club."

Fifty years later, his teammates still remember Dick's quiet leadership.

"We used to go from the ballpark to his room and we'd get a fifth of scotch and drink and just talk baseball," Carlos May recalled.

"I don't look at myself as a leader — I'm a professional ballplayer (and) that's what they pay me for, to do a job," Dick explained to *Newsday*'s Sandy Padwe during the 1972 season. "This stuff about measuring a ballplayer, how do you do it? Look at a guy like [utility infielder and former teammate] Tony Taylor. When I was with the Phillies, he would hit .250. But if there was a guy on second, Taylor would sacrifice himself a lot and get the runner to third with a ground ball. I want to do those things as much as hit home runs. Both things win ball games. And ballplayers who can do both can really help."

Dick recounted examples of how he taught teammates, in the 1972 interview with Chass. "One night I was on first and another guy was on second and Bill Melton was at bat," Allen recalled. "The guy on second steals third and is out. I naturally have to go to second, and that leaves first base open. After the game, the other guy asked me if that was a bad play and I said 'Yeah, you got to let Melton swing the bat. You can't let the other team pitch to him with an open base.'"

Dick could be equally helpful to pitchers. "Hell, I've never thrown a pitch in my life," Allen told Chass. "I just remind them of game situations. Like one night there was a man on first and our pitcher kept throwing over to keep him close to the bag. Meanwhile, he also threw two balls to the batter. I just went over to him and said: 'You take care of the batter and let the catcher take care of the runner.'"

Rory Clark remembered Allen consoling phenom relief pitcher Bart Johnson on June 3, 1972 in a game at White Sox Park against the Yankees, the day before Allen's "Chili Dog" heroics. The Sox dropped the Saturday contest, 18-10, in 13 innings after Johnson gave up eight runs in the 13th. Johnson was demoted to Triple-A as a result.

"[Manager] Chuck Tanner didn't get anybody up in the bullpen," Rory Clark recalled. "He was just determined that Bart Johnson was going to get himself out of the inning. And by the time it was over, we were down 18 to 10. And so Bart was pissed, but he was not a vocal guy. I think he hated Chuck Tanner from that moment on. They did not like each other. And when Bart came into the clubhouse, Dick sat down with him and talked him off the ledge. He was that kind of guy.

The '72 White Sox probably comprised the most relaxed clubhouse that Dick Allen had ever been a part of — a marked change from the tense rooms of which Dick was the centerpiece during his time with the Phillies. Now, he was one of the cut-ups before many games — and he loved it.

Dick remained controversial, however, when it came to the media. In a 1972 profile in *Ebony Magazine*, the slugger was said to have started requesting payments for interviews because "it's something I don't really care about." He was alleged to have told newsmen to "see my agent," who happened to be his brother, Hank, in order to set up any interviews.

His alleged requests for cash from reporters was never confirmed by Dick or anyone close to him. But he did admit to frustration with the press, going back to the savage treatment he had received from the Philadelphia media during the 1960s. "They keep writing things like…saying 'I'm changed, I'm a new person,'" Allen complained to Sandy Padwe. "I didn't know there was anything that bad about the old me. I don't care what they write. One guy cuts me, someone else writes a sympathetic story. It all evens out."

Mr. Allen's approach to the media was business-like, without a lot of camaraderie. "He wasn't effusive and personable with them because he had been hurt by the press a lot of times," Clark said. "He talked to the media all the time, but he was very matter-of-fact. And the press didn't like that. They wanted him to be 'yucky and jokey.' But he wasn't that way at the time."

Tanner told reporters that his top player deserved different treatment than his other players. "The pressures are tough," Tanner said. "When other guys miss buses or are late, nobody says anything about it because they're not the superstar.

"If Dick Allen eats left-handed in a restaurant, they're gonna write about it and wonder what happened to his right hand. He's magnetic. When he walks, people look at him. Whatever he does, they watch. I know he eats in his room a lot of times because when he goes into a restaurant people want to talk to him. He's sort of a bashful-type individual and he just wants to play baseball."

Tanner was instrumental in protecting Dick from the Chicago media in a way that his managerial counterparts never did in Philadelphia. Tanner's son, Bruce, who pitched briefly for the Sox under Tony LaRussa in 1985, was a 13-year-old batboy for the 1972 team. He remembered one specific time when his father shielded Dick from the media when he was late for work – even by the unique Allen standards of timeliness.

"It was 30 minutes before the game and he wasn't at the stadium and these reporters were in my dad's office," the younger Tanner said. "And they were hounding him pretty hard — like 'Where's Richie, why is he not here?' Finally, my dad said, 'Listen, it's 30 minutes before the game. You guys got to clear out, get out of here — Dick will be here.

"So, it's game time and Dick's not there. So eight guys go running on the field. And first base is empty for the National Anthem. And I'm like, 'Holy cow, like he's not here!' And about halfway through the Anthem, you know, I heard his spikes coming down the runway from the clubhouse to the dugout. And when that final note of the Anthem hit, I suddenly saw Dick hit the top step of the dugout and sprint out to his position. It was unbelievable!"

While Dick was in Chicago during 1972, he was living apart from his wife, Barbara, his daughter Terri, and two sons Richard, Jr. and Heron, who remained on his farm near Allentown, Pa. He started off in a hotel in the southwest suburbs, before moving to a two-bedroom townhouse in the same area. When Hank was signed as a utility player for the team, he moved in with his brother. "It used to take us about 45 minutes to get into the city," Hank recalled. "We had to leave early enough to beat the heavy traffic."

By mid-summer, seven-year-old Richard, Jr. (known to family as "Doobie") joined his father in Chicago, and lived with him in the suburban apartment, which was filled with all the accoutrements of a swinging 1970s man — a couch, a waterbed and a quadraphonic sound system. "I remember the very heavy '70s look with the couch and the colors and all that," Doobie Allen said. "I remember my grandmother (Era) visiting and sitting in the waterbed. She sunk down, and we had to help her out. When she looked in and saw the apartment she was like, 'Tsk, tsk, tsk, tsk.'"

Richard, Jr. had frightening early memories of trash dumped on the family's lawn, broken windows and ever-present boos from angry fans at Connie Mack Stadium in Philadelphia. The contrast to his father's enthusiastic welcome in Chicago, with all its embedded racial conflicts, was astounding.

"What I remember most is the walk-up music from [Sox organist] Nancy Faust," he said "It used to give me goosebumps on my arms, and it still does. I can still hear 'Jesus Christ Superstar' on that deep organ."

Even Doobie couldn't escape the barrage of line drives from his father. "They used to call me a stadium rat, because I liked to walk around the stands during the game," Richard, Jr. said. "One time I remember walking around and he hit a foul ball. He hit a foul ball, it missed the side of a vendor and almost hit me."

Following the All-Star break, the White Sox resumed their chase of Oakland. On July 28, Dick smashed his 25th homer, leading the Sox to a 5–0 blanking of the Royals at Sox Park.

Then on Monday, July 31, at the Twins' Metropolitan Stadium, Dick Allen did something that had only been accomplished by a handful of players in the history of baseball. He hit not one, but two inside-the-park home runs in the same game, both off future Hall of Famer Bert Blyleven. Dick was the first American Leaguer to accomplish the feat since 1932.

With center fielder Bobby Darwin in futile pursuit, Allen legged out a three-run homer to right center in the first inning. Four innings later, he again bedeviled Darwin with another elusive drive, this one to left center, with one runner on base. The Sox cruised to an 8-1 victory.

Future Sox teammate Jim Kaat could only watch Allen's drives in astonishment from the Twins' side.

"When he hit those two out to Bobby Darwin [the balls] just kind of knuckled their way out there," four-decade lefty Kaat said in an interview in the summer of 2021. "That was a memorable day, because we had that huge center field and once the ball got past Bobby, there was no chance."

Nearly 40 years later, Blyleven recalled: "He (Allen) was a tough out. You could see the bat he swung was a 40-ounce bat, like a telephone pole. He was so strong and so quick that the barrel of the bat went out so quickly.

"The two inside-the-park home runs he hit involved Darwin, a converted pitcher. The first one short-hopped Bobby. He came in and tried to make a shoe-string catch, and the ball eluded him and went all the way to the wall, which was 402 (feet) at the old Met. It was a three-run homer. Next at-bat, it was like a knuckleball. Darwin came in like he was going to catch it. The ball went past him again. A two-run inside-the-park home run."

The Allen rope-a-dopes with Darwin were a fitting end for the first 3½ months of the season for an AL newcomer cementing his status as a Most Valuable Player candidate.

"What couldn't he do?" remembered Wilbur Wood, his All-Star teammate. "What couldn't he do? He could do everything."

Dick Allen Historic Home Runs at Comiskey Park

A. 6/7/74 (508'): Carlton Fisk, "This was the longest drive I ever saw".

B. 5/1/73 (490'): Hit tower platform on left field roof and bounced over.

C. 8/23/72 (480'): Landed in 7th row in center field bleachers.

D. 7/23/72 (450'): Landed in 4th row of upper deck in deep right center field. Hit off Hall of Famer, Gaylord Perry.

E. 4/26/72 (465'): Rising line drive which broke chair in 10th row of left field upper deck.

F. 5/12/72 (475'): Landed in 1st row of upper deck left center field.

G. 6/22/73 (468'): Line drive off upper deck facade in deep left center field.

H. 8/4/74 (458'): Hit the top bleacher wall just left of dead center field.

I. 7/16/74 (455'): Hit batting cage in center field.

J. 8/20/72 (463'): Hit high into left center field deck.

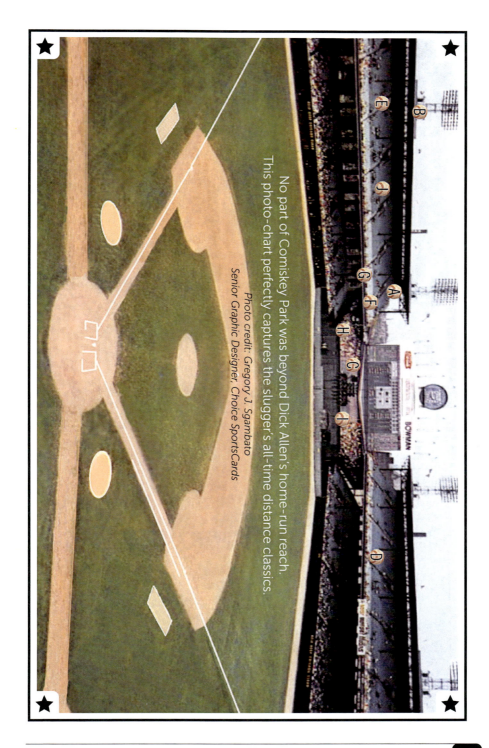

No part of Comiskey Park was beyond Dick Allen's home-run reach. This photo-chart perfectly captures the slugger's all-time distance classics.

Photo credit: Gregory J. Sgambato
Senior Graphic Designer, Choice SportsCards

Dick Allen was known as one of the best baserunners of his era. Here he takes out a Cleveland Indians fielder at second base.

Photo credit: Leo Bauby Collection

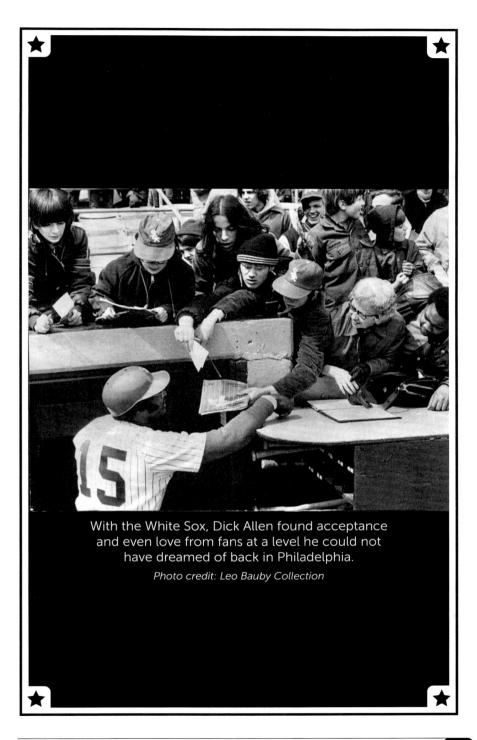

With the White Sox, Dick Allen found acceptance and even love from fans at a level he could not have dreamed of back in Philadelphia.

Photo credit: Leo Bauby Collection

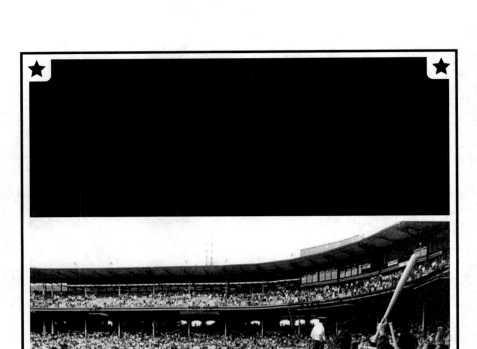

The fans who stuck around for the entire second game of the June 4, 1972 Bat Day doubleheader celebrate Dick Allen's signature moment of the 1972 season.

Photo credit: Leo Bauby Collection

CHAPTER 13

Wilbur Wood –
The Blue-Collar Innings Eater

> **"Wilbur Wood was beyond Old School. He was Old Testament. He was the last vestige of a time when men named Rube and Mordecai and Smokey Joe and Grover strode as giants upon the land …. When Wilbur Wood hung it up, it left no one to stop the meek 5-inning starters and 4-pitch bullpen specialists from inheriting the earth."**
>
> *– Josh Wilker, "Cardboard Gods: An All-American Tale Through Baseball Card with 1 Stick Bubble Gum."*

On a lazy Saturday afternoon, Aug. 12, 1972, in Oakland, the Chicago White Sox were playing in game 107 of the strike-shortened season. Having erased an 8½ game deficit since July 19, the Sox entered the day one game behind the A's in the American League Western Division race.

Catching up to Oakland with six weeks left in the season had set off pennant fever in Chicago. The Sox relied heavily on the indefatigable arm of Cy Young candidate Wilbur Wood and the bat of Dick Allen, who appeared to be a runaway MVP winner. Matched up against John "Blue Moon" Odom, Wood took the mound at the pitcher-friendly Oakland Coliseum, shooting for a 20th victory that would lift the Sox into first by a mere percentage point.

The third contest in this four-game showdown was scoreless until the top of the ninth inning, when Dick, who had already notched two hits in the game, led off with a triple. He scored the game's first run on Carlos May's sacrifice fly. The 30-year-old lefty Wood, with his thinning wheat-blond hair tucked neatly under his red Sox cap, had allowed just one hit, a single by left fielder Brant Alyea, through eight frames. But with two outs in the bottom of the ninth, Alyea — who had been in the A's minor leagues before his call-up days earlier and not had a base hit since May 12 – homered to tie the score, 1-1, visibly upsetting the normally stoic Wood. He slammed the resin bag in disgust.

"It was a high knuckler and when it left my hand and hit the bat, I knew it was gone." Wood said after the game.

"I kicked the mound a bit and said a few cuss words, but it was just a bad pitch, that's all it was. The thing to remember is that I got away with seven or eight bad pitches before then when they hit one. I feel I can always bounce back."

Wood quickly regained his composure and began tossing his knuckleball again to keep his team in the game and send it into extra innings. He walked Gene Tenace before getting Dave Duncan to ground out to second base to end the 9th inning.

The Sox eventually won, 3–1, in 11 innings on a dramatic two-run home run by Ed Spiezio off future Hall of Fame closer Rollie Fingers. Wood pitched all 11 innings, not uncommon for teams' aces of the era, to gain his 20th victory. Wood worked a quick bottom of the 11th, getting Bert Camparenis and Joe Rudi to ground out before striking out Sal Bando, looking.

Spiezio, who had played on the Cardinals' 1964 and 1967 World Series champions as a backup, said his homer into the left field seats was the happiest moment of his baseball career, which stretched back to playing for Nielsen's Service Station in Joliet in 1961.

He had been struggling, falling into an 0-for-13 slump, and had homered just once since joining the Sox in July. But this blast was well-timed, catapulting the White Sox into first place only two years after the franchise practically finished out of the AL when the team-record was 56-106.

The 11th inning started with Allen getting another hit, but he was caught stealing second base on a controversial call. May walked and Spezio stepped up to the plate.

Spezio told himself "to wait, wait, wait…" Fingers started him out with a fastball, which he sliced foul down the right field line. Next pitch was a slider. "I waited and I was ready," said Spiezio, who ripped Fingers' second pitch over the left field wall at the spacious Oakland Coliseum.

After the thrilling game, Spiezio and Wood posed for a celebratory picture printed in the *Sporting News* and the smiles on both of their faces told the story. The Sox were on top, and Wood became the majors' first 20-game winner of 1972, and a rare consecutive 20-win Sox pitcher after going 22-13 in 1971. Along with Tigers lefty Mickey Lolich, Wood was the busiest starting pitcher in the AL in the early 1970s.

He had an outside shot at winning 30 games with an estimated 15 starts left in the season. But all "Wilbah" talked about was winning both No. 21 and the pennant. He had been close in 1967 as a Sox reliever when the team collapsed late in the final week of the season amid a frantic four-team American League race. "I want to be in first place on October 4. That's my goal," he said, enjoying the jovial and very loud locker room.

Wood seemed to have a top publicity man in *Chicago Today* columnist Rick Talley, writing positive baseball news about a knuckleballer he considered baseball's premier pitcher. This was better than years of sniping at sclerotic Cubs manager Leo Durocher. In his post-game column, Talley wrote: "Wilbur Wood, Mr. Average American and baseball's most ignored superstar. Smokes cigars, drinks beer, jokes about getting a hair transplant. Loves to fish, spend time with kids, and doesn't believe in pressure."

"Pressure. Forget it. You win or you lose. The sun gonna shine tomorrow. You do it or you don't," Talley quoted Wood.

As all the scribes gathered around him in the wild, postgame celebration, Wood fielded a question about whether the 1972 White Sox could go all the way. "I think we've got an excellent opportunity," he replied with an earnest smile and a lit cigar in his mouth, knowing the White Sox had developed team chemistry with their new slugger Allen leading the way.

Dick Allen was the muscle, while Wood was the glue, a reliable stopper, fueling the hard-charging Sox' surge to win 15 of their last 19 while the defending AL West champion A's had lost eight of 10. Sox manager Chuck Tanner was convinced that his young team, led by the veteran leadership of Wood eating up innings on a two day's rest routine, and his "co-manager" Allen's superman heroics would win the AL West.

"We'll take the pennant now," said Tanner, ignoring the fact that Melton, 1971's American League home run leader, was on the disabled list for the season. Meanwhile, center fielder Jay Johnstone was batting .180, and his three catchers – Ed Herrmann, Tom Egan and Chuck Brinkman – were batting a dismal .233, .202 and .133, respectively. He touted the fact that his team was 31-13 in one run games.

August 12, 1972

American League West at a Glance:

- *Chicago White Sox 62-45 .579*
- *Oakland Athletics 63-46 .578*

"The White Sox are coming, tra-la-la-la, The White Sox are coming, tra-la-la-la..." trumpeted Harry Caray on the Sox' small radio stations right after Wood's triumph. Not since 1967 had the Sox been on top this late in the season, and thousands of Sox fans fiddled with their AM radios in an attempt to follow their first-place team on the West Coast.

Despite being the franchise's most important series since September 27, 1967, WFLD-TV, in its final year of that five-year contract, failed to broadcast any of the entire four-game series. As a lame-duck carrier, about to be acquired in part by Kaiser Broadcasting Co., WFLD did not want to spend extra money on AT&T long-line charges from the West Coast and on-site production personnel.

The Cubs were not really in the hunt for the NL East crown despite Billy Williams' stellar, near-Triple Crown season that was equal to Dick's production. So, there were no realistic dreams of a Chicago Subway Series come October.

Against the backdrop of the two presidential election conventions, the summer of 1972 saw fan interest in the Sox surge. "We should support the most exciting team in baseball. They are playing their hearts out," wrote one fan in a letter published in the *Tribune*.

The Sox-A's showdown may have been the single greatest series played in Major League Baseball in 1972. The action included everything you could want: Tight games, great pitching, timely hitting, extra innings and unexpected heroes.

"You have a bunch of guys who want to win a pennant and they're going to do it," said Tanner. "Here you got the Cy Young winner and the most valuable player on the same team. In my book, Wilbur Wood and Dick Allen are shoo-ins."

The effect of the strike-shorted season loomed as teams were left with an uneven number of games on the schedule. The Sox and A's could not tie because the A's had a 155-game schedule compared to the White Sox' 154. After the weekend set, the Sox had 47 games remaining while the A's had 46, including 11 against the two front-runners in the AL East, the Orioles and Tigers.

Dick's two-inside-the-park home run bonanza against the Twins to close out July 1972 jump-started the late season surge of the Sox. They took eight wins in nine games before heading to Oakland for the showdown series.

The Sox' early August 1972 West Coast swing

Wood was the Sox' most reliable man in their dog days surge. He beat the lowly Rangers in a complete game as part of a Sunday doubleheader sweep on Aug. 6, then outdueled Nolan Ryan, 1-0, in Anaheim on Aug. 9, cutting the A's lead to 3½ games.

Wood induced former Sox outfielder Ken Berry to hit into a game-ending double play. Starting the twin killing was third baseman Spiezio, whose defensive skills at third helped partly compensated for Melton's loss at bat. With runners at first and second, Spiezio snagged Berry's grounder, stepped on third and threw to Dick at first to end the game. Wood picked up his 19th win and sixth complete-game shutout.

Wood was also the hero at the plate as his seventh-inning bloop single chased home Buddy Bradford from second base for the game's only run.

The Sox had quickly cut a seemingly-safe A's lead of 8½ games down to one.

Boldly insisting that the pressure was on the "other guy," the Sox battled Oakland for 17 innings in the first game of the four games on Thursday night, Aug. 10. The marathon went past the bewitching hour and was eventually suspended in a 3-3 tie due to the mandatory American League 1 a.m. local time curfew. Bleary-eye listeners back in Chicago were up until the middle of the night for the first of two memorable wee-hours games from Oakland.

From the dugout, A's starter Ken Holtzman, who had thrown the first seven innings of this extravaganza, could only watch as Oakland nearly blew the game in the 13th inning when the Sox took a 3-2 lead.

Holtzman, who had been traded to the A's from the Cubs for outfielder Rick Monday in November 1971, began to have nightmares of the A's repeating the late-season collapse of his Cubs blowing their 10-game lead over the Mets in August 1969. "It's déjà vu all over again," said the left-handed starter, borrowing from Yogi Berra.

Thursday night's suspended game resumed before the regularly-scheduled game on Friday, Aug. 11 and went two more innings before Joe Rudi's two-run homer off Bahnsen won it for Oakland in the 19th.

The Sox had endured some revenge from their former star pitcher Joel Horlen, released by Chicago in the spring. Horlen pitched the innings 15, 16 and 17 before Catfish Hunter entered the game to pick up the win. The Athletics wanted no part of Dick Allen. In the first inning, they walked him intentionally, and in extra innings passed him four more times.

Undaunted by the heartbreaking two-day loss, the Sox rebounded to win, 1-0, in the regularly-scheduled Friday night game delayed by Chicago-based A's head honcho Finley's typical lineup meddling. Finley and manager Dick Williams argued for 27 minutes on the phone about who would pitch.

Under Finley's directive, suspended-game winner Hunter drew the assignment. He pitched eight innings, giving up the lone run in the first, when Pat Kelly led off with a single and with two out stole second. May dumped a single over shortstop Bert Campaneris to score Kelly. Sox lefty spot-starter Dave Lemonds, like Holtzman a former 1969 Cub, and reliever Cy Acosta combined for a two-hitter.

In 2009, in an interview with Sox historian Mark Liptak, Wood reflected back on that epic series. "It was draining, especially on the position players," he said. "In a big series like we had with Oakland, a lot is expected of players… we had kept knocking on the door that season trying to catch those guys [and] that becomes draining, too. Because we were in a pennant race, we had to play our guys every day. That race was so close, you just couldn't give guys time off."

Wood's long journey to pitching excellence

Before he became *The Sporting News*' American League pitcher of the year in 1972, Wilbur Forrester Wood, Jr. had a long journey to ace status coming out of Belmont Mass., just west of Boston.

Born on Oct. 22, 1941, Wood still had his distinctive Boston accent as he turned 80. He played multiple sports growing up. He was his high school's starting quarterback. He also played hockey and had dreams of being a left-handed goalie in the NHL.

"If you want to know the truth, hockey was my favorite of all of them because of the practices we had," said Wood. "Obviously I loved baseball and liked football, but it was just the way we had practices for hockey that made it a lot of fun."

He led Belmont High School to the state baseball championship in 1959, his junior year, as a "self-described fastball-curveball pitcher." Wood already had experimented with the knuckleball at age 12, trying to imitate his father, who threw a palm ball as a semi-pro player.

"I had thrown a knuckleball since I was a kid," he told Bob Vorwald of WGN in 2010. "My dad had a pretty good palm ball that acted a lot like a knuckleball since it didn't have any rotation on it. When you're a kid you want to try to do what your dad can do, so I came up with throwing the ball on my fingertips and came up with my knuckleball."

Around 15, Wood began to play on a semi-pro team in Belmont, where he mixed in the knuckler with his two other pitches. The squad was populated with ex-professional baseball pitchers who tried to convince him to stop experimenting with the "fool pitch."

In high school, young Wilbur relied on his very good curveball and an average-speed fastball, but Wood did not use the knuckleball because his confidence in the pitch was low. This conventional two-pitch arsenal was good enough to produce four no-hitters and a 24–2 record in high school. He drew interest from a number of major league teams before signing for a $30,000 bonus with the hometown Red Sox after he graduated from high school in 1960.

Before signing, Wood had a tryout in 1960 with the Milwaukee Braves, where Roland Hemond, who was the team's assistant farm director, went to Milwaukee to watch the workout.

"The scout from Milwaukee, Jeff Jones, wanted to try to sign Wilbur," Hemond recalled in 2014. "Wood threw a pitch and hit Del Crandall, the Braves catcher, with a pitch and they kicked him off the field. So, one bad pitch and he was eliminated from being signed by the Braves." But Hemond and Tanner changed Wood's pitching career forever when they permanently tapped him as a starter, which and helped earn them the *Sporting News* MLB Executive of the Year award and American League Manager of the Year Award, respectively.

"He was a chubby little guy who didn't throw very hard. I watched him throw batting practice and I couldn't get very excited," remembered Hemond about that tryout with the Braves.

After a year at Waterloo in the Class D Midwest League in 1960, Wood was invited to spring training and made his major league debut with Boston at 19 on June 30, 1961.

Wood went 0–5 for the Red Sox in several trials over the next four seasons before the team sent him down to Triple-A in Seattle of the Pacific Coast League in May 1964. "The little son-of-a-gun just couldn't throw hard enough," recalled Boston manager Johnny Pesky.

After Wood posted a 15–8 record for the Seattle Rainiers, the Pittsburgh Pirates purchased his contract in September 1964. He got into three games in the remaining month of the season. In 1965, the Pirates used Wood mostly in relief in before sending him back to the minor leagues in 1966 even though his ERA was a respectable 3.18.

He thought about quitting baseball and joining Wilbur Wood, Sr. in the plumbing business. But his first wife, Sandy, told him to give baseball one more year and he had a great season in 1966 with the Class AAA Columbus Jets of the International League with a sparkling ERA of 2.40 in 225 innings. The now-veteran hurler was named the International League's Most Outstanding Pitcher, leading in complete games (15) and shutouts (eight). This performance caught the attention of Gordon Maltzberger, a scout for the White Sox, who recommended him to General Manager Ed Short.

On Oct.12, 1966, Wood's contract was purchased from Columbus by the White Sox, with whom he'd spend the final 12 years of his career. Later, the Sox sent left-hander Juan Pizarro to complete the transaction with the Pirates.

One knuckleballer mentors another

Despite the stellar year as a starter in Columbus, Sox manager Eddie Stanky immediately informed Wood that he would be the ballclub's mop-up man when he arrived at spring training in March 1967.

He was fortunate that the White Sox had future Hall of Famer Hoyt Wilhelm, an ageless 44, in the bullpen to mentor him and forever change the arc of his career. Under Wilhelm's tutelage, Wood developed from a marginal pitcher into star-quality due to the knuckleball, first as a top reliever, then as an ace starter.

"When I got to the White Sox, my record was poor and my fastball was a few yards too short," Wood said. "I told myself I was going to do anything. I needed to change, period. Being with Hoyt Wilhelm, it was pretty simple: If I'm going to do anything, I have to do it with the knuckleball 'cause my fastball isn't good enough. I just made my mind up. I'm going to go out there and throw knuckleballs and I'm going to throw more knuckleballs.

"My pitch had a tendency to break down and away from right-handed hitters. Hoyt's was unpredictable: When he threw it, it could go all over the strike zone.

"The wind could change how the pitch was moving as well. The area around home plate in most of the stadiums that I pitched was where the wind would blow after it bounced off the stands, or in some parks like the old Metropolitan Stadium in Minnesota, just come right in and bounce the pitch around. A knuckleball acts by having the wind push against the seams.

"I was fortunate because I was always able to throw strikes with the knuckleball. That was my biggest asset. I was always around the plate. Eddie (Herrmann) never even had to put down a sign, he knew what I was going to throw, I knew what I was going to throw, and the fans knew what I was going to throw."

The confidence to throw his knuckler full-time made Wood's career. "And it (1967) was a make-or-break year. I had to start to do something because I hadn't done anything. I mean, the Red Sox, a few cups of coffee, and with Pittsburgh, I didn't pitch too much.

"And when I came over to the Chicago White Sox, I had made my mind up then and there that I was just gonna throw the knuckleball. Bury it. Up until then, I was throwing the curveball, fastball, occasionally a knuckleball."

Wilhelm, one of the all-time masters of this unique pitch, told Wood, "You either throw the knuckleball all the time or not at all. It's not a part-time pitch." Utilizing tips and analysis of his pitch from Wilhelm, Wood blossomed into one of the most effective, and durable, relievers in baseball by adopting that approach and sticking with it.

"And the big thing…and this was right in spring training (1967), right from the get-go…Hoyt said, 'Listen, you're gonna throw the knuckleball, you have to throw it 80, 90 percent of the time sometimes or more.' And he said, 'You can't mix it with the curveball or your slider. Because then your wrist is where it shouldn't be.' And I made my mind up: 'Hey, I'm throwing this knuckleball and it's hell or high water, it's make or break.' I guess, boy, it worked out well."

In 51 games (including eight starts) in 1967, he had a 4–2 record, four saves, a 2.45 ERA, 47 strikeouts, 28 walks and 95 hits allowed in 95⅓ innings pitched.

Wood began spring training in 1968 feeling confident about his decision to be a full-time knuckleballer. He continued to seek out Wilhelm's help to fine-tune it. In particular, Wilhelm helped Wood make adjustments when the ball was hung or flat. And going into his second spring with the White Sox, Wood further adjusted his windup with the help of pitching coach Marv Grissom.

"I used a full windup at the start of [the 1967] season. Then in midseason, I went to a half-windup," Wood said, "Grissom talked me into not using my windup at all."

The alteration paid immediate dividends. First, it gave Wood one of the best pickoff moves to first base in the game. Second, it made his occasional fastball and curve more effective because they were even less anticipated without a windup.

In 1968, Wilhelm developed a bad arm, while Bob Locker, the other mainstay late-innings man, was also hurt. Wood nevertheless led the league with 88 appearances, setting a single-season major league record with 13 wins, 16 saves and an ERA of 1.87 for a team that won just 67 games. He was named the American League Fireman of the Year.

Wood saved 15 games in 1969 and 21 games in 1970, both for terrible Sox teams. From 1968 to 1970 Wood led the American League in games pitched each year. His 386⅔ relief innings over that three-year span were the most in baseball, despite those Sox teams being collectively 104 games under .500.

Becoming a heavy-duty starter – and a star

In the spring of 1971, Johnny Sain became the White Sox pitching coach and inherited a pitching corps that in 1970 had recorded the highest earned-run average (4.54), allowed the most hits (1,554), yielded the most home runs (164) and gave up the most runs (822) of all 12 American League teams. The Sox had finished dead last in team pitching in the AL.

Under Sain's leadership in 1971, the White Sox finished fourth in the American League in team pitching. The staff ERA was 3.12. They placed three pitchers in the top 15 of the American League, including a 22-game winner in Wood, who had won only a little more twice that many in his previous *eight* years in the majors. Sain nurtured two of Sox brightest new prospects in Bradley, who won 15 games and posted a 2.96 ERA, and Johnson, who won 12 with an ERA of 2.93. As a team, the South Siders finished 79-83, good for third place in the AL Western Division in 1971 after having finished dead last the year before.

Sain admitted to author Pat Jordan, who published in 1973 *Suitors of Spring, The Solitary Art of Pitching, from Seaver to Sain*, "I don't know much about knuckleballs." But Sain did claim credit for converting Wood to the starter role and told Wood that he'd often pitch with only two days' rest between starts. Sain felt that as a knuckleballer, Wood put less strain on his arm than did other pitchers with more orthodox stuff, and he could therefore absorb the extra work with ease. Wood started 42 games in 1971.

A half century later, Wood recalled how much Sain meant to his career: "Johnny was good. And he believed that you had to throw the ball. In other words, you start a ball game, you don't just take off and rest for five days, six days and then pitch again. He believed in a four-day rotation, pitch every four days. And I think that's one of the biggest faults today, that the guys don't throw enough. I mean, you hear about everyone throwin' 100 miles an hour but it's...

it's different."

An injury to eleven-year Sox veteran pitcher Joel Horlen, who tore cartilage in his left knee sliding into second base in the last exhibition game of 1971, accelerated Wood's conversion. "I was going to do a 'pop-up' slide," Horlen said, and "when I threw my left leg back as I hit the dirt, I heard a loud pop in my knee. The leg was locked into a 90-degree angle. I just couldn't bend it back."

After surgery on April 5, Horlen made it back on the field in just 29 days when he pitched two innings of scoreless relief against Boston. But his injury forced the Sox to make Wood a fourth starter, which Wood initially resisted.

"I enjoyed pitching in relief, because I knew when I went to the park that there was a chance I'd get in the game," he said. "When you are a starting pitcher, you pitch — then sit for three or four days. I used to take ground balls in the infield on days when I wasn't pitching just to keep busy, and I'd run a little bit, but sitting around just wasn't for me.

"That was a strange situation, because even before the [Horlen] injury I was almost traded. It's true; the Sox had a deal in place with Washington. I was going to be traded for Darold Knowles. But I was holding out that year. I was fighting for more money, and I never signed a contract. So, the trade was null and void.

"It was pretty apparent that Chuck didn't want me in the bullpen. He didn't like a shit-baller coming out of the bullpen. He wanted hard-throwing guys, and we had players like Terry Forster and Goose Gossage coming up, so I became a starter."

Sure enough, the trade attempts continued. Prior to breaking camp and heading north, Roland Hemond tried to deal Wood once more. He offered him to the California Angels in a package deal for young pitchers Dave LaRoche and Lloyd Allen.

"Roland Hemond said it and it's true: 'Sometimes the best trades are the ones you don't make,'" remarked Wood, looking back at how his career would have turned out differently.

"I was a little apprehensive at first doing this (starting), it was just like before any game you're always a little nervous. But when you start having success, you get comfortable, and right away I had success starting. I was tickled pink that things turned out the way they did."

Wood didn't win his first game as a starter in 1971 until May 2, but by the All-Star break he had a 9–5 record and ranked second in the American League with a 1.69 ERA. "I never got any work because of all the off days early in the season." he said.

The 1971 season was the start of an incredible run of success. In 42 starts, Wood amassed seven shutouts, a save, 334 innings pitched, 210 strikeouts, 22 complete games and an amazing ERA of 1.91. His control — especially for a knuckleballer — was the best in the American League with only 62 walks, computing to one walk for every 21⅓ batters faced. He even led the major leagues with 21 sacrifice bunts.

Implementing Sain's advocacy of short rest, Wood made his first start on two days' rest on June 30, an 8–3 complete-game victory over the Milwaukee Brewers. From then until the end of the season, he started 14 times on two days' rest, going 8–4 with a 1.86 ERA in those games. The Sox won 10 of the 14 starts. "The more he pitches, the more it helps the club," Sain said about Wood in August 1971.

Sain was not surprised by Wood's initial success as a starter. "I guess they always said, 'Poor Wilbur, he just doesn't have enough natural ability to pitch in the big leagues,'" he said at the time. "What they call natural ability is standing six-four and being able to throw a ball 100 miles per hour. Well, it turns out that he has as much God-given ability as any man I've ever met. He can throw the knuckleball and it requires a natural feel."

Following the 1971 season, Wood finished third in the Cy Young voting behind Vida Blue and Mickey Lolich and ninth for the AL MVP award, also captured by Blue. His Wins Above Replacement (WAR) in 1971 was a staggering 11.5 compared to Blue's 9. Any WAR about 8 is considered an MVP-caliber season, according to Sabermetrics.

Based on that, Wood's '71 season was one of the best for Major League pitchers after 1920, exceeded only by Roger Clemens (11.6 in 1997), Steve Carlton (11.7 in 1972) and Dwight Gooden (11.9 in 1985).

Tanner and Sain thought Wood deserved the 1971 Cy Young Award. Looking back 50 years later Wood wishes he won it. "Honestly, I didn't think about the Cy Young back in those days," he said. "At the time, it wasn't that important to me. Looking back, would I have liked to have won it? Sure."

A three-man rotation, by necessity

The short-rest experiment with Wood was considered a success, and the White Sox plan for 1972 was for more of the same. "Wood is proof that pitchers can work more often," Sain told David Condon of the *Chicago Tribune* on March 12. "I've known many who could do the job with only two days' rest…But Wood has to be tops."

In spring training, 22 year-old starter Bart Johnson reported he had injured his knee in an off-season basketball game. He was slated to be part of the starting rotation after a solid 1971 campaign in which he had back-to-back games with 12 strikeouts in September. The Sox hoped to at least use Johnson out of the bullpen, but he was limited to a mere nine appearances and went 0-3 before being shipped out to the minors in June, eventually having knee surgery in September 1972.

With Johnson out of the rotation, the Sox slated Wood, Horlen, Bradley and Bahnsen as starters. Rookie left-hander Dave Lemonds would be counted on to be a spot starter.

Horlen was the White Sox' Players Association representative in 1971 and 1972, and argued in favor of the strike that delayed the opening of the latter season. He clashed with Sox general manager Stu Holcomb, and was released at the end of spring training, on April 2, the day after players voted for the strike. Horlen had been lauded by Tanner for his "true grit" coming back in 1971 after his knee surgery, but Holcomb's poorly-conceived release of the veteran hurler took place nevertheless. Without Horlen and any other in-house candidates, the Sox essentially contracted to a three-man rotation. Wood, Bahnsen and Bradley ended up starting an astonishing 130 of 154 games in 1972.

Wood thus compiled ironman numbers: *376 2⁄3 innings*, 49 starts, eight shutouts, 24 wins and an ERA of 2.51. Wood himself was never concerned about throwing that many innings and comfortable with his heavy workload.

"I didn't think about it that much," he said. "I was throwing the ball well. I had been in a groove the entire season. I wanted to give it a shot, I enjoyed it. I also didn't like down time, just sitting around. So, when they said, 'Do you want to pitch every second day or third day?' I said 'Sure.'

"People said I didn't get sore because all I threw was the knuckleball, but that's not true. I'd get stiff and sore, and in those days, pitchers never used ice. I didn't get as sore as if I was throwing, say, a slider, because I wasn't putting the pressure on my elbow and shoulder, but I did get sore."

Did overworking Wood and other starters cost the Sox the AL West title?

While Wood claimed he could throw the knuckleball morning, noon and night, careful analysis of the pitching records in '72 showed that signs of fatigue plagued all three Sox starters. Even Wood evidenced some wear and tear. He failed in his last seven starts to get his 25th win. Collectively, the starting rotation slowed down considerably over the last six weeks of the season. From opening day through August 19, it had an overall record of 53–37 (.589) with a 2.92 ERA; over the remainder of the season, just 10–18 (.357) with a 3.61 ERA.

Both Bradley and Bahnsen felt that the two-day rest really affected them down the stretch. Tommy John agreed, saying in 2011: "Tanner and Sain were big on pitching on two days' rest, three days' rest, and they had Tom Bradley. Bradley could pitch. God, that son-of-a-gun could throw the ball…they rode him right into the river, man. And Bradley, I thought, was never the same pitcher after pitching in Chicago in '71 and '72."

Bradley's post-White Sox pitching record supports John's criticism. After starting 40 games in 1972, Bradley only started 61 more games over the remainder of his career, going 23–26 with a 4.56 ERA, and threw his last major-league pitch at age 28. He developed a rotator cuff tear in 1974, which he blamed on his two years in Chicago.

However, during the first part of 1972 neither Bahnsen nor Bradley had any issues with pitching on short rest. In a June 2 story, "More Work? Really It Works," Bradley told the *Chicago Tribune*'s George Langford: "I actually feel stronger in the games with only two days' rest." Bahnsen agreed. "I've felt strong," he said about starting games on short rest. "I think they have shown that a lot of the theory of rest is a mental thing."

Fifty years later Bahnsen said: "So, I didn't want to pitch with two day's rest, though. I told Wilbur that. But they wanted to go — Tom Bradley and myself, Bradley would pitch for three days, then two days. Wilbur's number of starts could be huge, but we were different, not capable of starting nearly 50 games. But they wanted him to go out there as often as he could go."

According to Don Zminda in a 2016 article in *Baseball Research Journal* entitled "Working Overtime: Wilbur Wood, Johnny Sain and the White Sox Two-Days' Rest Experiment of the 1970s," Wood started 25 times on two days' rest during the 1972 season, the most short-rest starts for any major league pitcher since at least 1914. Bahnsen and Bradley each started eight games on two days' rest, and Lemonds made three short-rest starts.

Wood posted a 2.62 ERA in his 25 starts on two days' rest in 1972. As a group, White Sox starting pitchers posted a 3.04 ERA in their 44 starts on two days' rest in 1972, a figure actually a shade lower than the club's 3.12 ERA in their 110 starts with three or more days' rest. Overall, the team's 44 starts with two days' rest between starts was the most by a major league team since the 1918 Philadelphia Athletics.

"I feel no difference, physically or mentally, between two and three days of rest," said Wood about his workload. "Everybody thinks I should be more tired, but I am not."

When Wood lost his final chance to win his 25th (October 1 in a 1-0 loss to Texas), Tanner sent him home. Wood gave up his chance to start his 50th game on October 4 and break Ed Wash's franchise 1908 record of 49 starts.

After the A's won the AL West crown, Joel Horlen spoke up and stated the

Sox lost out on winning the title due to his release on the last day of spring training.

"You could single me out that I made a difference in X number of games for the A's...take away X number of games and tack them onto the White Sox and see what happens…" said the bitter Horlen in a Ron Bergman article in the *Sporting News* in October 1972 with the headline, "Horlen's record with the A's Avenges Chisox Release." A familiar complaint from the era reared its head again: Sox GM Stu Holcomb was blamed for being cheap.

Bergman wrote that although bitter about the circumstances of his release, Horlen kept his feelings to himself until the A's beat out his former team for the division title.

"The White Sox didn't win this year because they were short of pitching," Horlen said. "They told me in spring training they didn't need another starter and I couldn't relieve. They just never found anybody for a fourth starter this year beyond Wilbur Wood, Tom Bradley and Stan Bahnsen. I feel strongly they didn't want to spend the money, I mean my salary, for insurance," Horlen had a deceptive 3-4 record for Oakland as a spot starter and long reliever with 32 appearances, and ERA of 3.00 and 84 innings pitched.

In the first three times he faced the White Sox, Horlen pitched shutout ball over 9⅓ innings. In total, Horlen appeared in five games against the Sox in 1972, allowing just two runs.

While one can debate if the three-man rotation hurt the Sox' chances to win the American League Western Division, one also needs to analyze Wood's batting statistics. He had a terrible year at the plate and set an American League record for the most strikeouts in a season for a pitcher with 65 in 125 at-bats. Oddly, Wood batted right-handed, exposing his pitching arm to being hit by a pitch. Hitting was the one thing he did not learn from Johnny Sain, who was an excellent hitter in his career. In fact, Sain struck out zero times during the 1947 season (118 at-bats) and had a career batting average of .245 over his 11-year career.

Fortunately for Wood, the American League instituted the designated hitter in 1973 and he only batted two more times in his career.

Off-the-chart 1972 numbers

Despite having a terrible September, Wood's less-obvious numbers for the 1972 season were also staggering. His 376⅔ innings represented 27% of the 1,385⅓ innings thrown by the entire staff. Wood faced 1,490 batters and averaged only one walk for every 20⅓ innings pitched. His control of the unpredictable knuckleball was spectacular, pitching 10 games with no walks and another stretch of nine straight without walking more than one man.

Wood's innings pitched were the most in the AL since Walsh's 393 in 1912. His 49 starts not only tied the 63-year-old White Sox mark, it was also only two fewer than Jack Chesbro's 51 for the 1904 Yankees.

Wood was seventh in the MVP voting, finishing behind Cleveland future Hall of Famer Gaylord Perry. Of course, Dick Allen won the MVP almost by acclamation.

However, if one uses Sabermetrics WAR to evaluate a player's value to his team, Wood beats Allen:

Wins Above Replacement 1972 AL

1. *Perry: CLE 11.0*

2. *Wood: CHW 10.3*

3. *Allen: CHW 9.3*

Wood's contribution to the '72 White Sox was remarkable. There have only been 22 seasons in which a pitcher generated a pitching WAR of 10.0 or higher, and only seven pitchers did it twice: Wood in 1971 and 1972, Bob Gibson (1968-69), Randy Johnson (2001-2002), Sandy Koufax (1963, 1966), Steve Carlton (1972, 1980) and Tom Seaver (1971, 1973).

Although the Cy Young award went to Perry, Wood was named AL Pitcher of the Year by *The Sporting News* and their headline said it well: "In AL Allen, Wood rate as the Best."

Chuck Tanner was very disappointed that his ace fell short of the Cy Young. The skipper was aware that Wood lost five of his final seven starts. "Far too much is made of what they're calling his September slump," Tanner said then. "He really didn't slump in his pitching. We just didn't score any runs for him." Tanner called Wood one-and-a-half pitchers because of his ability to eat up innings, adding, "In the seventh starts he made trying for his 25th, we scored only 12 runs for him. If we had given any kind of support at all at the plate, he could have won 30 games."

Wood's enduring legacy

In a four-year span from 1971 to 1974, Wood pitched more than anyone since the Dead Ball Era; and his statistics are unimaginable in today's game. He won at least 20 games each season, led the AL with 24 in 1972 and 1973, and his 90 wins were the most in baseball — two more than future Hall of Famer Catfish Hunter. He averaged 348 innings per year.

Despite his accomplishments, Wood is typically overlooked among top pitchers of his era, in favor of Jim Palmer, Tom Seaver, Nolan Ryan, Steve Carlton, Catfish Hunter and Perry.

Wilbur Wood never had his moments on the big stage because he never got into the postseason. He was named to the American League All-Star team three times (1971, 1972 and 1974), but pitched only once, a two-inning outing surrendering two hits and one run in 1972. The Sox record during those years (just one winning season) contributes to the lack of attention, as does Wood's relatively short time as a starter (and thus fewer career wins) in comparison to the aforementioned Hall of Famers. Wood also lost a major league high 69 times during this stretch and in 1973 became the first pitcher since Walter Johnson in 1916 to win and lose at least 20 games in the same season.

But in relishing his new role as a modern pitching ironman, Wood enjoyed phenomenal success with his new routine of pitching twice per week. He started 42 games in 1971, 49 in 1972, 48 in 1973, 42 in 1974, and 43 in 1975, giving dramatic new meaning to the phrase "innings eater."

Wood was one of the most popular Chicago athletes in the 1970s in part because he wasn't 6-foot-5 with a sculpted body. Reliable Wilbur looked like your Uncle Steve or Cousin John. He was an everyman. And all Sox fans could relate to a blue-collar guy who somehow found a way to consistently get major league hitters out again and again.

Famed baseball writer Peter Gammons in a 1973 *Boston Globe* piece thought Wood could pass as a plumber or even a beer taster in a brewery. In fact, in the off-season Wood lived in Hinsdale, Ill. and was a plumber.

White Sox beat reporter Edgar Munzel wrote in *The Sporting News*, "There isn't anyone in the major leagues...who looks less like a ballplayer. He's a chubby, pot-bellied guy with thinning blond hair, blue eyes, and a pleasant round face."

Wood led the American League in 33 different categories during his playing days, most of them in the positive column. They included leading the league in appearances, games started, games finished, innings pitched, batters faced, wins and getting hitters to ground into double plays.

He had scoreless inning streaks of 29 in 1973 and 27⅔ in 1972. He tossed three complete-game two-hitters, with two of those lasting 11 innings. He also added nine complete-game three-hitters. Wood twice started both ends of resumed doubleheaders.

He liked pitching at Comiskey Park. "I appreciated the fact it was a big ballpark and because of the size of the ballpark, if you made a little mistake, your outfielders would catch mistakes on the warning track," Wood said.

He also liked how the grounds crew would groom the field for the home team but denied ever being aware that the baseballs were put in a refrigerator to "deaden them up."

He was an all-time fan favorite, playing for three teams that were contenders: 1967, 1972, and 1977. He was named to the Chicago White Sox All-Century team in 2000.

His career was cut short in May 1976 when he took a Ron LeFlore liner up the middle off his left kneecap, shattering his patella. Longtime Sox GM Roland Hemond remembered visiting Wood in the emergency room in Detroit. "All Wilbur wanted was a cigarette and a beer," Hemond said. The veteran pitcher missed the rest of 1976 — his only stint on the disabled list.

Wood returned as a spot-starter on the 1977 "South Side Hit Men" Sox team that smashed all team hitting records, but he was not the same pitcher. He admitted he was gun-shy throwing inside, as he was fearful of getting drilled again.

After baseball, Wilbur ran a seafood business and was a pharmaceutical representative in his native Boston area. He hated flying after several close calls when travelling to call on doctors.

In his baseball career, Wood was dogged by unflattering physical descriptions of himself, along with suggestions that throwing a knuckleball was somehow less demanding than a fastball. All of that gave the impression Wood's success was the result of a fluke pitch and that he didn't need to work hard or be fit to play.

Scoffing at such notions, Tanner once offered a different perspective: "He's a stubborn competitor and has ability and courage to go with it." Always quick to point out that pitching is more difficult than hitting, Johnny Sain suggested that Wood's success rested as much on his mental preparation as physical abilities. "Wilbur has tremendous poise. He has the perfect temperament. Wood never gets rattled," Sain observed.

"I don't think people realize or understand Wilbur Wood was a pretty good athlete," said eight-year Sox teammate Bill Melton. "His legs were in great shape. Everybody's asking, 'How is Wilbur Wood?' When I go to old-timers' games. I saw Woody a couple years ago in Chicago, and actually Woody looks better now than most retired players, 'cause Woody looks the same. Hair is the same. Physique is the same. He looks really good."

Wilbur Wood was a late-20th Century throwback to baseball's past. There will never be another pitcher like him. No one will match the 376⅔ innings he logged in 1972 en route to earn that *Sporting News* American League Pitcher of the Year award — and, of course, the truly everlasting gratitude of Chicago White Sox fans.

Two masters of their craft. Nancy Faust (left) lets knuckleball ace Wilbur Wood sound a few notes on her organ.

Photo credit: Leo Bauby Collection

White Sox ace lefty Wilbur Wood pitches against the Milwaukee Brewers on Aug. 17, 1972 at Comiskey Park, notching his 21st victory in an 8-6 win. Wood's 376 2/3 innings pitched in 1972 will never be surpassed by another MLB pitcher.

Photo credit: the Associated Press/Charles Knoblock

CHAPTER 14

Arthur Allyn's UHF Folly

Arthur Allyn no doubt stewed. In the middle of his White Sox ownership, he dreamed big dreams of a new stadium in the under-developed south part of downtown Chicago, but he also faced a broadcast conundrum.

Allyn was hemmed in by the Cubs on WGN, who benefited from a sweet deal of below-market rate rights fees from owner Philip Wrigley. The Sox owner looked at other big-league franchises, and except for the New York teams, the majority of televised games were road contests. The Lords of the Game protected their home gates – which in aggregate was not growing by leaps and bounds in the 1960s. Allyn could not televise most weekend road games on WGN with the station locked in to Saturday and Sunday afternoon contests at Wrigley Field. At the same time, he was not going to give away all his trademark home night games on TV to make up for the airtime barriers created by the Cubs schedule.

Most particularly galling was the Sox outdrawing the Cubs by 500,000 in 1964, almost doubling the Cubs home attendance in 1965 and, even in an off-year, outpacing Wrigley Field gatherings by more than 350,000 in 1966. If more road games were offered on TV and the Sox were winning, it might produce even higher attendance from the impulse ticket purchases which were predominant in an era of modest season-ticket numbers.

A solution could ostensibly come via the Sox' own outlet on TV's high band – UHF. As 1965 progressed, plans for Field Enterprises' WFLD-TV, Chicago's second UHF commercial station on Channel 32, were announced. Allyn was billed as a tough negotiator on broadcast deals, garnering $200,000 more a year in broadcast rights fees than the Cubs despite considerably fewer games on TV. As the businessman with the butterfly collection began tossing around ideas, he apparently did not pay attention to the fine print about UHF.

Ultra High Frequency television, originally covering channels 14 through 83, had been approved by the Federal Communications Commission to expand the medium's reach after the original allotment of VHF channels 2 through 13 was fully assigned. But the approval of UHF proved to be the introduction of technology outpacing the market's ability to support the system.

As with radio in the early 1920s and the internet in the mid-1990s, many entrepreneurs, well-funded and otherwise, quickly jumped in to start UHF stations, only to back out when audiences and advertisers proved scarce. Television sets manufactured before 1964 were not required by the FCC to have UHF tuners. Adding UHF capability boosted the price of sets, already relatively expensive. So, huge numbers of TV homes in large and medium markets simply could not select UHF channels for viewing.

Early on, UHF could succeed only when a VHF channel was not allocated to a smaller market when all the available VHF assignments were given to larger cities nearby. Viewers in "UHF islands" such as Peoria, South Bend, Ft. Wayne, Scranton/Wilkes-Barre, Youngstown, Fresno and Bakersfield were forced to buy UHF-compatible TV sets or tuner converter boxes. Some markets such as Central Illinois, Rockford, Madison and Springfield, Mass., had one VHF channel and multiple UHF stations.

The technological disadvantages meant that UHF could not compete with established VHF stations, including those in bigger markets owned by the three major networks or publishing companies. And when a startup UHF station had the chance to switch to a VHF frequency that was later allocated to its market, it jumped at the chance, as did longtime ABC affiliate KTVI in St. Louis. And even when staying on UHF, a preferred destination was the lowest channel possible. Stations assigned to, say, Channel 61, campaigned with the FCC to get down to Channel 17 or 22.

Eighty-two UHF stations were on the air in mid-1954, but only *24* were still operating a year later. Meanwhile, factory-equipped all-channel tuners dropped from 20% in 1953 to only 9% in 1958. Converters remained available, but were hardly the answer. By 1961, just 5.5 % of new TVs could receive UHF, an all-time low in the history of the spectrum.

Clear reception was also a challenge. No matter if the UHF tuner was internal or an added converter, viewers often needed the dexterity of a safecracker to twist the radio-style dial for Channels 14 to 83. That stood in contrast to VHF tuners that clicked and locked in, channel-by-channel, from 2 to 13. The result was often-snowy video from UHF transmitters that were not as powerful as their VHF counterparts, for UHF's range was but two-thirds of VHF. Hilly or mountainous terrain was an added impediment.

Chicagoan Newton Minow, the outspoken John F. Kennedy-appointed FCC commissioner, wanted more diversity of content to counter what he famously called a "vast wasteland" in conventional TV programming in 1961. So he and his agency backed the All-Channel Receiver Act of 1962, which is how all TV sets shipped via interstate commerce came to be required to have factory-equipped UHF tuners from mid-1964 onward. Minow wanted to give UHF station operators a fighting chance to succeed. But even though the law *required* UHF tuners, many years would pass before the turnover of old sets and purchase of new ones would elevate UHF to near-complete tuner penetration in all markets.

"The all-channel legislation took about 10 years to make UHF television viable," was Minow's after-the-fact analysis at age 95 in 2021 as probably the last living major JFK appointee.

Multiple UHF channels and licenses had been granted to Chicago, but no major operator moved to activate any into on-air service due to the lack of all-channel tuners. Radio stations such as WIND and WCFL had licenses. The license held by Field Enterprises, publisher of the *Sun-Times* and *Daily News*, was originally for Channel 38. Theater and television impresarios Harry and Elmer Balaban were the first owners of the Channel 32 license.

But only entrepreneur John Weigel, a former broadcaster who had a short stint as a weatherman on WENR-TV in 1952, acted. He counted his pennies to begin WCIU-TV on Channel 26 from tiny studios and offices atop the Board of Trade Building in downtown Chicago on Feb. 6, 1964, breaking the static lineup of four commercial Chicago TV channels that had existed since 1953. Weigel purchased used equipment, including the transmitter, while paying all employees just $100 a week – basically a secretary's wage in '64. Although Mayor Richard J. Daley offered his greetings for the sign-on, WCIU's inaugural night merited just a three-paragraph story in the *Chicago Tribune*.

Weigel cobbled together programming where he could for his meager seven-hour-a-day schedule. Opening Night featured a New York Knicks at Philadelphia 76ers basketball game. Longtime baseball radio and on-line reporter Bruce Levine, then a South Shore teenager, remembered buying a UHF converter for $18 — "a whopping sum in those days" — so he could watch promised St. Louis Hawks NBA games. Remembering TV's wrestling roots, Weigel aired a "Texas Rasslin" show. But the most distinctive 1964 WCIU offerings in 1964 were two-hour bullfights from Mexico at 8 p.m. Saturdays. Ethnic programming was a staple from the start.

WCIU could not even broadcast films in color until 1974, a decade after WBBM-TV and WLS-TV acquired their color film chains and, soon afterward, studio color cameras. So the little station was not capable of carrying, let alone paying rights fees for, a local sports franchise.

WFLD-Channel 32 would be different. Field not only owned those two of the four Chicago daily newspapers, but also *World Book Encyclopedia*. And running the fledgling station would be Sterling C. "Red" Quinlan, the market's most senior – and eclectic – TV executive.

Quinlan had started as a jack-of-all-trades at the original WBKB-Channel 4, Chicago's first TV station, in the late 1940s. He moved up the executive ladder and finally landed as general manager of ABC-owned Channel 7. He constantly tinkered with local, live programming to fill daily schedule holes the parent network couldn't yet occupy due to thin finances. In turn, Quinlan helped prop up the entire network with healthy local advertising sales.

After turning down the presidency of ABC's owned-and-operated stations division, Quinlan bailed out of WBKB (later renamed WLS) in early 1964. He was the perfect guy to get a new operation off the ground.

At Channel 32, ad rates would be crimped by the low level of UHF penetration, requiring an initial outlay of cash from Field Communications, a newly-created subsidiary of Field Enterprises, to cover start-up losses. As 1966 dawned, just 823,000 of Chicago area's 2.5 million TV households could receive UHF. Color TV sales were booming as network prime-time schedules were increasingly in color, and those new sets did come with UHF tuners. But not everyone could afford $400 to $600 for a new color console, or even a new black and white set.

As Quinlan conceived WFLD going into its Jan. 4, 1966 sign-on, the station would not be just another repository for off-network reruns, old movies and a couple of kids shows. WFLD would partner with the *Sun-Times* and *Daily News* to produce several daily "Newscope" programs, combining studio-based anchor Patrick Muldowney with live shots of reporters reading copy from the city rooms of both papers in their riverfront barge-like building, now the site of Trump Tower.

"Newscope" quickly won a Chicago Emmy Award in 1966. An Opening Night documentary featured award-winning *Daily News* photographer Henry Herr Gill displaying his photo collection from the combat zone in Vietnam. Quinlan promised to do "30 to 40 of these things (documentaries) a year." The *Daily News* hailed WFLD as the "Station of Tomorrow."

While championing variety and ahead-of-their-time creative shows, Quinlan craved a live sports presence. "We'll be big in sports," he promised. Quinlan desired a nightly 8 to 10 p.m. sports block. He aired Illinois, Loyola and DePaul basketball games from the start, the NBA All-Star Game and non-revenue sports from the Big Ten that more established stations had not yet picked up (an all-sports cable outlet was still basically a sci-fi fantasy in 1966). Winding the clock back to early 1950s TV, WFLD dispatched a mobile unit to Ridge Bowl for live bowling broadcasts. Quinlan also had plans for a nightly sports program.

The presence of a very familiar Chicago face who had previously hosted a weekly show for Quinlan at Channel 7 in 1959 perhaps caught Arthur Allyn's eye more than any other program on Channel 32. After all, Allyn was once part of this headliner's ownership group with the Chicago White Sox.

Bill Veeck, always a raconteur, began hosting a half-hour show at 10:30 p.m. weeknights in the spring of 1966, and Quinlan would soon syndicate "Barnum Bill" as part of nascent plans for even greater programming production and distribution. Veeck went into familiar territory by hosting sports-themed shows with Bud Selig, then trying to land a major-league baseball team for Milwaukee to replace the Braves, and Johnny Unitas talking about the physical hazards of quarterbacking.

But the worldly Veeck delved in a slew of real-world themes such as abortion and interracial marriage. Five years later, and now a gentleman squire on Maryland's Eastern Shore, Veeck was always rumored to have renewed interest in baseball ownership. At this point, his supposed cravings were limited to the Cubs, in whose employ he began his career, or the Washington Senators. He returned to Chicago for one weekend day each week, usually taping six shows.

From an exposure standpoint, Allyn logically should have not been restless about his WGN deal, given WFLD's newbie status, the minority percentage of UHF penetration and the now-established schedule of scattered home and road White Sox night games on Channel 9. In addition, the White Sox benefited from ancillary WGN programming.

As Opening Day neared every year, WGN annually aired a half-hour special for each Chicago baseball team, previewing the season. In 1964, WGN sports editor Jack Rosenberg helped rig up wireless microphones, then a novel technical advancement, on Sox slugger Dave Nicholson and catcher J.C. Martin to provide extra color on their spring-training rounds in Sarasota. And in 1966, WGN debuted a weekly "Sports Open Line" live studio show at 9 p.m. Mondays, hosted by Jack Brickhouse, featuring an audience and calls from viewers. New Sox manager Eddie "The Brat" Stanky alternated as a weekly guest, depending on which team was home, with Cubs counterpart Leo Durocher also appearing.

But Allyn was obviously antsy. By 1966, his financial standing reportedly was declining. The Sox finished with their poorest record (83-79) since 1950 and were never in contention. Attendance dropped for the second straight season, dipping under one million for the first time since 1958. WGN's "Park-Ruddle News," the first dual-anchor 10 p.m. newscast in Chicago history, advertised "Exclusive Chicago Baseball Highlights." That meant a couple of minutes of Cubs videotape from that day's game, and perhaps one or two Sox clips hurriedly edited for the newscast from action in an 8 p.m. night game.

Over at Marina City's new office building, Quinlan remained equally anxious for a big sports rights deal. Who approached whom is pretty much lost to history, but with just eight months on the air and only a 4 p.m.-to-midnight broadcast schedule, WFLD moved to land its first major Chicago pro sports team as 1966 progressed.

"I had the money to spend," Quinlan told The Video Veteran in 2002. He tossed at Allyn a maximum $1.25 million annual offer if all 162 White Sox games were telecast. Allyn likely felt the prospective payout was manna from heaven.

The base payout was $1 million annually for a minimum of 129 games. The Sox had received just $900,000 for TV-Radio rights in 1966, according to the Nov. 14, 1966 issue of *Broadcasting* magazine. Prior to signing with WFLD, Allyn also sealed a new radio rights deal with clear-channel, NBC-owned WMAQ-Radio for $350,000 in 1967 and $375,000 in 1968.

The story of the November 10, 1966 contract signing for Sox telecasts was significant news — the first UHF station in the country to land a big-league baseball franchise, with the contract running for five years, starting in 1968, plus a five-year option. Dillman recalled a motivating factor on the WFLD side for the deal: The promotion of sales of UHF converters that would benefit the entire station schedule. To Quinlan, the Sox had the veneer of a contending franchise; future troubles as yet unforeseen.

Allyn's deal with WFLD would remain the outlier in baseball for many years to come. Most teams' flagship TV stations were larger VHF outlets who would sometimes pre-empt prime-time network programming — usually summer reruns — for baseball. UHF stations' connections with teams were limited to affiliates on the flagship outlet's network.

In 1972, according to Tom Shaer, a baseball and broadcasting historian and former Boston and Chicago sportscaster, the Red Sox had a choice of more money by moving to UHF WSBK (Channel 38) after years of telecasts on CBS affiliate WHDH-TV (Channel 5), which had lost its license. The other, lower bidder for the team's rights was Westinghouse-owned NBC affiliate WBZ-TV (Channel 4). As the late Red Sox general manager Dick O'Connell told Shaer, his team opted for the safe bet and assured all-market exposure of WBZ. If a team wanted to keep guaranteed reach to all TV homes and peace among its core sponsors, they remained with the established, maximum-exposure outlet.

The tenor of the Broadcasting article basically painted a picture of Allyn jumping his WGN contract as he craved the big Field Enterprises payout. Ben Berentson, the vice president and general manager of WGN-TV, said his Sox deal provided for renewal negotiations to commence between June 1 and Aug. 31, 1967. But Allyn countered WGN had already begun negotiations earlier, and he refused their terms. Berentson said the talks were part of an informal lunch, were not actual negotiations and believed the WGN contract was still in effect.

If Allyn fancied himself as an expert in sales and distribution, he was taking a reckless gamble. Quinlan said at the time his White Sox deal was signed that Nielsen estimated just 40% of the Chicago market was UHF-equipped, only a small increase since WFLD began. As Allyn bit on the numbers, cash and otherwise, Quinlan optimistically projected 72 to 78 % UHF penetration by 1968, which would have meant an all-time Chicago-area boom in new TV set sales and converter purchases in just one year's time. Red always looked at the sunny side of life.

As with Quinlan's programming plans for WFLD, the new Sox deal had starry-eyed goals. WFLD projected a regional baseball network stretching into downstate Illinois, Iowa, Wisconsin, Indiana and western Michigan. In addition, Field Communications planned a new UHF station on Channel 24 in Milwaukee, as another outlet for its baseball telecasts. Then-WFLD Director Dave Dillman recalled the plan was that Channel 24 would re-broadcast WFLD's signal by picking it up over-the-air with a high tower to save AT&T line charges. The Brewtown station would thus add a potential 500,000 homes for viewership, boosting advertising rates – as went Field Communications' optimistic thinking.

But long before WFLD employed its four newly-purchased Marconi Plumbicon color cameras to televise games from Comiskey Park, Allyn witnessed his leap at a pot of gold starting to go sour.

The projection of a Midwest network was beaten to the punch by WGN-TV on April 3, 1967. The station announced a schedule of 25 Cubs games for its new "WGN Continental-Chicago Cubs Baseball Network."

13 road night games, 10 Sunday home games and two holiday games were offered on the network for the 1967 season. WGN was able to market the network coming off that 10th-place Cubs 1966 season likely due to a far-flung fan base throughout the Midwest originally developed in the team's old glory days. These fans typically did not travel to Wrigley Field – except perhaps for an annual summer Sunday outing with the Cardinals or a holiday doubleheader — but they still desired games on television. Some White Sox home Sunday and other games, including the recent uptick in home prime-time contests, had been televised on WGN in preceding years while the South Siders were contenders, but no such regional network had been desired by the station. Otherwise, WGN would have logically booked the AT&T lines to distribute such Sox telecasts.

"For years stations in downstate Illinois, Michigan, Wisconsin and Iowa have wanted this type of service," said a WGN spokesman. "Now we have worked out the legal and contractual basis by which we can serve them."

In setting up the network one year in advance of the Sox start on WFLD, WGN effectively staked out the high ground in the Midwest. In the limited-channel universe of the times, two stations in smaller markets were not likely to program baseball against each other. A big prize was CBS affiliate WISN-TV (Channel 12) in Milwaukee, giving the Cubs a VHF outlet in the second-largest market on its network. And the projected Field Communications UHF station, Channel 24, was not yet on the air.

Meanwhile, even though its White Sox status appeared to be as a lame-duck carrier, WGN actually increased its number of televised games to a record number for 1967. WGN scheduled all 41 Sox home day games along with 23 night and twi-night doubleheader home contests. The station had normally televised just the first game of a twi-nighter. That left just 18 Sox home games blacked out in Chicago. 13 Sox road games also were scheduled, bringing the total to a healthy 77 telecasts.

Jack Brickhouse's philosophy had always been to "never take the first 'no' for an answer," and he appeared to send a message to Allyn to not vacate his video bully pulpit. Brickhouse and baseball TV director Arne Harris reportedly had lunch to dissuade Allyn from his defection, to no avail.

"The big mistake was not realizing what they needed most of all was exposure, not money," Brickhouse said two decades later in *Thanks for Listening*, his autobiography.

On May 23, 1967, Red Quinlan again time-tripped to his broadcast past for another major WFLD talent acquisition, which hardly elevated the anticipation level or spurred purchase of new sets or UHF converters to watch the Sox.

Despite only two years of baseball announcing experience early in his career (at the end of the 1930s) Jack Drees was hired as the new Sox play-by-play voice. A 6-foot-6 former Austin High School basketball star on Chicago's West Side, the 50-year-old Drees was known for everything *but* baseball. He had worked for Channel 7 as the nightly sportscaster in the early and mid-1950s. Drees also did play-by-play for the station's Monday prime-time package of Illinois and Northwestern basketball in the second half of the 1955-56 season.

Drees was best known for horse racing, having worked top races and serving as broadcast media director of Arlington Park prior to his 1950s sports run on Chicago television. He also called the filmed races for WGN's weekly 9:30 p.m. Saturday night "Let's Go to the Races" show, in which Jewel grocery stores' customers played off cards, hoping their selected horse would bring home a winner and modest cash awards. But no Chicagoan seemed to know anyone who ever got a payout; a typical viewer's horse always got nosed out in the stretch.

Other highlights on Drees' resume included lead TV announcer on the Illinois Boys Basketball Semi-Finals and Finals broadcast every March from Champaign. He also handled St. Louis Cardinals football telecasts and college football on Saturdays. But for baseball pizzazz in a market expecting an animated, even homer-ish announcer, Drees was sorely lacking.

As the spring of 1967 progressed after Drees' hiring, Allyn suddenly had unexpected competition for space on the sports pages. The Cubs would not start out 4-16 as in the previous April. A young core — revolving around middle of the lineup staples Billy Williams, Ron Santo and Ernie Banks – that had looked promising in the final two months of '66 kept their heads above water in the early going of '67.

Then the Cubs really took off. From June 7 to July 3, Durocher's up-and-comers went on a 22-5 run to grab a tie for first with the Cardinals. The increased TV exposure throughout the Midwest helped pack Wrigley Field in numbers not seen in decades. With some fans storming the field in celebration after the final out and winning pitcher Fergie Jenkins needing a cordon of four ushers to get him to the locker room, big portions of a crowd of 40,000 refused to leave the ballpark after the July 2 victory over the Reds. Amazed Cubs players peered out of their clubhouse entrance in the left field corner at the spectacle. The throng was satisfied only when grounds crew members hoisted the Cubs flag atop the scoreboard yardarm to signify a first-place standing.

The city was at its highest fever pitch for baseball since the "air raid" sirens went off for the Sox pennant-clincher of 1959. Cubs excitement hadn't reached this level at any time since the city's schoolchildren were let out early on Sept. 28, 1938 to listen to 3 p.m. radio broadcasts of the pennant-on-the-line game with the Pirates which ended more than 2½ hours later on Gabby Hartnett's "Homer in the Gloamin." And, of course, there was the last Pennant-winning year of 1945.

The Cubs enjoyed more good timing on WGN-TV. A structural change to the station's 10 p.m. news starting in the spring of 1967 ensured the team's meteoric rise would gain prime publicity. WGN lured John Drury, stuck for years as No. 2 anchorman behind the venerable Fahey Flynn at CBS-owned WBBM-TV, to become lead anchor at 5:40 and 10 p.m.

Drury's newscast – also featuring newly-hired Harry Volkman as weatherman and Wendell Smith anchoring sports as the first Black regular on a Chicago 10 p.m. newscast – was expanded to 25 minutes. The extra time played into the day-night advantage in publicity the Cubs had long enjoyed over the Sox. WGN had hours to work with reels of two-inch-wide videotape to cull and edit Cubs highlights. If an 8 p.m. White Sox night game was shown, though, the Drury show was cut to 15 minutes, coming on after the game or at 11 p.m. Thus, the night crew had less time to edit and squeeze Sox highlights into a much smaller time slot.

WGN knew it possessed a valuable commodity in its color game videotape highlights. The station marketed its exclusivity as a lure for fans to switch from better-rated 10 p.m. newscasts on the three network-owned stations to Smith's segment 15 to 20 minutes into Drury's show. Thwarted from using WGN's highlights (before inter-station courtesy started in the 1980s), WBBM, WMAQ and WBKB/WLS began sending crews to Wrigley Field to film large portions of the games. Motorcycle couriers would pick up the film and rush it back to downtown studios for developing. Editors could process the film and air it on 6 p.m. newscasts. Pre-game filmed interviews also could be used. But film-developing time prevented such use from an 8 p.m. Sox game for 10 p.m. newscasts.

The Cubs' action-packed games seemed to overshadow a kind of plodding Sox encampment in first place. Riding a pitching staff that was more effective top to bottom than the Dodgers of Koufax and Drysdale, with a 2.45 team ERA for the season, the Sox seized the top spot in the American League on June 11 for a full two-month stay.

But the damage of win-now trades made by Veeck and General Manager Hank Greenberg after the 1959 season had now fully come home to roost. The duo had dealt away five top young home-grown position players. Fifties lefty ace Billy Pierce said all the pitching-rich Sixties Sox teams needed were one or two run-producers. Instead, Arthur Allyn's front office fielded a slew of top-of-the-lineup table-setters and bottom-of-the-order fill-ins miscast in RBI roles. The Sox thus lacked a star-caliber offensive presence since Minnie Minoso's second tour of duty in 1960-61. The position-player roster almost mirrored manager Eddie Stanky's own playing past as a gritty-but-limited-talent contributor over 11 MLB seasons.

During the July 4 televised game at Comiskey Park, the three-four-five Sox hitters were third baseman Dick Kenworthy, center fielder Ken Berry and shortstop Ron Hansen. Berry and Hansen totaled 15 homers for 1967 while Berry led the regulars with a .241 average. Lefty Tommy John did his job shutting out the Orioles, 4-0, in two hours, five minutes. Nobody at the ballpark or home was kept up late for work the next morning. But compared to the crosstown Cubs throwing both power and pitching at the consumer, the Sox offered somnolent TV in an era when baseball was ripped for being too slow compared to the NFL. Allyn, Stanky and GM Ed Short seemed determined to bring back the "Dead Ball Era" while giving a sneak preview of 1968's "Year of the Pitcher."

"The Sox weren't a fun draw," said the now-60-year fan Ron Eisenstein, recalling his grade-school-age fandom on the Far South Side in 1967. "The pitching was unbelievable. But when you grew up as a Sox fan, you just didn't come to expect 12-9 games."

The likes of Dick Allen and others claimed Comiskey Park's 375-foot power alleys in left and right center were actually 15 feet longer, but longtime legacy groundskeeper Roger Bossard says that was never so. Whatever the case, the top brass still should have developed or traded for a certified RBI man. Pete Ward led the '67 team with 18 homers and 62 RBI. The power-short Cardinals would score more than enough runs in a similarly big ballpark throughout the 1980s.

Instead, all the Sox could come up with were the likes of Chicagoan Moose Skowron, Rocky Colavito and Ken Boyer — all in their baseball dotage.

Management did everything in its power to thwart offensive production to protect a staff of sinker-ball pitchers.

"The park was tailored towards them," Berry recalled to White Sox historian Mark Liptak in 2019. "The infield grass was kept high so that our infielders could get the balls, our pitchers were basically ground-ball type guys and the area around home plate was always a swamp. When you stepped in, you could see the water seep up around your spikes. We weren't that bad of hitters...it's just that it was very difficult to get ground balls through our infield."

And batting sightlines were a problem in the glare of the exploding scoreboard Bill Veeck had installed back in 1960.

"It was very tough for hitters to see in those days," Berry recalled. "(The scoreboard) had all the team names on it, numbers, lights and so on. Light would reflect off it. It was hard to see at the plate. It wasn't like the backdrops they have today. Also fans could sit in the bleachers then, it wasn't kept empty or with a black background like today."

Meanwhile, the Cubs in 1967 installed the new-fangled Astroturf in blocked-off bleachers in center field as a green batting background. Continuing to astound baseball, they again tied the Cardinals for the top spot in the National League with a 3-1 win in St. Louis in the first of a three-game series on Monday, July 24. For the first time in station history, WGN aired an entire three-game road series. Interest was so high, WGN added the July 26 rubber game with no White Sox home night game scheduled.

The WGN programmers and station salesmen were well-rewarded. But they still could not foresee how thoroughly the results would pre-empt the Sox' future attempt to build a Midwest TV network, long before the first flip of a switch from the baseball remote truck of WFLD in 1968.

For the Cubs' July 24, 1967 game, some 1.5 million viewers in the Chicago area tuned in — a 46 share (percentage of households watching TV at the time). The next day, another Chicago-area 46 share was recorded, and WGN also fed that game to stations in Rockford, Peoria, Champaign, the Quad Cities, Milwaukee, Madison and Marion, Ind. The regional audience was gauged at an astounding 3.5 million. The July 26 game was again picked up by all the stations except Madison and Marion. Throughout the Midwest, a lot of decisions about making a future day trip to Wrigley Field were cinched on those steamy nights. The groundwork for the Cubs as destination viewing on television and in person was firmly laid.

By mid-August, though, the Cubs began falling out of the race as the Cardinals lapped the National League. That left the White Sox still firmly in one of the most bunched-up American League pennant races in history, dueling daily for the top with the Red Sox, Tigers and Twins. Strangely, though, Sox fans did not rush the Comiskey turnstiles to witness the South Siders' second close race of the decade. Attendance actually dipped to 985,000, some 5,000 fewer than the also-ran 1966 team. Soon after the season, Allyn would blame the languid gate on bad weather – Chicago suffered a number of rainy weekends in 1967 – and bad press.

But the attendance drop was through no fault of WGN. Loyal to the very end of its Sox contract, the station added, on short notice, the Sept. 26-27 games in Kansas City to its schedule. The Sox entered the two-game final-week series with the lowly Athletics just one game out of first place, the race getting more frantic by the day. The Sept. 26 contest was rained out, necessitating a twi-night dou-bleheader the next day. WGN faithfully televised both games – which the Sox lost 5-2 and 4-0 – a twin dip that would be ruminated about for a half-century to come. Chicago then dropped its final three games of the season at home, all televised, against the tail-ending Washington Senators. The WGN era was over. The South Siders and their suffering fans could not imagine what was yet in store for them on the field and on television.

Arthur Allyn literally felt like a million bucks. He had a new season coming in 1968 after an entire winter separating the franchise from the downer finish of 1967. And the amateur entomologist had his new WFLD contract in hand with the station ready to televise 144 games, generating a rights fee above the $1 mil-lion base. On WMAQ Radio, Allyn had a signal equal to the Cubs' WGN Radio with comparable five-state Midwest daytime coverage and dozens of states at night. New color TV sets were flying out of Polk Brothers and Sears showrooms, although not at the rate to make Red Quinlan's 72 % UHF penetration predic-tion for 1968 come true.

The Sox owner could even cheer *Daily News'* TV critic Dean Gysel's review of competing Cubs and Sox telecasts. WFLD's South Side TV debut was the Cubs-Sox City Series exhibition game on April 6 in Milwaukee, the first of 10 games the Sox would play at County Stadium in 1968. The game took place de-spite the first pitch being less than 48 hours after Martin Luther King Jr. was as-sassinated in Memphis. Baseball would cancel all pre-season and Opening Day contests for two days in the wake of the tragedy, encompassing a national day of mourning and urban rioting.

Admittedly not a baseball fan, Gysel penned a snarky April 8 review of much of the video coverage, claiming he experienced "ennui" watching a game. He wrote that WGN's crew provided slightly more action, offering instant replays while WFLD did not. Gysel also wrote WGN's color was brighter on his set.

But the contrasting announcing styles caused Gysel to aim plaudits at Jack Drees. He ripped Jack Brickhouse as a homer and did not understand his catch phrases like a "blue dart." Drees was praised as "straightforward and just informative." Gysel was "pleasantly shocked" that Drees seized the ongoing narrative and asked the Sox' Tommy Davis for his reaction to King's murder.

"WFLD has a fresh opportunity to strike a blow for electronic journalism and against one of the cannons of hometown sportscasting by allowing Drees to be a reporter of a sports event instead of just a house man," Gysel concluded.

In the front of his mind, Gysel likely was giving an edge to a fellow Field Enterprises subsidiary's underdog operation against the 20-year-old powerful, cash-gorged flagship of Tribune Company's broadcasting division. But his words of praise would turn out to be among only rare accolades sent WFLD's way in its five-year stewardship of Chicago White Sox telecasts.

In and outside of baseball, and in the corridors of WFLD's Marina City offices and the *Sun-Times/Daily News* Building a short block away, Arthur Allyn's grand financial stroke was being further undercut, and quickly.

Cubs owner Phil Wrigley had old-school sensibilities. He felt he had a "gentleman's agreement" with the Sox to share WGN-TV. That sensibility included the 1964 Cubs season opener in Pittsburgh not being televised so the Sox home opener, played at the same time, could be aired as per the station-sharing arrangement.

Now Allyn had broken the two-decades-long Chicago baseball-TV system for the sake of Red Quinlan's cash infusion. Never concerned about making the fastest buck – a reason why Wrigley Field remained lightless to the team's competitive detriment even past his 1977 death – Wrigley allowed WGN to replace its missing Sox games with a full complement of Cubs road games without a significant rights fee increase. Now appointment viewing throughout the Midwest on the new WGN Continental network, the Cubs matched, and exceeded, WFLD's planned schedule of games. Chicago media pundits knew the consequences. *Chicago Tribune* columnist Robert Markus wrote that Sox home night game attendance would be impacted by competing Cubs road night games on TV.

Whatever WFLD could do, WGN could considerably up that ante with its vast resources. When the initial 1968 TV schedule was revealed, WFLD televised no games from the West Coast. WGN's expanded lineup included seven West Coast games.

WFLD would never pop for the increased AT&T line charges to televise games out of Anaheim, Oakland and Seattle, in its one season as the Pilots in

1969. That meant a video blackout for the opening week of the baseball season in '69, as the South Siders made the three-city West Coast swing. Another week without TV games during a West Coast trip ensued in late June. White Sox fans had to paint pictures in their minds via Bob Elson's pedestrian descriptions on radio. In 1971, an unusual Opening Day doubleheader in Oakland was not televised, while WGN aired two twinbills among its 13 West Coast games.

WFLD's brand-new Plumbicon color cameras produced a clearer image compared to the nearly-decade-old monster TK-41 RCA cameras employed by WGN. But the latter station had the production edge thanks to replays and Arne Harris as producer-director. Harris, an off-camera character (like the unseen Carlton The Doorman on the 'Rhoda" sitcom) for Jack Brickhouse, was a veteran of the WGN baseball crew, working his way up from assistant director. He called for personality in his cameramen's panning of the stands, eventually gaining fame for his "hat shots" and female fans dressed down for the summer.

Meanwhile, UHF reception problems continued. Individual channel-clicking "detent" UHF tuners were years from the market. Tim Cronin, longtime Chicago suburban sportswriter and author, purchased his first color set as a teenager in 1970; it had a less-precise radio-style dial UHF tuner. *Sun-Times* gossipmonger Irv Kupcinet, boosting his Field Enterprises bosses' video outlet, may have touted Opening Night reception reports from viewers as A-OK for WFLD on Jan. 4, 1966. But in the real world, baseball fans had to battle snowy images as they tried to lock in WFLD's signal.

Initially beamed from a tower atop Marina City before switching to the new John Hancock Center in late 1969, WFLD boasted of 2.5 million watts from its Big John transmitter. But promotion of that tower of power was little help for viewers unable to tune the signal in clearly. For fans accustomed to WGN's crystal-clear image on Channel 9, long transmitted from a distinctive tower atop the Prudential Building, the sometimes-sketchy Channel 32 reception was, literally, a turn-off.

"The picture quality was bad for Sox games," said Bruce Levine, by now an experienced UHF tinkerer. "The team lost a lot of fans, in my opinion, because of (the poor video quality)."

Although Gysel the non-baseball fan panned Brickhouse, now a Cubs-only baseball man, the most ubiquitous broadcaster in the industry's history gave the Midwest audience what it wanted: Rah-rah homerism. He held back any criticism of the Cubs organization to protect WGN's golden goose of below-market rights fees and the resulting assured profits.

In contrast, Drees' more detached style and lack of a recent baseball broadcasting pedigree did not play well with his audience.

To Mark Liptak, watching intently then, Drees was an "East Coast horse-racing announcer" despite those personal and professional Chicago roots.

"Drees was awful and very monotone in his delivery," added Levine.

Drawing similar criticism was Elson. After four decades as White Sox radio announcer on WMAQ, the Commander's precise even-keel diction seemed out of place with the times and matched the Sox offense's dullard ways. If an announcer existed who could sell the Sox as the 1960s ended, he was not employed by either WFLD or WMAQ.

WFLD and the Sox did not help Drees with an impactful broadcast partner. His first boothmate in 1968 was garden-variety sportscaster Dave Martin, with no reputation in baseball. Martin was replaced in 1969 by former ace Red Sox pitcher Mel Parnell, who had no Chicago background, having worked on Boston games from 1965-68.

Parnell wanted out after the first year of a two-year deal, said Liptak. WFLD at first would not let him go, but Parnell recruited Sox legend Billy Pierce as a replacement, by Liptak's recollection, and the station bid Parnell farewell. The well-meaning Pierce lasted just one season with Drees in 1970, a perceptible lisp hindering his delivery.

The Comiskey Park broadcast booth revolving doors again swung open with White Sox PA announcer Bud Kelly teaming with Drees for two seasons starting in 1971. Kelly matched Drees with a thin baseball background, having been the morning man on WBBM-Radio in the mid-1960s before serving as a deejay on several FM stations.

Dress and his college of analysts were only the face of the WFLD dilemma for the Sox. Behind the scenes, Arthur Allyn had been undercut. Red Quinlan left the station just as his big rights deal got underway in 1968. "I told them — after I get this established I'm going to back off. I wanted to write," Quinlan recalled to the *Video Veteran* in 2002.

WFLD director Dillman said Quinlan never truly had the full Field Enterprises tailwinds as backing. The company's plunge into TV had been championed by boss Marshall Field IV, who died at age 49 in 1965, just three months before WFLD went on the air. With heir Marshall V too young to take over just yet, Field was succeeded by an executive from the World Book-Childcraft encyclopedia division of the business. The shift was perceptible in the lower enthusiasm for Quinlan's grand plans.

Quinlan left WFLD to write books and, at the invitation of Pakistani Prime Minister Zulfiqar Ali Bhutto, built up the country's TV network. Quinlan later said he "lived like a king."

Also departing WFLD in 1968 to return to the Field newspapers was news coordinator Herman Kogan. Despite rave reviews and awards for "Newscope," the collaborative TV station-print production faded after two years along with the other 1966 promises of creative programming. The new flagship television outlet of the White Sox quickly became less than Allyn and viewers were promised.

"You are so right about the big plans going up in smoke," said Herman Kogan's son, Rick Kogan, a Chicago journalism standout in his own right at the Tribune.

The White Sox existed like an island on a financially-struggling UHF station that now adopted reruns of "Rawhide" and "McHale's Navy," movies and "Divorce Court."

And, typical of corporate quick hooks of later decades, Field Enterprises began shopping WFLD to Metromedia, a large operator of independent TV stations such as WNEW in New York, WTTG in Washington, D.C. and KTTV in Los Angeles. No additional money would be pumped into a losing team's broadcasts, given the necessity of righting the financials for a prospective buyer.

Perhaps Quinlan could have come up with some creative solutions for his loss-leader Sox deal, had he stayed on. But when the Sox started out 0-10 in 1968, the die was cast. The team was even more snore-inducing than before, slugging just 71 homers and losing 95 games while finishing eighth in the 10-team American League. Just under 400,000 fans showed up for the 72 games played at Comiskey Park; the other nine regular-season contests had been scheduled in Milwaukee. Succeeding season loss totals of 94 and that franchise-record 106 ensured more stress on WFLD's bottom line with still no full-market penetration for UHF, which the station claimed was at 87% in 1970.

Meanwhile, on WGN and its network, the Cubs began to blow the Sox out of the market. Bill Gleason, self-proclaimed voice of the South Side, drinking fan in the *Sun-Times*, theorized the Cubs had seized the loyalty of the area's young fans after observing their presence in screeching numbers in a crowd of more than 33,000 for their Wrigley Field home opener on April 13, 1968 against the Cardinals. Only three days before, the Sox had drawn just under 8,000 for their delayed opener against the Indians at Comiskey Park.

The Cubs' record was hardly better than the Sox' mark in late June at 31-41, after going a big-league record 48 scoreless innings that month. But an ensuing 33-14 mid-summer run made for entertaining TV viewing and low-cost Wrigley Field day trips from all points of the Midwest to distract from the bad real-world news of 1968.

The strong second half was a prelude to a 1969 Cubs season that has been covered and analyzed to death through the ages. But the bottom line was: A mania took over a regional cultural landscape. The combination of a first-place team through August and all the attendant sideshows, often centered around manager Leo Durocher, made WGN-TV and radio a hyper-power, like the United States Military on Aug. 10, 1945. All Arthur Allyn could do in response, in near-obscurity, was commence negotiations to sell the White Sox to Bud Selig in Milwaukee.

In the White Sox' own backyard, a South Side mainstay staged a packed Cubs event on July 15, 1969. Some 12,000 showed up at 47th and Damen, just two miles southwest of Comiskey Park, for the Back of the Yards Council Fun Fair "We Love the Chicago Cubs Night." Such a turnout on the South Side would have been unthinkable in previous seasons. The only significant Cubs not in the house were Ernie Banks and Fergie Jenkins, attending a benefit softball game 15 miles away at Thillens Stadium organized by 17-year-old Les Grobstein, a future Chicago sports radio raconteur. Fergie actually pitched two innings there. The veteran star hurler also opened a new McDonalds in north suburban Skokie, but quickly ran out of his 100 photos and signed autographs on cups, napkins and any other solid object offered.

Meanwhile, over the humidity-producing corn and soybean fields extending out hundreds of miles from the Big Town, Cub Power was being beamed on an expanded TV network. Beyond the original 1967 stations, the outlets for Sunday, holiday and some weeknight road games now included Green Bay and La Crosse in Wisconsin; South Bend, Ft. Wayne and Terre Haute in Indiana, and Cedar Rapids and Des Moines in Iowa. This was the promised Chicago White Sox regional TV distribution of 1966.

The actual Sox network of mid-summer 1969 consisted of Milwaukee, Rockford, South Bend and Ft. Wayne. Fittingly, UHF independent station WVTV in Milwaukee carried the Sox on Channel 18 while more powerful CBS affiliate WISN still carried the Cubs on VHF Channel 12. Field Communications' Channel 24, projected in 1966 to be the Sox' Milwaukee outlet, *never signed on.* As Dave Dillman recalled, its planned transmitting tower was next to a country club, whose members virulently opposed such a blight on their sylvan sightlines. No station would activate Channel 24's license until 1980.

Red Quinlan's successors at WFLD would pump no more resources into Sox telecasts than mandated by contract. The initial schedule of 144 games was cut to the minimum 129. Ratings got a considerable boost from Dick Allen's explosive production in 1972. But the red ink had stained WFLD's coffers so much that they opted to not pick up the next five-year option. Further cost-cutting was underway, the sale to Metromedia fell through and Field Enterprises was now trying to sell at least part of WFLD to Kaiser Broadcasting, an operator of non-network UHF stations.

A final embarrassing episode during WFLD's baseball tenure took place during a crucial four-day weekend series in Oakland from Aug. 10-13, 1972. Six games out of first place to begin August, the Sox got hot and quickly closed in on the lead in the AL West, tying the Athletics at the top on Aug. 12. WFLD got caught with its pants down by not stepping up to televise at least part of the Oakland series. By then, WGN was televising Friday-through-Sunday Cubs games from the West Coast.

Station management used Jack Drees as an apologist before its Aug. 15 home telecast of a Sox-Brewers game at Comiskey Park to counter heavy media and fan criticism. Drees claimed WFLD did not have time to make the arrangements for a technical crew for the Oakland Coliseum. But, again, the bottom line was just that: Money.

The Sox' new owner John Allyn entered the middle of 1972 without a TV outlet for the next season. So, he stretched his already-thin finances to forge a solution. He could not go back and find space on WGN amid its nearly 150-games-a-year Cubs schedule, in spite of the attractive lure of the Dick Allen-led 1972 contenders. One other Chicago outlet remained — WSNS-TV (Channel 44).

Signing on in 1970, WSNS generated humor as an archetype of a low-budget TV station in the same manner of WCIU six years earlier. Original programming consisted of hours of "Instant News," a news-scroll on the screen, straight off wire-service teletypes. Management decided to jazz up the hours of tedium with something never seen before or since on TV: News delivered by an attractive Linda Fuoco, garbed in a revealing negligee. Fuoco was portrayed lying across a red satin sheet-covered heart-shaped bed. TV Guide even ran an article about the juncture of sex and news. Suffice to say, the show did not have staying power.

Soon WSNS reverted to news being read by conventionally-dressed female anchors such as Linda Marshall and Roz Deeter. Chuck Collins, just 21, hosted "Underground News." Psychic Irene Hughes had her own show. Paul Harvey's syndicated program also aired on WSNS.

Into this odd mix stepped Chicago's American League baseball team.

Beggars could not be choosers for Sox telecasting. John Allyn approached Don Nathanson of Grey-North Advertising about placing Sox games on WSNS. Nathanson, part of the WSNS's ownership group, had gained "Mad Men"-era acclaim for slogans like "Promise her anything, but give her Arpege," along with naming Dippity-Do hair gel and Flair pens.

The Sox would start a unique arrangement for a major-league baseball team: Paying for the airtime on a per-game basis. WSNS would simply be a "conduit" for the telecasts, as station boss Ed Morris told Clarence Petersen of the *Chicago Tribune* in 1972. Since WSNS was a small operation, WGN was contracted to provide the remote truck for Comiskey Park.

John Allyn named Marshall Black to head TV advertising sales efforts. But the brokering of time on WSNS and associated production costs put extreme pressure on the Sox' staff to make back the up-front cash outlay in sales, compared to all other franchises simply cashing rights-fees checks from broadcasters.

The WSNS deal put even more strain on Allyn's always-precarious finances, and was likely a contributing factor in the plucky owner literally running out of money to pay spring training hotel bills and nearly the final player payroll in 1975. Harry Caray relayed a conversation he had in late 1975 with Black about total TV sales revenue in recession-plagued 1975: $300,000. Caray did not break down or clarify the numbers, but the amount seemed paltry by any measure.

Mark Liptak said advertisers, to whom John Allyn apparently had business links, were recruited despite not normally being seen on baseball telecasts. Entities like Interlake, Inc., a steel manufacturer, and the International Brotherhood of Electrical Workers Union bought commercials, but they had no product to sell directly to baseball fans. Liptak even recalled ads for a chicken producer, again with no logical pitch to consumers. In his 1969 Artnell Corp. assets settlement with his brother, John Allyn retained a Georgia chicken farm. Mystery solved.

The Sox did not completely lack conventional baseball TV sponsors, to be sure. WFLD and WSNS featured Household Finance Corp., an age-old Sox sponsor, along with Zenith, Motorola, Commonwealth Edison, Jays Foods, Chevy, Chicagoland Oldsmobile Dealers, True Value Hardware, American National Bank and Drovers Bank, the latter a longtime South Side institution. Olympic Savings & Loan also sponsored the baseball clinics at area banks, the Soxettes and the Meet the Sox baseball dinners.

Watching from the sidelines in his post-FCC vantage points, UHF godfather Newton Minow could feel John Allyn's and the Sox' pain. "I agree that the Sox were hurt for a period," he said of their long, strange journey through the channel spectrum Minow had championed.

Falstaff, the Sox beer, was the prevailing suds sponsor during this era. Harry Caray was the Falstaff pitchman-for-hire, long before he became a "Cub Fan, Bud Man." He took full advantage of live beer commercials, quaffing the product on-camera against all the broadcast standards and practices at the time.

But Harry always was bigger than his medium, maybe even the FCC itself. He was one of the two quick benefits quickly derived from the brokered time on

WSNS. The Sox re-aligned the broadcast team to switch Caray from radio-only to the first three and last three innings on TV with the remainder on WMAQ, the division of TV and radio for much of the remainder of Caray's Chicago career. In a baseball TV-oriented market like Chicago, the lead broadcaster had to be on camera. Caray lured more viewers to the broadcasts as they bought new TV sets, now with easier and more accurate dentent UHF tuners as the 1970s progressed. With the team calling the shots, West Coast telecasts commenced on the first road trip to Anaheim, a month into the 1973 season.

Meanwhile, the White Sox got some high-profile ancillary programming on WSNS – but it came with a caveat befitting its leading man. Dick Allen was awarded an hour-long weekly show in his name on Sunday nights in the spring of 1973. Big names from other Chicago sports franchises were guests. But in keeping with his often-enigmatic personality, Allen was often absent from the host's chair. Substitute hosts drew praise, but "The Dick Allen Show" quickly lost steam without its star attraction.

While Allen was AWOL from his program, Caray became the front-and-center White Sox figure as his second year doing six innings on TV progressed. Providing Caray with a higher-profile medium proved to be a double-edged sword. As the team disappointed with a .500 record in 1974 and then collapsed into the AL West nether world without Allen in 1975, Caray reverted to his old St. Louis shoot-from-the-hip style with heightened criticism. Bob Waller, Caray's 1973-74 TV partner, was bounced supposedly for being too critical.

John Allyn's skin got as thin as his White Sox budget. Waller's 1975 replacement was good ol' boy former Sox and Cubs catcher J.C. Martin, a reported Allyn golfing buddy. Martin's Virginia drawl was hardly the second coming of Dizzy Dean. Caray likely cringed with Martin homilies: "Ah know a couple from Poplar Bluff that raise Hereford steers and cockleberries," "Y'know, in Yazoo City they serve grits with snacks," and "Big Jim Kaat just pounced on that ball like…like…like a big ol' puma!"

The WSNS arrangement, and Caray, survived the end of the John Allyn regime and the circuitous reversion to Bill Veeck ownership. Allyn's brief on-air "firing" of Caray on Oct. 1, 1975, only to have Veeck continue business as usual, simply attracted viewers to the broadcast Pied Piper even more, no matter what the record. Caray was teamed with unpredictable, no-filter Jimmy Piersall starting in 1977 for a true guerilla-theater-on-the-air show. The Sox telecasts, with almost all viewers by now possessing UHF tuners, finally achieved a kind of equality in the market with old-school WGN...if not in ratings, but in the bread-and-circuses entertainment befitting a Veeck production.

So the dynamic trio of John Allyn, Dick Allen and Caray had brought the

Sox to more solid footing, even if additional drama loomed for the franchise's future. Allyn blocked a move to Milwaukee coming and to Seattle going. He stretched his finances to afford Allen and further increased Caray's visibility, ensuring he'd be the face of TV baseball in Chicago until his last broadcast in September 1997.

John Allyn could not yet reverse the 1966 money-hungry decision of his brother, Arthur, but he took actions to induce viewers to find Sox telecasts on UHF.

If Veeck-to-Arthur Allyn-to-John-Allyn-back-to-Veeck was a completed circle, so were future Sox broadcast homes. WFLD came back as the over-the-air TV home from 1982 to 1989, with cable's penetration progressively leveling the playing field between VHF and UHF. Field Enterprises had actually regained control of the station as the Sox returned.

In 1981, star *Sun-Times* columnist Mike Royko hatched an idea to Marshall Field V to buy the Cubs from Bill Wrigley, last of the three generations of Wrigley men to own the Cubs, and actually switch their telecasts from WGN to WFLD. Charlie Finley, who had just sold his Oakland team, would run the baseball end of the franchise. But, in Jack Brickhouse's vernacular, the deal was "a day late and a dollar short." Wrigley felt uncomfortable selling to anyone but his longtime broadcast partners — in a way, de facto minority Cubs owners — at Tribune Company, who sensed the shifting broadcast landscape and moved quickly to protect WGN-TV's legacy programming and the roughly 500-plus hours of airtime it filled, annually.

Years later, after Fox bought WFLD, the non-cable rights reverted back to WGN for 30 seasons — 10 more than the original run — to complete the circle. Hawk Harrelson, with enough catch-phrases to rival Brickhouse, helmed the broadcasts through the 2005 White Sox World Championship season and well beyond. When WGN's 72-season baseball-TV run came to an end in 2019 as the Cubs and Sox opted to put all games on their own cable outlets, its final telecast was, fittingly, on the South Side: A Sox-Tigers Saturday night game at Guaranteed Rate Field.

The Sox had foolishly left their reliable, powerful TV outlet in 1967, simply for money. The deal proved a fistful of dollars often is not a panacea. In the end, though, the South Siders had made it all the way home to Good Ol' Channel 9.

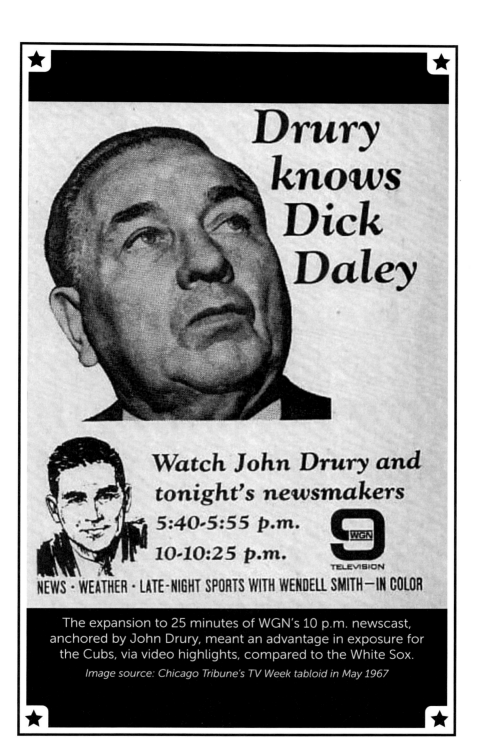

Drury knows Dick Daley

Watch John Drury and tonight's newsmakers

5:40-5:55 p.m.

10-10:25 p.m.

9 WGN TELEVISION

NEWS · WEATHER · LATE-NIGHT SPORTS WITH WENDELL SMITH—IN COLOR

The expansion to 25 minutes of WGN's 10 p.m. newscast, anchored by John Drury, meant an advantage in exposure for the Cubs, via video highlights, compared to the White Sox.

Image source: Chicago Tribune's TV Week tabloid in May 1967

White Sox owner Arthur Allyn (right) and GM Ed Short flank
longtime manager Al Lopez upon signing another contract.
Lopez came back to replace Eddie Stanky in the middle of a
1968 season that sent Sox fortunes on a severe downslide.

Photo credit: Leo Bauby Collection

WFLD, the White Sox's new TV outlet for 1968, was fortunate to land Sears as a sponsor when it went on the air two years previously. But UHF penetration was still only a minority of the market, and Sears had to remind consumers its new sets had channels 14 through 83.

Newton N. Minow, FCC Chairman, testifies before a Senate subcommittee on May 23, 1961, weeks after delivering his "vast wasteland" speech. He backed the All-Channel Receiver Act of 1962, which mandated that all TV sets be factory-equipped with UHF tuners from mid-1964 onward. Minow wanted to give UHF stations a fighting chance to develop an audience but, in reality, it took 10 years before there was near-complete market penetration of UHF receivers. Low penetration made Art Allyn's decision to leave WGN to go to WFLD Channel 32 ill-advised as the White Sox lost out on exposure.

Photo credit: the Associated Press

CHAPTER 15

August 22, 1972: 'Goose'

"How about that job Gossage did!"

– Chicago White Sox manager Chuck Tanner to assembled media after his team defeats the New York Yankees 5-4 on Aug. 22, 1972 at White Sox Park.

By the time the New York Yankees returned to Chicago, on Aug. 22, 1972, the White Sox had taken control of the baseball scene in Chicago. The team started the day with a 67-48 record, only half-a-game back of the first-place Oakland A's in the American League Western Division. Dick Allen was continuing to make his case as a potential AL MVP, with a league-leading 30 homers and 87 runs batted in to go with a .313 batting average.

"The resurgence of the White Sox and Yankees to contending status in both of their respective divisions has been quite a relief for their fans. In Chicago and New York, the ardent rooters have returned, saluting rediscovered heroes with the fervor of an old-time revival meeting," noted *Chicago Tribune* writer Bob Logan.

Meanwhile, the crosstown Cubs, a consistently competitive team since 1967, had dropped to 12½ games behind National League East-leading Pittsburgh, although the North Side still had a .521 winning percentage on August 22. The Cubs had their own MVP candidate in left fielder Billy Williams, who was mirroring Allen's offensive production: A league-leading .334 average with 25 homers and 84 RBI.

But even the Chicago media had begun to view the North Siders in an unfavorable light when compared to their South Side counterparts. *Chicago Tribune* beat writer George Langford, who covered the Sox during the first half of the 1972 season, moved over to cover the Cubs after the All-Star break. He filed this dour report from San Diego in the August 22 *Tribune* sports pages:

"The Cubs don't work together, generally. Their concern for themselves was brought home dramatically to this writer when compared to their cross-town compatriots — the White Sox — a group of players obviously trying to work for a common goal."

At Chicago's City Hall on LaSalle Street, the city's top fan, Mayor Richard J. Daley, was preparing to go to the Sox-Yankees game that evening. And on this late August morning, Daley would need the respite at White Sox Park, as he continued to lick his wounds after a humiliating defeat in July in Miami Beach, where he and his 58 other elected Democratic convention delegates representing Illinois were ousted in favor of the more diverse group.

The next day, Daley was slated to meet with the Democrats' candidate for president, the liberal-leaning Sen. George McGovern, across the street at Cook County Democratic Central Committee headquarters in the Sherman House

Hotel. The storied 1925-vintage venue would close in the next year, eventually to be replaced by the modernistic Helmut Jahn-designed Thompson Center.

The McGovern meeting was an event about which Daley was decidedly unenthusiastic. "I think he must clarify his position on the various issues," Daley would tell reporters. "(But) I'm confident we'll win Illinois."

Off-the-record, Daley remained furious at McGovern, blaming him for the embarrassment in Miami Beach, and savagely attacking the South Dakota senator in a recent call after McGovern said he wasn't directly responsible for the ouster of his hand-picked delegates. "McGovern, don't give me that b.s.... I know better," was what Daley reportedly told him, according to city gossip columnists.

Daley would be in his box seat at the ballpark when McGovern landed at Midway Airport later that night.

As Daley left City Hall to pick up his limo for the trip to the game, he probably was enlivened by news that six Black alderman, all Daley supporters, sent McGovern a letter that day, warning him about Rev. Jackson, an adviser on the candidate's campaign. "(Jackson) is trying to hoodwink the McGovern people into believing that Jackson alone is interested in registering black voters," wrote the six Black aldermen, led by veteran Claude Holman of the 4th Ward, long Daley's mouthpiece in City Council chambers. "Beginning with the election of Mr. [Mayor] Daley in 1955, it has been the Daley commitment and political leaders who get the vote out in Chicago."

One who signed the letter, 6th Ward Alderman (and future Chicago Mayor) Eugene Sawyer, also took the time on that day to lambaste NBC-TV's John Chancellor. Reporting that week from the Republican National Convention in Miami Beach, anchorman Chancellor unflatteringly compared some sycophantic young GOP delegates to Daley-sponsored delegations of the past:

"In past conventions, we've seen Mayor Daley pack the hall with 6th Ward sewer workers," Chancellor would report. "Now we have the Republican equivalent."

Sawyer, whose 6th Ward had turned only within the last few years from all-White middle class to all-Black middle class constituents, was offended by the connotation that his ward — which contained the Chatham, Gresham and Park Manor neighborhoods — was filled with sewer workers.

"Will you tell him that the 6th Ward is full of more than its share of doctors, lawyers and other professionals?" Sawyer asked a *Chicago Tribune* reporter.

Despite the increasing independence from the machine which Black politicians and voters would show in ensuing years, some of the Black aldermen remained in thrall of Daley. Former Illinois State Senate President Emil Jones, Jr., then a state representative, recalled a hotel elevator trip he made with Daley at the 1976 Democratic Convention in New York. Also on hand were several Black aldermen who had already pushed the buttons for their respective floors before Daley got on. But in Jones' recollection, none dared get off the elevator, passing up their floors, until Daley debarked.

Away from City Hall, conventions, courtrooms and offices, some of those 6th Ward doctors and lawyers were probably joining Daley at the game. That's because White Sox-Yankees games were long the marquee matchups at 35th and Shields. And on the night of August 22, the Sox were facing an equally resurgent team, which was only a game-and-a-half behind AL East-leading Detroit after being mostly non-competitive for the previous eight years.

The glory days of the rivalry were the 1950s and 1960s, when Mantle, Berra, McDougald and Ford battled Minoso, Fox, Aparacio and Pierce in a first-division war that the Yankees would ultimately win far more often than not. The Sox interrupted the Yankees' dynasty just once with the semi-surprising 1959 pennant, timing the surge for a season when the dynastic Bronx Bombers had a rare pratfall, finishing slightly over .500.

"The Yankees at Sox Park were usually the highlight of the season," remembered Roger Wallenstein, the longtime Sox fan, post-game radio broadcaster and vendor. "It was usually a four-game weekend series with a doubleheader on Sunday and over 100,000 in total attendance."

On this night, more than 43,000 fans complemented Daley and his entourage. Also in attendance: Baseball Commissioner Bowie Kuhn, who was in Chicago to witness the resurgence of the White Sox up close and to give the team clearance to start printing playoff tickets, priced $7 and up.

The commissioner and mayor got to see Allen wallop a game-winning two-run home run over the center field fence in the fifth inning to pace the Sox. This was the 15th time that Allen had produced the winning run in 1972.

But the real story was in the bullpen. Starter Stan Bahnsen had his usual problems with his old team, giving up four runs and getting yanked after just 1⅔ innings. But in the top of the fifth with the Yankees up 4-3, Rich "Goose" Gossage replaced lefty Dave Lemonds and worked out of a bases-loaded jam. The Sox' "kiddie corps," Gossage and Terry Forster, closed out the game with 4⅔ scoreless innings. Gossage picked up the win — his third straight without a loss. Forster notched his 21st save.

After the game, Tanner was showering his rookie right-hander with praise. "How about that job Gossage did!"

It was one of the many revelatory moments for Gossage, turning 21 midway through his first of 22 major league seasons, which would include nine All-Star appearances, three World Series, 1,502 strikeouts and 310 saves, numbers that booked a 2008 induction into the Baseball Hall of Fame. He is one of only eight relief specialists in Cooperstown. The others are Lee Smith, Trevor Hoffman, Mariano Rivera, Hoyt Wilhelm, Rollie Fingers, Dennis Eckersley and Bruce Sutter.

But that 1972 Sox team stands out as a cherished baseball memory for Goose — because it was his first big-league experience…and because of Dick Allen.

"It ranks up there with the '78 (World Series champion New York Yankees) team that I played with," Gossage recalled nearly 50 years later from his home in Colorado Springs, Colo. "It ranks up there and is maybe even more special because it was my first.

"Everything was my first. Everything was fresh. Everything was brand new and incredible. I was in total awe of the whole experience. It was something I wish every baseball fan could do and experience. I had four or five 'out of body' experiences – the first year walking into original Yankee Stadium, playing in that great cathedral of Comiskey Park and the bombs that Dick hit. I never saw balls hit like Dick hit that year, ever again."

Allen was more than just an explosive, one-of-a-kind hitter to Gossage. He was also, in 1972, a mentor.

"Dick was the smartest baseball man I'd ever met," Gossage said. "The education I got, all the money in the world could not pay for it. He took me under his wing and taught me — from the greatest hitter that I ever saw hit, that I ever saw in person play the game, he was the greatest baserunner I ever saw. Little did I know, I'm a rookie, I am watching the greatest player that I will ever watch. It was something to behold. I never forgot that."

Gossage, Only 20, Fires Bullets on Chisox Mound

The Sporting News - June 17, 1972

Richard Michael Gossage was the fifth of sixth children who grew up in a one-bedroom house in Colorado Springs. Gossage was one of the many live arms uncovered by the White Sox scouting staff in the 1960s and 1970s. He was taught baseball initially by his father Jake, a failed gold prospector who died when Gossage was a junior at Wasson High School in Colorado Springs.

Young Rich Gossage, talking to reporters in 1972, credited his older brother, Jack, for tutoring.

"He was always telling me to throw harder," he told Chicago sportswriter Jerome Holtzman. "I'd be throwing as hard as I could and he'd say, can you throw harder than that? Sometimes I'd cry…[But] that was his way of helping me."

Bill Kimball, the Sox' chief scout in the Midwest for almost 30 years, discovered Gossage while he was pitching for Wasson High, and signed the pitcher for an $8,000 bonus as a ninth-round pick in the June 4, 1970 first-year player draft.

Kimball's scouting report for Gossage, now in the Baseball Hall of Fame, is concise and prescient:

"Good Prospect...Has the good live fastball...
With the good loose arm."

Almost immediately, young Rich began impressing Sox personnel, starting with his first campaign in the Gulf Coast Rookie League, where he struck out 21 and walked only six, exclusively using his high-90 mph fastball.

Gossage moved up to Appleton in the Class A Midwest League in 1971. Already on the big club's radar, Chuck Tanner and Johnny Sain directed their attention toward him during spring training. When the season started, Tanner also made a special trip on a White Sox off-day to the Quad Cities, where the Appleton Foxes were playing a road game, to help Gossage develop an alternative to his dynamic fastball.

"I could command my fastball, but I had no idea what a breaking ball was," Gossage recalled. "Chuck flew [to the Quad Cities] in a little puddle-jumping plane, a little bitty plane. Johnny Sain had showed him (Chuck) how to throw a change-up and he flew there and showed me how to do it. It was that simple."

With his new off-speed pitch, Gossage dominated the Midwest League as a starter in 1971, finishing the year with an 18-2 record and getting invited to the big club's spring camp in 1972, where he was expected to have a good shot to make it to Chicago. But Gossage had a slow start; it was then that he encountered the unique inspirational skills of Tanner.

"I'm getting knocked around because I don't have my fastball yet," Gossage remembered. "So (Chuck) calls me into his office and Sain's in there with him. Chuck threw me this pad and on the top sheet he's got the roster of all the pitchers that made the team. And there's my name crossed out. I go, 'What is this?' He says, 'That's the roster that's going north.' I said, 'So my name is crossed out?' He goes, 'Yeah.'

"So, I go, 'I'm not going north?' He said, 'No, unless you start pitching better.' I went off on him. I said, 'I'm the best fucking pitcher you've got in this camp.' He stood up and I stood up and Johnny's between us, like we're going to go at it. I'm fucking mad and I go, 'I'm the best fucking pitcher you got in camp,' and he goes, 'Well, why don't you go out there and fucking prove it?' I said, 'Give me the fucking ball and I'll go fucking prove it, OK?' That was all I needed. It was great. I think it was his way of waking me up."

But like all the other players on the big club, his debut would be delayed by the strike: The 13-day players' walkout started on April 1. Gossage was stuck in Chicago.

"My sister was in Chicago, but she wasn't there at the time," Gossage recalled. "So I had to spend one night out on the town. I didn't have a credit card, so I couldn't get a room somewhere. I didn't have any money at all. Finally my sister returned. So we got in her car and drove all the way back to Colorado Springs."

When the strike ended, Gossage joined the team in Kansas City, where he finally got a chance to meet his new teammate, Dick Allen, who had signed his contract on the day the strike started. While he was in Florida during the spring, Dick Allen rarely even made it to Payne Park.

"I'm throwing on our day off in Kansas City before Opening Day, working with Johnny Sain," Gossage recalled. "I'm on the mound for the first time since spring training. Now, tomorrow is the first game. I'm throwing on the side and I had never met Dick Allen. He walks up and steps in the box, nobody around but me, Johnny Sain and the catcher."

"Dick, was a specimen, man. I'm a young kid and don't know quite where the ball is going and I'm throwing 100 mph. I said, 'Oh my God, I'm going to kill Dick Allen right here, and he's going to beat the shit out of me.' I was petrified and scared to death. My adrenaline started and I'm throwing hard and he's looking at every pitch. He's got a bat in his hand and he's standing there like he's really studying me and getting ready for the game. So, after my session with Johnny, Dick comes up to me and says, 'Hey, son, that's one of the greatest arms I've ever seen.' He said always keep a sleeve on it. Always keep it covered. He said, 'Never pitch without long sleeves.' I said, 'Yes sir.' And I never did…and I never had any arm problems."

Gossage got into his first major league game in Kansas City on Sunday, April 16, walking one while not giving up a run in a 2-1 loss.

His stunning fastball reportedly could approach triple digits, which was still a rarity in major league baseball of the early 70s. Teammates and coaches were in awe of this ability.

"His fastball is nasty," Rick Reichardt told reporters back then. "Very nasty."

"What amazes me about him is his poise, which is exceptional for a 19-year-old kid," added third-base coach Joe Lonnett. "And every time he works, he's more relaxed and confident."

But in those first few weeks, Gossage sometimes struggled with his control. Outside of Sain, Dick was a main confidant to Gossage. They would sometimes meet up in the Holiday Inn hotel bar off Interstate 55 in southwest suburban Hickory Hills, where Dick stayed for part of the 1972 season. Other times, they'd chat in the clubhouse. The message that the veteran would continuously make to the rookie: Challenge hitters.

"Dick said, 'You've got to pitch inner half,'" Gossage said. "He'd tell me: 'That left elbow that's sticking out there, kind of toward the plate, that's your target'. I said, 'Dick, geez, if I miss in, that's right at their heads.' He goes, 'Goose, that's the best thing that can ever happen to you, is that you dust a couple of those guys, knock them down. Every guy in that dugout is watching. They want no part of you.' I was so afraid I was going to hit somebody and then Dick got me over that. I drilled [only] three people intentionally in 22 years."

While Allen was in Gossage's one ear, Johnny Sain was in the other. The man who former Yankees pitcher and "Ball Four" author Jim Bouton called "the greatest pitching coach who ever lived" was setting his sights on this youngster. His goal was to make Gossage a more well-rounded pitcher, with an additional breaking pitch that could be used as an alternative to his fastball.

"I really never ran into anybody quite like him ever since then," Gossage said.

Sain taught Gossage how to throw a "slurve," a slider-curve combination pitch that Sain had pioneered during his days hurling for the Boston Braves in the late 1940s.

"I had no preconceived ideas of what a breaking ball was, so to run into Sain and be taught those mechanics of a devastating, freaking 'slurve,' oh my God, it was a thing of beauty to watch it progress and to see what I did," Gossage recalled.

"I threw it hard, 91, 92 mph right at (a batter's) hip as hard as I could and it broke big. John, as I've said many times, taught me the breaking ball in bullpen sessions and with home exercises."

Bart Johnson, Terry Forster and Gossage provided the heat out of the bullpen. All three relievers threw 90-plus MPH, something few other bullpens could match back then.

"You didn't want to be in the bullpen at that time," Gossage said. "It was a junk pile where old starters went that could not start anymore. There were a few good relievers, Lindy McDaniel, Sparky Lyle, Dick Radatz [years earlier] with Boston was awesome. Hoyt Wilhelm, he's basically in the Hall of Fame as a reliever. But in 1972, you still didn't want to be in the bullpen. But that was starting to evolve. And Johnny and Chuck were going to change it, by using multiple guys out of the 'pen.

Johnson remembered Forster and Gossage as hard throwers, although not in the 100-mph range.

"I wouldn't put myself in a class of Forster and Gossage, the two of them were something special," Johnson recalled in a radio interview. "I thought Terry threw the hardest, 93, 94, 95 at times. Actually, Gossage, I thought, was more like a 90 guy when he first came up, but he only played like seven games in his high school senior year in Colorado. So, he never had much baseball in him. Terry and I came from California and, of course, we played a lot more than him."

Gossage believed that Forster had the best stuff he'd ever seen: "He threw as hard as I did and usually hard throwers like me when they throw hard like that, the ball is a livelier ball. Terry threw 98 and heavy."

Forster and Gossage had been roommates when Goose was called up to the Class-A Appleton Foxes during the final few weeks of the 1970 season. Duane Schaffer, another member of that 1970 Appleton pitching staff, later become a longtime scout and Director of Player Personnel for the White Sox, responsible for drafting standout future Chicago pitchers such as Jack McDowell and Mark Buehrle.

"Terry and I were best friends," Goose recalled. "He made it to the big leagues in 1971, one year before I did. In the big leagues, Terry and I started playing a game called 'burnout,' where we'd play catch, but throw these balls as hard as we could. He would kill me throwing those balls. We come out one day and he goes, 'Let's go play catch. Let's go play our game.' I said, 'No, you win.' I took my glove off, held up my hand, and my whole palm of my hand was purple/black. I had a bone bruise, I thought I'd have to go on the disabled list because I couldn't catch the ball back from the catcher."

By late August, the tandem of Gossage and Forster in the bullpen had been fully established by Tanner.

"They were just such power pitchers," Bahnsen said of the duo, 50 years later. He was often relieved by the Forster/Gossage tandem in 1972.

"I remember one time in '72, we faced Nolan Ryan out in LA, and he was throwing like at 100 or 101," Bahnsen said. "And Forster, who's left-handed, was right at that. He was like 99. Those guys, when they came in, if we were ahead in the eighth inning by one or two runs, we were going to win that game with those two guys."

"We were ready at any point past the fifth inning," said Gossage, who would end his 1972 rookie season with a 7-1 record and a 4.28 ERA in 80 innings pitched. "It was exciting, just driving into the ballpark with the opportunity and the thought that, man, tonight I might get in the game. But I had to get over the disasters because you walk that tightrope every day being the hero or the goat – how do you handle being the goat? It's everything. Johnny Sain told me I'm going to have to get over the disasters. Think good things and good things happen. Think bad things and bad things will happen."

Ironically, Gossage had "lost" his fastball in 1974, after concentrating too much on the breaking ball repertoire that Sain had taught him. "Chuck called me into his office that year and said I had lost a foot off my fastball," Gossage remembered. "I had just gone backwards. I temporarily lost my fastball in the process of learning how to throw a breaking pitch. It's not an alibi. When you get to the big leagues it is a learning process. Johnny Sain told me exactly what was going to happen. "

Gossage and Forster continued to anchor the Sox bullpen in the three years after 1972. And when Gossage regained his fastball in 1975, he took on the closer role from Forster, recording 26 saves and winning Fireman of the Year.

Goose spent one more year with the White Sox, when Bill Veeck bought the team and installed Paul Richards as manager. Richards asked both Gossage and Forster to join the starting rotation.

"I ended up 9-17 with 15 complete games (as a starter in 1976)," Gossage said. "I don't think I got one game saved. But I enjoyed starting. I'm a workhorse, give me the ball. I prided myself on finishing what I started. All I was in the minor leagues was a starter, so I already had that mentality."

Veeck, realizing that he would never be able to afford Gossage and Forster long-term, traded both to the Pittsburgh Pirates in the winter of 1976. He got back slugger Richie Zisk in the deal, who would make crucial contributions to the exciting, offensively talented 1977 White Sox — "The South Side Hitmen."

Forster went on to have a solid bullpen career for the next 10 years with various teams, including the Dodgers and Braves.

And Gossage established himself as baseball's top reliever, a star who displaced Lyle with the New York Yankees as a free-agent signee in 1978. The Goose registered 20 or more saves in every year between 1978 and 1986, with the Yankees and San Diego Padres.

With the Yankees, Gossage rode the postseason roller-coaster. He picked up his only World Series ring in 1978, pitching six innings of scoreless baseball in three appearances to help New York win its second straight Fall Classic against the Dodgers.

But dramatics often cut the other way in baseball's autumn. In a much-rerun video highlight, Gossage yielded a two-out, three-run homer to fellow Hall of Famer George Brett in the seventh inning of Game 3 of the 1980 American League Championship Series at Yankee Stadium, powering the Royals from behind for a three-game sweep. Goose also pitched in the 1981 World Series for the Yankees and the 1984 National League Championship Series against the Cubs, as the closer for the Padres who, shockingly, came back from a two-games-to-none deficit with three straight wins in San Diego.

Within four years, Gossage became enmeshed in the one of the innumerable Cubs front-office blunders spanning both the Wrigley family and Tribune Company ownership.

New Cubs general manager Jim Frey had not liked closer Lee Smith's deportment during the 1987 season. So at that year's Winter Meetings, Frey rushed the Hall of Famer out of Chicago, literally in 30 minutes according to Cubs official Gordon Goldsberry, for the first player package offered by the Boston Red Sox. But projected ninth-inning man coming back from Boston, Calvin Schiraldi, was soon pegged as too nervous to close. Frey then had to trade clutch hitter Keith Moreland to the Padres for Gossage.

Working on breaking pitches to counter a diminished fastball at age 35, Gossage had his worst year ever as a closer in 1988 as a Cub with just 13 saves and a 1.489 WHIP. He heard plenty of boos. The sight of manager Don Zimmer waddling multiple times to the mound with a determined purpose, to pull Gossage, was a similar low point in his career. Gossage lasted just one season at Wrigley Field.

Despite the near-nightmare with the Cubs, Gossage hung on as a setup reliever through age 42 in 1994, eventually playing for nine teams.

His pioneering success as one of the game's great closers — and one who routinely pitched for more than a single inning — was what eventually got him elected to the Hall of Fame in 2008. When Gossage became eligible for enshrinement, relievers were still a new concept for Cooperstown; it required nine years of writers' voting before he finally was elected.

During the Goose's Hall of Fame acceptance speech, he made sure to mention his mentors on the 1972 White Sox who helped guide him to success: Tanner, Sain and the man who energized that Sox team and Chicago back in 1972: Dick Allen.

"Dick Allen was the greatest player I ever played with," Gossage told the crowd in Cooperstown. "He taught me pitching from a hitter's perspective."

Gossage enjoyed a truly special induction weekend. Dick and Tanner made a surprise appearance to see their old White Sox colleague get enshrined.

Dick had mentored Goose long before the ace reliever became famous for his signature Fu Manchu mustache and menacing 6-foot-3 frame. Gossage was slated for induction into the Hall of Fame on July 28, 2008 and Dick decided to travel to Cooperstown to support his teammate.

Together with Tanner, fondly remembered as their rookie manager, Dick's plan was to simply show up in the presence of Goose, whom Dick had taught how to pitch inside and understand hitters. That time and attention 36 years earlier made the then-20-year-old hurler a lot better in his inaugural season of 1972.

In an odd coincidence, Goose's career ended with the last strike in August

1994. Gossage would be the only player who could claim the distinction of a career bookended by strikes. But there was no strike in the bucolic upstate New York village where the National Baseball Hall of Fame had stood since 1939.

Gossage had secretly hoped that his first manager, and the player who had influenced him the most in his 22-year career, would be there for his Hall of Fame induction. He was certain that Dick, his mentor, would have already been inducted into this select fraternity of baseball immortals. Yet, the mentor would see his charge get into Cooperstown while he waited for the recognition he privately felt he deserved.

Dick was now living on and off in the Wampum, Pa. house he built for his beloved mother, Era, with the bonus money he received in 1960 for signing with the Phillies. She had died in 1993 and he moved into the house. Now, he drove 13 miles north from his rural Wampum home along state route PA-18 to stop off in New Castle and pick up Tanner.

The old skipper had just endured surgery to clean out a clogged artery in his neck but was determined to surprise his star pitching pupil. Roland Hemond was waiting for them in Cooperstown to help pull off this surprise for Goose.

Motoring along the Beaver River in his silver 2007 four-door Impala LT sedan, Dick looked forward to seeing Tanner, the ultra-enthusiastic long-ago manager whom he alternately called Homey or Lefty. Like Dick, Tanner still resided in his birthplace. The Cooperstown trip triggered thoughts of that magical 1972 season, when the slugger/MVP nearly led the White Sox into the postseason.

The player thought the manager looked a bit frail when he got into the car because he had lost weight and the incision on his neck looked fresh. He was worried about his former manager, who would pass away three years later in 2011.

During the long drive to Cooperstown, they talked about their time together and how Hemond — the architect of the 1972 White Sox — had brought them all together.

"Homey, we almost did it. We almost won it all that year," remembered Dick, looking at the man whose familiarity with his personality made him the first manager to help nurture and maximize his talent. That made the time in Chicago a success. "We almost made it to penthouse in '72," the driver told his passenger.

Four years later, Dick would recall how special that time was, driving up to Cooperstown.

"We talked about the team and the guys on the squad and how special they were," he recalled. "When I came to Chicago, I was about 28, 29, maybe gonna be 30, and like I mentioned, would be like that lady with the biological clock. Well, when I got to Florida in '72, I felt like I'm back to Triple-A. I took a look from center field and I'm like, 'Golly, second base-shortstop? Where's my World Series ring? That's a high school bunch.' But Chuck had talked to Mama and she had insisted I be in Chicago with Chuck."

Allen got Tanner to laugh when he reminded his skipper: "Remember, Lefty, we went to Kansas City and opened up in '72 and I hit a home run off of Dick Drago that put us ahead in the ninth…we lost it late and again the next day and the following day, we came home to Comiskey 0-3 to start the '72 season. I remember you coming in that clubhouse after the third one which we gave away, clapping, 'That's OK, gang, we'll get 'em, we'll get 'em.'"

Tanner said: "And after we gave those ball games away you came into my office, and I asked, 'Well, would you handle this on the field?' You said, 'Nope, we'll do it together, OK?' And that's how we did it in 1972."

Meanwhile, Hemond helped keep Allen's and Tanner's road trip to Cooperstown under wraps to surprise Gossage.

"Chuck called me and said, 'I'm gonna be with Dick and we're going to Cooperstown to see Goose since he's going into the Hall of Fame,'" Hemond said. "They arrived on that Saturday morning. They arrive to the hotel and they say, 'Where's Goose?' I said, 'Well, there's a golf tournament, let's go to where the golf course is,' which was not far from the hotel. I go into the dining room and Rich is there, he just completed his lunch. I said, 'Hey Rich, a couple of friends are here to see you.' He says, 'Who are they?' I said, 'I'm not going to tell you.'"

Goose looked up in astonishment to see Dick and Chuck.

"When Roland came in," recalled Gossage, "I was wondering who the heck told me somebody was out front, because that weekend was a blur, and I sat there, and Roland said there's somebody out front wants to see you. Well, I go through the Pro Shop and I go out and, Oh my God, here's Dick and Chuck. It was one of the neatest things that's ever happened to me in my life. And to have those two drive all the way from Pennsylvania to Cooperstown and turn right around just to tell me congratulations, and to see me. I can't tell you what that meant to me, to have those guys here, especially when I knew Chuck was having some health problems at the time."

Dick, Goose and Chuck embraced and enjoyed the special moment, only to have other Hall of Famers join in the fun.

Reggie Jackson came over: "Dick Allen, my idol, I grew up in Philly, I'll always remember what you did as a rookie."

Then Gaylord Perry came up: "Dick Allen, you beat me with a home run in the 15th inning."

Next, Carlton Fisk appeared, flattering Allen by impersonating Dick's batting stance.

"When you see great players show such respect and admiration for a man who had talents superior to anyone who played the game, it's special." recalled Hemond on one of the multiple occasions when he spoke about this memorable reunion at which his daughter, Susan, photographed the four men together.

Gossage addressed the national media as part of the induction weekend program. He also named the five people who had the most impact on his Hall of Fame career as a closer. All happened to be from the White Sox: pitching coaches Ray Berres and Johnny Sain, Hemond, Tanner and Allen.

He then paid Dick the ultimate compliment: "Dick took me under his wing. He was the single most knowledgeable baseball guy I've ever been around and the greatest player I've ever seen in that MVP season. He did it all. And there's not an ounce of BS in Dick."

Dick and Tanner were supposed to address the national media about Gossage's breakout rookie year at the Saturday afternoon press conference before Sunday's induction ceremony. But they quietly left Cooperstown and drove home to Pennsylvania.

Later, Allen would reveal how proud he was of his star pupil, but admitted that seeing Jackson, Perry, and Fisk — his peers — hurt. He had never even gotten close to joining them in Cooperstown and he did not want to stick around and let anyone know about his private disappointment, especially if a reporter asked him why he was not in the Hall of Fame.

"Gossage would look back many times at the visit of his two compadres, once saying, The only thing that would have topped off that is to go into the Hall with Dick."

Rookie Goose Gossage (foreground) and bullpen mate Steve Kealey watch batting practice before a 1972 game at Comiskey Park.

Photo credit: Leo Bauby Collection

Dick Allen's mentoring of Goose Gossage in 1972 helped develop the 21 year-old into a future Hall of Famer.

Photo Courtesy of David Fletcher

CHAPTER 16

Aug. 23, 1972:
Eyewitness to Allen's
Center Field Thunderbolt

By George Castle

If swiveling one's neck was a handy talent for witnessing Dick Allen's 1972 long-distance classic home runs, then such dexterity served double duty on the dog-day afternoon when the White Sox MVP touched another ZIP code with his heavy lumber.

Hours before Dick set off a mad scramble in the faraway center field bleachers for his seventh-inning long shot off the Yankees' Lindy McDaniel on Aug. 23, I ensured my neck was properly warmed up, on the lookout for a couple of Sox fans from the ol' neighborhood who'd roast me alive if we crossed paths in Comiskey Park.

The personal radar swept 360 degrees as a friend and I worked our way from 35th Street, into the ballpark and grandstand seats past third base. But I never saw Ron Eisenstein and his Sox-fan chum — we will call him Steve — that pleasant afternoon. Eisenstein later claimed he was in the house.

Neither being the type to crawl under rocks in shame during the Sox' mere 56-win season two years before, both would have crowed like bantam roosters at the sight of me, a chastened Cubs fan. Here I was, a Jewish third-generation follower from West Rogers Park, five miles northwest of Wrigley Field, confident of the North Siders' supremacy even in the near-misses of the Leo Durocher years starting in 1969. And here was Steve, a North Side Sox rooter who also boosted non-Chicago teams in other sports, and transplanted South Side "Pill Hill" resident Eisenstein never wavering in their pride in Sox fandom through some of the franchise's darkest days since the Black Sox scandal.

Nothing fazed them through the White Sox' Syd O'Brien/Gerry Janeski era. Voluble Cubs like Ron Santo and Milt Pappas seemed to particularly irk the long, lanky Steve. Now the worm turned, radically, as Dick put the Sox on his shoulders and carried them all the way into first place with 10 days left before our senior year at Mather High School commenced. Meanwhile, the Cubs were mired as an also-ran, 10 games behind the defending World Champion Pittsburgh Pirates, unable to beat the "Lumber Company" head-to-head. Left-handed Buccos hitters like Al Oliver clobbered ace Fergie Jenkins while bad-ball-hitter Manny Sanguillen literally hit pitches that first bounced in the dirt.

Despite our very different baseball allegiances, the Sox fans and I, along with another friend, existed in a tiny bubble within a larger bubble back in West Rogers Park. We were teenage fans who were in an apparently small minority in the neighborhood. Despite the short, half-hour bus-and-L trip to Wrigley Field, Cubs love seemed to be in short supply at Mather in the wake of the hoopla of the late Sixties.

I remembered attending the freshman orientation assembly at the high school as August 1969 came to a close. Dr. Gerard J. Heing, the principal, concluded his remarks with a big, loud wish to cheer on the Cubs to a pennant. Surprisingly, Heing drew a tepid response with no cheers. That belied the so-called Cubs Mania of the day. After all, only six weeks before, some 12,000 showed up at the Back of the Yards Council's Cubs Night only two miles southwest of Comiskey Park. But over the four years at Mather, none of this enthusiasm seemed to infect the average student.

On the first or second day of high school in 1969, I made small talk with Steve, who also was in math teacher Clarence Starling's home room. "Me and a lot of other kids won't be here in October," I told him, cognizant of the Cubs' six-game winning streak that brought the team's record to a season-high 84-52. I hadn't read the fine print or paid attention to *Tribune* writer Dick Dozer's questioning of Leo Durocher two weeks earlier about whether or not his players were getting tired. Nor did Steve and I know of the behind-the-scenes machinations in the White Sox executive suite on almost the same day — when John Allyn blocked brother Arthur's bid to sell the team to Bud Selig and move the White Sox to Milwaukee.

Steve cynically responded: "Where will you be?" "At the World Series, in Wrigley Field!" I gleefully shot back. But that World Series at Wrigley Field would not be played for another 47 years nor would "a lot of other kids" be available to talk baseball over the next four years.

The social climate was smack dab in the middle of turbulent times due to the Vietnam War. Much of the Mather student body walked out amid a nationwide Moratorium anti-war protest later in the fall. I followed suit — but just to get out of school. My attention was focused on pouring over the sports sections of three newspapers each day to read every word on the Cubs and baseball. I was popular with the local females only when they needed to borrow my *Sun-Times* to read Ann Landers during study hall. Eppie Lederer's frequent message to them was: "Good girls don't."

Mather was extremely cliquish, and cross-migration from one group to another at lunch tables was expressly forbidden. I had no idea what other students did with their non-classroom time. The neighborhood was quiet with no high-profile teen hangouts. In another century, senior citizens Faye Birnbaum-Rosenberg and Larry Rosen both recalled Lerner Park, near the Winston Towers high rises, as a gathering spot. Rosen told of trips to concerts at the Kinetic Playground at Clark and Lawrence, about three miles away. Mather was overwhelmingly Jewish. You could shoot a cannon down its halls on the High Holidays and Passover, and not hit anybody, students or teachers. Mather also had a reputation as a "drug school," although in my bubble I did not smell anything pungent and sweet. I was almost cloistered.

On our long walks to school down Washtenaw Avenue, I'd argue Cubs vs. Sox with Steve. He never gave an inch, even as his team's losses mounted. I soon met Eisenstein, who, opening his freshman year, stayed with an aunt three blocks from Mather while his family prepared to move from the far South Side to a Georgian home at the corner of California and Greenleaf avenues. My observations about the Sox had to be second-hand, via the newspapers or my newly-purchased UHF converter box with its loop antenna for our 1963 Zenith black-and-white set. Comiskey Park was distant, not well-attended and seemingly unreachable compared to the daylight-only, easy-public-transportation commute to Wrigley Field.

The majority of night-game visits to Comiskey Park were by car. My spend-no-dime-before-its-time single mother never owned a car, plus she was too scared to drive, anyway. My father, equally thrifty, declined to put me on his insurance for his 1965 Dodge Coronet. The low-cost used car was kept through 1971, representing the first car I drove outside of driver's ed. Travel at night via CTA buses and trains was increasingly deemed unsafe in the early Seventies, putting a premium on access to a car for any kind of social life not in the immediate neighborhood.

But teenagers always will press their boundary lines. In the baseball bubble, that meant taking the "Howard-Englewood" L south of downtown for a Sox day game. With Steve and Eisenstein singing the praises of a revived Chuck Tanner-managed team in 1971 that tickled the .500 mark on Aug. 22 before slumping, curiosity pushed me to the outer limits of travel for a teenager without wheels.

Some frowned on a North Side kid going a short distance within the South Side, given the prejudices of the times. But a friend and I took the plunge for a Sox-Twins Labor Day doubleheader on Monday, Sept. 6, 1971, enduring the airport-level noise of the L's open windows going through the subway, this time beyond the Loop. We got off at 35th Street, four blocks east of the ballpark. We had never seen the huge Stateway Gardens housing project, whose northern border abutted 35th Street, up close. We kept on walking past the project and Illinois Institute of Technology (ITT) campus buildings, across the Dan Ryan and through the turnstiles to a seat in the right-field upper deck.

My only memory was of a bright, sunny, late-summer day, a final respite before the grind of Mather resumed for junior year. Until I looked over the box score, I did not remember Bill Melton's 28th homer in the first inning, on his way to the American League home run title or, mondo bizzaro, reliever Steve Kealey's three-run homer in the eighth (the DH was still two seasons away) that provided needed insurance runs in the 6-3 Sox victory. I know we departed midway through the nitecap, to leave plenty of daylight travel time for the 45-minute L trip back to the Loyola stop in Rogers Park.

Dick Allen's arrival on the South Side, planned during the 1971 winter meetings brought us back for more in 1972. I don't know how we were able to get out to a Wednesday afternoon game on April 26 — that seemed late for Chicago Public Schools spring break. Until working on this book, I did not remember Mike Andrews' clutch grand-slam homer and Allen's 10th-inning walk-off clout. But the narrative did jog the memories from deep in my historical recesses. The lasting images of the sunny afternoon in the right-field lower deck were Cleveland rookie Buddy Bell's long blond hair sticking out of the back of his cap, and busted Cubs star Adolfo Phillips romping in center field in the final days of his big-league career. Except Phillips never played in the game — Del Unser was the Cleveland center fielder. The memory must have been Phillips roaming center in batting practice.

Another weekday game, likely in June, brought this memory: Released Cubs closer Phil Regan warming up in the Sox bullpen down the left-field line, observed from a perch in the left-field lower-deck stands. Sox game patronage was restricted by my summer stockboy position at the downtown Goldblatt's department store. I worked Saturdays, and Sundays were split between seeing my father and going to see the Cubs.

Thus, it was somewhat unusual that another long L trip commenced on August 23. This time, the expedition's goal was to watch the AL East contending Yankees try to stop the White Sox, who were a robust 68-48, a half-game up over the Oakland A's in first place. We took our seats beyond third base, the fourth different location in four games so far. We figured Steve and Eisenstein would be in the right or left-field stands somewhere (Eisenstein later said he liked the right-field upper deck).

Again, little other detail was filed away except for the astounding winning homer hit by Allen and the supporting cast of my experience: Yankees reliever Lindy McDaniel and Sox announcer Harry Caray, doing his shirtless matinee broadcast from the center field bleachers with a fishnet at the ready.

We just gaped at the blast, almost good enough for two homers with the ferocity and firmness with which it was struck. In the distance, the ball, unlike most high-fly-type homers, seemed fated to bore a crater into whatever it made contact with. Anyone who got in its way was taking life and limb in hand, yet a posse of Sox fans tried to nail the ball.

Caray could not have caught it, but still waved his fishnet as part of his schtick. Harry was already a showman and the Comiskey Park Pied Piper. He made us gnash our teeth in August 1969 when he crowed through the humidity, "The Cardinals are coming, tra la, tra la," on KMOX Radio's booming 1120 AM signal. We took great care on our table-top AM-FM radios now to tune in Harry at much lower wattage on the rigged-up Sox network.

Mark Liptak, assembling the material that would make him a Sox historian in future decades, was closest to the clout.

"I was sitting in the center field bleachers to the right of Harry Caray's location, maybe about halfway up," Liptak said. "Allen's blast was more of a frozen rope and the thing that I remember was seeing Bobby Murcer, the (Yankees) center fielder, back to the fence looking up and the ball was still on a line. It was not quite coming down yet."

I was so keen on dodging Steve and Eisenstein that I had no idea another Sox fan had journeyed from his North Side home to get a closer view of the launching end of the titanic homer.

Mark Schultz had a big South-Side-team-loyalty pedigree in his family. Grandfather Isadore Schultz had owned the White Sox Shoe Repair Stand, a few blocks from the ballpark, back in the day. Father Sol Schultz ensured they'd have great seats between home and third, 10 rows back. 'Dad always walked up to the box office and asked, 'What do you have on the baseline?'" the younger Schultz said. "We had a great view. I remember that pitch. Lindy McDaniel, an old-timer, threw a fastball down the middle and he destroyed that pitch. We had the feeling this guy (Allen) could do anything."

Allen became one of seven players to reach the center field bleachers. The list began with Jimmie Foxx in 1934 and Hank Greenberg in 1938 and later included Alex Johnson in 1970, Richie Zisk in 1977, Tony Armas in 1984 and George Bell in 1985.

McDaniel, in his 17th full season at age 36, represented a telling Cubs connection. His prime days as an effective Chicago closer for the North Siders blip-of-a-revival team in 1963 already were a decade in the past. He had netted the great return of Randy Hundley and Bill Hands in a trade to the Giants. Schultz's remembrance of the hittable fastball belied McDaniel's forkball specialty. He had pitched against Allen for five years in the National League, but perhaps his memory slipped when working to Allen in 1972.

Schultz could re-create the scene with his pen and drawing pad. He later specialized in editorial cartoons for the Lerner Newspapers at the same time I was their North Side Sports Editor.

I eventually discovered Eisenstein was a reasonable guy who would not have lorded over me with the Sox banging at the door of glory while the Cubs played out the string under Whitey Lockman. Turns out he was a "reasonable" Sox fan who did not froth at the mouth at the mere mention of the Cubs, a team which his club never played in league competition. I could not, then and now, understand the obsession many Sox fans have with the Cubs, one that is not reciprocated going from the North Side southward.

"There were times I had a little bit of an inferiority complex," Eisenstein said. "The Cubs were the talk of radio and the papers. The Cubs were the pretty boy and had the cozy ballpark. But I never had that kind of hatred. In reality my hate was there for the Yankees. It was just jealousy and two cultures, North Side vs. South Side."

Meanwhile, I retreated further into my baseball bubble. I had the option of skipping Mather graduation ceremonies — attendance was actually optional at this point — on a blistering-hot Sunday, June 10, 1973 to watch the Cubs outslug the Reds, 9-7, at Wrigley Field. I do not recall attending any Sox games in '73.

Still car-less finishing out my college freshman year, I hopped rides with Eisenstein to some Sox night games in 1974. I also started my journalism career in April that year as Friday and Saturday overnight *Chicago Tribune* city-room copy clerk, getting to meet the likes of David Axelrod and Clarence Page early in their careers. Billed as a contender for 1974, the Allen-led Sox were initially an attraction, so Eisenstein and I went to several Friday night games, and he dropped me off at Tribune Tower on the way home. Such door-to-door service sure beat the slo-w-w-w local 151 Sheridan CTA bus. On the way to work, I endured as it made all stops down Sheridan Road and the inner Lake Shore Drive all the way to Michigan Avenue. My mother, nervous about night L travel, persuaded me to take this turtle-paced route from Devon Avenue all the way downtown.

I learned on the car trips that the Comiskey Park neighborhood was actually not chock full of urban terrors. Eisenstein usually parked on Shields Avenue on the 3100 or 3200 blocks, depending on the size of the crowd. The neighborhood was quiet, with some residents sitting out on their front porches watching fans go by. In future seasons, I'd park in the same area with my first car, a brown 1965 Buick Special with a battered left rear door; my uncle had acquired it for $75 at the Oldsmobile dealership where he worked as a salesman. I named it The Brown Beauty.

Two months before I began driving "Brown Beauty," just in time to avoid nighttime winter CTA travel to Tribune Tower, I took my final L trip to Comiskey Park on Aug. 8, 1974, the day Richard M. Nixon resigned as president. Befitting the sour mood of the day, the under-performing Sox lost to the California Angels, 6-4, blowing a one-run lead in the eighth inning.

Allen followed Nixon out the door five weeks later, and a memorable Sox era concluded with a whimper and regrets. There'd be plenty of bread and circuses under the second Bill Veeck ownership that began in 1975 — Caray singing in seventh innings, Nancy Faust playing "Na Na Na Hey Hey Hey, Good-Bye" on the ballpark organ, Disco Demolition Night and the only shorts ever worn as baseball uniforms.

But nothing beat baseball action at its best. The memory never fades, for I saw an MVP show why he deserved the award by muscling up like no one else in the game, hitting a thunderbolt to the center field bleachers as Caray whiffed at it with his net. Tens of thousands were wowed — including a Cubs fan hiding out from what were then his Sox superiors.

The Dick Allen home run swing was generated by tremendous bat speed.

Photo credit: Leo Bauby Collection

Fans scramble for Dick Allen's monster homer into the faraway center field bleachers off Lindy McDaniel, while a shirtless Harry Caray waves his fishnet on Aug. 23, 1972.

Photo credit: Leo Bauby Collection

Dick Allen smiles in a visiting locker room during the 1972 season. The White Sox, led by Allen, were the one of the top road team draws in the American League in 1972.

Photo credit: Leo Bauby Collection

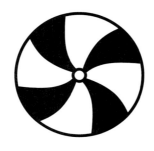

CHAPTER 17

September 7, 1972:
Comiskey Park Magic:
Allen Blasts No. 33,
Wood Wins No. 24

By David Fletcher

Nineteen-hundred seventy-two would be a transformative year for the City of Chicago, the Chicago White Sox, their marquee star Dick Allen — and myself.

Politicians and social activists alike were stunned when Mayor Richard J. Daley's ironclad machine rule was being challenged for the first time in the wake of State's Attorney Ed Hanrahan's handling of the Fred Hampton shooting. Daley's kingmaker role in the Democratic Party was damaged as his preferred candidate, Edmund Muskie, did not get the Democratic presidential nomination. Instead, a fractured Democratic Party was stuck with George McGovern to run a doomed race against incumbent Richard Nixon, who had been strategic to withdraw most U.S. ground troops from Vietnam prior to the Presidential campaign getting underway in earnest.

The White Sox franchise, led by the 30-year-old prodigiously talented and enigmatic Dick Allen, emerged from the ashes of a string of terrible seasons and an aging, decaying and empty ballpark perceived as being in a bad neighborhood. Allen's season for the ages in 1972 brought back the excitement on the South Side, and his feats had rescued the franchise that had one foot out the door to leave Chicago.

Dick had become the Sox' first African American superstar and his star power in the summer of 1972 would forecast the future popularity and impact of Michael Jordan. Unlike his years spent in Philadelphia, Chicago embraced Dick. The fans — including large numbers of African American rooters — returned to Comiskey Park, suddenly the hottest ticket in town.

Chuck Tanner's handling of Dick in 1972 was a stroke of managerial genius, and it was not a surprise when he was named Manager of the Year by *The Sporting News*. In essence, by not "managing" him, Tanner had coaxed a career-best pinnacle performance out of a player whom many had previously believed was a temperamental underachiever.

For me, personally, 1972 was a transformative year for a 17-year-old middle class White kid from Glen Ellyn, a western suburb of Chicago, about to leave my parents' home and start my pre-medical studies at the University of Illinois in Champaign in late September.

Like other baseball-loving youths in the Chicago area, my bedroom was adorned with the June 4, 1972, *Sports Illustrated* cover of Allen, photographed on the dugout steps before a game, merrily smoking a cigarette while juggling three baseballs. Sadly, I would discover 50 years later that those same cigarettes had caused the lung cancer that would claim his life in December 2020.

Why did this Black baseball player from the seemingly-mythical town of

Wampum, Pa., win over White kids like me growing up in the suburbs?

After graduating from Glenbard West high school in June 1972, I had one last summer to enjoy before college. While the Vietnam War was supposedly winding down, the military draft still loomed over me. As a male born in 1954, I would be subject to the next draft lottery scheduled for March 1973. I could not yet foresee the lottery would simply be a bureaucratic exercise with the Vietnam peace accords signed in January 1973. The last draft call was on Dec. 7, 1972, and the authority to induct 19-year-olds expired on June 30, 1973. But I didn't think about the draft in that summer of '72. My more immediate priorities were trying to get laid, hanging out with my friends and following Chicago baseball.

At Glenbard West, I was the sports editor of the school paper and had written a story about Opening Day at Comiskey Park being cancelled in April 1972 because of baseball's first strike.

The delay in the timeless tradition of Opening Day that year was an introductory jolt to me about the loss of innocence and that things in life would not always be fair and what you expected.

Growing up in white bread Glen Ellyn, I was fortunate to have outstanding liberal parents, Archie and Dottie Fletcher, who did not enforce a curfew. My mom and dad were truly one-in-a-thousand by the standards of the times. They allowed me to bring girls to our house, rather than confine mutual exploration to the back seat of a car. This was a perk that friends also enjoyed at my house, and earned my best friend Gary Kowal the nickname "Boxer Shorts" when Dottie caught him with his skivvies down in the company of a girl in our walk-out basement.

His father, Edward Kowal, was the assistant state's attorney for Du Page County, and later a judge. We both got into some trouble that summer for a stupid act of immaturity when caught breaking windows at our high school baseball coach's house. We were able to avoid trouble because of Boxer's father, who got the vandalism charges dropped and our records wiped clean. So, my privilege helped me avoid derailing my life, unlike people of less-fortunate circumstances. I also was fortunate that I had not gotten caught earlier for another stupid teenage act when I egged the house of Blackhawks player Bobby Hull when he signed a huge contract with the World Hockey Association in late June 1972. The Golden Jet lived on the fifth hole of the Village Links, where I also lived.

I interviewed for my school the soon-to-be-outgoing Illinois governor, Richard Ogilvie. But that did not compare to the earlier thrill of meeting Daley in 1969 at the infamous Chicago Amphitheater. I was manning the booth at the Junior Achievement trade show for a company called Mazco that manufactured wooden coasters. Here was this larger-than-life figure, who just walked up to the booth with his entourage in tow and wanted to talk to me. Those five minutes I had with him as a 14-year-old west suburban kid were indelible. He was the ultimate retail politician.

Glen Ellyn was considered a liberal community in the middle of very conservative Republican DuPage County; it was the home of William Ayers, the son of the president of Commonwealth Edison. Ayers was part of the radical Weatherman bombers and would later become an issue in the 2008 presidential campaign because of Barack Obama's relationship with him. Bill Ayers also attended Glenbard West as did his brother John, who was in my 1972 graduating class.

Despite the village's reputation for being accepting and more liberal than most of DuPage County, it was virtually all-White and all-Protestant. The only Jewish kid at Glenbard West was our class president Larry Krupp, who was a huge White Sox fan.

The Chicago area in the late 1960s and early 1970s was still a hotbed of racism. I was fortunate that my parents instilled in me to be tolerant, not prejudiced.

In 1968, after the Martin Luther King assassination riots, my parents wanted to expose our family to another world and volunteered to foster a young Black girl from the Far South Side. She stayed with us only briefly, but the experience was an eye-opener.

That same year, as an eighth-grader, I caused quite a controversy when I asked one of the two African American males in our school to go with me to Bobby Rivers' dance studio to learn ballroom dance. This triggered a lot of fireworks, and it was sad to see the reaction when he was not allowed to come into the studio. That was one of the first times I really got to see what it was like to be in the shoes of a minority person.

And I had no clue about the racism Dick Allen, who had become my favorite ballplayer in 1972, had faced in his life. Later I would learn about his harrowing 1963, being the first African American baseball player to suit up in Little Rock, Ark. and all the racism he experienced in his first stint in Philadelphia.

Starting in early August 1972, when the Sox came back from 7½ games down to take over first place after Wilbur Wood won his 20th game in Oakland, Chicago was overcome by rabid White Sox pennant fever. The Sox had pushed Cubs coverage "below the fold" in the sports sections of the city's then-four daily newspapers.

Like most Chicago-area residents, I sometimes found following the White Sox a challenge because of the team's limited radio network with low-watt (at night) WTAQ-AM LaGrange as its flagship station. But with the excitement that

Harry Caray brought to covering those games in the summer of '72, you found a way to keep up with this exciting team led by Dick Allen. Better yet, you actually went to the ballpark and watched in person with ticket prices easily affordable and seats always available.

As early September 1972 rolled around, the Sox were still in contention to win the AL West flag and had received Major League Baseball's permission to print American League Championship Series playoff tickets. I hoped I could snag a set once they went on sale.

My first day of college was fast approaching and my earthly possessions were organized to haul down to Champaign. I would be able to attend one more Sox game before leaving home. Adult responsibility was calling me and whatever shreds of innocence that remained would soon be slipping away.

Boxer Shorts and I would go the final game of the two-game set between the Athletics (again in first place) and the Sox. It was a must-win for the South Siders, who had dropped the previous game against Oakland.

We left Glen Ellyn, headed to Comiskey Park. Driving down the Eisenhower Expressway, one could still see some of the damage on the West Side from the 1968 riots.

We were both getting ready to start our freshman year. In the car we sang along with Rod Stewart, who had a new hit song, "Maggie May." The lyrics "It's late September and I really should be back at school" resonated with us. We knew that life would never be the same.

Once we were going south on the Dan Ryan in my mother's brown 1971 Chevy Nova, we could see out in the distance the large light towers of Comiskey Park that lit up the late summer twilight sky as we rushed to get there before the 8 p.m. start time that was standard for that era. We couldn't listen to the pregame show because of the weak signal of WTAQ-AM. And since the car, like most others, did not have an FM radio, we could not listen to WEAW.

A warm Thursday night with a hazy sky and scattered clouds greeted the big crowd as the sun set over Bridgeport, to the west. The throng's mood was somewhat somber due to murder of the Israeli Olympic athletes in Munich two days before. On the Athletics, former Cubs pitcher Ken Holtzman and first baseman Mike Epstein, both Jewish, wore black armbands, as did right fielder Reggie Jackson.

While saddened by the tragedy in Munich, Boxer Shorts and I were still excited to see Wilbur Wood go for his 24th win. The cagey veteran knuckleballer would face off against 22-year-old Vida Blue. In 1971, Blue had an astounding first full season: A 24-8 record, leading the American League in ERA (1.82) and shutouts (eight) and winning both the Cy Young and Most Valuable Player awards. I knew that Blue had missed the first part of the '72 season because he had held out for a new contract. He had publicly battled the A's front office for a better deal, and that had affected his pitching, but still Blue had a sub-3.00 ERA for the season.

We witnessed a dream September baseball matchup. The defending division champion A's led the upstart White Sox by four games. The two teams with the best records in the American League were squaring off to decide which would win the division. The Sox had only 23 games left in the season to make up the deficit. The concept of going for a wild-card playoff berth was science-fiction at a point when divisional play, and the postseason consisting of only four teams, was just a few years old.

Almost 35,000 fans showed up for the game. Considering that this was a weekday night with schools already in session, the size of the crowd was fantastic and demonstrated how special this ball club was to Chicago. I knew that just two years earlier the Sox attendance was horrible and there were two September home games that drew fewer than 700 fans.

We parked south of Comiskey Park near the corner of Pershing Road and Princeton Avenue. I could always count on that area to have open spots, and there were no meters.

Occasionally I would have a young kid who lived in the neighborhood ask me for a buck or two to "watch" my car. In all my time going to games in this era at Comiskey Park, I never perceived the neighborhood as being bad.

Despite the large crowd, we were able to get from the ticket office a couple decent reserved seats in the lower deck along the left field line for $3 each.

In the bottom of the seventh, with the White Sox ahead, 3-0, future Hall of Famer Rollie Fingers came into the game for the A's. Sox No. 8 batter Luis Alvarado started off the inning with a single and was sacrificed to second by Wood. Leadoff man Pat Kelly drew a walk, putting runners at first and second with one out. Mike Andrews struck out swinging. This brought up Dick, the star attraction, with two outs and ducks on the pond.

The slugger had already driven in one run in the first inning with a sacrifice hit, followed by two strikeouts, which finished with the crowd cheering him each time as he swung his monster 40-ounce bat and whiffed.

Comiskey Park was rocking. The young, good-looking blonde organist Nancy Faust, perched above home plate, was whipping the crowd into a frenzy when she started banging out the opening notes of "Jesus Christ Superstar" as Dick walked up to the plate. She would later be credited with inventing walk-up music in 1972 with her use of that song every time he strolled to the plate. The crowd loudly sang along with Nancy's music:

Jesus Christ Superstar

Jesus Christ Superstar

Do you think you're what they say you are?

On a 1-2 count, Dick muscled a line-drive bomb to center field where the bullpens used to be — and one of his favorite destinations for his Comiskey Park homers in 1972. The packed ballpark erupted as the Sox led, 6-0. The man had come through, hitting his 33rd home run and driving in four more runs, hiking his league-leading total to 96.

This home run would be the start of torrid pace where Dick put the White Sox on his shoulders for the rest of the pennant drive. From September 7 through September 12, he knocked in 16 runs, including four game-winners, all against AL West rivals Oakland, California and Kansas City.

The crowd stayed the whole game and cheered loudly in the top of the eighth, when Bert Campaneris tried to score from third base on a fly ball to center field, only to be blocked at the plate by "Fort Herrmann." A team leader, Sox catcher Ed Herrmann seemed to specialize in the art of denying home plate to runners attempting to score.

The crowd was in a raucous mood from the start of the game until the final out when Wood got Epstein to ground into a double play. Game time: Two hours and 18 minutes, something you don't see today. The Sox' 6-0 win over A's would bring them back to three games behind with only 22 remaining.

Boxer Shorts and I got back to Glen Ellyn around midnight and drove around looking for action in the final few days before departing for college. The Sox were still in the hunt and by September 12 would cut Oakland's lead down to two games, knowing they had a pair of contests left with the A's, out west, in two weeks.

That Sunday, Sept. 10, I had to leave for Champaign. My father dropped me off in the parking lot of Scott Hall, my dorm, across the street from Memorial Stadium. No more time for summer foolin' around — time to embark on my studies with the eventual goal of getting into medical school.

Since I had gotten an FM receiver as part of a new stereo system, I could follow the Sox the rest of the season on WLRW-94.5 FM in Champaign and listen to Harry Caray and Ralph Faucher call the games. I was out of signal range of Sox video flagship WFLD-TV (Channel 32), and no central Illinois station picked up Sox games on a network like Champaign's WCIA-TV (Channel 3) did with the Cubs.

The Sox' 11th inning 1-0 loss in Anaheim on Friday, Sept. 15 was a heartbreaking radio experience. The game ended after midnight, and the Sox fell four games out.

In a thoroughly memorable season 50 years ago, I got to watch Dick Allen perform at the pinnacle of his career. Even today, his iconic *Sports Illustrated* cover still adorns my bedroom wall. They don't make colorful players like the '72 MVP anymore.

Pitcher Tom Bradley and batboys Rory Clark and Jim Riley greet Dick Allen after home run.

Photo credit: Leo Bauby Collection

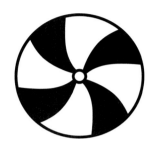

CHAPTER 18

September 1972:
The White Sox Weren't
Supposed To Be Here

The White Sox finished August 1972 with a 71–52 mark, 1½ games back with 31 games left, including four more against the front-running Oakland Athletics.

With Dick Allen now a national baseball sensation due to the heroics of the Chili Dog homer and other legendary long blasts, fans in other cities were coming out to watch No. 15. By season's end, Dick's team attracted 936,579 customers on the road, which pleased the other American League owners.

He would be featured in a splashy story in Ebony, "The Importance of Being Dick Allen" written by Louie Robinson right after the White Sox split a four-game set with Oakland in mid-August.

Roberson wrote: "The importance of being Dick Allen to the game of baseball is said by a fellow member of the profession, Reggie Jackson, Oakland, another star performer.

"Says Jackson: 'Allen is good for players, is good for fans, he's good for the owners because he brings people into the park, he's one of the most valuable players to come into the league.'

"The White Sox, Jackson believes, are 'playing over their heads' because of Allen's presence of in their lineup.

"Jackson, who hailed from Philadelphia and watched in marvel Allen's 1964 Rookie of the Year season as a senior in high school, noted:

'American League hasn't seen too many good black players anyway.'"

A three-game series in New York Sept. 1 to 3 was a pennant battle for both teams. The Yankees were 2½ games behind in the AL East. Both teams had hopes to win their respective divisions and facing each other in the ALCS.

Dick's desire to finally play on a winner fueled him that last month of the 1972 season. He was haunted by the Phillies' astounding 1964 collapse from a 6½-game lead with 12 to play.

His one-man-wrecking-crew dramatics frightened Yankees fans. They had heard radio broadcaster Phil "Scooter" Rizzuto shouting "I don't believe it. I don't believe it" over and over again into his microphone for nearly a minute before his partner, Frank Messer, informed listeners that Dick Allen had just beaten the Yankees with the now-famous one-out, three-run walk-off homer off Sparky Lyle. And they had heard Allen's 460-foot blast into the center field stands at Comiskey Park off Lindy McDaniel a mere 10 days earlier.

As the pennant race heated up, Dick had become the central player in baseball, electrifying the sport and resuscitating a White Sox franchise that had not won a world championship since 1917.

Characteristically, when Dick, who was still in the running to win the Triple Crown, came up in the first inning, a couple of the Yankee fans in the bleachers uncurled a banner:

'Save our monuments! Walk Allen!'

Despite the presence of Dick Allen, his team's road woes continued. They fell, 4–0 and 2–1 to the Yankees and dropped 2½ games off the pace.

The second loss was a heartbreaker. Dick hit the ball hard three times, reaching base with two singles and an error. He was now leading in all three Triple Crown categories, including a .319 average.

Dick also nearly beat out an infield hit in the top of the eighth inning; many of the traveling Chicago scribes thought he was safe. The Sox also had two other close calls at second base go the Yankees' way: Carlos May tried and failed to stretch a single into a double, also in the eighth, and Dick was thrown out attempting to steal in the fifth.

The next night, Wilbur Wood finally stopped the Sox' four-game losing streak with a magnificent 99-pitch shutout. He threw 72 strikes, walked no one and even notched an RBI when he was walked with the bases loaded. Wood nearly had to leave the game when he took a rocket off his left thigh in the third inning but stayed in to complete the 5–0 victory.

Oakland had also won that day, so Wood's 23rd victory could only keep the Sox 2½ games out. This was his 41st start, challenging Ed Walsh's 1908 team record of 49.

Sox manager Chuck Tanner had planned the rest of the season so that Wood could start nine more games.

White Sox fans' hopes were high for a Labor Day doubleheader at Comiskey Park against the Twins. Nearly 34,000 came out, but the Chicago faithful left in despair due to missed opportunity and — according to Tanner — missed calls. Minnesota swept the Sox, 2–1 and 4–0.

The White Sox left 15 men on base in the twinbill and, to make things worse, poor umpiring plagued the White Sox. With Chicago ahead, 1–0 in the seventh inning, the Twins scored two runs on Jim Nettles' double. Umpire Bill Kunkel called the ball fair, although TV replays showed Sox right fielder Pat Kelly two to three feet in foul territory when the ball bounced off his glove.

Later in the game, after plate umpire Jerry Neudecker called a high strike on Rich Morales, Tanner shot out of the dugout to argue the call. As Tanner jawed with Neudecker, a fan in left field unfurled a bed sheet with a large eye chart emblazoned on it.

Comiskey Park erupted. The umpiring crew, which had called many of the Sox' games since the All-Star game (and Tanner felt was inept), demanded the removal of the banner before play could resume.

The Sox came back on Tuesday night, September 5, with a 5–2 win to salvage one game against the Twins, pulling within three of the A's. The leaders arrived in Chicago for the anticipated two-game set starting Wednesday afternoon.

With Oakland owner Charles Finley watching from above the first base dugout, the A's pounded Tom Bradley and the Sox, 9–1.

The ever-optimistic Tanner brushed off the loss that dropped his team to four games out: "We'll be back tomorrow."

"Tomorrow" turned out to be a gorgeous, hazy late summer Thursday night, Sept. 7. Some 34,000 fans filled Comiskey Park, hoping to will the White Sox back into contention with only 23 games remaining.

Wood, seemingly a shoo-in for the Cy Young, pitched a seven-hit shutout, gaining his 24th victory and pulling the Sox to again three games behind the A's. Dick hit his 33rd home run in the 6–0 thrashing and ended a "mini-slump" in which he had not homered in two weeks and had not driven a run in ten games. During this mini-slump, he had still hit safely in 16 of 17 games.

The final Comiskey Park game against the Athletics saw Dick begin hitting at a torrid pace.

The Sox' final doubleheader of the year was scheduled for Friday night, Sept. 8, against the Angels. They had played in an exhausting 17 twinbills on the year. In the opener, Stan Bahnsen pitched his fifth complete game in his 38th start of the season, scooping up his 17th victory thanks to four Allen RBI. The Sox, however, dropped the nightcap, 9–4, leaving them 3½ games behind Oakland.

The following afternoon, September 9, the Sox held off the Angels, 3–2, on the brilliant relief work of Goose Gossage and Terry Forster, who relieved starter Eddie Fisher and combined to toss 6⅓ innings. Forster got the win, which put the Sox 2½ games behind the A's, who lost to Texas, 3–2.

The Sox had high hopes for Sunday's game, the finale of a nine-game home stand, with Wood going for his 25th win.

But the snappily played 1-hour, 57-minute contest ended with a 5–1 loss, which meant the White Sox finished the homestand 4–5 and again dropped 3½ back.

The following night, Mr. Allen clubbed his franchise-record 34th homer with a runner on in the fifth inning to lead the White Sox to a 2–1 victory over the Royals in Kansas City. "More important to win," said Dick, who added that the previous home run record, set in 1971 by fallen teammate Bill Melton, mattered little to him now. Forster relieved Tom Bradley with two out in the ninth and collected his 23rd save. Even better, Oakland lost a doubleheader in Minnesota, allowing the Sox to creep within two games of first place.

The next evening, the A's dumped the Twins 7–4 and the Sox, led again by an Allen homer and a strong start from Bahnsen, beat the Royals 6–0. The South

Siders were 78-59, while the 80-57 Athletics knew they were the beneficiaries of one extra game on their schedule due to the strike.

On Wednesday, Sept. 13, Wood — again trying for win No. 25 — fell short when the White Sox lost, 6–4, to the Royals. Stung by base-running gaffes and poor defense, the Sox went down in a game they should have won. Meanwhile, the A's beat the Twins, 8–0, to yet again lead the Sox by three games. This was the final turning point in the race.

The team then flew to the West Coast for a three-game series with the Angels followed by two more in Oakland. They had only 16 contests left to make up the three games on the front-runners.

Tanner reflected a lot on the season that had gone by in a whirlwind. In his second full season as a big-league manager, he still had a chance to make it to the postseason. His handling of Dick (or lack of handling, as some saw it) had received plenty of commentary. Some were critical and others, like Harry Caray, were touting him as the "Manager of the Century." In future years, Caray would hardly be as charitable to Tanner, as the Sox' fortunes declined.

Fans and the press did not know that Allen hadn't not received any more special treatment than the 24 other White Sox players. No one knew then, for example, that Tanner regularly let Wood fly home between starts.

Tanner's managerial style was different from the traditional "my way or the highway" skipper. He did not publicly berate his players when they made mistakes. He spoke privately to them behind closed doors. The closest that Tanner would come to berating Carlos May for poor baserunning, for example, was by stating: "We will have to work on that next spring." Tanner did make sure to publicly praise his players when they excelled.

He knew that if Bill Melton had been healthy, his team would have won the AL West hands down. Ed Spiezio played a decent third base, but he was not the defending American League home run champion.

On the off-day before the critical California West Coast swing, Tanner went on record saying that Allen's 1972 season was the "greatest year of any baseball player he has ever observed." And Tanner didn't mind acknowledging that he spent a major portion of his career on the bench.

"I got a good look at guys like Ernie Banks, Hank Aaron, Eddie Mathews," he said "Don't take anything away from these players. They were all great. But Dick Allen is doing more for the White Sox this year."

What the press did not know was how much Dick Allen played hurt in September 1972. He dealt with the continued chronic effects of the injury suffered in August 1967 when his right hand went through a headlight while he was pushing a car (rumor had the injury happening in a bar fight). Also, Dick's right shoulder bothered him and he suffered from shooting pains in his right knee, nagging lower back pain and a bad toe. But he kept quiet about his ailments, lest the opposition know he was not 100 percent. Dick was on a mission to get to the postseason "Promised Land" that had eluded him at almost the last second in 1964.

Before the first game in Anaheim, Dick was batting .315, but Tanner insisted: "He would be 20 points higher if he weren't trying so hard to help us win. He's chasing bad pitches sometimes because he wants so badly to knock in runs for us." He had struck out 118 times to this point.

Dick was also winning games on the bases with speed and cunning. He had already stolen 15 bases in 20 attempts. In contrast, Carlos May had been caught stealing in 15 of his 36 attempts.

California delivered a backbreaking 11-inning loss to the South Siders on Sept. 15. Bradley pitched his heart out, but lost 1–0 when, with two out in the bottom of the 11th, Leo Cardenas plated Curt Motton with a single to right field.

In the top of the inning, Bradley had doubled, but was cut down trying to reach third base on Walt Williams' failed sacrifice bunt attempt. Bradley fell to 14–14 despite fanning nine and walking just one. Worse yet, Oakland upped its lead to four games with a win at home against Texas.

Allen was determined to keep his club in the race, so on Saturday, September 16, he took matters in his own hands. He took Nolan Ryan downtown with a massive blast to deep center in the fifth inning with a man on, driving in the game's only two runs.

Forster came on in relief of Bahnsen with no outs and the tying run at the plate in the ninth. He quickly got three outs to notch his 25th save, helping Bahnsen earn his 19th win.

The White Sox improved their record to 79-61, but the A's beat Texas, 4–0, to keep their four-game lead.

On Sunday, September 17, the Sox again pinned their hopes on Wood. Dick again did everything he could to win the game even though the opposition continued to pitch around him. In the sixth, with the White Sox down, 2–0, Andy Messersmith walked Dick with one out. Allen promptly stole second, his 19th steal of the year, and scored on Mike Andrews' single to center.

Unfortunately, the Sox did not score again, and Wood fell to 24–14. Chicago fell to five games behind the A's, who swept their weekend series at home with Texas.

The Sunday loss exposed one of the team's greatest weaknesses, demonstrating what it would need to contend. Not since aging Luis Aparicio was traded away to Boston in 1970 did the Sox have an adequate shortstop, one who could both catch the ball and contribute something at the plate.

Sox shortstop Luis Alvarado's lapses in the field in the second inning led to an unearned run; he loafed on a pop fly in short center that he should have caught, enabling Doug Howard to score from first base. In the third inning, Alvarado failed to cover second base on a steal that led to another unearned run.

Alvarado and Rich Morales, who shared the position for the '72 Sox, contributed little at the plate. Alvarado, hitless in the game against the Angels, was mired in a 1-for-36 slump and Morales was not much better.

Meanwhile, in Oakland, despite winning the division in 1971 and fielding a star-studded lineup with a lot of thunder, fans stayed away, much to the dismay of owner Finley. The twice relocated franchise had not set the turnstiles on fire since arriving in the East Bay in 1968.

The A's, with the best record in the AL, drew an average of just 6,300 patrons in their weekend sweep of Texas and had only drawn 859,771 for the year — roughly 300,000 less than the Sox.

As it stood on Tuesday, Sept. 19, the A's magic number was at nine.

"If we can sweep our two games here. I still feel we'll win it," said the unfailingly optimistic Tanner.

A soft-spoken Dick appeared on Harry Caray's pre-game radio show. Caray wanted Allen to talk about his 1973 contract, but No. 15 would not take the bait. He wanted to concentrate on winning. Eight years after witnessing the Cardinals overtaking the Phillies at the very end in 1964, he knew it could be done again.

In a game reminiscent of the 17-inning suspended contest in mid-August, the White Sox and A's battled into the early hours of September 20, before the Sox came out 8–7 winners in 15 innings. Loyal fans back home were especially bleary-eyed, staying up until the middle of the night to follow the encounter. Rookie infielder Jorge Orta slugged a homer in the top of the 15th, and Gossage, who came into the game in the 13th after Dave Duncan had hit a two-run home run to tie things, picked up his fifth win against no losses in relief.

So, the Sox would live to fight another day, four games back, but now had to face Holtzman. Wood remained in search of his elusive 25th win; this would be his fourth try.

The talent-stacked A's, upgraded with the acquisitions of Matty Alou in right field and Dal Maxvill at shortstop, outslugged Wood and the Sox, 6–3, with homers by Sal Bando and Reggie Jackson. Rollie Fingers replaced Holtzman in the top of the sixth inning with a 5–2 lead and the bases full, and got pinch-hitter Pat Kelly to ground into an inning-ending double play.

After the game, A's manager Dick Williams was certain his team had captured its second straight division title. Up five games with 12 to play (only 11 for the Sox), Williams summed it up: "They had to win two to catch us. We beat a tough pitcher, the best in the league."

A frustrated Wood admitted that his pitching was "pretty bad" in the loss.

The next day, in Arlington, Tex., Bahnsen joined Wood in the 20-win circle, beating the Rangers 8–4. It was his fourth victory in 15 days.

For the first time since 1920, two White Sox pitchers had won 20 games (that club had four 20 game winners: Ed Cicotte, Red Faber, Lefty Williams and Dickie Kerr). Forster's two scoreless innings earned his 26th save.

The 8–4 win, and the A's 5–3 loss in Kansas City, gave the Sox temporary hope, again cutting Oakland's lead to four games.

But by now, it was obvious that Dick Allen was hurt. Tony Muser took over at first base in the top of the fourth after Dick was hobbling on one knee.

The next night, Sept. 23, the Sox, knowing the A's had won their matinee game over the Royals, kept their faint hopes alive with a 4–3 victory against the Rangers. Gossage picked up his fourth win in relief. Allen made a pinch-hit appearance.

On Sunday, September 24, the White Sox continued to cling to life with a 7–4 win, sweeping the three-game set from Texas. As they had done all year, the team kept battling. Despite clearly ailing, Dick ripped his 37th homer and drove in four runs. Gossage picked up another victory in relief of Wood, running his record to 7-0. It was the fifth time the ace knuckleballer failed to win his 25th game.

Oakland split its doubleheader against the Royals, meaning that the Sox picked up a half-game in the standings and were 3½ out…but the A's had cut their magic number to five.

The Royals came into Chicago on September 26 and handed the Sox a heartbreaking 2–1 loss. Kansas City's 23-year-old rookie, Steve Busby, who had won the final game of the 1971 College World Series for champion Southern California, went the distance and allowed just five hits. In the seventh, Dick and Carlos May opened with base hits, but Busby got Rick Reichardt and Spiezio to strike out and Ed Herrmann popped up to end the rally.

May homered in the ninth with one out, but an undaunted Busby got Reichardt and Spiezio to end things. The A's lead was now four games with seven games left.

For Tanner, the day had started out well, with news that he was given a contract extension through 1975. "I want to stay in Chicago the rest of my career. I could not work for a better man than Mr. Allyn."

Tanner's entire coaching staff received contract extensions as well. Roland Hemond, however, was without assurance of 1973 employment, which upset

Tanner, already disenchanted with the White Sox' economizing measures.

The White Sox needed a miracle to get into the postseason but did not get it. Wood again missed win No. 25 as the Royals edged the Sox, 4-2, and fell 5½ games off the pace as the A's split a twinbill against the Twins.

This was the final home game of the year, and only 4,752 fans showed up to say good-bye to the 1972 White Sox.

Dick Allen, battling to the end like Davy Crockett at the Alamo, got his league-leading 113th RBI in the first with a ringing double to right field, scoring Jim Lyttle, given a start in center field to spell the slumping Reichardt.

Dick came up in the bottom of the ninth with the Sox down, 4-1. He went down swinging, but the scant crowd gave him a rousing standing ovation as he walked slowly back to the dugout. He looked up into the stands and held his bat high in salute. Chicago had accepted him for what he was. It was a fitting tribute to a Most Valuable Player.

For the second game in a row, Melton's replacement, Ed Spiezio, made the last out of the game, killing a rally. It would turn out to be his final at-bat in the majors.

Wood had not won since defeating the A's on September 7. He made no excuses. He did not have a sore arm.

After the A's defeated the Twins 8–7 on Sept. 28 to eliminate the White Sox from contention, Tanner offered his superstar first baseman a rest. After playing in every one of the White Sox' first 148 games, he accepted Tanner's offer to go home and rest his ailing knee.

And so, Dick Allen, Cy Acosta, Moe Drabowsky and Ed Spiezio did not make the final road trip to Texas and Minnesota. Drabowsky's long career dating back to 1956 with the Cubs would end when the Sox soon released him. Spiezio was nursing nagging injuries, including broken ribs, but made no excuses about failing to produce in clutch situations. Acosta was facing minor eye surgery.

May was still in a battle with the Twins' Rod Carew for the batting crown. Tanner was upset that Carew was rested against the A's, who, with their Thursday night win against the Twins, clinched the division. Carew's average had slipped to .317.

The Sox won their first two games in Texas with Tom Bradley earning a 5 – 1 complete-game win in Friday's opener. There was no celebrating.

Season finale

After his seventh try for the elusive 25th victory, falling 1- 0 to the Rangers, Wood took up Tanner's offer to go home for the year after pitching the Herculean 376⅔ innings. He finished tied for the team's all-time record for starts.

The Sox went to Minnesota and won, 6-4 and 5–4, but lost the finale, 14–2. Gossage made his first career start and suffered his first career loss, lasting only three innings. He finished the year at 7–1 with a 4.28 ERA.

The Sox ended the year 87–67, the second-best record in the AL and the fourth-best in baseball.

The A's beat the Tigers 3 games to 2 in a hard-fought ALCS, then won the first of three straight World Championships by edging the Cincinnati Reds in seven games. They took the crown despite Reggie Jackson missing the entire Fall Classic with a major leg and knee injury suffered in Game 5 at Detroit.

What Allen played through to make it to the final week was a profile in courage.

His 1967 injury was potentially career-ending. Co-author Dr. David J. Fletcher examined Allen's right hand when he was in Chicago in 2012. Fletcher was amazed that he could have ever returned to competitive baseball.

His fourth and fifth fingers (which are innervated by the ulnar nerve) were basically non-functional and he had lingering effects of chronic neuropathy. He could not make a full grip with his hand. He had to change positions because it was still difficult for him to grip and throw a ball with his injured right throwing arm.

Dick rehabbed on his own and in private, constantly squeezing a rubber ball while dealing with psychological demons that this injury caused. Dick was determined to not let his career end with a freak accident. To build strength in the hand, he took a construction job laying bricks. His will to recover from this type of injury demonstrates what kind of character he had.

Dick arrived for 1968 spring training wearing a golf glove for extra support to protect his hand from the vibratory shocks from his damaged ulnar nerve ("funny bone"). He later recalled being fined for using unlawful equipment, but later that year, more major leaguers began wearing such gloves. He and original glove user Ken Harrelson had started a trend.

A lot more than met the eye went into Dick Allen's MVP award, which he received six weeks after the season ended. Years of physical and mental pain and toil, plus sheer will and belief in his knowing how to win led the man to true greatness.

Late in the 1972 season, the White Sox were given permission to print playoff tickets.

Photo credit: Chicago White Sox

White Sox players, in their red pinstripes of the era, at batting practice in June 1972. From left to right: Walt "No-Neck" Williams, Mike Andrews (in the batting cage), Tom Egan, Bill Melton, Tom Bradley and Coach Jim Mahoney, leaning on the cage. '71 Home Run Champ Melton was lost for the season later that month, and the Sox were edged out in September by the Oakland A's for the AL West Division Championship.

Photo credit: Leo Bauby Collection

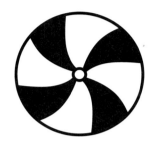

CHAPTER 19

October 3, 1972: Forster the pitching phenom and base burglar, pre-Letterman

During the next-to-last game of the 1972 season, 20-year-old Terry Jay Forster was finishing his second season as major league pitcher and sitting in the bullpen at Metropolitan Stadium in Minnesota waiting for the call to go into the game. Fewer than 3,000 fans were in the stands to watch two teams close out the season.

Forster had made it to the major leagues at the age of 19 — after appearing in just 10 games in the minors with the White Sox' Class-A team in Appleton, Wis.

"In 1972, I didn't have a care in the world. It was a very exciting time in my life," recalled Forster 50 years later, way off the grid after moving to Ottawa, Canada to work in his wife's construction business and raise four daughters.

Though disappointed that the Sox would not be going to the postseason after battling Oakland for the AL West lead into late September, Forster knew he would have other opportunities in the future to earn a ring. He had a fantastic year and was challenging the Yankees' Sparky Lyle as the best reliever in baseball.

The young left-hander was savoring the night before, when he earned his 29th save of the year by finishing out a 6-4 win against the Twins. The feat had set the Sox team record for most saves in a season, surpassing future Hall of Famer Hoyt Wilhelm's mark of 27, set in 1964.

For the year, Forster had appeared in 62 games, all out of the bullpen, totaling 100 innings with a 2.25 ERA — second-best on the Sox staff after Cy Acosta's 1.56 and 104 strikeouts. His 6-5 record reflected the battle scars of being put into pressure situations with games on the line all year long.

The year before, Forster, still a teenager, had made the 1971 White Sox as a non-roster invitee and was quickly baptized by fire in do-or-die situations. On April 23, 1971, in his first appearance Yankee Stadium, less than a year out of pitching for Santana High School in Santee, Calif., Forster entered a 5-5 game in the bottom of the 11th inning. He had inherited a bases-loaded, no-out situation. Four pitches later, he had retired the side and sent the game into the 12th.

During the 1972 campaign, Forster was almost named to the 1972 American League All-Star team. He would finish second to Sparky Lyle in the *Sporting News* Fireman of the Year award with 35 points (29 saves plus six victories) compared to Lyle's 44 points (35 saves and nine wins).

Though disappointed that he was not named a '72 All Star, the kid received a nice surprise after All-Star break.

"In those days they only took one relief pitcher and you had John Hiller from Detroit, Sparky Lyle, Rollie Fingers and one of those guys always seemed to get picked," Forster recalled. "And so, they didn't take me, and Stu Holcomb had called me up to his office at Comiskey Park. And I thought maybe I was in trouble; I don't know what the heck was going on. I went up there and he tore up my contract and gave me a $3,500 raise. How many times does that happen?"

In his 1972 breakout season, Forster did not serve up a single home run. The homerless streak, from the end of 1971 through the beginning of 1973, ultimately covered a span of 137⅔ innings and was the longest streak ever for pitcher except for Babe Ruth (who pitched in the dead ball era). The career mark of 0.42 home runs per nine innings for Forster is sixth-best for major league pitchers with 1,000 or more innings.

"As long as he can get people out, he's got a job, White Sox manager Chuck Tanner said late in the 1972 season. "We figured we had to make a spot for this kid as far back as a year ago, only we weren't quite so sure just then where it would be."

At the close of the season, Sox pitching coach Johnny Sain told Phil Elderkin of the *Christian Science Monitor*: "The one thing you don't ordinarily do with the kids this age is rush them. But since Forster already seemed to have most of the fundamentals, we went ahead a little faster than normal. He's a kid we can work with because he listens. During spring training I'd see him learn something in the morning and then make it work in the game that same afternoon."

Forster sensed the confidence from the field staff at the time: "Chuck [Tanner] has been great to me; he's never second guessed me — not even once — and on those days I am not getting people out, he never complains. He just gives me a pat and tells me will get 'em tomorrow. He never stops building your confidence."

While sitting in the Metropolitan Stadium bullpen reflecting back on this success in his young career, Forster had to focus on the game at hand against the Twins. He was ready to come in and earn his 30th save if Tanner called upon him if the Sox tied the game or took the lead.

However, the current situation was dire because the South Siders were trailing the Twins, 4-3, with two out in the top of the ninth and no one on base. Down to their last bullet, Sox first baseman Tony Muser, subbing for Dick Allen, tripled. Pinch hitter Ed Herrmann was intentionally walked, his American League-leading 19th intentional pass of the year. Pitcher Jim Geddes went in to run for Herrmann. Suddenly, Forster believed he was going to pitch the bottom of the ninth.

Sox right-handed hitter Hank Allen, Dick's brother, was about to face Twins right-handed reliever Wayne Granger when Tanner unexpectedly shouted out to Sain, "Get Forster a bat!"

So instead of grabbing his glove and warming up for a mound appearance, Forster ran in the from bullpen and started swinging some bats in the on-deck circle, readying for his first big league pinch-hit appearance.

The 6 foot-3, 210-pound left-handed batter calmly ripped a shot into center field to tie the score, 4-4, driving in Muser and sending Geddes to third base. Taking a normal lead off first base, Forster saw third-base coach Joe Lonnett flash the straight steal sign.

"I couldn't believe they are wanting me to steal second base," recalled Forster. He took off for second base and while sliding into the base, the ball thrown by Twins catcher George Mitterwald sailed into center field and Geddes, who became the trailer runner, was able to score easily to allow the Sox to take a 5-4 lead.

Forster's bat and legs, not his arm, had earned the White Sox their 87th win of the season to go 21 games over 500. The unlikely offensive hero was credited with both a game-tying RBI and what turned out to be his only career stolen base.

"After the game, the clubhouse was crazy loud and everyone was riding Terry about his speed and his hitting ability," remembered Hank Allen, who himself had to live down having a pitcher pinch-hit for him.

Forster's theft would be the last stolen base by an American League pitcher until 1997 (interleague play), due to the inception of the DH rule in 1973.

Forster had already established himself as an excellent hitter. When the White Sox drafted him, they planned to have him pitch and play first base at Appleton.

Roving minor league instructor Deacon Jones influenced the offensively-adept Forster to concentrate on pitching in July 1970. Deacon Jones' wife was the Rosa Parks of baseball when she refused in 1962 to sit in the segregated section of the White Sox minor league affiliate ballpark in Savannah, Ga. Her action led to NAACP picketing and the eventual move of the franchise to Lynchburg, Virginia in 1963.

Forster had been drafted in the second round (erratic shortstop Bee Bee Richard was the Sox' first pick) and No. 30 overall in the June 1970 MLB draft.

"When I went to Appleton my first year...I sat for the first two weeks, because they didn't know if he was going to be a first baseman or a pitcher," Forster said. "We had an intrasquad game and I pitched three innings. Deacon Jones came in and said, 'Hey, I think you're going to be a pitcher, but we want you to play first base, too,' and I said OK. He said this, I'll never forget, 'When you get up to hit, if that ball hits you, I'm going to come in from third base. I'm going to kick your ass.' They wanted to protect me. So, after the game the next day in Appleton I decided to just pitch and not play first base."

While the then-18 year-old focused on pitching the rest of his first pro season, he still showed flashes that he could hit better than most pitchers. He was 8-for-26 for a .213 average in his brief, two-month stay at Appleton.

In 1971, as a White Sox rookie, Forster went 2-for 5. In fact, his .397 lifetime batting average (31 hits in 78 official at-bats) is the highest for any major leaguer in history with either 50 at-bats or at least 15 years of major league experience. His best season as a hitter was 1972 when he was 10-for-19 (.526), all singles — with one run scored and three RBI. Forster had a total of 22 plate appearances with two sacrifice bunts and one walk. His 1972 OBP was an unworldly .550 in 1972 and over his 16-year career, he had a .413 OBP.

Co-author David Fletcher used to rib Dick Allen that Terry Forster had a better year in '72 with Forster's 1.076 OPS/218 OPS-*plus* (OPS+) versus Dick's 1.023 OPS/199 OPS+.

After the DH arrived in 1973, Forster batted only once again (1973) until being traded to the National League in 1977. Hitting again, he went 9-for 26 (.346). Chuck Tanner, then the skipper of the Pirates, did use Forster as a pinch hitter three times that year.

While Forster didn't show much power (no home runs in his career), he did make contact. In 1972, he only struck out twice in 22 plate appearances, compared to Wilbur Wood's record-setting low for pitchers of 65 strikeouts in 144 plate appearances.

During his career, Forster had four doubles and a triple.

One wonders why Tanner did not regularly use him as a pinch hitter

"Chuck was more of a traditionalist in baseball," Forster said. "He wanted to win, he'd do what he had to do to win, but he also was very sympathetic to average ballplayers because he himself was not the superstar, the All-Star coming up. I don't think he really wanted to show up anybody. He said, 'If I hit you, then you can't come in the game late to pitch.'"

In the '72 off-season Forster was rewarded for his batting prowess. He got a $3,500 contract to be a hitter in 1973, along with $17,500 for being a pitcher, only to see Holcomb try to take the hitting dollars away when the DH rule went into effect that year.

"After the 1972 season, I signed my contract as a pitcher and I signed my contract as a hitter," Forster said. "Wow. Nice, I didn't even know that split contract like that existed. Then the Sox tried to take the $3,500 away from me because we went back to DH. And so, Marvin Miller of the Players Association said, 'No, you got to pay him, it's not his fault that the owners voted for (the DH).'"

Forster's status as player of many talents stemmed from his old-school status as a teenage phenom signed out of high school who punched an express ticket to the major leagues. In his 10 games for the Appleton Foxes in 1970, Forster went

6-1 with a 1.33 ERA as a starter.

He was so impressive in his half-season in A ball, he made White Sox' parent roster the following season right out of spring training.

The promising southpaw joined an elite group of pitchers who were in the major leagues as teenagers. Most notably, Bob Feller went from Van Meter, Iowa to the Indians at age 17, and Walter Johnson joined the Senators at 19. Forster's contemporaries who made their debuts at 19 included Hall of Famers Jim Palmer and Bert Blyleven along with lefties Ken Holtzman and Don Gullett. Later, Dwight "Doc" Gooden was baseball's pitching sensation at 19 while Fernando Valenzuela made his debut at that same age.

Forster pitched in all four years at Santana High School outside San Diego and attracted hundreds of scouts who came to watch him pitch (and hit). The strapping lefty, 200 pounds as a senior, went 10-0, possessing a mid-90 mph fastball. He also played basketball, including duels against future UCLA star Bill Walton.

Forster would have been a higher pick in the 1970 draft, as he was considered one of the top three prospects, but teams were scared to pick him because he had a bad back. His hometown Padres had the No.1 pick and took a pass.

In 1971, Forster admitted to *Chicago Sun-Times* White Sox beat writer Edgar Munzel that he had chronic back problems, "But nothing that interferes with pitching. There's a bone missing in my lower back that separates the vertebrae. The summer after eighth grade, it was so bad I was on crutches for a couple months. I recovered from it and ever since my sophomore year in high school I've been getting along fine by wearing an elastic brace." Over his 16-year career, Forster's lower back never prevented him from pitching, but he did have on-going treatment.

Bat boy Jim Riley recalled Forster's back issues. "He wore a brace of some sort. I think [trainer] Charlie Saad used to work on it."

"In 1970, I went to Appleton Wisconsin for the second half of the year, and I was 6-1 there and came back home after the season ended," Forster said. "Some people said, 'Hey, are the White Sox going to bring you up the last month of the season?' and I wasn't even aware that the major league teams did that. And I said, 'No, I haven't heard anything.' And I wanted to go back home more than anything else. Well, anyway, I think the White Sox they'd finished — or were about to finish — the season in Anaheim."

The White Sox had, in fact, pulled him out of his final game on September 1 at Appleton and flew him to Chicago to discuss a possible last-month '70 season call-up. But Sox GM Ed Short and manager Don Gutteridge both got fired mid-month and Forster never was summoned, as the new team brain trust of

Tanner, Sain and Roland Hemond took over. They did arrange for Forster and his parents to meet them in the visiting clubhouse in Anaheim when the Sox closed out their calamitous 1970 season.

The team itself was hardly an attraction for the Forsters when the Sox lost the entire four-game series to the Angels to finish at a definitely-last-place 42 games out. Forster was then informed that after just 54 innings of pro baseball, he would be a non-roster invitee to spring training in 1971.

"After we left (Anaheim Stadium) my dad, mom and I and were talking about it on the way home. And my Dad said: 'Don't get too excited about it.' He said that because guys worked hard their whole careers just to get up there."

"Well, the next year, I go to the spring training, and I always thought that major league pitchers threw the ball 100 mph and anywhere around the plate, and had great curveballs. And when I went to spring training, I saw some of these guys throwing. I said, 'Jeez, we had three pitchers on my high school team that good.'

"So, I had decent workouts and stuff, but I wasn't pitching in any of the games. It just so happened we're in Sarasota, we're playing at Payne Park, where we trained at the time and we're playing the Boston Red Sox; I'll never forget this.

"I think it's ninth or 10th inning of the game and Johnny Sain gets up, and he's looking around in the stands where I was sitting. And he looks at me and says, 'I think he's on our team,' but I'm not sure until he says, 'Hey, come here. You're the left-handed top prospect. Yo, get in that clubhouse. Get your uniform on because you're pitching the next inning.'

"It was extra innings, we ran out of pitchers and, you know, I'm so excited. I'm sure I fell down once or twice running over to the clubhouse. Got my uniform on, hurried to come out to hurry up, go down and warm up. I warmed up and I think got into the last two innings and we won the game. Because of him coming to the stands and I was in the right place, right time, I might not ever get a chance to be looked at."

In 1971 spring training, Forster had a 1.75 ERA, best on the team. He fanned 11 batters in 13 innings pitched.

"And how I knew I made the team (in '71) is because we stayed at the Sarasota Hotel," he said. "It might have been a 15-story-high hotel. A bunch of us were around the elevator and Roland Hemond got on it toward the end of spring training. He said, 'Hey Terry, are you anxious to see your mom and dad out west (the Sox were to start the season in Oakland) next week?' And I said, 'What's Roland talking about?'

"I thought I was going to go down to Double-A ball and those others in the elevator looked at me, you know, and their mouths drop off and sure enough I made the final cut, and I was on the team. So that's…that's how I knew about it."

Forster made his White Sox debut on April 11, 1971, against the Minnesota Twins at Comiskey Park. He was brought in to relieve Bart Johnson in the sixth inning with Cesar Tovar and Rod Carew on base. Forster got Tony Oliva to pop out to third. In his second inning of work, Forster allowed a single to Harmon Killebrew, but then struck out Rich Reese and got Jim Holt to ground into a double play.

In his rookie season, he appeared in 45 games (three starts) and had a 2-3 record with a save.

As the '71 season wound down, *The Chicago Tribune* reported that the Terry Forster "experiment" was working exactly as planned and that the Sox' decision to allow the 19-year-old to learn his craft at the major league level under the tutelage of Sain instead of in the minors was paying off.

"Last year at this time I only had two pitches, a fastball and curve and I used a big windup," Foster said then. "Now I have two fastballs, two curves, two sliders and a changeup; I pitch with a no-windup delivery because it gives me better control and makes my fastball more alive. Johnny Sain taught me all that."

According to Forster, Sain also showed him how to make a fastball sink and how to throw his curve ball with both an overhand and three-quarter sidearm motion.

Forster called Sain the "greatest pitching coach who ever lived. He was a special pitching coach. I think that he was probably 30, 40 years ahead of his time. He was there to help you, he'd show me different things to do with the ball. He said, 'Hey, try it. So, that's all I'm asking. If you don't like it, don't use it. Yeah, but I'm here to help you guys.' Look what he did for Jim Kaat to speed up his windup, he got 120 more wins.

"I remember Johnny, he always told me every year you're in the big leagues, you have to improve something. He said, if you don't improve in one area, you're not going to be in the big leagues a long time and he says I don't know if it's getting bunting, fielding your position, or holding runners on. But that was something we always worked on with him and then we see other pitchers running stuff. You can't run the ball over the plate. He said I'd rather have you guys throw every day than to run every day. He was just ahead of his time. He was very intelligent."

As a teenage rookie, the hard-throwing Forster nearly averaged a strikeout per inning in 1971. And he was in great demand throughout baseball. After the season, he was almost traded to the Dodgers – for whom he'd later pitch – in the Dick Allen deal.

Until interviewed for this book, Forster never knew that Dodgers GM Al Campanis wanted both Tommy John and him in exchange for Dick. Hemond refused to part with his budding star in December 1971. Campanis would finally nab Forster, for the '78 season, as the Dodgers first-ever free agent signing.

Despite pitching for 16 years in the majors, Forster would never save as many games as he did in 1972 (29). In his career, Forster pitched for the White Sox (1971-76), Pirates (1977), Dodgers (1978-82), Braves (1983-85), and Angels (1986). He finished his career with 1,105⅔ innings pitched, 127 saves and a lifetime ERA of 3.23.

After pitching exclusively in relief during 1972, Forster started 12 games in 1973 because Tanner needed some help in the rotation. With Cy Acosta flourishing in the bullpen, the manager experimented with Forster in the rotation until Jim Kaat was claimed off waivers in August. Forster completed four games in 12 starts. Overall, he was 6-11 with 16 saves and a 3.23 ERA over 172⅔ innings in 1973.

The Chicago rotation gained some stability in 1974 thanks to 20-win seasons from fast-working veteran workhorses Kaat and Wood. This starting rotation depth allowed Forster to go back to the bullpen full-time. He paced the American League in saves with 24 and was named its Fireman of the Year, logging a busy 134 innings in relief.

The workload finally caught up to Forster in 1975, as he managed only 37 innings, though he was still effective (2.19 ERA). He injured his left elbow on a pitch to Reggie Jackson; with Forster sidelined, Goose Gossage claimed the role of closer.

When Chuck Tanner refused to accept a demotion to coach third base by new owner Bill Veeck after the '75 season, his replacement, Paul Richards, made the contentious managerial decision to put *both* Forster and Gossage in the starting rotation. This move turned out to be a disaster: Forster went 2-12 and Gossage 9-17. Even after their poor seasons as starters in 1976, with free agency looming, they were dealt together to the Pittsburgh Pirates for Richie Zisk and Silvio Martinez. They would again play a year for their skipper, Tanner, who (after one season in Oakland) moved on to his greatest success managing Pittsburgh. Tanner knew how to use the pair effectively.

Both left the Pirates after becoming free agents for the first time following the 1977 season. While Gossage signed with the Yankees to replace Sparkly Lyle, Forster's Dodgers salary was the then-big figure of $170,000. In 1978, Forster went 5-4 with 22 saves and a 1.94 ERA in 47 appearances. He also hit .500 (four-for-eight), with a double and two RBI. He was the victor in the deciding game of the 1978 NLCS with a perfect 10th inning and two strikeouts. But he had left elbow surgery after the season.

With the Dodgers, Forster came back and earned a World Series ring in 1981, pitching against the Yankees. In two World Series games, he threw two innings. After pitching for the Atlanta Braves, the southpaw spent his final season on the Angels' 1986 ALCS-bound team but did not pitch in the postseason.

Forster had by now gained some unwanted fame for his persona. He was constantly battling weight problems, and his eating habits began attracting national attention due to the fact the Braves games were broadcast nationally on TBS. In June 1985, host David Letterman made Forster a national celebrity by calling him "A Fat Tub of Goo" on his NBC's Late Night show. Letterman said he had seen Forster, by now of stout build, on cable TV and made several cracks about his waistline, sticking him with the insult, "A Fat Tub of Goo."

On July 29, 1985, Forster got a chance to face off with the man who gave him that nickname that he is forever stuck with and which would make him the butt of jokes the rest of his career and life.

"The first nine or 10 times I saw it on tape, I thought it was really funny," Forster said. "But then about the last 20 or 30 times I saw it, and everybody was talking about it, I said, well, I don't know how this is going to go over. But I came home that night, and I realized my wife says worse things about me."

Letterman said he had second thoughts about his comments. "It just started out as kind of a joke," he said. "Then I'm driving home, and I thought to myself: Now wait a minute, I just went on network TV...and I called a man a fat tub of goo. And regardless of how funny or not funny a person might think that is, if you start thinking about it, that's not a real flattering thing to say."

Forster said: "My first reaction was that this guy dogged me, I'm going after him, and I'm going to sue him. And then after I took a shower and looked at myself in the mirror, I said, no, the guy's right. How can I sue him? You know, I haven't always been this big. It just sneaked up on me."

Forster agreed to meet the funnyman face to face on the post-midnight show. Letterman brought out two baseball cards, the first from Forster's 1971 season with the White Sox, the other his current Braves card. Both cards, Letterman noted, showed Forster's weight as 210 pounds. "It's amazing what a little money will do for you," Forster said, whose comedic chops on that infamous appearance matched Letterman.

For a short time, Forster tried to cash in on his "Fat Tub of Goo" notoriety. His gastronomic proclivities and ability to make fun at himself secured him a four-minute music video entitled, 'Fat Is In' that failed to dent the MTV charts but can be watched on You Tube.

Forster would struggle with his weight the rest of his career and even went to a weight-loss program that he paid for after the 1985 season.

"I've always had a little trouble on the scale," confessed Forster that year. "I remember with the Sox, our manager, Chuck Tanner, would come up to me the first day of spring training and say, 'Terry, you must have worked out hard all winter. You look like a Greek god.' Then, around July, he'd come up to me and say, 'Terry, now you just look like a Greek.' I'd tell him I'm a growing boy. I guess I'm still growing."

On April 1, 1986, Braves manager Tanner, the same man who had promoted him to the majors at age 19 with the White Sox, released Forster because of his weight. He had a clause in his 1986 Braves contract about his weight and didn't meet his weight-loss goal, but was able to latch on with the Angels in 1986. In 1987, still struggling with weight, Forster got a minor-league deal with the Twins and was almost a part of their 1987 world champion team, but Minnesota general manager Andy MacPhail hesitated when he said he was in better shape than Forster.

Despite his comedic fame, two decades into the 21st century Forster's profile was almost subterranean after moving to Canada. Gossage, with whom he had been paired for so many years on the White Sox and Pirates, did not even have his phone number. Yet, emotionally, Forster feels as much a part of the memorable early '70s South Side squads as any teammate.

He was among a triumvirate of young flamethrowers —Johnson, Gossage and Forster— whom the White Sox developed in the early '70s.

Johnny Sain was a man way ahead of his time when he proposed in 1973 that Johnson, Gossage and Forster each pitch one inning when the Sox had the lead or were tied going into the seventh inning. But Tanner rejected this strategy, which would become adopted as the industry standard decades later.

Forster was "The Natural" 12 years before the Robert Redford movie was released when he started his baseball career. Drafted out of high school by the Sox. In the Major Leagues as a 19-year-old. Remarkable.

Over 16 MLB seasons Terry Forster could dominate hitters like few others, while having that uncommonly good stroke at the plate for a pitcher. He was 12-for-24 in his first two MLB Seasons before the bat was taken out of his hands with the advent of the DH in 1973.

And on one early fall night in the Upper Midwest, Forster's crazy legs beat the throw to second base and earned win #87 for the 1972 Chicago White Sox.

That was all quite adept for a "Fat Tub of Goo."

No American League batter was comfortable facing young lefty reliever Terry Forster in 1972. Forster was like the Michael Kopech of his era.

Photo credit: Leo Bauby Collection

CHAPTER 20

November 15, 1972:
Chili Dog MVP

After a season in which he dominated the American League, Dick Allen made his triumphant return to Chicago and White Sox Park on Nov. 15, 1972. Long after the season ended and a few weeks after the rival Oakland A's had won the World Series, the man's exploits during the season were still an indelible memory for Sox fans.

Now, their hero was back for the day, driving in from his farm in Allentown, Pa., to meet with a full house of sportswriters at the ballpark. The reason: Dick was chosen as the American League's Most Valuable Player, with all but three scribes in the Baseball Writers Association of America voting for the 30-year-old slugger.

In his first season in the AL, Dick had dominated with 37 homers, 113 RBI and an over-the-top OPS of 1.023. He was the second Black player in Chicago baseball history to win an MVP after the Cubs' Ernie Banks captured back-to-back honors in 1958-59. But this award was truly in the spirit of an MVP: He had put his team on his back and carried them into surprise contention.

"He has just been tremendous for us," White Sox Director of Player Personnel Roland Hemond said, as he presented Dick to the journalists attending. For Hemond and owner John Allyn, it was a particularly proud moment. Roland, along with manager Chuck Tanner, had persuaded the owner to let them trade for the future MVP almost one year earlier. The trade created tremendous financial risks for a team which had perilously low attendance of just under 500,000 only two years earlier. Allen's $135,000 salary was the highest in baseball, so there were questions about the Sox' ability to afford him.

And yet, that gamble paid off enormously. Dick's exploits — combined with charismatic, unique radio broadcasts of Harry Caray and the ground-breaking in-stadium entertainment from young organist Nancy Faust — were instrumental in bringing fans back to the South Side. The franchise drew 1,177,318, third-best in the American League and more than twice their draw in 1970, and the team regained solvency.

Bill Veeck, who was watching the White Sox closely from his Maryland home, had estimated that Allen's 1972 "crowd pleasing, crowd drawing" season was worth $750,000 in added income: Extra season tickets, the new radio deal and much more concession sales. All nicely funded Allen's salary.

But to the White Sox and their fans, Dick Allen meant more than dollars. He meant survival — and hope. Here was a team that lost 106 games in 1970. In 1972, with Allen, the team won — in a strike-shortened season — 20 more games than it lost. That's a turnaround of 70 games in just two seasons.

So Dick was treated as a savior as he returned to Chicago on this chilly fall day. "It's as big a thrill for me as it is for Dick," said Tanner, also basking in the glow of that AL Manager of the Year Award from the *Sporting News*. Hemond's *Sporting News* Executive of the Year Award was the first ever for a Chicago White Sox executive in the 36-year history of that honor.

Dick's teammate, Wilbur Wood, finished seventh in the MVP polling and finished second in American League's Cy Young Award ballots, with the Indians' Gaylord Perry earning nine first-place votes to Wood's seven. The knuckleballer posted a 24-17 record with 49 games started and 376⅔ innings pitched, the most in baseball since Grover Cleveland Alexander logged 388 innings in 1917.

Wood actually had a higher WAR (Wins Above Replacement) value than Dick in 1972 — 10.3, compared to 9.3. Mr. Allen made sure to credit his teammate for the brilliant year on the mound, saying, "The way I look at it, I'm sharing this award with him."

The Most Valuable Player displayed his humble side as he talked to the press about the honor. He did not think he would win the MVP, believing that it would go to Joe Rudi, who led his A's to a World Series championship. But Dick said he wouldn't be completely satisfied until the White Sox won a pennant with him. "Baseball is more and more an individual game, but I am one of those guys who happen to believe it is still a team game," he said. "And our team became tighter than pantyhose two sizes too small."

The supreme sentiment that came from this press conference was Dick's love of his new home city. "The fans of Chicago have done a lot for me," he said in an emotional moment. "I don't say I've been fair to the people in baseball, but sometimes they haven't been fair to me. Coming to Chicago made a human being out of me.

"I'd like to end my career right here in Chicago. You can trade me if you want, but I'm coming right back."

Years later, Allen would recall in his autobiography the moment he realized his Chicago experience would be different from Philadelphia, St. Louis and Los Angeles:

"Whenever I was traded to a new team, the front office would set up a press conference," he wrote. "I was always good box office, and management knew it. It was like a circus, and I was the main attraction. The first question I got in Chicago was 'What shall we call you, Rich, Richie, or Dick?' Know how many times I heard that? So I said what I always said: 'I prefer to be called Dick, but I just want to be a winner.'

"So next day, I open the Chicago papers and there I am — 'Dick Allen.' I go to the park, and everybody's calling me Dick — the ushers, the clubhouse guys, the fans. First time. First city to call me by the name my mother gave me at birth. I'd about given up. I made up my mind right then and there that Dick Allen was going to pay back Chicago for the respect they were giving me."

Allen's comment only enhanced his enthusiastic reception from all corners of the metropolitan area. He professed to never feeling as welcome as in Chicago. However, a subset of the populace viewed a Black superstar, or any entertainer, far different than a potential neighbor next door or schoolmate. Allen's press conference was staged at a time when a tribal Chicago was again engulfed in racial drama, especially on the Southwest Side, the ancestral home for many White Sox fans.

> **"Well, you know…I like black people. But there comes a time when they have to walk their road, and I have to walk my own."**
> – *Bill Gushing, 19-year-old White Gage Park resident during race riots in Chicago in November 1972*

In Gage Park, the White ethnic neighborhood southwest of Bridgeport and Back of the Yards, the newly integrated high school was the scene of violent combat between Black and White students. The area — including nearby Marquette Park — had been a target of an open housing campaign led by Dr. Martin Luther King, Jr. in the 1960s. As a result, Gage Park High School began admitting Black students the late '60s, and by 1972, African Americans accounted for 37 percent of the school's population.

White parents revolted by staging a boycott at the start of the 1972 school year, with about 300 white students staying home for the first two months of classes. Their goal focused on having the school transfer about 600 Black students to "relieve overcrowding."

That boycott was unsuccessful, and when those White students returned to the school, the violence began, culminating with a two-day riot that started on the same day when Dick made his triumphant return, "The school grounds had become the scene of almost guerrilla warfare tactics by more than 100 White students who ran through the area in groups of two and three, attacking Black students as they entered or left the school," the *Tribune* reported on Nov. 17, 1972.

"The fighting throughout a two-square-block area surrounding the school came to a head in a rock-throwing melee shortly after lunch. About 120 Black students left the school and confronted a band of about 100 White students lined up across the street. As police broke up the group, a second band of White students attacked from the opposite direction."

"It's a powder keg," Gage Park school security director Edward Brady said at the time. "The racial hatred has gone too far." The school would end up closing for two days, and it took a seven-point security plan to help create an uneasy truce among the Black and White students. But ultimately, many of the White families would eventually leave the school and the neighborhood, mirroring the White flight that was going on throughout the South and Southwest sides. By 2018, Gage Park High had a student body that was still over one-third Black, well under one per cent White and approximately two-thirds Latino; Mexican Americans had expanded throughout Southwest Side neighborhoods in the preceding 30 years. They constituted a potentially strong new fan base for the Chicago White Sox.

At Chicago's City Hall on this November day, Mayor Richard J. Daley's floor leader, Ald. Thomas Keane, pushed through a successful resolution to redistrict the city's 50 wards. Keane was forced to redraw the maps in an effort to avoid a suit filed in the U.S. Court of Appeals, challenging ward boundaries established in 1970. The suit alleged that the 1970 map didn't acknowledge the growing number of Blacks and other minority groups that were expanding by increasing numbers in South Side neighborhoods. The suit was filed by a diverse group of politicians and activists, which included Ald. Bill Singer and Rev. Jesse Jackson, the men who had successfully challenged Daley's delegation at the Democratic Convention in Miami back in July.

Daley, meanwhile, was proposing a record nearly $1 billion city budget for 1973, one-third of which would go to police and fire protection in the city — all this, while endorsing a $30 million property tax cut. The budget also called for more than $150 million for Streets and Sanitation; despite his national reputation within the Democratic party, Daley always prided himself most on his ability to provide the basic needs for the neighborhoods. "It's another resounding call to maintain the status quo," said longtime Daley foe Leon Despres, the alderman representing the city's 5th Ward, home of the progressive Hyde Park neighborhood.

On the surface, it was a bad month for Daley. His reputation as a presidential kingmaker had just taken a major hit. In the U.S. elections a few weeks earlier, Sen. George McGovern was soundly defeated by incumbent Richard Nixon. McGovern carried Chicago by 170,000 votes, but his showing in the city was still disappointing, compared to the turnout for Dems running for the White House in past elections. McGovern only narrowly won Daley's own 11th Ward, with 15,000 votes to 11,000 votes for Nixon. Daley also saw progressive Democrat Dan Walker get elected Illinois' governor, after beating party-endorsed Paul Simon, Daley's hand-picked choice, in the primaries before knocking off incumbent Republican Richard Ogilvie. A capable public servant, Ogilvie fell on his sword, committing political suicide by backing the first state income tax.

Perhaps most significantly, Daley saw Black voters rebel against his political machine and support moderate Republican candidates in two significant races.

In the U.S. Senate, African Americans helped re-elect incumbent Republican Chuck Percy over Democratic machine candidate Roman Pucinski. But, most astoundingly in the Cook County State's Attorney race, Bernard Carey beat Edward Hanrahan, the surly tough guy once seen as a possible successor to Daley before Hanrahan's role in that ill-fated 1969 police raid in which the two Black Panthers were killed. Although Hanrahan and 13 fellow defendants were acquitted earlier in 1972 on charges of obstruction of justice, Black voters had the last word. Eleven of 14 Black wards broke from the machine's script to throw out an incumbent Democrat, an unprecedented event for the era that scarcely was repeated in the ensuing decades.

African American voters were long considered a straight Democratic ticket vote in Chicago, especially under Daley, who worked with Rep. William Dawson, the longtime African American Democratic U.S. Congressman, to turn out the vote on the South Side for the Democratic Party's machine. Critics called the practice "plantation politics." But Hanrahan's campaign outraged Black Chicago, which joined forces with Republicans in the surrounding Cook County suburbs to defeat Hanrahan. Rev. Jackson even showed up at Carey's campaign headquarters on election night.

The rebellion of the decades-long reliable inner-city electorate had been telegraphed the previous March, when former 1930s U.S. Olympic hero Ralph Metcalfe, who succeeded Dawson in Congress, split with Daley on the issue of police brutality. Two Metcalfe friends, both dentists, had been roughed up in traffic stops. Metcalfe launched a campaign of appearances, bringing light to the age-old issue of police brutality that would have worldwide reverberations a half-century later with George Floyd and other Black victims of illegal police behavior, formalized as "Black Lives Matter." Metcalfe unleashed harsh criticism at the "Irish" mayor (Daley) and "Irish" police chief (James Conlisk, named an unindicted co-conspirator in the Hampton case).

"The last of the old-style city political organizations is not dead," wrote the Associated Press' David Goldberg. "But it's declining slowly under the wave of a...more discriminating electorate that refuses blindly to follow orders from the top."

Some national reporters speculated that the turmoil showed Mayor Daley's decline. But on this November week in 1972, Daley was in a good mood. There was one election on Nov. 7 that he continued to celebrate: His son, Richard M. Daley, would win an Illinois Senate seat, in the 23rd District. The younger Daley enjoyed his first win at the polls and the start of his slow rise to power in a

play baseball. Sure, some little kid might come up for my autograph. I still don't want to sign it. What does it mean? People want my autograph so they can show it to someone else and say 'See, I got Dick Allen.' Autographs don't mean anything to black people. I can walk in the ghetto and out of 500 people five might ask for my autograph. A lot of people will want to shake my hand, though, and I'm happy to do that. That means something."

Despite all the controversy, the veteran slugger had an outstanding first half of the 1974 season. Echoing the competitive starts in 1972 and 1973, the White Sox kept pace with Oakland and the young, talented Kansas City Royals. After a slow start, they rebounded in July and had a respectable 49-45 record at the All-Star break, good enough for second place behind the two-time world champion A's. Dick was once again voted as a starter in the All-Star game, after leading the majors in homers during the first half with 26 and ranking second in the AL with 70 RBI.

The All-Star Game was played at Pittsburgh's Three Rivers Stadium, just 30 miles from his mother's home in Wampum. But Dick's image took a beating in what should have been a celebratory homecoming for him. He missed the pregame workout and media sessions and showed up only 42 minutes before game time. When he arrived, he sparred with the press. "I'm a ballplayer, not a politician," Dick told them. "I can't stand around signing autographs and small-talking. I don't have anything to say. Nobody wants to hear me anyway." When reporters asked about the late arrival, Dick said: "I don't know where I was. I took a plane. I was home." The national media's response to his tardiness was harsh. "It must be nice to make $250,000 a year and be bigger than the game that pays you," the *Philadelphia Inquirer's* Frank Dolson wrote.

After the All-Star game, the Sox began a slow drop in the standings. Dick continued to drop hints about retiring from baseball. "It was kind of a mental, emotional thing with him at the time," his brother Hank recalled.

"When he broke his leg, I think that that took a toll on him because he wasn't able to do some of the same things physically on the field. And I'd say from an emotional standpoint, that that took some of the starch out of him. A couple of times, when I talked with him after the games, it didn't seem like he was putting his heart and soul into it, so I asked him one time after he'd struck out and three or four times in a game, I asked him, 'What's the problem? You don't look like yourself. You're going at things half-assed, not putting your heart and soul in it?' He said, 'I'm just tired.'"

When talking to African American reporters, Dick would complain about being used by the baseball system to bring fans into the ballpark. "(I feel like) a potential slave awaiting his turn in the 'meat market,'" he told the *Chicago*

Defender's Tony Blackwell. He told the *Defender's* Norman O. Unger that he was anxious about the White Sox attempting to trade him. "They didn't come right out and say so, but I felt it was coming," Allen said. "Except for the fans which I was bringing into the ballpark each day, I had practically outlived my usefulness."

Dick injured his shoulder in August, then suffered serious pain in his lower back. And by early September, he began missing games, primarily due to that bad back. The team dropped below .500 at this point, and Oakland was running away with the division, on the way to its third straight world championship. Dick then began dropping cryptic hints about an early departure. He had cleaned out his locker at the conclusion of the Sox' homestand on Sept. 1 and paid off the clubhouse attendants, a practice players usually do at the end of the season.

On September 14, Dick met with owner John Allyn at his offices in downtown Chicago. He told the financially-strapped executive about his troubled physical and mental state — it was at a point, the player told the owner, where he was considering walking away from the game. Allyn surprised Dick with a diffident response: "By no means is this slavery. You can go any time you want." That was all Dick Allen needed.

With the White Sox at 72-75 and in fourth place in the AL West, 11½ games behind the A's, Dick arrived at Comiskey Park several hours before an 8 p.m. game against the Angels. He took batting practice, then called his teammates together in the clubhouse. Choking back tears, he told them he was retiring. "This is hard for me to say," he said. "I've never been happier anywhere but here. You're still going to be a good ball club without me. You've got a good manager in this guy." He then pointed to Tanner, standing nearby in the room. Then, Dick broke down in tears and left the Chicago White Sox clubhouse for good. By the time newspapers reporters found out about his actions, the larger-than-life man who had dramatically changed the franchise's fortunes in 1972 was long gone.

"I might not have left if John Allyn had said something different to me," Dick told *Chicago Tribune* baseball writer Richard Dozer years later.

Tanner later admitted that Allen had been periodically talking about retiring during the last few months of the 1974 season. And Melton told the media at the time that Dick was disappointed in the team's production, and that factored into his retirement. "I wasn't shocked," Melton said. "He came over here to win, and we didn't do it. The fact he doesn't foresee winning in the near future is why he retired."

"We were puzzled, but I don't know that anything Dick did totally surprised people, because he was his own man," Jim Kaat would say years later. "He lived in the same (suburban) apartment complex that I did and I know he mentioned he was frustrated. He was leading the league in homers even in the last month of the season. He was having a great year, but the team wasn't, and he had regrets about that."

But outside of his teammates, Dick Allen's retirement was seen as quitting on the team. "Whether from past scars or not, he eventually turned on everyone who was his friend: The Chicago press, players and fans, and eventually his manager," wrote Dave Nightengale of the *Chicago Daily News*. "He became the greatest enigma I've ever known."

"It was like he had let me down as a kid when he when he just decided to walk away," said Scott Rosenbaum, a team batboy and the son of the team's longtime batting practice pitcher, Glen. "This guy is really awesome, and you could tell he was a star, just the way that people were around him, the newspaper guys. You couldn't get a newspaper guy into the clubhouse in 1969 or 1970 and now reporters from everywhere were coming in when Dick was there. It was a completely different feel inside the clubhouse because he was there. And then he just left. It was weird to me as a kid. But I didn't know that he had played hurt for so long and had gone above and beyond, but you don't really see that — you see this guy that quit."

Dick had his last great season in 1974. In only 482 at-bats, he still managed to lead the American League with 32 homers. He also drove in 88 runs with a .301 batting average. He was tops in both slugging percentage (.563) and OPS (.938). The productive season capped off one of the best 10-year stretches of a player in major league history. From 1964 to 1974, his OPS (.940) was second among all players who played in at least 1,000 games during that period. Only Hank Aaron was higher (.941). All the other players in the top 10 of OPS covering '64 to '74 period are in the Hall of Fame. Dick also ranked second to Aaron in slugging percentage (.554) and was in the Top Ten in homers, RBI, batting average, runs scored and walks.

Mr. Allen might have been the greatest enigma to himself. He too rashly pulled the plug on his good thing with the indulgent Sox. By early November, Dick had changed his mind; now he was considering returning to baseball. He intentionally decided not to file his retirement papers with the league — if he had done so, he would have been ineligible to return for 60 playing days.

"Everybody says I'm retired except me," Allen told the Associated Press from his farm in Allentown, Pa. "I'm only retired if they don't want me back. I'm going to play somewhere next year, even if it's Jenkintown, Pa." He said he had given some thought about playing in Japan in 1975. But he added: "If I play ball in the United States, it'll be in Chicago. It's a great sports town."

After the roller-coaster 1974 season, the feeling was no longer mutual. The

White Sox did not want Dick Allen. Tanner, the close family friend who was instrumental in getting him to come to the team, was being perceived in the media as the weak enabler of Dick.

"It was Richie Allen who managed Tanner and not Tanner who managed Allen," Jerome Holtzman would write in the *Sporting News*. "Regardless of what any bleeding hearts might say, it is team discipline that helps win pennants. Discipline is considerably more important than 10 extra Richie Allen home runs."

Although he wouldn't come out directly and say it, Tanner felt burned by Dick's actions during the 1974 season. "Tony Muser is my first baseman," the manager told the *Associated Press*. "If Allen came back, how could we be certain for how long before he might quit again." Hemond agreed. In October, he got a surprise call from Phillies owner Ruly Carpenter, who was looking to bring Dick back to the Phillies in 1975. The two teams worked out a deal to trade him to the Phillies for outfielder Bill Robinson and cash. But Dick vetoed the trade.

At the winter meetings in New Orleans in December 1974, Hemond struggled to find a taker for Dick. "We want equal value for the guy," Hemond would say. "But no one wants to take him. But we've got to do something. We can't let it stay in limbo." Hemond wound up sending Dick to the Atlanta Braves for a mere $5,000 in cash and a player to be named later, a shockingly low amount for the man whom Hemond later credited with saving baseball on the South Side, "We traded Allen because when he failed to formally retire, he violated his contract," Hemond said. "By doing that, he let us down."

The transaction outraged Dick. He called Hemond to say he didn't want to be traded. He then sent this telegram to Braves GM Eddie Robinson: "Received your message. However, at this time, I must decline. Thank you for your interest in me. I wish you continued success." Echoing Curt Flood's refusal to be traded from the Phillies to the Cardinals five years earlier, Dick Allen was now challenging baseball's century-old reserve clause which still held each player in perpetuity to the team that "owned" him.

Now it was the Braves' turn to try to find a taker for this hard-to-understand character. Again, only the Phillies were interested. A key figure from Dick's career surfaced to move the arrow back to his baseball roots. He met with John Ogden, the man who scouted him for the Phillies 15 years earlier, along with former Phillies great Richie Ashburn and some of the young Phillies, including future Hall of Famer Mike Schmidt, who would form the team's pennant-contending squads of the late 1970s. Dick finally agreed to a trade from the Braves to the Phillies, with catcher Johnny Oates, in exchange for minor leaguers Jim Essian, Barry Bonnell and $150,000.

Dick spent the next two years with the Phillies. But Chicago remained a fond subject for him. He returned to the city in June 1975, when the Phillies made their first trip of the season to Wrigley Field. There, he met with the *Chicago Tribune's* Robert Markus. "I don't always understand [Allen], but I find him honest, if contradictory, and I like him," Markus wrote.

"The thing that bothers me the most about my three years in Chicago is that we cheated the fans, and they don't deserve that," Dick told Markus. "The team just seemed to be getting farther and farther away from being a winner. When I came here I said we could win within three years. That first year we were only 2½ games out of first with two weeks to play. The next year it was 10 games out and then 15. We got worse every year."

He also took the time to criticize his old friend, Chuck Tanner: "You may remember that when I came to Chicago there was some doubt on my part as to whether I wanted to come. But I decided to come as a favor to Tanner. When I came, Tanner said I'd always have a job with the Sox. Then they traded me." Dick conveniently omitted the fact that he had quit first.

Dick posted decent, but noticeably declining, numbers with the Phillies in a part-time role in 1975: 12 homers, 62 RBI but a career low .233 batting average. He would rebound in 1976 slightly, hitting 15 homers, driving in 49 runs, batting .268 and sporting an impressive .826 slugging percentage in another part-time role for the NL East division winners.

But Dick's stay in Philadelphia would again come to an end after a controversial incident where he celebrated the division-clinching game for the Phillies in Montreal with a group of Black players and Mike Schmidt separately in the clubhouse from the rest of the team. This incident came after Allen threatened to boycott the playoffs if his longtime Phillies friend, Tony Taylor, was left off the postseason roster. An apparent rift was exacerbated between White and Black players on the Phillies. Once again, Dick was in the center of a Philadelphia controversy with race as the primary point. After the Phillies were swept by the Reds in the National League playoffs, Dick left the team as a free agent.

His last year in the majors was 1977, when he had the one-time opportunity to become a free agent, under the terms of the new, game-changing Collective Bargaining Agreement that the owners very reluctantly agreed to adopt. Dick's problem was that teams were shying away from him. New Cubs manager Herman Franks, who witnessed the peak Dick Allen while with the Giants in the mid-1960s, wanted him for the North Side. But management, led by owner P.K. Wrigley and GM Bob Kennedy, refused to consider him.

"I've always liked the guy," Franks told *Chicago Tribune* columnist Rick Talley. "I brought up (his) name at the club meetings last month but got pretty much a negative reaction. Everybody wants to know what made me think I could handle Allen when nobody else could."

It was likely the Cubs weren't going to sign a controversial player after trading two-time batting champion Bill Madlock, who had desired a $1 million contract spread across three years. Subtle racial overtones hovered over the Madlock deal, so Dick was also kryptonite to the Cubs.

Eventually, another Chicagoan would take on the previously-shunned free agent — one who was as controversial as the brilliant slugger. Finley, whose Dynasty A's of 1972-73-74 had been decimated due to trades and free agency, took a chance on the wandering native of Wampum, Pennsylvania. Finley was an innovator, the man who introduced colored shoes and brightly colored green-and-gold uniforms to baseball and encouraged his players to grow facial hair. Like John Allyn, this owner was being priced out of the game due to increasing salaries of players with the onset of free agency. By 1977, only pitcher Vida Blue remained from those great teams. Dick's decreasing value made him a bargain buy for Finley. He would end up paying just $150,000 for one year.

Dick's last season in Oakland would start well — the A's were above .500 and he was hitting .303 with four homers and 23 RBI at the start of May. But the shoulder and back pain that persisted during his last year in Chicago flared up again in Oakland. The average and power dropped by early June.

Perhaps it was appropriate — it certainly was ironic — that Dick Allen's career came to an end at Comiskey Park in 1977. The A's traveled to the South Side June 18-20 for a four-game series against the White Sox, resurgent under owner Bill Veeck. The "South Side Hit Men," who were in first place when the series started, won the first three games. During the fourth contest on a Monday night, Dick did not play. He was frustrated by his health and falling batting average. He was also being heckled by Sox fans near the visitors dugout.

"Some guy called me a bastard by the dugout that night in Chicago," Dick recalled. "Maybe I took it too personal. Later, (Manager Bobby) Winkles asked if I wanted to hit. We were ahead by a bunch of runs and I said no. I didn't really want to, but I would. When he didn't use me, I thought it was OK to take my shower early."

Chicago was still Finley's hometown. He decided to make an unannounced visit to the clubhouse during the game, caught his new player in the shower and immediately suspended him for a week without pay. Dick then stayed away *another week* after the suspension was lifted, before calling Finley to ask that his lost pay be reinstated. When that was refused, he jumped ship. So his last game in the majors turned out to be June 19, 1977 at the erstwhile South Side Baseball Palace of the World that he helped save only five years earlier.

But Dick never officially retired. There was no interest among any major league teams by spring training 1978, so he turned up without advance notice to the A's camp in Mesa for one last, sad attempt to make a major-league roster. The team indulged Dick slightly but did not take him seriously. He didn't have an assigned locker and was given a second-hand pair of pants.

But the man did again get to wear his custom jersey from 1977: The green-and-gold A's pullover with his hometown name of "Wampum" on the back along with the number 60, to commemorate his year of graduation before high school.

After his final departure, the nickname was removed and the jersey re-used. The stitch-mark outline of "Wampum" was still visible behind a different player's name.

During spring training, Dick had a chance to chat with Richard Dozer, who reported that Chicago remained on his mind. "That was the biggest mistake of my life," he said to Dozer about walking away from the Sox. Then Dozer wrote:

> *Allen turned inquisitive about the Cubs and Sox.*
>
> *"There's no place I'd rather end my career than in Chicago. Who've they got over there?"*
>
> *Informed that Bill Buckner, Larry Biittner and Dave Kingman gave the Cubs all the first-base protection they would need — and more — Allen wondered about the Sox. Their stock of first-sackers is just as deep: Lamar Johnson, Rob Blomberg, Reggie Sanders and Frank Ortenzio.*
>
> *"Would it be tampering if I talked to them?" Allen asked.*

Richard Anthony Allen's brilliant major league career officially came to an end two weeks later, as the A's cut him. "Baseball quit on me, I didn't quit on baseball," he would later say in his biography.

> ### "I maybe could have played longer and made more money if I was someone else, but Momma didn't raise no Uncle Tom. She wouldn't have been proud if I wasn't me."
> – *Dick Allen, before an Old-Timers Game at Comiskey Park - July 1987*

Dick Allen would be employed by the White Sox one more time. In late 1985, when Ken "Hawk" Harrelson was promoted from the broadcast booth to the general manager's position for the Sox, Dick was one of Harrelson's initial hires.

He signed a two-year contract to be a $40,000-a-year roving minor league instructor. After 12 years, Allen was back in Sarasota, once again wearing No 15 for Chicago's American League team, albeit in the newer White Sox uniform with the block "Sox" lettering across the chest on a navy-blue stripe. "Hitting is just a part of Allen's job," Harrelson told the media. "He can teach base running. And he can teach these kids how to think, how to play the game."

By this time, Dick's primary interest was his stable of horses. He joined brothers Hank and Ron to establish the Allen Racing Stable in Southern California, where they had about 30 horses. Hank was trainer and Ron was foreman. "I just help around, doing what I can, hot-walk, rub, whatever has to be done," Dick told Jerome Holtzman on a spring morning.

Dick had earlier dabbled in the game he loved, joining the Texas Rangers briefly in 1982 as a spring training hitting instructor. But his role with the White Sox would involve him working through the season, touring their minor league teams in Buffalo, Birmingham and Appleton, Wis.

Chuck Tanner's son, Bruce, was a pitcher for Triple-A Buffalo in 1986 and fondly remembers Dick's visits. "He'd come to see me and my roommate, Russ Morman, at our hotel in Buffalo," Bruce Tanner recalled. "I swear, he talked for an hour-and-a-half about baseball. And it was just when he left, we looked at each other, like that is one of the greatest things we've ever heard in our lives." Bruce Tanner said Dick was a big proponent of the game of "pepper," where one player hits brisk grounders and line drives to a group of fielders standing 20 feet away. "That's a game that they don't play anymore, but he just wanted to see the bat hit the ball."

The Dick Allen Sox return was short-lived. Hawk Harrelson was fired as GM after the 1986 season — moves such as dismissing longtime manager Tony LaRussa and assistant GM Dave Dombroski backfired on him. When Harrelson was dismissed, his hires, including Allen, were let go as well. Eventually, Hawk's colorful broadcasting style would make him a decades-long fixture on television for the White Sox after he returned in 1990, following a three-year absence. Harrelson was a worthy successor to the man he replaced in the booth, Harry Caray. Hawk eventually made it to Cooperstown in 2021 as a Ford C. Frick Award winner.

Dick Allen returned to old Comiskey Park one last time before the Baseball Palace was torn down. Back for an Old-Timers game in July 1987, he returned to his old clubhouse, dressed in a sharp blue suit and still looking as if he could play professionally. "This is the best town to play in," he said, as he dressed in yet another re-design of the Chicago White Sox uniform: The more conservative, script-oriented 1987 incarnation. "That one year here, 1972, was the most fun I've ever had in baseball."

Dick provided his own epitaph for his career before he stepped out on the field that summer day, "I loved the game itself," he told *Chicago Tribune* columnist Bob Verdi. "If it had been just the games, that would have been fine. But all the other stuff, I had it with that. Labels. Once you get a label in this game, it sticks like glue, especially if your skin is black. And I had the label of a bad boy. Was I too good a ballplayer to play with so many teams? Well, I like to think I could play a little."

He then proceeded to take the field for the American League Old-Timers. Batting fourth that day, he was for that moment the old Dick Allen — hitting a bullet of a line drive to National Leaguer Dick Groat, before leaving Comiskey and Chicago one last time.

The old park was torn down after the 1990 season. And, during that last season, Dick's old teammate, Bart Johnson, was touring the Sox clubhouse. Johnson, by then a scout for the White Sox, had gone to one of the back rooms of the clubhouse, where he made an amazing discovery.

"He was in the back of the equipment room under the stands, and, in an old cupboard back there, he found Dick Allen's Most Valuable Player award," recalled Glen Rosenbaum, who was about to go out and pitch batting practice. "Dick didn't even take it."

Dick later said, "I've never taken that trophy home from the clubhouse. Every player on that team that year was a piece of that trophy. That's why I left it in the clubhouse. Like the biggest thrill I had was when Chuck Tanner got Manager of the Year in 1972, that meant more to me than winning anything. Much more than me winning the Most Valuable Player award that season." Those thoughts were expressed in *The Batter Pitchers Hate to Face*, an article by Larry Johnson in the October 1974 issue of *Baseball Digest*.

The Sox shipped the award to its rightful owner. "Not that I didn't want it," Dick would say after receiving it. "It's that we all had a part of it that season."

The MVP trophy and Rookie of The Year award are now safely in the hands of his son, Doobie.

Separate from those major awards, *Baseball Digest* selected Dick as their 1972 Player of the Year, and quoted him after that honor, "I've had everything from baseball except the joy of playing on a winner."

It was an epitaph, in a way, for the personal effort by Dick Allen in carrying the White Sox back to respectability, contention and profitability. He was the best day-in, day-out player in the American League in 1972 — on the field and on the bottom line.

Clubhouse attendant Jim O'Keefe (left) holds Dick Allen's 1972 American League MVP award during a pre-game ceremony on May 4, 1973 in front of a full house at Comiskey Park. O'Keefe prepared the chili that Allen (center) spilled on his uniform before he hurriedly changed and belted the most famous White Sox homer of 1972. The Chicago Sun-Times' Edgar Munzel (right), the city's senior baseball writer in 1973, addresses the crowd.

Photo credit: personal collection of Jim O'Keefe

Dick Allen acknowledges the cheers of a Friday night Comiskey Park crowd in May 1973 after accepting the MVP trophy for his outstanding 1972 season.

Photo credit: Johnny Reyes

The Return of Dick Allen and the Team That Saved Our Sox.

CHICAGO BASEBALL MUSEUM

JUNE 24-25 2012

U.S. CELLULAR FIELD

1972 MVP

Dick Allen Tribute on June 26, 2012.
Artwork by Grant Smith, Grant9Smith.com

Jim Geddes, pitcher. Now 72 years old and living in Naples, Fla., Geddes pitched in five games with one start in 1972. He followed that with six games, including one start, in 1973.

Rich "Goose" Gossage, pitcher. He posted a 7-1 record in 1972, his rookie season. Three years later, Goose led the American League in saves (26) for the first of three times in his career. Gossage is still known as Rick to family and friends. A member of the 2008 Hall of Fame class, he resides in Colorado Springs, Colo., promotes youth sports and speaks all over the country.

Roland Hemond, player personnel director. In little more than two seasons at the controls, he turned the White Sox inside out and was named Executive of the Year in 1972. He spent 16 years in the Sox front office. The 92-year-old resided in Colorado after finally retiring from baseball in 2019 until he died in his sleep December 12, 2021.

Ed Herrmann, catcher. In five consecutive seasons (1970-74) with the team, Herrmann reached double figures in home runs. In 1972, he gunned down a league-high 50 percent of would-be base-stealers. The former Kansas City Royals scout remained active in youth baseball in the San Diego area until his death in 2014.

Stu Holcomb, general manager. Known best for his work as Purdue University football coach and Northwestern athletic director. He was general manager of the ill-fated Chicago Mustangs soccer team before replacing Ed Short in the White Sox front office. Holcomb died at 66 on Jan. 11, 1977.

Bart Johnson, pitcher. His athletic talent was such that UCLA head coach John Wooden recruited him to play basketball. After a solid 1971 campaign, the right-hander sustained a knee injury in a basketball game and was limited to nine appearances in the next season. Johnson spent 30 years in the White Sox organization — 12 as a player and 18 as a scout. He died in 2020 from complications of Parkinson Disease.

Jay Johnstone, outfielder. In 1970, he was acquired with Bradley and Egan from the Angels in a deal that helped turn the Sox around. Johnstone had a 20-year major-league career, including three seasons (1982-84) with the Cubs. He owns two World Series rings – one with the Yankees and one with the Los Angeles Dodgers. He died in 2020 due to complications from COVID-19.

Steve Kealey, pitcher. He and Bart Johnson were teammates at Torrance (Calif.) High School, which produced several major league players. Kealey's three-run homer against the Minnesota Twins on Labor Day 1971 was the only one by a White Sox pitcher in 25 years. The 75-year-old resides in Abilene, Kan.

Bud Kelly, television announcer. The former disc jockey and Comiskey Park PA announcer spent two seasons (1971-72) with Drees in the TV booth. He also filled in on Blackhawks telecasts for two years. Kelly last worked for KLIV radio in San Jose, Calif. before his retirement in 2008 after 60 years on the air. He resides in Arizona.

Pat Kelly, outfielder. The fleet right fielder set the wheels in motion in 1972 with 32 stolen bases, which ranked fourth in the American League. Kelly later served as an ordained minister in Maryland. He passed away on Oct. 2, 2005, at 61. His brother was Leroy Kelly, the former Cleveland Browns halfback and Pro Football Hall of Fame member.

Dave Lemonds, pitcher. He's the answer to this trivia question: In 1972, which White Sox pitcher was the fourth starter in their three-man rotation? The Cubs selected the left-hander first in the 1968 draft, one spot ahead of Johnson, his future teammate. Lemonds was one of three 1969 Cubs, along with reliever Phil Regan and outfielder Jimmy Qualls, on the 1972 Sox. Arm problems cut short his career. The Matthews, N.C., resident is 74.

Joe Lonnett, third-base coach. In 15 seasons, the former catcher was manager Chuck Tanner's first lieutenant with the White Sox, Oakland Athletics and Pittsburgh Pirates. World War II and Korean War veteran Lonnett died at 84 on Dec. 5, 2011.

Jim Lyttle, outfielder. A longtime backup outfielder, the left-handed hitter batted .232 in 84 at-bats in 1972, his only season with the White Sox. Lyttle played on four teams in his eight-year MLB career. He is 75 years old and lives in Boca Raton, Fla.

Carlos May, outfield. The 1972 season was the best of his nine with the club: .308 batting average, 23 stolen bases. Believed to be the only player to wear his birthday (May 17) on the back of his uniform. Now, the 73-year-old serves as a White Sox community relations representative. Resides in Matteson, Ill.

Bill Melton, third baseman. On the heels of consecutive 33-home run seasons, Melton sustained a herniated disc in 1972 and was never quite the same. Melton remains in the game as a studio analyst on White Sox telecasts and with community work for the organization. He is 76 years old and lives in Phoenix, Ariz.

Jim Mahoney, coach. A former major-league shortstop, Mahoney joined Chuck Tanner's coaching staff in 1972 and remained with the Sox through the 1976 season. He is now 87 and lives in Hawthorne, N.J.

Al Monchak, first base coach. In 1940, Monchak played briefly with the Philadelphia Phillies before World War II interrupted his career. He was deployed to the 11ᵗʰ Armored Division and fought under Gen. George Patton in the Battle of the Bulge. As a manager, he guided four minor-league teams to championships. Like Joe Lonnett, he followed Tanner to Oakland and Pittsburgh. Also, Atlanta later in his career. Monchak died at 98 on Sept. 12, 2015.

Rich Morales, shortstop. Nine years after the White Sox signed him as a free agent immediately following his graduation from Westmore High School in Daly, Calif. in 1963, Morales had a career-high 71 starts at the unsettled shortstop position in 1972. He went on to become a manager in the Cubs farm system, among others. The 78-year-old makes his home in Pacifica, Calif.

Tony Muser, first base. Recalled midway through the 1972 season, he was primarily a defensive replacement in late innings. Yet he hit a respectable .279 in 61 AB. He was an effective pinch hitter in 1972, batting .333 in 12 appearances during August and September 1972. Muser was the Kansas City Royals manager for four full seasons and parts of two others, after serving as a Cubs coach. Currently, the 74-year-old is a roving instructor in the San Diego Padres organization. He lives in Los Alamitos, Calif.

Dan Neumeier, pitcher. Neumeier pitched in three games in relief and posted no record during three innings of work. Now age 73, he lives in Lodi, Wis.

Jim O'Keefe, clubhouse attendant. The "chef" who made the chili with which Dick Allen garnished his hot dog and spilled on his jersey before slugging the most famous White Sox homer of 1972. Bridgeport resident O'Keefe was a clubhouse attendant from 1971-75, getting a close-up view of the entire Allen era. He stayed in contact with some of his co-workers and a few players. He gave up his cooking duties to spend 42 years with United Airlines, retiring as an IT principal engineer in June 2020. Now 67, O'Keefe lives in southwest suburban Woodridge, Ill. with wife Jeanine and Brandi, their Maltipoo dog.

Dennis O'Toole, pitcher. The ultimate cup-of-coffee player, O'Toole spread his 15 major league appearances (three in 1972), all in relief, over five seasons from 1969-1973. The Chicago native was the brother of the late Jim O'Toole, a top lefty starter and All-Star for the Cincinnati Reds in the early 1960s. Dennis O'Toole, 72, lives in suburban Des Plaines, Ill.

Jorge Orta, shortstop. Purchased from the Mexican League after the 1971 season, the 21-year-old made his major league debut five months later. A converted second baseman, Orta totaled 1,002 hits in nine seasons with the team. He later moved back to second for a number of productive seasons with the Sox. He was a member of the 1985 Royals team that won the World Series in seven games. At 71, Orta makes his home in Phoenix.

Jimmy Qualls, outfielder. He was a spare outfielder starting the season, appearing in just 11 games with 10 at-bats (no-hits) before being released, ending his big-league career. Qualls' claim to fame was breaking up Tom Seaver's perfect game with one out in the ninth at Shea Stadium as a Cub in 1969. Now living in Suter, Ill. the 75-year-old Qualls had worked a small farm while also unloading barges on the Mississippi River.

Phil Regan, relief pitcher. At 84, "The Vulture" was still coaching in the Mets organization in 2021, while making his home in Florida after a long residency in his native Grand Rapids, Michigan. Regan had a stint as pitching coach of the Mets' parent club as an octogenarian in 2019. Like Qualls, Regan ended his big-league career with his brief South Side stint. Ever cagey, he still won't confirm he applied Vaseline to the baseball during his prime as a closer with the Dodgers and Cubs.

Rick Reichardt, outfielder. A left fielder by trade, he split time with Johnstone in center field. In 1964, the University of Wisconsin two-sport star touched off a bidding war that resulted in a then-record $200,000 bonus and the establishment of the amateur draft a short time later. The 79-year-old is a part-time financial planner in Gainesville, Fla.

Lee "Bee Bee" Richard, infielder. The White Sox' first-round pick in the June 1970 draft, Richard was athletically gifted but fundamentally shaky. He was tried as the regular shortstop in 1971 but lost the job to Luis Alvarado and Rich Morales in 1972, playing in just 11 games that season. Richard resurfaced as a Sox backup in 141 games from 1974-76. He is now 73.

Jim Riley, bat boy. In his first of four seasons with the team, the Loras College graduate had a regular position near the home team bullpen down the left field line. Now 65, Riley resides with his wife and two children in northwest suburban Elk Grove Village, Ill., where he is a Zurich Financial account executive.

Vicente Romo, pitcher. Widely regarded as the greatest pitcher in Mexican League history, the reliever was acquired with Muser from the Boston Red Sox before the 1971 season when the Sox traded catcher Duane Josephson and Pitcher Danny Murphy. Romo played for five teams in eight years. In 1972, he was 3-0 and had a 3.31 ERA in 51⅔ innings pitched. His older brother, Enrique, was also a major league pitcher. He is 79 years old, and he lives in Cerritos, Calif.

Glen Rosenbaum, batting practice pitcher. An accomplished minor league pitcher, he compiled a 95-45 record in 11 seasons in the White Sox farm system. In all, Rosenbaum spent five decades with the organization, including stints as a coach and longtime traveling secretary. The retired 86-year-old still lives in his native Union Mills, Ind.

Johnny Sain, pitching coach. The outspoken Arkansan was a rarity: An accomplished pitcher who went on to become an equally successful instructor. He also liked to brag that he was one of the first major leaguers to get hair transplants. Sain coached nine 20-game winners (including White Sox pitchers Wood four times, Kaat two times and Bahnsen one time) and was with five pennant-winning teams. A four-time 20-game winner himself, he totaled 139 victories despite a three-year Navy stint in World War II. Sain died at 89 on Nov. 7, 2006.

Ed Spiezio, third base. The Joliet native filled in for Melton in the last three months of the 1972 season, after which he retired at age 30. A member of the 1964 and 1967 St. Louis Cardinals world championship teams, Spiezio later hit the first homer in San Diego Padres history. The Lewis University product lives in Morris, Ill. His son, Scott, also played in the major leagues. He turned 80 in October 2021.

Chuck Tanner, manager. His unbridled optimism and infectious enthusiasm played no small role in the Sox' success and his American League Manager of the Year selection. The ex-outfielder also had managerial stints with the Athletics, Pittsburgh Pirates and Atlanta Braves, and his 1979 Pirates team won the World Series in seven games. He passed away at 82 on Feb. 11, 2011.

Walt Williams, outfield. Known as "No-Neck" because of his short, compact build, the popular reserve filled in for Kelly against some southpaw starters. He was traded to the Cleveland Indians shortly after the 1972 season. Until his death in 2016, Williams lived in Brownsville, Texas, where he was director of a youth recreational center.

Wilbur Wood, pitcher. On the strength of 24 victories and 376⅔ innings pitched, the southpaw finished second for the Cy Young Award and seventh in the Most Valuable Player voting in 1972. The *Sporting News* feted him as the AL Pitcher of the Year in 1972. In July 1973, the Hoyt Wilhelm disciple started both games of a doubleheader against the Yankees in New York. Now 80, the former pharmaceutical sales representative resides in suburban Boston.

The 1972 team reunion on June 24, 2012 brought back Hank and Dick Allen, Bill Melton, Ed Spezio, Bart Johnson, Goose Gossage, Tom Bradley and Roland Hemond; 1972 MVP Allen throws a perfect strike to home plate.

Photo credit: Mike Gustafson, Owner Gustafson Photography
MikeGustafsonPhotography.com

EPILOGUE

Dick Allen, Chili Dog MVP

In Chicago, Dick Allen's career was reborn and so were the White Sox, Allen's fourth team in four years. He knew that he was expected to carry the Sox on his back in 1972, and the man was better than advertised.

Initially, Allen expressed doubts about playing for the South Siders, as he was unsure that he wanted to continue to play baseball after being shuffled around from Philadelphia to St. Louis to Los Angeles and now Chicago.

Because Sox manager Chuck Tanner had known Dick and his brothers since they were kids growing up in coal country outside Pittsburgh, he knew all about Dick's remarkable talent and old-school desire to win. Tanner's handling of Allen made his time in Chicago successful. Dick's numbers in his first year at old Comiskey Park bear repeating: A league-leading 37 homers, a career-high 113 RBI and 99 walks, earning that 1972 MVP award. He led the league in batting average going into September, but finished third, barely missing the Triple Crown.

"It was the best time of my baseball career," Allen said of his three seasons in Chicago, a recurring theme he would express the rest of this life, including his final interview in late November 2020 with the *Chicago Tribune's* Paul Sullivan.

In contrast to Philadelphia, Allen was, for a time, beloved in Chicago. When he stepped to the plate, legendary organist Nancy Faust's invented "walk-up" music of "Jesus Christ Superstar," ignited the fans into a frenzy. Famed movie critic Richard Roeper, who wrote the book *Sox and the City* following the White Sox World Series crown in 2005, was 12 when Allen came to the White Sox. He fell in love, writing later: "Dick Allen was Fonzie before anyone heard of Fonzie. He was that cool, mysterious, slightly dangerous loner, who had a unique style without ever once appearing as if he were trying to affect a style."

In 1972, Allen became somewhat of a "co-manager" with Tanner, acting as a veteran who wanted to impart his knowledge of the game to the younger players.

"He was the leader of the team," Tanner said in 2005. "He taught the kids how to play the game. They loved him, they listened to him. He was the best player I ever had and he should be in the Hall of Fame. I can't say enough about the things he did for me and for the team. He understood the game and the way it's supposed to be played."

After the 1972 season, Dick Allen became baseball's highest-paid player at $225,000 a year in a three-year deal. He had also helped Harry Caray rebuild his own popularity with a team more people wanted to hear about.

In contrast to the experience in Philadelphia, during his three-year stint in Chicago, Dick also earned admiration from some sportswriters steeped in old-school baseball ways. Jerome Holtzman was the dean of Chicago baseball writers and later Major League Baseball's first official historian who covered Dick in his Sox days. He proclaimed in 1992 that "Allen…is a member of baseball's royal family, one of the great sluggers of his time, perhaps of all time."

In 1973, Dick was on track to repeat as MVP. He started out batting .316/.394/.612. But the broken leg suffered in that collision at first base in Anaheim kept him out of all but just three more games that year. At the time of his injury, the Sox were one game out of first with a 37-32 record. Without Allen, the Sox tumbled to 77-85 and finished fifth in the AL West.

In September 1973, a *Sports Illustrated* article featured Dick in a lengthy piece entitled "Swinging In His Own Groove: When Dick Allen Crashed, So Did the White Sox, Which Tells A Lot About This Talented Eccentric Who Says Only His Image Has Changed." The feature deftly captured Dick's persona, what he meant to the White Sox and what coming to Chicago meant for him:

> *"Allen is the first black man, and indeed the only contemporary man of any color, to assert himself in baseball with something like the unaccommodating force of Muhammad Ali in boxing, Kareem Abdul-Jabbar in basketball and Jim Brown in football. He is perhaps the best all-round player in the game today; he is certainly the most independent and highest paid."*

In 1974, Dick put up numbers that placed him in contention to win another MVP award. Playing with back, shoulder and ankle injuries and feuding with new teammate Ron Santo made for unpleasant times.

When he left the team with two weeks remaining in the '74 season, the Sox were mired in fifth place, 11 games back at 72-75. Dick had not played since September 8. Yet, in just 128 games, he clubbed 32 homers, which was enough to win the American League home run crown for the second time in three years.

Dick left Chicago and retreated to his horse farm in Perkasie, Penn. to recover from his various injuries. He rejected a $2 million offer to play baseball in Japan as he contemplated a career as a horse racing entrepreneur. His attempt to get back with the White Sox for the 1975 season was as doomed as it was surprising.

Convinced that the racial climate had changed in Philadelphia, Allen was lured by future Hall of Famer Mike Schmidt and Dave Cash to come out of re-tirement and rejoin the Phillies. At the time, the Braves owned the rights to him since the Sox had sold his contract to Atlanta, and he never formally filed his retirement papers. Baseball Commissioner Bowie Kuhn began to investigate the Phillies for tampering. On May 7, 1975, they completed a trade with Atlanta for the right to re-sign Dick, who agreed to a $225,000 contract.

On May 14, 1975, 30,908 fans came to Veterans Stadium to see the prodigal son's return. He was given a standing ovation when he stepped into the batter's box in a Phillies uniform for the first time since the final game of the 1969 sea-son. Dick lined a two-out single to center, prompting another standing ovation.

The veteran slugger helped the Phillies win the NL East title in 1976, but suffered two injuries that cost him two months of playing time. He did make his only postseason appearance as the Phillies were swept three-in-a-row by the Big Red Machine in the National League Championship Series.

The End

Dick was told he would not be asked to return to the Phillies in 1977, but he felt there was still some baseball left in his body.

He was approached by White Sox owner Bill Veeck, who was looking for a new manager to replace one-year stopgap Paul Richards. Veeck offered a play-er-manager role with the Sox — but Dick turned it down, believing it was a gimmick. Veeck hired Bob Lemon for the job. During spring training on March 16, 1977, Charlie Finley signed Dick for the Oakland Athletics, but he feuded with Finley, who had promised him he would not be a DH.

So, following that June game, the second contest of a doubleheader in Chica-go, the city where he had enjoyed his greatest success, Dick Allen again walked away from baseball. He had played only 54 games with the A's. In his final at-bat, as a pinch-hitter, he struck out. How fitting that final at-bat was at Comiskey Park.

In 1979, Tanner unsuccessfully tried to lure him out of retirement to join the "We Are Family" Pirates. There was also that one-season (1986) stint as a White Sox roving minor league instructor and the even briefer time with the Texas Rangers.

The Retirement Years

Dick Allen's life after baseball was a Shakespearean tragedy, as his retirement years were challenging. He made income from appearances at card shows and sales on his website.

In 1979, a destructive electrical fire engulfed Dick's Perkasie, Penn. home and destroyed his horse stables. He had not insured the property and lost everything.

He turned over his MLB pension to his first wife, Barbara, after their divorce in 1981. Barbara Allen raised their three children, who all went to college.

The legend had become more of a ghost with virtually no connection to baseball, and what he did between the white lines was becoming more and more obscured by the passage of time. The enigmatic Mr. Allen was a mysterious figure who had rocketed through the big leagues, but wandered from port to port, never really finding a home — except possibly his three years in Chicago.

He worked at a few racetracks and tried to scratch out a living while waiting for a baseball job to turn up.

"I was running away from things for years," said Dick, who grew content with a life of seclusion and admitted he had become edgier and hurt about the racial abuse he suffered in his career.

He likened his life to "one of those always-singing, cheerful darkies on a plantation. Everyone thought we were happy, but they really had a time bomb in their hands and murder in their hearts."

His life had turned into a baseball version of a fading, broken down movie star who was once the matinee idol — in this case, one with enough talent to be another Babe Ruth with his tape-measure home runs. "Dick Allen's the strongest, most dangerous hitter I've ever seen," remarked future Hall of Fame pitcher Tom Seaver.

Dick Allen had become a modern-day Prospero, the complex and contradictory sorcerer character in Shakespeare's "The Tempest," with all the swirling conflicts and turmoil in his life.

While suffering through a long period of loneliness and hurt, things began to slowly turn around for the man. In 1987, he married his second wife, Willa King, who had grown up in East St. Louis and met Dick when he was with the Cardinals in 1970.

He began to play in some Old Timer's Games, including the one at Comiskey Park in 1987, where the 45-year-old White Sox legend, still lean and chiseled, confessed he was upset about being fired by the White Sox after the 1986 season.

In 1989, he published an autobiography *Crash: The Life and Times of Dick Allen*, in which he referred to himself in the third person as simply "The Ballplayer."

But the worst part of this self-imposed isolation from baseball was the loss of his first-born child, daughter Terri, who was murdered at age 27 by an ex-boyfriend in May 1991.

Dick kept his pain about Terri's tragic death to himself. Very few people in the baseball community were aware that their former colleague's daughter had been killed, including ex-teammate Goose Gossage, who was shocked when he finally learned about it nearly 24 years later.

In July 2004, Dick was recognized by the Baseball Reliquary, a quirky off-shoot of the Baseball Hall of Fame, to become inducted into The Shrine of the Eternals. Dick, Willa, son Doobie and grandson Tre traveled to Pasadena, Calif. for the ceremony. He was honored alongside Lester Rodney, the former sports-writer for the communist *Daily Worker* newspaper, and one of only two men still alive who was in the press box when Jackie Robinson broke the color barri-er. Older, distinguished and dressed to the nines, Dick asked everyone to stand and then shake hands and introduce one another, just like they did in his Baptist church back home in Chewton, the village outside Wampum. His speech talked about Little Rock and other trying experiences in his life and how family and faith helped overcome such challenges.

The road less traveled to Cooperstown

Wampum, Pa. to Cooperstown, N.Y. is 428 miles, a 6½-hour trip by car. But for 66-year-old Dick Allen, the journey seemed to have taken an eternity and the destination might as well have been a million miles away.

For decades, Dick had seen his contemporaries — Hank Aaron, Willie Mays, Sandy Koufax, Bob Gibson, Frank Robinson, and Roberto Clemente, among others — gain entrance to the Hall of Fame. Yet for 11 years, from 1964–1974, Allen's 165 OPS+ adjusted (On-Base Percentage plus Slugging Percentage, ad-justed for the era and the ballpark) was better than that of *any other MLB player*.

Despite being the highest-paid major leaguer during the early '70s and put-ting up career numbers that equaled or surpassed his contemporaries of the pitching-dominated era, Dick was not even close to gaining entrance to the one place that could finally validate his 15-year MLB career.

Through the years, Allen carried a very private pain, feeling that he had not gotten the recognition he felt he deserved.

Allen honored on 40th anniversary of '72 season

Dick Allen was responsible for a turnaround at a crucial time in the Sox fran-chise history and cemented the Sox' standing in town after they almost moved to Milwaukee three years earlier.

After his retirement as a player in 1977, Allen had been a reluctant hero. His last public appearance in Chicago took place at SoxFest prior to the 2000 season.

For several years, Dr. David Fletcher had asked Dick to step forward and be recognized for his many contributions to the franchise and the city. In 2012, the shy, reserved man agreed to accept an invitation to be honored.

The White Sox finally paid tribute to Dick over two days at U.S. Cellular Field. He threw out the ceremonial first pitch prior to the game against the Milwaukee Brewers on Sunday, June 24. One night later, Hemond, Allen and several former teammates, including Gossage, were honored at the Stadium Club.

In 2012, the White Sox wore replicas (sans the classic zipper as opposed to buttons at the front of the uniform) of the same 1972 red pinstriped uniforms for every Sunday home game.

Nearly 38 years had passed since Dick disappeared into the twilight one September evening. He acknowledged that quitting the Sox so abruptly was the "greatest mistake of my life."

On the city's streets, he was treated like a rock star. The-70-year-old Allen was recognized instantly with his trademark aviator-style glasses. Large numbers of fans came and gave him high fives and hugs. He made many media appearances and ended up on the front page of the *Chicago Sun-Times* with the headline "Sox Savior Returns."

The return to Chicago generated national exposure, and Dick was amazed by the size of the media contingent who showed up at his press conference — much larger than the cozy group of writers and radio reporters who covered his often-contentious Sox tenure from 1972-74. "Look what we have here," he said. "This is more than we drew in Philly."

Jeff Szynal, the Sox' senior scoreboard operator and unofficial historian, put together a memorabilia locker display that included his game-worn uniform along with a large blow-up of the iconic 1972 *Sports Illustrated* cover of Dick juggling those baseballs while that cigarette dangled from his mouth. The locker also included a set of '72 American League Championship Series Sox tickets the team printed in vain.

"If we had had Melton, we would have had a chance to turn those [unused playoff] tickets into reality," Dick said, wistfully.

The returning slugger did a half-hour live interview with David Kaplan on Comcast Sports Chicago. Kaplan was very excited that he got a chance to sit down with Dick, telling him he was a vendor at Comiskey Park in 1972. Kaplan had to call his ophthalmologist brother to surprise him with a chance to talk to Dick, who was the elder Kaplan's favorite player.

ME-TV's Kenny McReynolds, the sportscaster who had idolized Dick as a youth, also had him on his weekly sports talk show, as the media tour continued.

Dick Allen was clearly still the team leader, 40 years later. Riding on the team buses from the Palmer House to the ballpark for all the events, he sat in the front seat and would periodically stand against the front rail talking to his '72 teammates like they were ready to go battle the A's. "I will go back to being the skipper..."

Dick even threw a strike on the ceremonial first pitch at U.S. Cellular Field — from the full 60 feet, 60 inches away. "It was great to see so many of my former teammates again," he said, accompanied by his brothers, Hank and Ron. "It had been much too long."

Ten members of the 1972 White Sox attended the Monday night dinner. Most hadn't seen each other in decades. "I can't tell you how much we enjoyed this," former pitcher Tom Bradley said. "It was a night that none of us will ever forget."

"Whenever I speak with White Sox fans, it doesn't take long before one of them mentions the 1972 team," said Hemond. "No one left a greater impression than Dick Allen with his clutch hits and long home runs. Along with Bill Melton, Wilbur Wood, manager Chuck Tanner and others, he turned many people into White Sox fans forever."

Hemond was asked if he ever got an award, a certificate, a plaque, anything for winning the top MLB executive award in '72. He replied that he did not remember getting a plaque. "All I saw was the *Sporting News* naming me Executive of the Year and that was good enough for me."

"Pardon the interruption here, but you said he didn't get a plaque? Nothing? Did it get lost in the mail?" asked Sox historian Mark Liptak. Hemond said it didn't matter: "The pleasure this ball club gave me, and the people involved, Tom Bradley, Dick Allen, etc. and Chuck Tanner's great performance, along with the coaching staff. That's good enough."

Someone in the audience yelled, "We got to do something about this."

And so, four decades after being named Executive of the Year, Hemond finally got a plaque.

Hemond was deeply moved by this gesture and talked about how the '72 season was a turning point for the White Sox organization. He recalled the respect Dick had earned from his teammates. He then directly addressed him and said, "Without you, this would never have happened."

Organist Nancy Faust, who had retired two years earlier after 41 seasons, began to play the familiar chorus of "Jesus Christ Superstar" as Allen strutted up to the microphone to a standing ovation of 300-plus in attendance.

"The reason I'm here is because of Roland and Chuck and these people here at this table, Tom Bradley, he gave us six, seven, eight innings every time," he said. "This bunch here at the table, that '72 group, that's who truly should be honored, not me.

"This is where I wish my baseball career would have started," said the old slugger, who felt truly honored by the outpouring of affection for him from the city of Chicago.

Does Allen deserve a place in Cooperstown?

Few players' Hall of Fame credentials have been more vigorously debated than those of Dick Allen. Detractors, like Bill James, point out two main factors: That he was "a clubhouse cancer"-type who hurt his teams and that Dick "used racism as an explosive to blow his own teams apart."

Second, the man's career was cut short by injuries, illness and other factors, and he didn't put up big numbers like 500 home runs.

While baseball writers labeled him a clubhouse cancer, many others — including his teammates and managers — thought he was a good man who was just misunderstood.

However, nearly every major player and coach who was a part of Dick's career stepped forward to rebut the claims of his negativity in the clubhouse, including two of the game's greatest managers, Tanner and Gene Mauch.

Stan Bahnsen, the pitcher and 1972 teammate, said it best: "I actually thought that Dick was better than his stats. Every time we needed a clutch hit, he got it. He got along great with his teammates, and he was very knowledgeable about the game. He was the ultimate team guy."

Arguably, one of the most interesting personalities to ever lace up a pair of baseball spikes, Dick was one of the five most dominant hitters in an era chock full of future Hall of Famers, from 1964-74. Dick stands alone in the important OPS+.

OPS+Adjusted 1964-1974 Name	OPS+
Dick Allen	165
Hank Aaron	161
Willie McCovey	161
Frank Robinson	161
Harmon Killebrew	152
Willie Stargell	152
Roberto Clemente	151
Willie Mays	148
Frank Howard	147
Carl Yastrzemski	145
Al Kaline	140
Boog Powell	140
Billy Williams	139
Tony Oliva	137
Ron Santo	136

His career numbers are undeniably Hall of Fame-caliber: Seven All-Star Game appearances, six times hitting over .300, twice leading the league in OBP, seven times in the top three in the league in slugging, twice ranking as league home run champ, twice runner-up in home runs and three times the league leader in Adjusted OPS (OPS+).

Throw in a National League Rookie of the Year Award in 1964, for one of the most dominant rookie seasons of all time with a 9.6 WAR. Add in, for good measure, his historic 1972 MVP season, when he nearly got the White Sox into the postseason, and one would believe Dick had been somewhat of a lock for the Hall of Fame.

Unfortunately, statistics alone often don't get you into the Hall of Fame. Just consider the heavy politics in baseball and sports media, thicker than that of Chicago's City Hall. Relationships and media relations are even more important than cash, particularly when applied to the Baseball Writers Association of America (BBWAA) annual Hall of Fame vote. In both the writers' and various incarnations of the Veterans Committee, a super-majority of 75% of ballots is required — a level not even required for any action in a fractious Congress. Dick said when he came to Chicago in June 2012, "I don't not know what OPS+

means. I just knew what I did on the field."

Allen's chances were hurt by playing on five different teams and a perception as the quintessential outlaw rebel through much of his career, when he clashed with some sportswriters.

2014 Hall of Fame vote—A near-miss for immortality

Dick topped out at 18.9% of the HOF vote in 1996, his second-to-last year on the BBWAA ballot. In 2003, he only got 13 of 85 votes from the reformatted Veterans Committee, then comprised of all living Hall of Famers.

In 2011, Allen did not even make the ballot of the new Golden Era Committee which considered candidates whose contributions to the game were most significant from 1947-72. This omission prompted some controversy in baseball circles, including Stuart Miller's impassioned commentary: "Ken Boyer and Tony Oliva Are on the Ballot. Why Not Dick Allen?" in the *New York Times*, Nov. 10, 2011:

> *"Allen's story is complicated by his personality and the politics of his time. He was, at best, a prickly nonconformist who broke rules and irritated teammates. However, he was also subjected to racism, both blatant and subtle, which is what fueled some of his behavior."*

After he was left off that 2011 ballot (which resulted in the posthumous selection of Ron Santo), the 2012 Chicago Tribune helped elevate Dick's post-career legacy and finally got him on the Hall of Fame Golden Era, ballot two years later.

The Allen Hall of Fame Campaign

In late 2013, Richard (Doobie) Allen, Jr, Dick's middle child, asked a former Phillies groundskeeper, Mark "Frog" Carfagno, to help create a campaign that would help elect his father to the Hall of Fame. A Facebook group page called *Dick Allen Belongs in the Hall of Fame* was started and soon was up to 4,000 members.

Unlike several other candidates, Dick had no team on which he played trying to help him gain admission to the Hall of Fame. In 2014, the Phillies employed him as a community and fan development representative, and they honored his wishes by *not* publicly pushing for his induction.

The Minnesota Twins were actively campaigning for Tony Oliva and Jim Kaat (who spent far more time with the Twins than the White Sox). The South Siders were backing two players whose numbers were retired by the team: Minnie Minoso (No. 9) and Billy Pierce (No. 19), and had nothing in place to help Allen. The Mets campaigned hard for Gil Hodges, who managed them to their first World Series title in 1969.

Under Carfagno's leadership, a contingent of supporters in Philadelphia and Chicago, SABR members and other baseball historians began to speak out on Dick's behalf. These efforts were supplemented by political help from Philadelphia Mayor Michael Nutter and the New Jersey State Legislature.

Allen talked only sparingly about his Hall of Fame candidacy, as he believed his career statistics spoke for themselves.

Despite not campaigning, Dick began to elevate his profile after the 2012 White Sox Tribute. He and relatives operated *www.DickAllen15.com* along with social media sites for Twitter, Instagram and Facebook. The website sold Allen memorabilia and had dozens of videos highlighting his career. It also had a section on horse racing news, Dick's other passion — and one also enjoyed by the late Rogers Hornsby, whom Bill James called the most controversial player in baseball history followed by Allen.

In 2014, the Golden Era Committee's second meeting considered 10 candidates, and Dick was added to the ballot considered by the 16-members.

Between Bill Mazeroski in 2001 and Santo in 2011, no player had been selected by the various Veterans' Committees, which looked at Hall of Fame-caliber players no longer eligible for the BBWAA ballot.

The Saturday night before the Dec. 7, 2014 vote, several members of the Golden Era Committee gathered at the bar of Donovan's, a restaurant in San Diego's Gaslamp Quarter, where the full committee was scheduled to have a private dinner.

Sipping his drink at the bar was Golden Era Committee member Hemond, sitting next to U.S. Senator Jim Bunning (R-Kentucky), who tossed a perfect game on Father's Day in Shea Stadium for the 1964 Phillies. Rookie Dick Allen made a huge play at third base in that game.

Committee members said they had been bombarded with mail pitches by the various candidates. "The Tony Oliva book I got cost $15 to ship to me!" exclaimed an exasperated Don Sutton.

In competition with the nine other candidates on the ballot — including the other players with White Sox connections, Team Allen, led by Carfagno, believed that Dick had several strong supporters among the electorate that was gathered-around the bar stools. The Allen boosters took the opportunity to do some last-minute lobbying, believing they could count on 12 of the 16 votes — enough to push Dick over the top.

"I am optimistic about Dick's chances tomorrow." said Hemond, seeking the platinum recognition for the player who put him on the high-profile baseball map, those many decades ago.

Suddenly, Dave Dombrowski, then serving as the Detroit Tigers president, walked in and stopped to say hello, around the time that the jovial get-together was finishing its drinks.

Carfagno and Doobie Allen watched the Golden Era Committee members — along with Dombrowski — walk upstairs for their dinner.

"Dombrowski is not on the Committee. Where's (Bob) Watson?" yelled Carfagno, who was also with TV producer Mike Tollin. The latter had been working on an Allen documentary for years and would later produce "The Last Dance" documentary about Michael Jordan that premiered on ESPN in April 2020 to great response from a pandemic sports-deprived audience.

While this Hall of Fame fate was being deliberated, Team Allen hung around the San Diego Manchester Grand Hyatt Hotel on Sunday December 7, hoping and praying their efforts would pay off.

Before the vote, Dick waited at his winter residence in Tampa, Fla. for the announcement of an honor for which he had never campaigned. He was upbeat and forgiving of all the past slights in his life, and very touched by people remembering his career and all that he had to endure. As a strong practicing Christian, he said, "It is in God's hands. I did all I could on the field."

Dick knew he had a late surge of support around the nation with great stories written in the *New York Times*, *USA Today*, *ESPN The Magazine* and other publications.

As William C. Rhoden, who saw the man play in his MVP season in 1972, wrote in the *Times*, "The Dick Allen story has never been solely about statistics, but about perception and forgiveness."

On Monday morning, Dec. 8, 2014, the tally was announced. One could tell by the dour facial expression of Jane Forbes Clark that this vote was not going to elect *any* veteran player to the Hall. *MLB.com* columnist Barry Bloom had predicted a shutout the night before while roaming the lobby of the Manchester Grand Hyatt.

Allen and Oliva were the top vote-getters, each coming in just one vote shy with 11. Kaat also was close with 10 votes, Maury Wills garnered nine and Minnie Minoso eight. All others, including former White Sox Billy Pierce and Ken Boyer, got three or fewer votes each.

Fergie Jenkins, Dick's 1963 Arkansas teammate, was disappointed, overall, by the results but saw the vote total as very positive.

"His first time on the ballot — getting 11 votes — that is outstanding," he said.

Added Jenkins, "He needs to do some more public appearances before the next [2017] vote," a tactic Dick's peer, Billy Williams, also recommended.

In the audience, waiting for the announcement, was Doobie Allen. "It's a disappointment, but I am proud my Dad got 11 votes," he said. "I told my dad he lost by a whisker," referring to a horse racing term.

Hall of Famer and front office veteran Pat Gillick said Dick had a large groundswell of support. "It was his numbers," he said. "Look at this guy. He was a power hitter. He was a guy that got on base. He stole bases. He had to make position changes (because of injuries)…a lot of good qualities…Everyone talked about Dick being a real good teammate."

As for the widely-reported viewpoint expressed by Bill James' near-condemnation claiming "Allen did more to keep his teams from winning than anyone else who ever played major league baseball," Gillick rebutted that with specific statistical and anecdotal evidence.

Three months after the vote, Bunning told veteran Philadelphia sportswriter Stan Hochman about the behind-the-scenes deliberations inside the committee room. "I felt useless," Bunning said. "It was the most disappointing three days I've ever spent in my life!" That was quite a statement from someone who also served in the Senate, on top of enduring the shocking final-days collapse of those '64 Phillies.

Bunning knew what it was like to rejected by the BBWAA. In 1988, he came within 0.8 per cent of being elected to the Hall of Fame. He was finally enshrined in 1996, a quarter-century after his retirement, after being selected by the then-Veteran's Committee.

Bunning's account was the first peek into a clumsy, tainted, ill-conceived process designed to elect players rejected by the baseball writers after the standard 15-year period on the regular ballot. It's not pretty, and it helps explain why players from the 1960s and '70s have commonly drawn a blank from the various such committees.

The Senator's play-by-play revealed that the committee gathered in a room which could hold 50 and that "the 16 of us sat at a big, oblong table and we considered the 10 candidates in alphabetical order. Dick Allen was first.

"I spoke first. I came prepared and gave an impassioned speech supporting Allen's worthiness for the Hall of Fame. Someone said he hit 20 home runs that traveled more than 500 feet. No one, no one in baseball had ever hit that many homers that went 500 feet.

"Bob Watson didn't make it. They never told us why. If he'd been there, it might have made a difference for two guys, Allen and Tony Oliva, who also got 11 votes. It turned out Dombrowski had replaced him.

"I don't think writers should be [members of committees] voting on past-era players. Let it be only their peers, guys already in the Hall of Fame. And I intend to tell that to the Hall of Fame people. And I'm going to tell them they ought to narrow the list, cut it back from 10 names.

"Guys were angry after the voting was announced. I stuck around for the press conference, but nobody asked me a question. The questions went to the writers.

"To me, it was a wasted weekend. We were there to pick someone for the Hall of Fame. We didn't accomplish anything. OK, maybe Allen and Oliva will be at the top of the list in three years when they come up again.

"But who will be on the committee of voters? What will the rules be? Things have to change!"

Bunning died in 2017 before he could again advocate for his long-ago teammate.

Although Dick fell one vote short, the perception about him has changed, and the media coverage more recently has provided some better understanding of his complex behavior and the context of the times. A lot of optimism prevailed that the next go-around in 2017 would push him over the top.

But before that 2017 vote, the rules changed. The Hall of Fame went from three veterans-type committees to four, classified by "eras." The division hurt Allen's chances to get elected in his lifetime because his career was stretched over *two* of the newly-defined eras, rather than dominate one.

In 2016, the Golden Era Committee was renamed the Golden Days Era Committee. The old Committee had considered candidates whose achievements were from 1947-72. Now, the Golden Days Era Committee considers those whose greatest contributions to the game took place between 1950 and 1969. The Modern Baseball Era Committee looks at candidates whose top achievements fell within 1970-1987.

Until 2017, Dick did not know which era he fit into since his career crossed over those two eras. Supporters hoped he would be best considered by the Modern Baseball Era Committee, which was going to meet in 2017 for induction in 2018.

Instead, Dick was grouped into the Golden Days Era Committee that was not due to gather until the MLB winter meetings in December 2020, when he would be 78.

But Dick — who was undergoing cancer treatment — had his hopes snatched away in 2020 because the COVID-19 pandemic postposed the Golden Days Era Committee vote until December 2021, with enshrinement at Cooperstown scheduled for July 2022. The Hall received considerable flak because that Golden Days Era Committee did not meet virtually, in the same manner as had the rest of the winter meetings participants.

Allen's No. 15 retirement ceremony — September 2020

Dick Allen was perceived both as savior and villain in Philadelphia and Chicago. But that's the nature of baseball.

Always his own man, possessed of a sense of wanderlust, Dick could scarcely fit into the conservative baseball mold of the 1960s. Thus, he ran afoul of customs and other so-called norms, which frowned on African American players speaking up for themselves or most players of any color displaying independence.

But justice gained late is still justice. Disappointed that the Hall of Fame delayed the Golden Days Era Committee vote until December 2021, Allen's friends and family were buoyed by the announcement that the Phillies would retire Dick's No. 15 in the midst of the COVID-19 pandemic despite all ballparks were closed to fans. Allen would finally get the apology of sorts and redemption from the city of Philadelphia, which he had deserved for a half-century.

On Sept. 3, 2020, Phillies Managing Partner John Middleton engineered the ceremony at Citizens Bank Ballpark that allowed the city to finally honor and indirectly acknowledge how he was mistreated. Middleton channeled his nine-year-old baseball-fan self into 2020.

"I remember it was the first time I'd ever heard someone described as a phenom, and dared dream and even expect that my Phillies could win the pennant and eventually the World Series," he said. "It was the moment my fandom turned into a passion."

His voice cracking with emotion, Middleton recalled his halcyon days summering on the Jersey Shore in 1964: "I was crushed in 1969 when Dick was traded to the St. Louis Cardinals…In my idolization of Dick, I have been anticipating this moment for over 50 years. Now it is here. I am excited. Really excited…Retiring Dick's number is a really big deal for the Phillies, Philadelphia and, I hope, even for baseball."

Middleton recalled how a bunch of White suburban Philadelphia kids would choose up sides to play wiffleball and imitate the iconic Allen batting stance.

"For us, it had nothing to with race," he said, choking back tears. "It was all about talent —extraordinary talent — and we all wanted to be just like Dick Allen. Everyone wanted to be Dick Allen. So, there would be one Dick Allen on each team."

Middleton rattled off Dick's career statistics that elevated him to an elite status: "Dick's numbers would have been even more extraordinary had he played in a better environment. Some of the conditions he played in and lived with off the field were truly horrific."

Before the ceremony, when a small crowd of family and close friends wore specially-made Allen No. 15 COVID protective masks, Middleton shared why he picked the ceremony on September 3 to honor Allen's "Juneteenth" day. "It was the day in 1963 when Dick was promoted from Little Rock to the Phillies," he said.

Like Abraham Lincoln did during the depths of the Civil War, Middleton stressed that even during the middle of the coronavirus pandemic, the time was now to free Dick, whom he considered a civil rights pioneer. During the ensuing ceremony, Middleton reflected on the recent death of civil rights leader John Lewis as an inspiration for the ceremony. Middleton even quoted Lewis as to why he felt it was necessary now to honor Allen:

"When you see something that is not right, not fair, not just, you have to speak up. You have to say something; you have to do something."

Middleton added: "You still evoke in me the awe and wonderment of that nine-year old boy on the Jersey Shore. The Phillies organization is doing and saying something to correct what is historically not right and not fair and not just. Should this moment have occurred years ago? Unquestionably, yes…"

One to avoid self-aggrandizement in his life, Allen spoke for just a few minutes during the moving ceremony. He threw out his prepared speech and talked about his murdered daughter Terri.

He conveyed the pain and hardship he felt when the Phillies in 1963 sent him to Little Rock, Ark. and their Triple-A club. Being the first Black player ever on that team — in a community which had become the civil-rights flashpoint in the national consciousness only six years before —was terribly difficult. That his mother, Era Allen, convinced him to stay was a key act in his development as a baseball player and a person.

"God gave you talent and a place to show it," recounted Allen about his mother's encouraging words to her 22-year-old son. "Don't let them drive you out." His bat won over the fans by season's end, and he got promoted to the Phillies on September 3.

Many believed this recognition by the Phillies would be the momentum Allen needed to be elected the next time the Golden Days Era Committee met in December 2021.

The quiet Mr. Allen was truly touched by that day and the fact that his number was retired by the Phillies, yet he had secretly hoped the Chicago White Sox would do the same and retire his South Side red-pinstriped No. 15. He knew walking out on the Sox in September 1974 had partially burned a bridge with the team for which he had achieved his pinnacle success.

Dick's health began to slip away, and the Philadelphia ceremony would be his final public appearance.

Cancer claims Allen

"Better late than never" truly defined Dick Allen's baseball life. "Late," but properly credited, can sum up his epitaph. The man who saved the White Sox for Chicago with his Most Valuable Player season in 1972 died at 78 on Monday, Dec. 7, 2020, after a long illness.

A week before his death, the once-powerful slugger had a lengthy phone call with Bill Melton. It buoyed his spirits to talk about the '72 Sox.

Andy Woolley, who ran Dick's Twitter account, announced his death via a tweet at 1:22 p.m. on December 7: "With sadness in our hearts, we need to share that Dick passed away this afternoon at his home in Wampum." The message featured Dick in a White Sox jersey, rather than a Phillies jersey — that was Dick's choice of uniform to be remembered in.

On December 12, a Celebration of Life was held at First Baptist Church of Chewton, where he had worshipped during his entire life. Dick's interment was at Clinton Cemetery in Wampum on a ridge above the home he built for his mother, who is buried nearby.

The funeral arrangements followed COVID-19 pandemic restrictions, and among the small group, Dr. David Fletcher spoke about what Dick meant for the City of Chicago:

"I loved Dick and I wanted to give some perspective from Chicago. Before there was Michael Jordan in Chicago, there was this man. The three years in Chicago, he was beloved. We brought him back for a tribute in 2012 and it was unbelievable how much outpouring of affection there was; it just was tremendous.

"They say you don't want to meet your heroes when you grow up; this hero was better as a real person than as a mythical baseball player. Especially when I learned about Dick's profound Christian faith and the whole aspect of him growing up in an integrated, tolerant community, Wampum, then going down to Arkansas and what he overcame. And for me, this is very special, because as a White man, I have three African American grandchildren.

"One final thing, Nancy Faust was the organist for the White Sox for 41 years. She started walk-up music because of this man. She played

Jesus Christ Superstar when he came to bat. I was so honored to be there for Dick's No. 15 retirement, and I had a tape of Nancy playing Jesus Christ Superstar and he loved hearing it again. We recorded a little shout-out from him to Nancy that was priceless."

After his death, various perspectives showed that Dick had always been Hall of Fame worthy. Now, it would have to be posthumous. All the facts and statistics surrounding the controversial slugger got a new review: One of the game's best all-around players, a seven-time All-Star, MVP winner, Rookie of the Year and a 15-year career which spanned an era of pitching dominance.

Now, decades later, the clearer eye of history could put his performance and impact on baseball in better perspective. He was a man ahead of his time who overcame racism with dignity and grace.

In 2021, all Phillies uniformed personnel wore a No.15 armband on their sleeves to honor Dick Allen.

His death was big news in Chicago. "Dick Allen is a baseball legend — Hall of Fame or not. And his place in Chicago White Sox history is secure," wrote Paul Sullivan as part of the *Chicago Tribune's* full Sports section Page 1 coverage.

"We all loved him" blared the headlines above descriptions of how previously empty Sox Park filled up dramatically when Allen arrived on the South Side.

"The Sox suddenly started winning again, the ballpark got crowded and whenever Allen stepped to the plate with his 40-ounce bat, the moment seemed frozen in time," Sullivan wrote. "Everyone paid attention because every at-bat brought the promise of something you never had seen before. Maybe that's why Allen's death Monday at age 78 was felt by so many Chicagoans of a certain age. Allen's career on the South Side was a mere blip in our baseball-loving lives, lasting only three seasons from 1972 to '74."

Hall of Fame enshrinement eluded him in life

The only thing missing from his life story was induction into the National Baseball Hall of Fame.

Critics cite the fact that Dick left too much on the table and that his statistics are a bit thin because he had fewer than 2,000 hits (1,848) in a career that was cut short by injuries, illness, bad decisions and other factors beyond his control. Also, the man's defense was not stellar. One or two more seasons, however, and fewer missed games in his prime, might have netted him 400 or more homers and would have provided more numerical justification for a relatively early Hall of Fame induction.

However, Dick's Wins Above Replacement (WAR) stats prove his Hall of

Fame value, overall. He had seasons at 9.3 WAR (1972), 9.1 WAR (1964) and 7.8 WAR (1966.) Every eligible player with two 9+ WAR seasons has been inducted (except for Barry Bonds, who has been suspected of numbers inflated by PEDs).

As with other controversial players, off-the-field baggage Dick accumulated, much of it misunderstood, kept him from gaining entrance to the Hall during his lifetime. Now, in the era of "Black Lives Matter," Allen's career is seen in a whole new light and measured partially against the society in which he played and the injustices he encountered.

Had his life turned out differently, Dick would have amassed more fruitful seasons of numbers that would have cemented enshrinement much earlier. He should have been honored on the South Side for his rejuvenating the White Sox for Chicago. But not until 40 years later was Dick properly recognized for his heroic, one-man-wrecking-crew feats, in a special tribute and retrospective press conference at US Cellular Field.

Current Major League Baseball historian John Thorn said, as early as 1984, that Allen is the most "egregious omission" from the Hall of Fame. Andrew B. Distler wrote repeatedly that Cooperstown has refused to admit Allen, one of baseball's first Black superstars who was neither quiet nor grateful.

Distler penned a stirring essay, "As The Phillies Retired Dick Allen's Number, He's Still Waiting On The Hall of Fame," published on Sept. 3, 2020, on *TheUndefeated.com*, a top platform for exploring the intersections of race, sports and culture. He wrote: "While Allen's statistics match those of many white players in the Hall, his reputation as a troublemaker — the stereotypical 'angry Black man' — derailed his chances. When his next chance at induction comes up, it will be an opportunity for voters to reevaluate his career in the context of his life on the field and off — a life of racial abuse, being marginalized, being taunted by teammates and fans alike, of forever being treated as a 'boy' rather than a man. Induction wouldn't change the past. But it would finally recognize the accomplishments that make him more than worthy for inclusion in the Hall of Fame."

Hall of Fame Phillies third baseman Mike Schmidt, whom Dick mentored in 1975-76, as he had done for Gossage in 1972, also spoke at the No. 15 uniform retirement ceremonies:

"Dick, then Richie, broke into the Phillies in 1964. They were the last team to integrate in the NL. He became the star of the team, and he was a sensitive Black man who refused to be treated as a second-class citizen. He played in front of home fans who were products of that racist era.

"He had racist teammates, and there were different rules for whites and Blacks. Fans threw stuff on him. Thus, Dick donned the batting

helmet throughout the ballgame. They yelled degrading racial slurs, they dumped trash in his front yard at his home. In general, he was tormented from all directions. And Dick rebelled. He became labeled as a bad teammate and a troublemaker. My friend, those labels have kept Dick Allen out of the Hall of Fame."

Dick's bad Philadelphia and Little Rock experiences would follow him the rest of his career, and well beyond. That is why the honors of 2012 in Chicago and 2020 in Philadelphia provided him with a well-deserved sense of redemption.

One of the most touching remembrances of Dick's impact on Chicago was written after his death by David McGrath in the Chicago Northwest Suburban *Daily Herald* newspaper. McGrath had to explain who Dick Allen was to his daughter, born long after the slugger left baseball:

"I explained that there probably would have been no White Sox and no Comiskey Park for her to see, had it not been for Dick Allen. For we needed Superman or Jesus or somebody to save the Sox in 1972 and it was Allen who came to the rescue.

"In several previous years, through a series of lackluster seasons, attendance at Comiskey was dwindling. Ownership was contemplating moving the White Sox to another city...That possibility was unthinkable to my grandparents, my father and my uncles who had suffered with the South Side team for decades and who celebrated with the same kind of ecstasy as when wars end, when the 'Go-Go Sox' finally won the American League Pennant in 1959...

"We were starving for a hero. Even today, I need no photos to remind me of Dick Allen's physical presence when he put on that uniform. Though it's been almost 50 years, his image remains etched in my mind.

"At 5-foot-11, he was not that big for a ballplayer and of surprisingly average size for a home run hitter. But his wide shoulders, his erect, perfect posture, whether in the batter's box or in the field, made an imposing impression. At a distance, say, of a thousand yards, when it's impossible to delineate the features of a man's face, I could recognize Dick Allen, standing or walking, by his angle to the earth and sky.

"Allen's right-handed stroke was the most memorable for its poetry and power in motion: Elbows spread, hands at the letters, gripping a 40-ounce beast of a bat held vertically, no one looked more relaxed and confident in the batter's box. And then you knew why when he'd tip that bat forward as the pitch was made and then swing the barrel around in a quick, compact backswing that generated blinding bat speed and power to crush the ball.

"No matter the score, no matter the inning, no matter what was happening around you, you stopped what you were doing when Allen, statuesque, faced the pitcher. Each at-bat, we watched, hypnotized, like awaiting the lighted fuse on a stick of dynamite.

"I was saddened by Dick Allen's death, but I also felt a wave of gratitude and peace, rather like Hemingway's character Santiago in The Old Man and the Sea and how he smiled to himself and was sustained by thoughts of the 'great DiMaggio.'"

And so, despite controversies, Dick's status as one of the great all-around players of his era remains unquestioned and is finally recognized. A supremely talented player was honored better late than never as the mindset of the times finally caught up with the magnitude of Allen's feats in the 1960s and 1970s.

His older brother Hank, who was a teammate on the 1972-73 White Sox and retired in 2019 as a scout for the Houston Astros, said of his younger brother:

"I've witnessed firsthand, not a player, coach or manager has ever espoused such negatively about drinking or anything else other than being the consummate teammate on every team he's played on. Don't get me wrong by any stretch of an imagination, he's not an angel, nor did he pretend to be one. But he did stand up for his dignity and self-respect."

Hank Allen explained that Dick was a product of his environment:

"After enduring four years in the minor-league situations, he becomes somewhat of pioneer when he arrives in major leagues with Philadelphia, becoming their first outstanding minority player who is also faced with some of the same indignities he's had to face during his previous four years. Keep in mind you still have to perform, produce and try to maintain your sanity, dignity and self-respect. It's a tough role for anybody to be placed in, let alone a 22-year-old young man.

"Now with a better understanding of all that he's had to deal with in his entire career. Not to mention the injuries, lies, innuendos, accusations of alcoholism from such people like Bill James and others, I find it amazing he was able to accomplish the remarkable career he's had. Without a doubt because of his personification, perseverance and endurance, he's what a Hall of Famer is all about."

No matter the quality or passion of advocacy for Dick Allen's qualifications, induction into the National Baseball Hall of Fame — due to the 75 % vote threshold — is one of the most difficult accomplishments in American sports and popular culture. As the 2020s proceed, Allen backers will need to adhere to Dr. Martin Luther King's famous quote: "...the arc of the moral universe is long, but it bends toward justice."

In the Dec. 5, 2021 Golden Days Era Committee balloting in Orlando, Fla., Dick again received 11 out of a possible 16 votes, again falling just *one short* of induction. Meanwhile, a quartet of long-deserving stars — Minnie Minoso, Jim Kaat, Tony Oliva and Gil Hodges — were elected from the 10-person ballot comprised of candidates whose primary contribution to the game came from 1950-69.

Minoso had just eight votes in 2014, but jumped to 14 this time. He was the beneficiary of support from University of Illinois historian Adrian Burgos, Jr., a longtime advocate for Latin players. Minoso, who died in 2015, also was featured in a lot of pre-vote publicity for his historic status as baseball's first Black Latin player.

Kaat, a 283-game winner, had increased his profile in recent years as a network baseball color analyst, still going strong into his 80s. Interestingly, the durable lefty won 21 games with the White Sox in Dick's final Chicago season, 1974. Katt followed up with 20 wins for a mediocre Sox team in 1975. He likely was packaged with former Twins teammate Oliva in the minds of Golden Days Era Committee voters, including last-minute substitute Bert Blyleven, a Twins teammate of both and a Hall of Famer himself. Kaat and Oliva each received 12 votes.

Also named on a dozen ballots was Dodgers "Boys of Summer" stalwart Hodges, long a bridesmaid in voting in the numerous incarnations of the old Hall of Fame Veteran's Committee. Hodges candidacy apparently tapped into a sentimentality surge to dramatically boost his numbers.

Logically leading the support for Dick were his former teammates: Hall of Famers Fergie Jenkins, a holdover voting member from 2014, and Mike Schmidt, whom Dick mentored on the 1975-76 Phillies. Another member of the 16-man panel was Hall of Famer Joe Torre, a teammate on the 1970 Cardinals.

Other voters were Hall of Fame shortstop Ozzie Smith; former commissioner and Hall member Bud Selig; major league executives Kim Ng, Bill DeWitt, Tony Reagins, Al Avila and Ken Kendrick; former major league executive John Schuerholz; six-decade Dodgers radio announcer Jaime Jarrin, statistician Steve Hirdt and Jack O'Connell, a former baseball writer and longtime top officer in the Baseball Writers Association of America.

Doobie Allen again led his family's watch party nearby in Orlando. If his father's voice echoes in his head, it's the counsel of patience, even when it hurts to be patient. Baseball is a game of failure and near-misses, so success is even sweeter when finally experienced.

The best, most impactful ballplayer of his generation not yet inducted in the Hall of Fame, Dick Allen still awaits the call to Cooperstown.

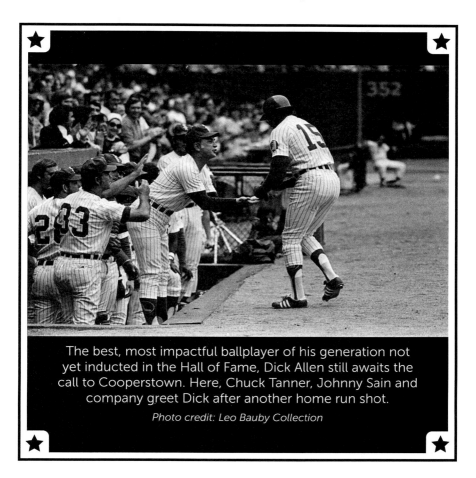

The best, most impactful ballplayer of his generation not yet inducted in the Hall of Fame, Dick Allen still awaits the call to Cooperstown. Here, Chuck Tanner, Johnny Sain and company greet Dick after another home run shot.

Photo credit: Leo Bauby Collection

(From left) Roland Hemond, Chuck Tanner and Dick Allen surprise Goose Gossage at the Hall of Fame induction weekend in Cooperstown in 2008.

Photo credit: Susan Hemond

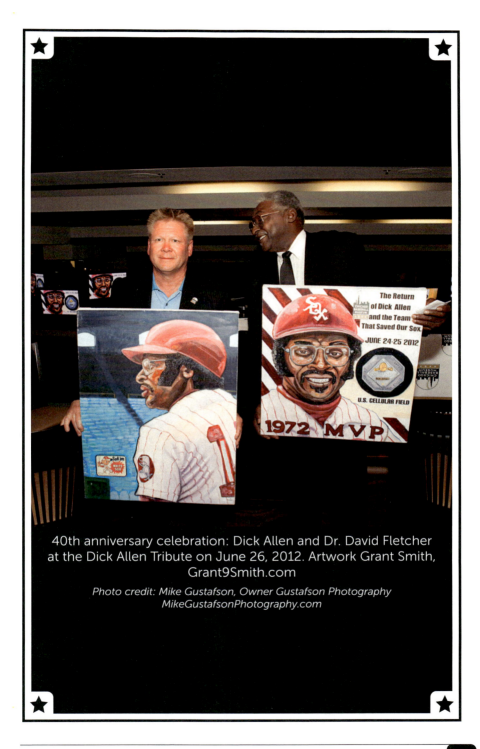

40th anniversary celebration: Dick Allen and Dr. David Fletcher at the Dick Allen Tribute on June 26, 2012. Artwork Grant Smith, Grant9Smith.com

Photo credit: Mike Gustafson, Owner Gustafson Photography
MikeGustafsonPhotography.com

Dick Allen (from left), Bill Melton and Goose Gossage pose with mascots the White Sox commissioned on the 40th anniversary celebration of the 1972 team on June 25, 2012.

Photo credit: Mike Gustafson, Owner Gustafson Photography
MikeGustafsonPhotography.com

Dick Allen addresses well-wishers at the 40th anniversary celebration of his MVP season at U.S. Cellular Field in 2012.

Photo credit: Mike Gustafson, Owner Gustafson Photography
MikeGustafsonPhotography.com

Dick Allen and wife Willa listen to a speaker at the 40th anniversary celebration of his MVP season at Guaranteed Rate Field on June 26, 2012.

Photo credit: Mike Gustafson, Owner Gustafson Photography
MikeGustafsonPhotography.com

Kenny McReynolds, who grew up rooting for Allen on the South Side, welcomes his former idol to his "Sports Edition" show on ME-TV in Chicago on June 12, 2012.

Photo credit: David Fletcher

One of the best baserunners of his generation, Allen slides under the tag of Yankees catcher Thurman Munson during a game at Yankee Stadium.

Photo credit: Leo Bauby Collection

SELECTED BIBLIOGRAPHY

Allen, Dick and Whitaker, Tim. *Crash, The Life and Times of Dick Allen*. New York. Ticknor and Fields, 1989.

Angell, Roger. *Five Seasons: A Baseball Companion*. New York. Ticknor and Fields, 1989.

Banks, Lacy J. "I'm My Own Man." *Ebony*, July 1970.

Blount, Roy Jr. "Swinging In His Own Groove." *Sports Illustrated*, Sept. 10, 1973.

Bouton, Jim. *Ball Four*. New York. Wiley, 1970 (1990 revised).

Brosnan, Jim. *The Long Season*. New York. HarperCollins Publishers, 1960 (2002 revised).

Caray, Harry and Verdi, Bob. *Holy Cow!* New York. Villard Books, 1989.

Castle, George. *Jackie Robinson West*. Guilford, Conn. Lyons Press, 2015.

Castle, George and Jenkins, Fergie. *The 1969 Cubs*. Dallas. Signature Strength Publishing, 2019.

Carmichael, John P. "The Barber Shop" (Arthur Allyn profile). *Chicago Daily News*, Sept. 25, 1969.

Chass, Murray. "Dick Allen: What It Takes To Keep Him Happy - And Why He's Worth It." *Baseball '73*, 1973.

Chass, Murray. "Dick Allen Returns To The Batting Cage." *New York Times*, Feb. 28, 1982.

Cohen, Adam and Taylor, Elizabeth. *American Pharaoh*. New York. Little, Brown and Company, 2000.

Condon, David. "Sox Not For Sale - John Allyn." *Chicago Tribune*, Sept. 26. 1969.

Condon, David. "Splitting of Artnell Starts Today; Many Activities Involved." *Chicago Tribune*, Sept. 26, 1969.

Condon, David. "In The Wake Of The News (A's celebrate 1972 World Series championship in LaPorte, Ind.)." *Chicago Tribune*, Nov. 16. 1972.

Condon, David. "Holcomb Discloses Feud With Tanner." *Chicago Tribune*, July 28, 1973.

Condon, David. "Allen: Chicago Treated Me The Best Of Any Town." *Chicago Tribune*, May 15, 1975.

Condon, David. "Veeck Deal Could Still Fail." *Chicago Tribune*, Dec. 10, 1975.

Conlin, Bill. "Dissension Brewing On Phillies?" *Philadelphia Daily News*, Sept. 29, 1976.

Costello, Rory. "Sam Hairston." *Society For American Baseball Research,* 2012.

Crews, Stephen. "McGovern Here For Daley Parley." *Chicago Tribune*, Aug. 23, 1972.

Dickson, Paul. *Bill Veeck: Baseball's Greatest Maverick.* New York. Bloomsbury Publishing, 2012.

Dolson, Frank. "Allen Makes It To The Game On Time – Barely." *Philadelphia Inquirer*, July 24, 1974.

Dozer, Richard. "Allen, Melton New Murderers Row." *Chicago Tribune*, Dec. 3, 1971.

Dozer, Richard. "Players Walk Out, And Allen Walks In." *Chicago Tribune*, April 1, 1972.

Dozer, Richard. "Strike Ends; Season Opens Tomorrow." *Chicago Tribune*, April 14, 1972.

Dozer, Richard. "National League Stars Win 4-3 In 10th." *Chicago Tribune*, July 26, 1972.

Dozer, Richard. "Allen's 2-Run Homer Beats Yankees." *Chicago Tribune*, Aug. 23, 1972.

Dozer, Richard. "Allen AL's Most Valuable." *Chicago Tribune*, Nov. 16, 1972.

Dozer, Richard. "Allen's 3-year pact - 675G!" *Chicago Tribune*, Feb. 28, 1973.

Dozer, Richard. "White Sox Cut Johnstone, Spiezio." *Chicago Tribune*, March 8, 1973.

Dozer, Richard. "Allen Defended By Tanner On 'Late' Arrival." *Chicago Tribune*, July 25, 1974.

Dozer, Richard. "Last Allen Sox Trip: A Walk." *Chicago Tribune*, Sept. 15, 1974.

Dozer, Richard. "Allen Bids Adieu To Chisox Fame, Fortune." *Sporting News*, Sept. 28, 1974.

Dozer, Richard. "Sox Will Not Claim Allen, Nor Seek Return." *Chicago Tribune*, April 30, 1975.

Dozer, Richard. "Veeck Gains Sox On Second Chance." *Chicago Tribune*, Dec. 11, 1975.

Dozer, Richard. "Allen Faces Last Rites Of Spring." *Chicago Tribune*, March 12, 1978.

Elmer, John. "Leaders See Hope Schools Won't Close." *Chicago Tribune*, Dec. 4, 1971.

Finkel, Jan. "Johnny Sain." *Society For American Baseball Research,* 2012.

Gleason, Bill. "Sox Fans Face Torturous Readjustments." *Chicago Sun-Times*, Dec. 5, 1971.

Herman, Edith and Crawford, William. "Gage Park High Closed After New Outburst." *Chicago Tribune*, Nov. 17, 1972.

Holtzman, Jerome. "Sox get Rich Allen, Bahnsen." *Chicago Sun-Times*, Dec. 3, 1971.

Holtzman, Jerome. "Richie Strolls In Same Day As Chisox Players Walk Out." *Sporting News*, April 15, 1972

Holtzman, Jerome. "Chisox Glad To Be Rid Of Allen." *Sporting News*, Oct. 12, 1974.

Holtzman, Jerome. "Dick Allen Walking Softly." *Chicago Tribune*, March 4, 1986.

Husar, John. "Ex-Sox Doctor Says Allen Could Have Finished Year." *Chicago Tribune,* Feb. 8, 1974.

Husar, John. "Allen Offering More Than Bat To Sox Surge." *Chicago Tribune*, April 27, 1972.

Jauss, Bill. "Fans laud Veeck, Daley." *Chicago Tribune*, Dec. 11, 1975.

Johnson, Larry. "Dick Allen: The Batter Pitchers Hate To Face." *Baseball Digest*, October 1974.

Jones, William. "Walker Demands That 3 Democrat Running Mates Quit City Ward Posts." *Chicago Tribune*, April 14, 1972.

Jones, William. "Daley Split Could Cost Race." *Chicago Tribune*, June 4, 1972.

Jones, William and Tagge, George. "How Singer Did It — And Daley Didn't." *Chicago Tribune*, July 12, 1972.

Kashatus, William C. *September Swoon: Richie Allen, the '64 Phillies, and Racial Integration*. University Park. Pennsylvania State University, 2004.

Kashatus, William C. *Dick Allen, The Life and Times of a Baseball Immortal: An Illustrated Biography*. Atglen, Pa. William C. Schiffer Publishing LTD, 2016.

Koziol, Ronald. "Bank Bomb Scare Renews Search For Weatherman Group." *Chicago Tribune*, Jan. 8, 1972.

Langford, George. "News Main Dish At Sox Luncheon." *Chicago Tribune*, Jan. 8, 1972.

Langford, George. "Allen Exits Sox Camp, Asks for Trade." *Chicago Tribune*, March 15, 1972.

Langford, George. "Opener Off, White Sox Practice At Home." *Chicago Tribune*, April 4, 1972.

Langford, George. "It Was An Opening Day That Wasn't." *Chicago Tribune*, April 7, 1972.

Langford, George. "Allyn Blames Owners from N.L." *Chicago Tribune*, April 12, 1972.

Langford, George. "Royals Owner Will Protest Sox Workouts." *Chicago Tribune*, April 14, 1972.

Langford, George. "Allen, Wood On. But Sox Off 2-1." *Chicago Tribune*, April 16, 1972.

Langford, George. "Sox, Carlos May Go On Spree." *Chicago Tribune*, April 19, 1972.

Langford, George. "Sox Win 7th Straight 7-5." *Chicago Tribune*, April 27, 1972.

Langford, George. "It's May Day! Sox Are In First." *Chicago Tribune*, May 22, 1972.

Langford, George. "Batty Day: 51,904 See Sox Sweep." *Chicago Tribune*, June 5, 1972.

Langford, George. "Melton Shelved For Year; Faces Surgery Next Week." *Chicago Tribune*, July 9, 1972.

Langford, George. "Reichardt, Andrews Regret Departure From Sox." *Chicago Tribune*, July 29, 1973.

Langford, George. "Anybody See Dick Lately?" *Chicago Tribune*, Aug. 10, 1973.

Langford, George. "Dick Allen Shows Up Early For Sox Training Camp." *Chicago Tribune*, Feb. 28, 1974.

Langford, George. "It's Wild! Sox Opener Ruined 8-2." *Chicago Tribune*, April 6, 1974.

Lewis, Allan. "Thomas Regrets Fight." *Philadelphia Inquirer*, July 4, 1965.

Lindberg, Richard. *Stealing First In A Two-Team Town*. Urbana. Sagamore Publishing, 1994.

Livingstone, Evelyn. "The Little Lady Behind Home Plate." *Chicago Tribune*, June 4, 1972.

Logan, Bob. "Sox 5-3 Victors." *Chicago Tribune*, July 23, 1972.

Logan, Bob. "Sox Sweep Indians As Wood Wins 15th." *Chicago Tribune*, July 24, 1972.

Markus, Robert. "Holy Cow! Sox Were In Danger of Losing 14-0 Lead." *Chicago Tribune*, April 20, 1972.

Markus, Robert. "Stops Along The Sports Trail." *Chicago Tribune*, Sept. 26, 1972.

Markus, Robert. "Bad Raps Stalking Dick Allen Again." *Chicago Tribune*, Aug. 28, 1973.

Markus, Robert. "Allen Almost Quit Friday, He May Yet." *Chicago Tribune*, April 7, 1974.

Merchant, Larry. "Allen Knows He's Better Than Good." *Philadelphia Daily News*, April 6, 1964.

Munzel, Edgar. "New Sox Will Have to Pay The Price of Success." *Chicago Sun-Times*, Dec. 4, 1971.

Munzel, Edgar. "Allen's Mom Prime Mover in Chisox Surge." *Sporting News*, Aug. 26, 1972.

Munzel, Edgar. "May Steals Chisox Show With Hot September Bat." *Sporting News*. Oct. 14, 1972.

Munzel, Edgar. "Tanner Hailed For Work As White Sox Manager." *Sporting News*, Oct. 14, 1972.

Munzel, Edgar. "You Made Me A Human Being, MVP Allen Tells Chisox Fans." *Sporting News*, Dec. 2, 1972.

Munzel, Edgar. "Allen's Leg Fracture Gives Sox New Case of Staggers." *Sporting News*, July 14, 1973.

Nathanson, Mitchell. *God Almighty Hisself: The Life and Legacy of Dick Allen*. Philadelphia. University of Pennsylvania Press, 2016.

Niesen, Joan. "The Spirit of St. Louis." *Sports Illustrated*, Sept. 22, 2014.

Nightengale, Dave. "Tom Bradley: New Hope For The White Sox." *Baseball Digest*, November 1971.

Nightengale, Dave. "The Human Side of Richie Allen." *Baseball Digest*, July 1972.

No Author. "White Sox Will Move Over to UHF in 1968." *Broadcasting*, Nov. 14, 1966.

No Author. "Faced With Trial, City Council Votes To Remap Wards." *Chicago Tribune*, Nov. 15, 1972.

No Author. "Ex-Sox Owner John Allyn Dies." *Chicago Tribune*, April 30, 1979.

Pacyga, Dominic A. *Slaughterhouse*. Chicago and London. The University of Chicago Press, 2015.

Padwe, Sandy. "MVP Dick Allen's Payoff." *Popular Sports*, September 1973.

Parker, Angela. "Rev. Jackson Suspended From Breadbasket Duties." *Chicago Tribune*, Dec. 4, 1971.

Peary, Danny. *We Played The Game*. New York. Hyperion, 1994.

Petersen, Clarence. "Our Fine 'Mare" Wishes Miller Well." *Chicago Tribune*, April 18, 1972.

Pratt, Steven. "'Honeymoon' Over For Lawlor, Langford." *Chicago Tribune*, April 6, 1972.

Prell, Edward. "Allyn Buys Out 2 Associates; Comiskey Asks For Meeting." *Chicago Tribune*, June 11, 1961.

Prigge, Matthew J. "The Forgotten Harry Caray-Bud Selig Beef of 1978." *Shepherd Express,* Jan. 18, 2016

Ritter, Lawrence. *The Glory Of Their Times*. Macmillan. 1966.

Robinson, Louis. "The Importance of Being Dick Allen." *Ebony*, October 1972.

Royko, Mike. *Boss*. New York. E.P. Dutton & Co., 1971.

Schreiber, Edward. "Daley Praises Muskie — But It's Not Official." *Chicago Tribune*, Jan. 8, 1972.

Schreiber, Edward. "Daley Still For Walker." *Chicago Tribune*, April 14, 1972.

Schreiber, Edward. "Jesse Trying To Hoodwink You, McGovern Is Warned." *Chicago Tribune*, Aug. 23, 1972.

Schreiber, Edward. "Daley Seeks Staff Trims, More Police." *Chicago Tribune*, Nov. 15, 1972.

Shnay, Jerry. "Players Relieved It's Over." *Chicago Tribune*, April 14, 1972.

Shrake, Edwin. "A Love Affair With A Loser." *Sports Illustrated*, March 29, 1965.

Soll, Frederic. "Hate, Fear Produce No Winner." *Chicago Tribune*, Nov. 17, 1972.

Smith, John Justin. "No sweeping changes for Sox: John Allyn." *Chicago Daily News*, Sept. 25, 1969.

Sweeney, Annie. "Ex-Sox Groundskeeper Bossard Dead At Age 80." *Chicago Tribune*, Feb. 1, 1998.

Tagge, George. "Dem Slatemakers Hear Unions Boost Simon Bid." *Chicago Tribune*, Dec. 3, 1971.

Talley, Rick. "White Sox Don't Want Dick Allen." *Chicago Tribune*, Oct. 8, 1974.

Talley, Rick. "Veeck Back For Another Battle." *Chicago Tribune*, Dec. 10, 1975.

Talley, Rick. "Stunning Veeck Takes Command." *Chicago Tribune*, Dec. 11, 1975.

Talley, Rick. "Tanner In, Caray Out, Hints New Sox Owner." *Chicago Tribune*, Dec. 11, 1975.

Talley, Rick. "Allen Offered To Cubs." *Chicago Tribune*, July 4, 1977.

Terry, Clifford. "Fans, It's So Hot On The Field Today That Our Third Baseman Is Melton!" *Chicago Tribune*, Aug. 3, 1975.

Vanderberg, Bob. *Sox: From Lane and Fain to Zisk and Fisk*. Chicago. Chicago Review Press, 1982.

Vass, George. "Chicago White Sox: A New Murderers Row?" *Baseball Digest*, August 1973.

Veeck, Bill and Linn, Ed. *Veeck As In Wreck*. New York. G.P. Putnam and Sons, 1962.

Verdi, Bob. "Dick Allen Returns With All His Old Intrigue." *Chicago Tribune*, July 27, 1987.

Watley, Philip. "Big Rally: We Don't Want The Crosstown." *Chicago Tribune*, May 22, 1972.

Wiedrich, Bob. "Tower Ticker (Daley-McGovern call)." *Chicago Tribune*, Aug. 23, 1972.

Wiedrich, Bob. "Tower Ticker (Daley rents tuxedo for son Michael's wedding)." *Chicago Tribune,* Nov. 15, 1972.

West, Gerald and Krizmis, Patricia. "Door To Success In Jobs Not Open To Us, Blacks Contend." *Chicago Tribune*, Dec. 3, 1971.

Wolf, David. "Let's Everybody Boo Rich Allen!" *Life*, Aug. 22, 1969.

Ziemba, Stan and Bukro, Casey. "Lakefront Plan Has Fans Foes, Few In-Betweens." *Chicago Tribune*, July 24, 1972.

Zminda, Don. *The Legendary Harry Caray: Baseball's Greatest Salesman*. Lanham, Md. Rowman & Littlefield Publishers, 2019.

Zminda, Don, *https://sabr.org/journal/article/working-overtime-wilbur-wood-johnny-sain-and-the-white-sox-two-days-rest-experiment-of-the-1970s/.* *Baseball Research Journal, Spring 2016.*

Dick Allen (right) and his son Doobie Allen (left) September 3, 2020.
Photo credit: David Fletcher

ORIGINAL 2021 INTERVIEWS

Goose Gossage, Fergie Jenkins, Billy Williams, Bud Selig, Dusty Baker, Jim Kaat, Newton Minow, Richard (Doobie) Allen, Jr., Hank Allen, Ric Allen, Willa Allen, Barbara Allen, Nancy Faust, Bill Melton, Wilbur Wood, Stan Bahnsen, Tom Bradley, Terry Forster, Carlos May, Phil Regan, Ron Kittle, Bruce Tanner, Roger Bossard, Jim O'Keefe, Jim Riley, Rory Clark, Glen Rosenbaum, Scott Rosenbaum, Roe Skidmore, Tom Shaer, Bruce Levine, Tim Cronin, Kenny McReynolds, Mark Liptak, Mike Pols, Tom Weinberg, Roger Wallenstein, Ron Eisenstein, Mark Schultz, Dave Dillman and a former top Chicago police official who preferred to remain anonymous.

Dick holds the runner on first.

Photo credit: Leo Bauby Collection

Walt "No-Neck" Williams circles the bases on June 26, 1972 after homering in the third inning off 1971 AL Cy Young Award Winner Vida Blue. Athletics third baseman Sal Bando watches as Sox third-base coach Joe Lonnett cheers on Williams.

Photo credit: Leo Bauby Collection

ACKNOWLEDGEMENTS

You usually can't judge a book by its cover. But in *Chili Dog MVP: Dick Allen, the 1972 White Sox and a Transforming Chicago*, the cover sums it all up.

Only a few artists in the world could capture the spirit of a book like Todd Radom, who let his imagination run with his take on the iconic 1972 *Sports Illustrated* photo of Dick juggling baseballs while puffing on a cigarette in the Comiskey Park home dugout.

Key characters of *Chili Dog MVP* surround Radom's period-piece cover. Harry Caray just starting out in Chicago, an angry Mayor Daley who sees his power slipping while his beloved White Sox contend for the AL pennant, a youthful, energetic Nancy Faust who would invent walk-up music, and the iconic Sox pitcher Wilbur Wood who represented everyman for the City of Chicago

We expected nothing less of Todd, who has been assigned many Major League Baseball artistic projects through the decades. One of his most prominent was the 1919-vintage White Sox uniform worn by the team in the wildly entertaining Field of Dreams Game in Iowa on Aug. 12, 2021. We see other projects similar to this book coming from our team of authors and editors, and thus we likely have not seen the last of Radom's cover majesty.

Within and without the book is the influence of Sharon Pannozzo. It's safe to say Sharon has publicized baseball, "Saturday Night Live" and a lot of impactful things in between.

If something needed to be done, if a person needed to be contacted, a phone call, e-mail or text from Sharon usually sufficed. She knows a ton of people in sports and media from her longtime positions with the Chicago Cubs and NBC. We made sure we put Sharon in her rightful place in the lineup to raise awareness of *Chili Dog MVP* while staying out of her way. You let your cleanup hitter swing on 3-and-0.

Some of us are tech Luddites, so the tag-team of Carol Kneedler, Marissa DeWeese and Heather Vining dragged us into the 21st century. From their base in Springfield, Ill. (which we have nicknamed "Lincolnburg"), they have tied up the little things that can throw monkey wrenches into a book project. Carol and Marissa are also spearheading the website, *ChiliDogMVP.com*.

Supplementing Carol and Marissa was on-line tutor Laura Staley, who answered the Luddite's questions that enabled 21st century-style editing over the tens of thousands of words that went into *Chili Dog MVP*.

Every editor needs an editor. And so, Tom Shaer, with his red pen in low-tech fashion, shaped up key chapters on plain ol' typing paper and later was the final set of eyes, proofreading and editing the entire manuscript. The first voice ever heard on Jan. 2, 1992, on "The Score", Chicago's first all-sports radio station, Tom used multi-media talents first developed as an Associated Press assistant covering the Boston Red Sox in 1977 to make the narrative of *Chili Dog MVP* flow more smoothly.

Tom's knowledge of baseball and broadcasting history was also invaluable. He came off the bench to deliver late-inning thunder and ensure that *Chili Dog MVP* would be a very special creative work and much more than a baseball book. Tom was the closer who earned a two-plus inning save like the 21-year-old future of Hall-of-Famer Goose Gossage and 20-year-old Terry Forster did in 1972.

The most grueling aspect of assembling a good-sized book is not the writing or researching/interviewing, but the transcription of long, taped interviews. To be accurate, the transcriber can only go a sentence at a time. Authors who've had to do double duty as their own transcriber feel like drilling holes in their heads in this process. So, thankfully, Ann Parkinson, Teri Sommer, and Roxanne Chumacas were the indispensable transcribers who made the writing team's life a lot easier.

We cannot be all-text, it is hard on the eyes. So kudos go out to longtime sports collector Leo Bauby for allowing us to tap into his collection of vintage photos from 1972 Comiskey Park. Still photography was baseball's most dominant visual image a half-century ago, and we're thrilled that Leo could share his treasures with us.

Two key images beyond Leo's cache are crucial to the presentation of *Chili Dog MVP*. The June 4, 1972 *Tribune Sunday Magazine* cover portrayed a glammed-up White Sox organist Nancy Faust posing with White Sox stars Bill Melton and Wilbur Wood. And a black and white photo from the same time period showed a shirtless Harry Caray in all his glory broadcasting from Comiskey Park's center field bleachers. We thank Tony Dudek of Tribune Content Agency for his courtesy in re-publishing these classics.

We also thank the *Milwaukee Journal-Sentinel – USA Today Network* for permission to print three key historical photos regarding the planned sale of the White Sox to Milwaukee by the group headed up by future baseball Commissioner Bud Selig.

Nancy Faust, the nonpareil organist, is a living, breathing example of "you can't beat fun at the ballpark," as her seventh-inning musical partner Harry Caray always said. Nancy provided some eye-opening documents and so many memories she could write and play songs about our work on this book. Her time at the keyboard has many, many years to go. Thanks also to Nancy's husband Joe

Jenkins in this process and for his willingness to haul her organ to events so she can entertain.

Although *Newspapers.com* provided access to vintage *Chicago Tribune* stories that were key to our research, not all papers of the time are so easily available online. Veteran Chicago sportswriter, author and radio "DXer" Tim Cronin, though, knew a way to access the late, sainted *Chicago Daily News* archives. Substantial perspective on Chicago baseball and broadcasting of the era was gleaned from the *Daily News*. Cronin also provided his perspective of the White Sox via radio and TV at the dawn of the 1970s.

The *Chili Dog MVP* team also had access to the Jerome Holtzman collection as described by the *New York Times* in their July 2008 obituary on Jerome:

> *Mr. Holtzman's baseball library, some 4,000 volumes, along with his meticulously catalogued collection of documents, articles and other papers, was purchased for $300,000 by the Chicago Baseball Museum, an institution yet to be built, that will emphasize baseball scholarship.*

> *"It might be the most significant private baseball collection in the world," said David Fletcher, the museum president.*

> *Jerome Holtzman, a homegrown Chicago sportswriter and columnist who wrote voluminously about baseball in general and Chicago baseball in particular, and whose mind and file cabinets were repositories of baseball history...*

Having access to the collection allowed the writing team direct use of hidden treasures including Johnny Sain's personal papers and theories on pitching.

A detailed book on a key time in White Sox history is needed in the marketplace. So we were thrilled to get the support of Scott Reifert, vice president of communications for the White Sox. Scott goes back decades in the front office and has seen it all, highlighted by the Sox's 2005 World Series run. But he also realizes there is an intriguing, dramatic backstory dating back even more decades that was waiting to be told.

Harry Caray's Restaurant impresario Grant DePorter and his staff get kudos for their willingness to host the gala rollout of this book. Everyone at HC's preserves the spirit of the man for whom the joint is named. Hopefully, the event will have happened April 2022 to officially acknowledge and celebrate the 50th anniversary of this very special team.

Dick Allen has long deserved to be enshrined in the Hall of Fame. We got crucial perspective from Goose Gossage, Billy Williams and Fergie Jenkins, three Hall of Famers who wholeheartedly support Dick's candidacy. Goose was especially generous in providing the Foreword, paying tribute to his earliest mentor among all teammates in a 22-year career from 1972 to 1994.

Mark Liptak was a witness to many of the events detailed in *Chili Dog MVP*, and he has turned those memories into an avocation as a White Sox historian. Mark graciously allowed us to tap into his previous interviews with Sox greats, which added to the narrative.

Roland Hemond was not available for new interviews for the book. But Dr. David J. Fletcher had so many encounters with Roland over the decades that the 15-year White Sox general manager contributed several chapters' worth of material that was already in the bank of their acquaintance. A 70-minute oral history on the '72 team filmed in June 2014 at the Green Diamond Gallery by director and filmmaker Paul Buchbinder of Paul Buchbinder Productions was also very valuable. Jay Hemond, one of Roland's three sons, confirmed key pieces of information. Sadly, Roland died in his sleep on December 12, 2021. They don't make colorful characters like the elder Hemond anymore.

So much "inside baseball" was provided by 1971-75 Comiskey Park home clubhouse attendant Jim O'Keefe, who grew up in neighboring Bridgeport. O'Keefe cooked the chili which the White Sox slugger slathered on his hot dog before being summoned to glory in the ninth inning on June 4, 1972. But O'Keefe's main recipe was the stories and contacts that he provided on an era never-to-be-forgotten by all those who participated.

Jim Riley and Rory Clark, who served as 1972 bat boys, joined clubhouse mate O'Keefe as major sources of help for book. Ziff Sustrunk, a 1973 bat boy, also provided inspiration for the book.

The erudite Tom Bradley, who started 40 games and pitched 260 innings in 1972, provided invaluable insight to the White Sox pitching staff.

Hemond contemporaries like former commissioner Bud Selig and Houston Astros manager Dusty Baker were also generous with their time. We thank Laurel Prieb for his assistance in getting in touch with his father-in-law Selig, who does not just sit back in his Milwaukee office as Commissioner Emeritus. Selig played a critical role in the status of the White Sox in Chicago, not only in almost purchasing the team in 1969, but also in the vote allowing Bill Veeck back into the game as Sox owner in late 1975.

Chili Dog MVP would be incomplete without the insight of the Allen family. Sadly, Dick Allen passed away just before the start of significant interviewing and research for this book. He knew the project was in development before his death on Dec. 7, 2020. More memories of the man and his family thus came from son Richard Allen, Jr., more popularly known as Doobie, and brother

Hank Allen, a longtime major-leaguer himself and teammate on the 1972-73 White Sox. Also helpful were Willa Allen, Dick's widow; Barbara Allen, his first wife; another brother, Ron Allen and nephew Ric Allen.

Andy Woolley, who handled Dick's Twitter account until his death, was an invaluable resource with the Allen archives. Mark Carfagno, who runs the Dick Allen Belongs in the Hall of Fame Facebook group, was a major help. Dick's longtime friend and teammate Howie Bedell was a major inspiration in getting things off the ground in 2008 by helping convince Dick to come to Chicago and be honored by the White Sox in 2012.

We truly appreciate Author David McGrath for permission to use his remembrance of Dick Allen published in the *Daily Herald* right after Dick's death in December 2020.

A special thanks to historian Willam Kashatus, whose 2004 book *September Swoon: Richie Allen, the '64 Phillies, and Racial Integration* (Keystone Books) was one of the first critical looks at the racial environment when Dick first started his career in Philadelphia. It helped explain how he reacted to harsh challenges as a 22-year-old African American.

We appreciate Brian Bernardoni's willingness to critically review the manuscript before publication.

Dr. David J. Fletcher's younger siblings Sally and Tom Fletcher were of great assistance. You hope big brother popped for some Frosty Malts when he took Sally and Tom to games back in the day. Jeffrey Fletcher, son of the co-author, helped on the project as did daughter Janine, an employment law specialist. She assisted in finding Nicole M. Murray of Quarles & Brady LLP to serve as the Entertainment and Intellectual Property attorney for F. Ferguson Productions, the legal entity for Dr. Fletcher's creative works.

More kinfolk helping included Casey Coon, otherwise known as Nurse Coon, otherwise known as the wife of David J. Fletcher. And whenever the good doctor got down, a four-legged personal therapy dog named Stanley Kup was there to pick and sniff out any ghost ballplayers coming out of the adjoining cornfields.

The SafeWorks Illinois family, present and past, in Champaign pitched in, led by Stacy Eichelberger. We also credit Stacey Benson. Ditto with Mary Scott, Chaley Shipley, Matt Dillon, Taylor Proctor, Amy Cook, Jen Watson, Dan Ogwal and Jason Cerezo.

Champaign, Illinois Attorney Steve O'Byrne served as F. Fergeson Productions, LLC corporate counsel.

A special thanks to Joe Coffman, owner of Box Seat, a Champaign baseball cards and collectibles shop, for driving Dr. Fletcher to Wampum, Pa. to research

Dick's ancestorial roots. Bryan Shirk also needs a shout-out for his invaluable assistance on this project.

The list of credits is long. Thanks to media types Paul Sullivan, Paul Ladewski, Phil Rosenthal, Steve Zalusky, Rob Feder, Chuck Garfien, the late John Reyes, SABR editor Jacob Pomrenke, Green Diamond Gallery owner Bob Crotty, Bruce Levine and Scott Merkin.

Kudos to Gary "Boxer Shorts" Kowal, Dr. Fletcher's partner-in-crime in 1972, who went to many games at Comiskey Park to watch those Sox, along with their fathers Judge Kowal and Archie Fletcher.

Finally, we want to thank our publisher Eckhartz Press. This boutique Chicago publisher was founded in Chicago in 2011 by Rick Kaempfer (Cubs fan extraordinaire) and his long-time collaborator and friend David Stern (a passionate Sox fan). They loved the project when we first pitched the book on Christmas Eve 2020. Eckhartz hired graphic artist Jeff Waggoner, who did a tremendous job with the book design. Jeff was flexible with the creative team's various late-minute editing changes to improve the quality of the end product. We hope that we can work with Rick, David and Jeff on future books.

We know we have missed a few people who helped out along the way on this book. We apologize for your omission.

Richard A. Allen III (Dick's grandson), Hank Allen (Dick's brother), Dick, Doobie (Dick's son) and Ron Allen (Dick's brother) at the tribute to the 1972 team at U.S. Cellular Field on June 24, 2012. "My father loved this picture a lot and it was the first thing you saw coming into his residence in Tampa where he lived the last few years of his life," revealed Doobie. Dick is holding the 1972 MVP trophy that was returned to him in 1990 when teammate Bart Johnson found it hidden at Comiskey Park.

Photo credit: Mike Gustafson, Owner Gustafson Photography

AUTHOR BIOGRAPHIES

John Owens, Author

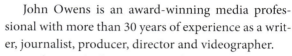

John Owens is an award-winning media professional with more than 30 years of experience as a writer, journalist, producer, director and videographer.

He has worked in a variety of capacities in broadcast, print and online — from producer to executive producer to director to videographer to writer to reporter.

Owens has produced numerous full-length documentaries and programs for broadcast and online platforms. His film "The City's Pastime" received the Chicago/Midwest Emmy Award for best historical documentary in 2005, and his film "Kenwood's Journey" won the Chicago/Midwest Emmy Award for best topical documentary in 2015.

Owens also received honors for his work from the Chicago Headline Club, the Illinois Associated Press Broadcasters Association, the Digital Edge Awards, the Telly Awards and the National Association of Black Journalists.

His work as a writer and reporter has been featured in the *Chicago Tribune*, *Los Angeles Times*, *Chicago Reader*, *Block Club Chicago*, *New City*, *Reel Chicago*, *Neiman Reports* and other publications.

Owens' broadcast work has been featured on the Decades Network, Me-TV, WGN-TV, CLTV, WYCC-TV (PBS), Fox News Chicago and Link-TV.

In addition, Owens is also an adjunct professor at the City Colleges of Chicago, where he teaches broadcast writing and interactive media.

He is also the President for the National Academy of Television Arts and Sciences Chicago/Midwest Chapter.

Dr. David J. Fletcher, Author

Dr. David J. Fletcher is a 1972 alum of Glenbard West High School in Glen Ellyn, Ill., where he played baseball. Sometimes taking three trains as a teenager to go to baseball games in Chicago, Fletcher attended some 20 White Sox games in 1972, and witnessed first-hand what Dick Allen meant to the city.

In 1980, he graduated from Rush Medical College, and practiced medicine in the U.S. Army. Along with his private medical practice Safeworks Illinois (*www.SafeworksIllinois.com*) in Champaign, Ill., Fletcher has become a noted baseball historian.

In July 2005, he was granted the Hilda Award at the Shrine of the Eternals 2005 Induction Ceremony of the Baseball Reliquary in Pasadena, Calif. The annual award acknowledges a person's unique passion and dedication to the game of baseball. Fletcher was recognized for his work for trying to clear the name of former White Sox third baseman and banned Black Sox George "Buck" Weaver. Fletcher created the website *www.ClearBuck.com* and is an expert on the Black Sox.

In 2005, Fletcher began efforts to develop the Chicago Baseball Museum (*www.ChicagoBaseballMuseum.org*), which would honor Chicago's many contributions to the national pastime. In 2007, the CBM, through Fletcher's efforts, acquired the private baseball library and papers of sportswriter and MLB's first official historian, Jerome Holtzman.

Fletcher and John Owens have teamed up before for "Buck O'Neil and Black Baseball in Chicago", a documentary written and filmed by Owens. The documentary aired on PBS and won the praise of White Sox owner Jerry Reinsdorf, who noted that the film was "vitally important for future generations." In September 2010, Fletcher screened the documentary at the Baseball Hall of Fame film festival in Cooperstown, N.Y.

For several years, Fletcher had urged that Dick Allen be recognized for his many contributions to the White Sox franchise. In 2012, he convinced the seven-time All-Star to participate in a two-day event at U.S. Cellular Field, co-hosted by the White Sox.

After the 2012 event, Fletcher became very close to Dick and his family. In September 2020, Dick personally asked Fletcher to attend the ceremony in Philadelphia to retire his Phillies uniform No. 15. Sadly, in December 2020, Fletcher also served as a pallbearer for Dick and spoke at his funeral in Wampum, Pa.

George Castle, Editor

Editor George Castle is one of the top authors and historians in baseball and broadcasting today.

An author of 21 books and historian for the Chicago Baseball Museum, Castle turned an avocation into a vocation. A native of Chicago's far North Side, he grew up in the cheap seats of Wrigley Field and old Comiskey Park, paying just $1 to get into the bleachers of the former in the early 1970s. Sometimes he'd splurge to spend $1.75 on grandstand seats.

On an off-day from his summer stockboy job at the downtown Goldblatt's Department Store, Castle was an eyewitness to Dick Allen's prodigious center field homer on Aug. 23, 1972, described in *Chili Dog MVP: Dick Allen, the 1972 White Sox and A Transforming Chicago.*

Castle began covering baseball in 1980 at both Chicago ballparks. Castle went on to write for a variety of newspapers and magazines. He founded "Diamond Gems", his own syndicated weekly baseball radio show, in 1994. Through spit, gum and wire, Castle kept "Diamond Gems" on the air for 17 seasons. Castle began his author's career with the first book published on Harry Caray after his death in 1998.

Castle has built longstanding connections to a number of Hall of Famers and top baseball personalities, who have helped him in his coverage. He co-authored *The 1969 Cubs* with Hall of Famer Fergie Jenkins in 2019.

He is a longtime North Suburban Chicago resident.